Restoring Free Speech and Liberty on Campus

This book addresses a major problem in contemporary American higher education: deprivations of free speech, due process, and other basic civil liberties in the name of favored political causes. Downs begins by analyzing the nature and evolution of the problem and discusses how these betrayals of liberty have harmed the truth-seeking mission of universities. Rather than promoting equal respect and tolerance of diversity, policies restricting academic freedom and civil liberty have proved divisive and have compromised the robust exchange of ideas that is a necessary condition of a meaningful education. Drawing on personal experience as well as research, Downs presents four case studies that illustrate the difference that conscientious political resistance and mobilization of faculty and students can make. Such movements have brought about unexpected success in renewing the principles of free speech, academic freedom, and civil liberty at universities where they have been active, while their absence at some universities has caused a steady decline in the importance of these principles.

Donald Alexander Downs is Professor of Political Science, Law and Journalism at the University of Wisconsin, Madison, and Research Fellow at The Independent Institute, Oakland, California. He has written four previous books, including *Nazis in Skokie: Freedom, Community, and the First Amendment*, winner of the Annisfield-Wolf Book Award; and *The New Politics of Pornography*, winner of the Gladys M. Kammerer Award of the American Political Science Association. Professor Downs has also published extensively in leading journals, encyclopedias, and professional books; lectured throughout the United States and in England and Scotland; and made numerous media appearances on radio and television to discuss issues of American politics and law.

*To my friends and colleagues in the Committee for Academic
Freedom and Rights, and to the many students who have
participated in the free speech and civil liberty movement at
the University of Wisconsin, Madison*

Life is hard to bear, but do not affect to be so delicate.

Nietzsche

Talk is cheap. Free Speech isn't.

Bumper sticker sold on Telegraph Avenue,
Berkeley, November 2001

Contents

Acknowledgments

Lewis Bateman, my editor at Cambridge University Press, has supported this project from the start and has provided the excellent editorial advice that is his hallmark. I also want to thank David Theroux, president, and Alexander Tabarrok, research director, of The Independent Institute. David has backed this project from its inception and given me useful information that has gone into the book. Alex gave me encouragement and superb editorial advice. He critiqued an earlier version of the manuscript, helping me to make it tighter and more focused on the human consequences of deprivations of liberty on campus.

Numerous individuals in the field contributed to this book by granting me interviews or providing me with relevant data and information. There are too many such contributors to name, and some have reason to remain anonymous. So it must suffice here simply to express my gratitude to these individuals, each of whom knows who he or she is. Of course, many were also participants in the events that I describe, so their names will appear in that capacity in the narratives that follow.

Several individuals at Wisconsin worked as research assistants in this project. Morgan Felchner and Sara Beachy did excellent work as tape transcribers and engaged in very helpful discussions with me about the project. It was always a pleasure to work with them. Mitch Pickerill collected material from newspapers, engaged in many probing conversations with me about the issues discussed in this book, and acted on behalf of free speech and civil liberty at Wisconsin. Mitch's combination of intelligence, scholarship, and commitment to liberty on campus and elsewhere has never failed to inspire me. Anat Hakim conducted penetrating research on cases concerning the University of Wisconsin faculty speech code and, along with her husband Martin Sweet, gave me stellar strategic advice in the pivotal years of the Madison free speech movement. Anat, Martin, and I go way back, and I have long benefited from witnessing the strength of their minds and character. Ben Thompson had many illuminating discussions with me about the subject matter of this book and enriched my thinking about the relevant issues, always with his distinctive acuity. Ben also wrote a senior thesis on the recent history of free speech controversies at the *Badger Herald*, a work that presented important and fascinating information. Ben was also a formidable leader of that paper along with other students whom I depict in the book. Katie Harbath was an invaluable assistant in a way that highlighted her all-purpose abilities. She conducted interviews, filed state freedom-of-information requests on her own initiative, coordinated a number of aspects of the research, and generally kept me on track. Katie's assumption of many weighty responsibilities on campus – including her work at the *Badger Herald* – stands as a model of campus citizenship.

I also want to thank Sharon van Sluijs for her nonpareil editing advice after my first major draft. In addition to providing excellent technical assistance, Sharon combined a mastery of language with an exceptional understanding of the issues at stake in this book and helped me clarify numerous critical points. In addition to being a first-rate editor, Sharon challenged my mind.

The Department of Political Science at Wisconsin deserves mention for two reasons. First, the department named me to a Hawkins Professorship, which has provided me with research funds to gather data and to travel to New York City, Philadelphia, Berkeley, and elsewhere. This project would not have been possible without these ample funds. Second, the department has remained hospitable to a diversity of viewpoints and has consistently fostered an environment conducive to those who challenge various campus orthodoxies. I know too many faculty members in other departments at Wisconsin or elsewhere who envy me for belonging to such a department.

My colleagues in the Committee for Academic Freedom and Rights (CAFR) merit special recognition. We have experienced many challenges together, and I shall always treasure my association with them and the opportunity I had to join them in political action. These colleagues were indispensable to the pro-liberty changes that have taken place at Madison in recent years. My CAFR allies have taught me many things, the most important of which are to stand up in a responsible and effective way for what you believe and to seek out souls who share a belief in academic freedom. Nor shall I ever forget the friendship and association that these individuals have afforded.

Equally important are the dozens of students who have participated in the Madison free speech and civil liberty movement over the course of the past decade or more. A few of these students have been named here, while the others appear in the narratives of Chapters 6–8. Most of these students have taken classes with me, and it has been an honor and a delight to teach them and also to work with them in the movement. Indeed, the opportunity to get to know such students, along with my CAFR friends, constitutes what I consider the highlight of my career at Wisconsin. Without these students, none of the free speech and civil liberty victories at Wisconsin would have come to pass. I also extend thanks to those students who have performed similar service for these causes at the other universities that I portray in my case studies – Columbia, Berkeley, and Penn.

Hasdai Westbrook stood out by performing many noteworthy tasks as a student, research assistant, and ally. First, Hasdai engaged in important free speech and civil liberty conflicts at Wisconsin as a member of the student government, as an editorial page editor of the *Badger Herald*, and in his individual capacity. He and I worked together on some key issues, some of which are portrayed in this book. Second, Hasdai conducted and transcribed many interviews and discussed their implications with me at length. Third, he interacted with me and challenged me more than anyone in terms of the sifting and winnowing of the issues with which this book deals. Hasdai had remarkably acute and discriminating instincts for the normative, political, legal, and psychological nuances of civil liberty conflicts, and he possessed a congenital disdain for moralistic bullying. He left a special mark on this book through his intellectual contributions and his example.

Finally, I want to thank my wife, Susan, and my children, Jacqueline and Alexander. They have consistently supported the principles that went into this book and have prodded me when I have wavered. More important, they are classic examples of the virtues that attend independent, self-reliant minds. I thank them for this and so much more.

Preface

This book focuses on the threats to free speech and civil liberty that have sprung up on America's campuses following the wave of so-called progressive reforms instituted in the late 1980s and the 1990s. The most important reforms included speech codes, broad antiharassment codes, orientation programs dedicated to promoting an ideology of sensitivity, and new procedures and pressures in the adjudication of student and faculty misconduct. Although these measures were laudably designed to foster civility, tolerance, and respect for racial and cultural diversity, they too often had illiberal consequences. Rather than improving the campus climate, the new policies often provided tools for moral bullies to enforce an ideological orthodoxy that undermines the intellectual freedom and intellectual diversity that are the hallmarks of great universities.

Following in the wake of several other books, this book tells the story of how and why this turn of events took place.[1] But it goes one step further than previous literature: this book explores how faculty, students, and even administrators can retrieve liberal principles of freedom on campus through conscientious political commitment and mobilization. I present two case studies of how such mobilization can make a difference, and two case studies of how the absence of such commitment leaves liberal principles in the lurch. My hope in writing this book is to show how liberal principles of freedom and individualism can be restored in a way that adds integrity to the pursuit of diversity in the contemporary university.

Although this book stresses the threats to academic and intellectual freedom posed by speech codes and related policies, it should be noted that freedom is also threatened by other sources, especially in the post–September 11

---

[1] There is an extensive literature on the uses and abuses of speech codes and similar policies, most of which is cited in this book. Perhaps the magnum opus of this literature is Alan Charles Kors and Harvey A. Silverglate, *The Shadow University: The Betrayal of Liberty on America's Campuses* (Free Press, 1998).

world. To begin, the modern university has long been engaged in industrial and governmental research that coexists uneasily with the university's erstwhile mission of open discourse. Such research benefits society and brings needed money into the university. But the benefits sometimes come at a price that includes limitations on speech and discourse. This trend has accelerated in recent years as state support has declined while the costs of higher education have escalated. Today, many universities engage in research with government agencies and corporations that require recipients to maintain silence about the nature of the research. Though understandable in certain contexts, the extension of such gag orders poses a challenge to the idea of an open university.[2]

Terrorism and the reaction to it also have brought about new threats to academic and intellectual freedom. Terrorism in itself is a threat, of course, as such groups as al Qaeda are bent on destroying the very fabric of liberal freedom in the world. On the other side of the ledger, such private groups as Campus Watch have begun monitoring classes and denouncing faculty whose views they consider unpatriotic. And some institutions of higher learning have jeopardized academic freedom by the way they have responded to public pressure exerted against faculty members who made intemperate statements after the September 11 attacks. A recent report by the American Association of University Professors cites several such cases, which have typically involved statements by faculty blaming America for the attacks or denouncing America as the real villain in the world. Such cases have generally been resolved in ways that constitute qualified victories for academic freedom. Despite strong pressure from trustees and the public, no faculty member has lost his job in these cases; but some received reprimands, which do represent formal sanctions.

Two less equivocal victories for academic freedom merit mention. In one case, Professor Nicholas De Genova of Columbia University sparked a firestorm when he called for "a million Mogadishus" during the war in Iraq, leading alumni and more than a hundred members of the United States House of Representatives to call for his dismissal. (Mogadishu refers to the shooting down of a U.S. Army helicopter and the killing and mutilation of U.S. troops in Somalia in 1993, subsequently dramatized in the movie *Black Hawk Down*.) Columbia president Lee Bollinger, who wrote an important book defending free speech in the mid-1980s, publicly criticized De Genova's comments, yet defended his right of free speech, declaring that "under the principle of academic freedom, it would be inappropriate to take disciplinary action." Though perhaps chastened, De Genova was not punished. In another case at City College of New York, Benno Schmidt, vice chair of the

---

[2] See, e.g., John W. Sommer, ed., *The Academy in Crisis: The Political Economy of Higher Education* (Transaction Books for The Independent Institute, 1995). On academic freedom, tenure, and the organization of higher education, see Ryan C. Amacher and Roger E. Meiners, *Faulty Towers: Tenure and the Structure of Higher Education* (The Independent Institute, 2004).

board of trustees, intervened on behalf of several faculty members who made similar remarks a few weeks after the September 11 events. Schmidt stated that "the freedom to challenge and to speak one's mind [is] the matrix, the indispensable condition of any university worth the name."[3] In the end, the board dropped the matter. Schmidt's intervention supports a major theme of this book: the importance of countervailing power and of strong institutional or political commitment to free speech and academic freedom principles. Indeed, during the 1990s Schmidt gained a national reputation as probably the nation's leading administrative champion of free speech in the face of the challenges posed by speech codes and similar policies. His stance in the City College case shows that he is not selective in applying his principles.[4]

One case that appears to have been resolved less fairly concerned a professor at Orange Coast College a few weeks after September 11. Several Muslim students accused him of calling them "terrorists" and "Nazis" and of stating that they were similar to the individuals who drove the planes into the World Trade Center. A thorough investigation concluded that there was no basis on which to sustain the charges and that the statements had been misreported. Nonetheless, the administration placed the professor on administrative leave and sanctioned him with a reprimand.[5] This case appears to fit the pattern of repression that was already taking place under the reign of speech codes, as the professor was accused (apparently unfairly) of offending minority students. Unfortunately, the evidence supports the conclusion that this particular type of repression has continued unabated since the September 11 attacks, as I show in Chapter 1.[6]

Finally, a case the American Association of University Professors (AAUP) calls "grave" involved Sami Al-Arian at the University of South Florida, who was arrested in February 2003 for providing material support for terrorism. Though dismissal would certainly be merited if such claims were substantiated or had a sufficient basis in evidence, the administration decided to dismiss Al-Arian well before such evidence became known in response to the public furor that had arisen surrounding the case. (The furor was triggered by a campaign conducted by Bill O'Reilly on *The O'Reilly Factor* television show.) Both the AAUP and the Foundation for Individual Rights in Education (FIRE) have opposed the university's actions in this case.[7]

---

3 "Academic Freedom in a Time of Crisis," Report of an AAUP Special Committee, p.20, available at http://www.aaup.org/statements/REPORTS/911report.htm. The other cases discussed here are from this report.

4 On Schmidt's role as a prominent speech code critic in higher administration, see Timothy C. Shiell, *Campus Hate Speech on Trial* (University of Kansas Press, 1998), pp.53–66. Bollinger's book is *The Tolerant Society: Freedom of Speech and Extremist Speech in America* (Oxford University Press, 1986).

5 "Academic Freedom in a Time of Crisis," p. 20.

6 See, e.g., the extensive set of cases in which the Foundation for Individual Rights in Education has been involved, at www.theFIRE.org.

7 "Academic Freedom in a Time of Crisis," pp. 20–21.

Those who maintain that the faculty in these cases should be immune to criticism misunderstand the concept of the marketplace of ideas. Taking verbal heat for making controversial statements is itself an indispensable part of the very "matrix" of free speech. It is part of the give-and-take of debate.[8] But free speech principles dictate that no one should be sanctioned for saying controversial things in appropriate forums and that institutions with which such speakers are associated should make it clear, as Schmidt and Bollinger did, that such rights will be protected.

Another area of concern is the new array of powers the federal government has amassed in the war on terror. There is little evidence at this point of the effects of these measures on academic and intellectual freedom, but there is reason for appropriate vigilance and concern. The USA Patriot Act and other new laws have significantly expanded the government's power to search and survey political groups and individuals on campus and elsewhere in the name of national security, and it requires universities to produce enormous amounts of information about personnel and students from foreign countries or who work with a long list of materials and subjects. In addition, laws have greatly broadened the categories of "classified" and "unclassified but sensitive" material and research.[9]

New laws also substantially enhance the power of the Federal Bureau of Investigation and the Central Intelligence Agency to conduct domestic searches and surveillance in the name of national security. Some expansion is necessary, given the fact that al Qaeda and its allies probably have cells inside America's shores. Only a fool would maintain that government power should not change at all given the present dangers confronting America. On the other hand, the FBI has demonstrated in the past that it is capable of abusing such power, as shown by the highly intrusive surveillance and infiltration of activist groups that it conducted in the 1960s and early 1970s, most of whom posed no danger to national security. (Antiwar groups, civil rights activists, campus radicals, and even environmentalists were among the targets of the FBI program known as COINTELPRO, which stands for "counterintelligence programs."[10]) Richard Nixon also ordered such searches and surveillance under the contrived guise of national security.[11]

Unlike the threats concocted in the imaginations of Richard Nixon and COINTELPRO, however, al Qaeda and similar groups are actual threats to the security of the United States. And the federal government rightfully

---

[8] See Jonathan Rauch, *Kindly Inquisitors: The New Attacks on Free Thought* (University of Chicago Press, 1993).

[9] For more extensive discussions of the various measures, see "Academic Freedom in a Time of Crisis"; and David Cole and James X. Dempsey, *Terrorism and the Constitution: Sacrificing Civil Liberties in the Name of National Security* (New Press, 2002).

[10] See Cole and Dempsey, *Terrorism and the Constitution*, pp. 6–7, 73–76.

[11] See, e.g., my colleague Stanley I. Kutler, *The Wars of Watergate: The Last Crisis of Richard Nixon* (Norton, 1990), pp. 97, 585–86.

possesses greater power to combat actual threats to national security than it possesses to combat normal crime.[12] But this recognition should not give the national government carte blanche in the war against terrorism. While the line between national security surveillance and traditional domestic law enforcement has legitimately shifted due to our present circumstance, it must nonetheless be carefully monitored and maintained in a meaningful form.

The major problem with the Patriot Act is that it defines "terrorism" very broadly, thereby posing the danger of collapsing the distinct realms of domestic and national security law enforcement altogether. The act expands the definition of terrorism beyond previous antiterrorism laws to cover virtually any group carrying out or planning violence or destruction of property.[13] Under previous approaches, the government limited the scope of the definition of terrorism to a short list of groups designated by the secretary of state. The new definition could be applied to domestic political advocacy groups engaged in civil disobedience that have nothing to do with the type of international terrorism that now threatens the nation. Americans should not be reassured by the Justice Department's pledge that "these hypothetical examples are just that – hypothetical, since the authority in the bill would never be used in that way."[14] Revisions of the Federal Intelligence Surveillance Act (FISA) contribute to the watering down of the distinction between domestic law enforcement and national security enforcement by making it much easier to conduct national security surveillance on the domestic front. According to two knowledgeable commentators, in conjunction with the expanded definition of terrorism, this change "greatly expands the power of federal authorities to apply the relatively loose standards of FISA to investigations of both U.S. citizens and residents that only tangentially touch on national security."[15] Thoughtful judicial review and conscientious monitoring by the citizenry are called for to maintain an appropriate balance between security and liberty.

As mentioned, this book does not deal with these new threats to liberty; but the lessons I hope to teach are relevant to this domain. After all, the commitment to liberty should be consistent across the board. Although the record is less than sterling, the AAUP report on the status of academic freedom concludes that universities today appear to be doing a better job of protecting controversial speakers from attacks in the name of national security and patriotism than they did during previous eras in which national

---

[12] In general, see Donald A. Downs and Erik Kinnunen, "A Response to Anthony Lewis: Civil Liberties in a New Kind of War," 2003 *Wisconsin Law Review*, pp. 385–412.

[13] USA Patriot Act, 115 Stat. at 376.

[14] Michael T. McCarthy, "Recent Developments, *U.S.A. Patriot Act*," 39 *Harvard Journal on Legislation* (2002), pp. 435, 450.

[15] John W. Whitehead and Steven H. Aden, "Forfeiting 'Enduring Freedom' for 'Homeland Security': A Constitutional Analysis of the USA Patriot Act and the Justice Department's Anti-Terrorism Initiative," 51 *American Law Review* 1081 (2002), p. 1103.

security fears were prominent, such as the McCarthy era and the Red Scare following World War I. "Incidents involving outspoken faculty members have been fewer than one might have expected in the aftermath of so momentous an event as September 11. Moreover, with few exceptions – at least one of them grave – the responses by college and university administrators to the events that have occurred have been reassuringly temperate."[16]

Unfortunately, institutions of higher education have continued to repress speech and ideas deemed contrary to the ideology of sensitivity that lurked behind the speech and harassment code movements of recent times. One case representing the continuing presence of progressive censorship took place at San Diego State. A few days after the September 11 attacks, Zewdalem Kebede, an Ethiopian student at San Diego State University who understood Arabic, overheard some Saudi Arabian students laughing about what happened in New York and Washington. Upset, he challenged them and asked them why they did not "feel shame." A heated exchange ensued, and campus police had to order the students to disperse. In what appears to be a parody of the spirit of progressive censorship, the campus Center for Student Rights wrote Kebede a letter accusing *him* of engaging in "verbally abusive behavior to other students." Eventually, the case was dropped, but only after Kebede's actions were reviled in public and a warning letter was placed in his file.[17]

During most of the twentieth century, threats to campus free speech and academic freedom came mostly from the right, and from *outside* institutions of higher learning. The new attacks on free thought that arose in the later 1980s turned this pattern on its head: they have arisen from leftist sources *inside* the ivory tower. It is for this reason that the new battles over free speech have sometimes taken on the characteristics of civil wars. The new type of censorship is "progressive" in aspiration, not "reactionary." What this and other books reveal, however, is that progressive censorship has a way of producing illiberal, repressive consequences that are just as detrimental to open universities and minds as traditional forms of censorship. With the return of the more traditional threats to free thought after September 11, it is possible that the advocates of progressive censorship will realize the errors of their ways for the simple reason that it is their ox that is now being gored once again. It remains to be seen whether this is true.

Whatever the case may be, it is time for all institutions to commit themselves to a more consistent approach that shows respect for free speech, academic freedom, and civil liberty for all members of the academic community,

---

[16] "Academic Freedom in a Time of Crisis," p. 19. The "grave" case is the University of South Florida case discussed previously. On past transgressions against academic freedom due to national security concerns, see Anthony Lewis, Kastenmeier Lecture, Address at University of Wisconsin Law School, September 30, 2002. In 2003 *Wisconsin Law Review*, p. 257. For a more specific focus on academic freedom, see Neil Hamilton, *Zealotry and Academic Freedom: A Legal and Historical Perspective* (Transaction, 1998), chs. 1, 2.

[17] See Jason Williams, "Student: Attack Praised," *Daily Aztec*, October 17, 2001.

regardless of their views or political pedigree. Accepting this responsibility means addressing threats to academic and intellectual freedom that emanate from causes and sources *within* the university, not just those that arise from without, as is the case with threats stemming from the war against terrorism. In this book, I attempt to show how political commitment on campus can help to bring about this retrieval of liberal principles.

PART I

INTRODUCTION AND BACKGROUND

I

The Return of the Proprietary University

The New Politics of Free Speech and Civil Liberty

The lore of history has indelibly linked three words in the public's imagination: "free speech" and "Berkeley." The free speech movement (FSM) at Berkeley witnessed the rise of a mass student mobilization and the first illegal takeover of a campus building – Sproul Hall – in United States history. FSM was the fountainhead of modern student political activism. And at its inception in the 1960s, it was all about free speech – at least in theory.

FSM was originally motivated by the desire to win for students the same rights of free speech and expression that citizens enjoyed in the world outside the realm of academe. This objective later blossomed into a broader movement in American higher education that eliminated or cut back in loco parentis policies, which curtailed student freedoms on the grounds that college students are not yet prepared to assume the full rights and responsibilities of adults.[1] The first major target of student protest at Berkeley was the wall of separation that University of California authorities had erected between politics and the university. In the 1930s University of California president Robert Sproul initiated policies banning such activities as the use of university buildings for holding partisan political exercises. By 1964 students were not permitted to solicit for political purposes or to hand out materials "distributed on University property to urge a specific vote, call for direct social or political action, or to seek to recruit individuals for such action."[2]

---

[1] See, in general, David A. Hoekema, *Campus Rules and Moral Community: In Place of In Loco Parentis* (Rowman and Littlefield, 1994).

[2] Katherine A. Towle, Dean of Students, University of California, Berkeley, "Use of Campus Facilities, Including Entrance at Bancroft Way and Telegraph Avenue and 'Hyde Park' Areas," September 21, 1964, FSM Records. Cited in Robert Post, "Constitutionally Interpreting the FSM Controversy," in Robert Cohen and Reginald E. Zelnik, eds., *The Free Speech Movement: Reflections on Berkeley in the 1960s* (University of California Press, 2002), pp. 401–21.

A 1944 restatement of Sproul's 1936 prohibition expressed the philosophy behind the policy succinctly:

The function of the University is to seek and to transmit knowledge and to train students in the processes whereby truth is to be made known. To convert, or to make converts, is alien and hostile to this dispassionate duty.... The University is founded upon faith in intelligence and knowledge and it must defend their free operation.... Its obligation is to see that the conditions under which questions are examined are those which give play to intellect rather than to passion.[3]

Sproul's policy was not dismissive of free speech and inquiry as principles. On the contrary, it was intended, however naively, to protect these goods in the university context from outside forces. Political activists pursue causes, not truth, pitting them in some fundamental sense at odds with the pursuit of truth. Truth has a way of being inconvenient to any cause. As Hannah Arendt wrote, "it may be in the nature of the political realm to be at war with truth in all its forms ... a commitment even to factual truth is felt to be an anti-political attitude."[4]

The University of California's policy was premised on some key liberal assumptions about the nature of knowledge and the function of the university, assumptions that had held sway since the rise of major research universities in the nineteenth century. These assumptions included the belief that truth and reason are in some fundamental sense distinct – however imperfectly – from such forces as passion, power, and history; and that the university's primary mission is to ensure the academic freedom of properly trained professors and their students. In its most advanced incarnations, the liberal concept of the university embodies a commitment to "cognitive rationality" and "radical individualism," and to the idea of the university as a special, relatively autonomous space where "the cultivation of rational thought and analysis" is valued more than in the outside world.[5]

But the post–World War II era unleashed forces that would tear down the wall of separation between truth and politics at Berkeley and elsewhere. New political and moral obligations cried out for attention, beckoning students to make the university more relevant to society. The civil rights and other progressive movements brought the problems of racism, poverty, and oppression to the fore, while economic and corporate expansion made American

---

[3] Regulation 5, 1944, on file in the FSM collection of the Bancroft Library, University of California, Berkeley. Sproul's statement remains the authoritative pronouncement of the University of California with regard to academic freedom.

[4] Hannah Arendt, "Truth and Politics," in Peter Laslett and W. G. Runciman, eds., *Philosophy, Politics, and Society* (Basil Blackwell, 1967), p. 113.

[5] Bridgette Berger, "Multiculturalism and the Modern University," in Edith Kurzweil and William Phillips, eds., *Our Country, Our Culture: The Politics of Political Correctness* (Partisan Review Press, 1994), pp. 15–24. On the historical rise of the special "space" of the university, see Sheldon Rothblatt, *The Modern University and Its Discontents: The Fate of Newman's Legacy in Britain and America* (Cambridge University Press, 1997), ch. 2.

life appear more impersonal and less authentic in many students' eyes. Forces swept through universities that rendered the separation of truth's pursuit and politics seem quaint, if not hypocritical. During the 1950s universities across the land succumbed to loyalty oath controversies and other disputes thrust upon them by McCarthyism. The University of California was afflicted with one of the most intense loyalty oath conflicts, threatening the very viability of Berkeley as an institution. UC president Clark Kerr managed to avert disaster by painstakingly forging a compromise that included the firing of more than one hundred faculty members who were or had been members of the Communist Party, while retaining faculty members who refused to sign the oath simply out of principle.[6]

More broadly, the very complexion of higher education was undergoing a radical transformation. Universities had evolved into what Kerr christened the "multiversity" in a famous book: a large, impersonal, bureaucratic institution without a soul or central mission, a land where faculty research and grants take precedence over the commitment to undergraduate teaching.[7] The multiversity was awash in military research and other work servicing the corporate state. In addition to targeting free speech policy, FSM turned its wrath on what it considered the moral impoverishment of the modern university as an institution. As FSM leader Mario Savio proclaimed in a famous speech, "There is a time when the operation of the machine becomes so odious, makes you so sick at heart, that you can't take part.... You've got to put your bodies upon the gears and upon the wheels, the levers, upon all the apparatus, and you've got to make it stop."[8]

But it was a seemingly minor deed that broke the dike protecting the university from the politics outside. The fall of 1964 was marked by increased student activism in the name of civil rights, social justice, and peace. It also happened to be the time that the university learned that a twenty-six-foot sidewalk area in front of the entry to the campus at the intersection of Bancroft Way and Telegraph Avenue belonged not to the city of Berkeley – as the university had long assumed – but rather to the university itself. In response to this discovery, the university promptly applied its rules against political solicitation and advocacy to the area for the first time. Student political activists were not pleased, as Robert Post relates. "The yawning

---

[6] Clark Kerr, *The Gold and the Blue: A Personal Memoir of the University of California, 1949–1967*, vol. 1, *Academic Triumphs* (University of California Press, 2001), chs. 1, 9. On the loyalty oath controversy at the University of California and other campuses, see Ellen W. Schrecher, *No Ivory Tower: McCarthyism and the Universities* (Oxford University Press, 1986).

[7] Clark Kerr, *The Uses of the University* (Harvard University Press, 1963).

[8] Savio speech, in Editors of the *California Monthly*, "Chronology of Events: Three Months of Crisis," reprinted in Seymour Martin Lipset and Sheldon S. Wolin, *The Berkeley Student Revolt: Facts and Interpretations* (Doubleday Anchor, 1965), p. 163. This book is an excellent compilation of primary and secondary sources assembled right after FSM's victory in late 1964.

disparity between freedom of speech as enjoyed by citizens and freedom of speech as defined within the institutional confines of the University was thus starkly exposed."⁹ Student activists and a handful of faculty founded FSM in the name of classic libertarian ends: to tear the wall of differential treatment down in the name of free speech and equal civil liberties. A key FSM platform declared that "civil liberties and political freedoms which are constitutionally protected off campus must be equally protected on campus for all persons.... The Administration may not regulate the content of speech and political conduct."¹⁰

But like most powerful political movements, FSM was complicated and tapped the full range of human motivation and aspiration. Its libertarian side reached out to those with a thirst for knowledge, moral commitment, and meaning. A less libertarian side appealed to communitarian impulses that were not always consistent with individual conscience. The movement was torn between the libertarian and moralistic impulses that Paul Berman analyzes in his book on political movements inspired by the student upheavals of the 1960s, *A Tale of Two Utopias*. Berman draws a line between movements bent on "moral reform" and those devoted to expanding the franchise, citizenship, and liberty. The latter comprised the "movement for political and cultural enfranchisement," which has historically included labor, abolitionism, civil rights, the women's movement, and the gay and lesbian movements. Moral reform movements, however, have too often degenerated into coercion and authoritarianism. Liberty movements are ultimately more successful and humane because they simply strive to expand the benefits of freedom to individuals and groups previously excluded by prejudice. Liberty movements are principally "campaigns to lead one sector of society after another upward from the gloom of bottom-place standing in the social hierarchy into the glorious mediocrity of the American middle class."¹¹

Free speech was important to FSM but mainly as the vehicle by which to address more substantive political concerns, including the nourishment of solidarity.¹² In "We Want a University," a manifesto dedicated to the students who took over Sproul Hall to further the cause, the authors (calling themselves the "free speech movement") announced their commitment to a

⁹ Post, "Constitutionally Interpreting the FSM Controversy," p. 405.
¹⁰ FSM Platform, quoted in *Daily Californian*, November 13, 1964. Cited in Post, "Constitutionally Interpreting the FSM Controversy," p. 402.
¹¹ Paul Berman, *A Tale of Two Utopias: The Political Journey of the Generation of 1968* (Norton, 1996), pp. 186–87.
¹² FSM steering committee member Jack Weinberg noted, "Free speech has been the issue, and virtually all the FSM supporters identify with the FSM demands. The roots, however, go much deeper. The free-speech issue has been so readily accepted because it has become a vehicle enabling students to express their dissatisfaction with so much of university life, and with so many of the University's institutions." Weinberg, "The Free Speech Movement and Civil Rights," in Lipset and Wolin, *The Berkeley Student Revolt*, pp. 221–22.

new kind of "loving community." Their language echoed the romantic ideas of such antilibertarian critics of alienated bourgeoisie society as Rousseau, Marx, Weber, Durkheim, Tönnies, and Heidegger:

Although our issue has been free speech, our theme has been solidarity. When individual members of our community have acted, we joined together as a community to jointly bear the responsibility for their actions. We have been able to revitalize one of the most distorted, misused, and important words of our century: comrade. . . .

For a moment on December 8, eight hundred and twenty-four professors gave us all a glimpse – a brief, glorious vision of the university as a loving community.[13]

Many FSM activists yearned for an intense educational experience that moved the mind and the soul. But their commitment to solidarity, comradeship, and organic community also contained elements that could smother individual independence of mind. Before long, part of the FSM ideal led to an insistence on the "right politics" rather than to freedom as a means to attain knowledge and individualistic self-discovery. In an interview, one of the four original faculty advisers to FSM, renowned Berkeley philosopher John Searle, related that things began to turn "within six months": "We won in December [1964] and in the following semester, by September, there was no question the situation had deteriorated. What happened is very simple and I'm sure it's a permanent feature of protest movements. Namely, to the extent that they are successful, they are taken over by the extreme elements. The moderate liberal students went back to their studies and the radicals got control."[14] As the 1960s wore on, free speech itself began to suffer at the hands of political causes. Opinions deemed detrimental to preferred political causes encountered problems in the public forum. As Searle observed, "There were periods when it was really bad. If you were in favor of the war in Vietnam, life was very difficult for you. I wasn't in favor [of the war], but I can tell you that there was no free speech [on that issue]. You could not have people come on campus to defend government policy. They'd be shouted down. . . . there was no free speech for people who weren't [what we now call] 'politically correct.'"[15]

In the aftermath of FSM's great victory in December 1964, Berkeley political scientist Albert Lepawsky wrote an insightful essay that pinpointed the

[13] Free Speech Movement, "We Want a University" (Dedicated to the 800), in Lipset and Wolin, *The Berkeley Student Revolt*, pp. 209–12. On the darker side of this communitarian revolt against bourgeoisie liberal democracy, see Bernard Yack, *The Longing for Total Revolution: Philosophic Sources of Social Discontent from Rousseau to Marx and Nietzsche* (Princeton University Press, 1986).

[14] Interview with Berkeley philosophy professor John Searle, August 2001. Searle went on to become an administrator and adviser to the chancellor on student affairs. He wrote an anatomy of the 1960s student movements, *The Campus Wars: A Sympathetic Look at the University in Agony* (World Publishing Company, 1971). In this book, Searle wrote that the student movements of the 1960s were often best understood as "religious movements" (p. 5).

[15] Interview with John Searle.

profound choices that Berkeley and other institutions now faced. Lepawsky conceded that political engagement constitutes a proper part of liberal education, especially in a time of democratic ferment. He also acknowledged the alienation generated by the multiversity. But Lepawsky fathomed a contradiction at the heart of FSM that would later come to haunt higher education in America: the status of free speech and thought as universal principles in contrast to the ends of political movements. What if free speech empowered movements deemed detrimental to FSM, the antiwar movement, or civil rights movements? Would free speech then be tolerated? With the traditional belief in the distinctive intellectual ends of the university now rendered suspect, just what were the criteria for determining the proper ordering of priorities? What if political commitments were valued more than what Lepawsky called the "cultivation of the intellectual freedoms"? Sensing an imminent sea change, Lepawsky cautioned that universities would lose their moorings if they allowed political commitment to marginalize the pursuit of truth and the freedom of speech and inquiry:

The main task we face is preserving the university not merely as a free political community but primarily as an institution which is privileged to be an intellectual sanctuary within a greater society that is now in political flux.

After all, the university's prime mission resides not in political activity but in the cultivation of the intellectual freedoms. . . . it is imperative that no one facet of the university's activities, certainly not the political, should dominate its overall responsibilities for the cultivation of the intellect. . . . any conflict between the intellectual and political way of life must be resolved in favor of the primacy of the intellectual over the political.[16]

With the political genie out of the bottle at Berkeley, the big question over the next decades would be whether institutions of higher education could promote and sustain the priorities Lepawsky championed. In some telling respects that I discuss, they have failed. Even at Berkeley, one of FSM's lasting legacies is not free speech but censorship by the students themselves.

New Threats to Free Speech and Civil Liberty

Lepawsky's concern about politics superseding the "cultivation of the intellectual freedoms" was among the most prescient observations of the FSM crisis. The problem was not that the wall separating politics and the university had come tumbling down. The rise of equal speech rights out of the ashes of in loco parentis was inevitable and positive in many respects. Nor need the introduction of politics into the university send chills up educators'

---

[16] Lepawsky, "Intellectual Responsibility and Political Conduct," in Lipset and Wolin, *The Berkeley Student Revolt*, p. 272.

spines. Engagement with the political and historical worlds can invigorate the university, especially in the liberal arts.[17] A problem arises only when the intellectual freedoms are consigned to secondary status in situations and contexts that matter.

In March 2000 Berkeley celebrated the FSM legacy in an official ceremony at which the university announced the opening of the Free Speech Movement Café in the undergraduate Moffit Library, part of a $3.5 million gift to the university from a former librarian. The bequest features a wide assortment of books in the social sciences and humanities, an extensive FSM archive, and the café "where students could discuss ideas and revisit the FSM's struggle to shape their university."[18] The heritage of FSM still reigns over the Berkeley campus, above and beyond the FSM Café.

In addition, Berkeley remains a hotbed of student activism. The Sproul Plaza area – the epicenter of the free speech movement – is a veritable bazaar, presenting an astonishing and intriguing array of student groups promoting their political views and wares, including, to name but a few, the Berkeley ACLU; College Democrats; College Republicans; the International Socialist Organization; the Muslim Student Association; various Asian student groups; students against the war on terrorism (Stop the War); students in favor of the war on terrorism (Pro-America); antisweatshop activists; pro-life and pro-choice groups; students advocating affirmative action based on race (highlighted by BAMN, for "By Any Means Necessary"); groups representing various philosophical, political, and religious orientations. In terms of student political activism, the FSM legacy is alive and well.

But not all is well with the deeper spirit of free speech at Berkeley, at least not in the public forum of speakers and print. The public forum has been notably hostile to ideas deemed incompatible with various causes for more than two decades, spawning several prominent incidents of suppression at the hands of counterdemonstrators. And Boalt Law School has witnessed some political campaigns that have suffocated open and honest discourse, especially in the wake of the passage of Proposition 209 in 1996, which eliminated race-based admissions in the state university system. The situation at Boalt in 1997 and 1998 motivated several students from across the political spectrum to publish a set of essays in an unusual book designed to provoke a discussion on the status of open and honest inquiry in the school – a hope

[17] See Jose Ortega y Gasset, *Mission of the University* (Norton, 1966), pp. 88–89. Ortega was a great defender of the university's distinctive intellectual mission, which included engagement with the world. "Not only does [the university] need perpetual contact with science, on pain of atrophy, it needs contact, likewise, with public life, with historical reality, with the present, which is essentially a whole to be dealt with only in its totality.... The university must be in the midst of real life, and saturated with it." By "science," Ortega means higher theoretical and philosophical thought.

[18] Martin Roysher, "Recollections of FSM," in Cohen and Zelnik, *The Free Speech Movement*, p. 140.

that was disappointed. One of the book's editors described the reason for the manifesto in his own essay:

Many Boalt students act as if their education is threatened whenever any conservative view is expressed. One conservative opinion per class is more than they can stand.... almost any time a lone conservative tried to raise his or her voice during my years at Boalt, things got ugly. Fists, rather than hands, were raised. Eyes rolled. Glares flashed. Intolerance radiated. Diversity of mind was declared dangerous and unwanted....

What excited me most about attending law school at UC Berkeley was its legacy of being an intellectually free university. I presumed Boalt Hall would be the ideal place to expose myself to a true diversity of perspectives.... I was angered that, in seeking truth, I was denied an encouraging environment in which to explore my view.[19]

Another example is the manner in which Berkeley – along with some other schools – reacted to the now famous advertisement that conservative journalist-provocateur David Horowitz sent to student papers in late February 2001, arguing against the idea of government paying monetary reparations for slavery. Though hard-hitting, the ad was not racist according to any standard definition of the term, and it was debated civilly in many forums outside of universities (its text is reproduced in an appendix to this book). Of the fifty-two student papers that received the ad, twenty-seven rejected it outright (which was within their editorial rights), twelve ignored it, and thirteen published it. Of these thirteen, six later apologized, often under great duress. At Berkeley, the *Daily Californian* immediately apologized when faced with angry students and promised never to run such an offending piece again. When Horowitz came to Berkeley to give a public lecture a short time later, the atmosphere was very intense, and he was unable to complete the question-and-answer period following his address due to the unruliness of the audience. It was as if the university consisted of a giant defense mechanism against unwanted ideas. Unfortunately, this type of reaction in the public forum is no stranger to the Berkeley campus, as many other controversial speakers have had their addresses either obstructed or limited by hostile audiences. I discuss some of these cases in a later chapter.

Throughout all of these incidents, a salient fact stands out: no organized group of faculty and/or students has arisen at Berkeley to resist or criticize what has happened to free speech in the public forum.

As is well known, Berkeley is not an isolated case of the restriction of liberty on America's campuses in recent years. Although they remain complex institutions in which a variety of objectives and values compete, institutions of higher learning have been busy since the later 1980s circumscribing and restricting the freedom of speech and due process rights in the name of

[19] David Wienir, "The History," in David Wienir and Marc Berley, eds., *The Diversity Hoax: Law Students Report from Berkeley* (Foundation for Academic Standards and Tradition, 1999), pp. 19, 34. Interview with David Wienir, June 2001.

promoting a variety of causes, including promoting civility and making the university a more hospitable place for minorities and other groups considered to be oppressed. Inclusiveness is a laudable goal, as is the respectful treatment of students and colleagues. As presently envisioned and practiced, however, the so-called diversity movement has too often restricted the diversity of ideas on campus and has violated individual rights. *The Shadow University: The Betrayal of Liberty on America's Campuses* by Alan Charles Kors, a University of Pennsylvania history professor, and Harvey Silverglate, a noted civil liberties attorney, is the definitive work chronicling this state of affairs. According to Kors and Silverglate, there has arisen a "shadow university," composed of select faculty, students, and administrators, that too often forsakes the 1960s promise of openness and intellectual challenge in favor of the suppression of liberty in the service of political causes. In the name of promoting civility and diversity of race, gender, sex, and culture, too many institutions of higher learning have fostered a rigid orthodoxy of belief:

The *best* aspects of that decade's [1960s] idealistic agenda have died on our campuses – free speech, equality of rights, respect for private conscience and individuation, and a sense of undergraduate liberties and adult responsibilities. What remain of the '60s are the *worst* sides: intolerance of dissent from regnant political orthodoxy, the self-appointed power of self-designated "progressives" to set everyone else's moral agenda, and, saddest of all, the belief that universities not only may but should suspend the rights of some in order to transform students, the culture, and the nation according to their ideological vision and desire.[20]

In 2000 Kors and Silverglate established the Foundation for Individual Rights in Education (FIRE) in Philadelphia to provide legal and policy assistance to individuals and groups whose rights have been threatened on campuses across the country. The major problems have concerned censorship, due process violations, unequal treatment under the law, and ideological indoctrination in various contexts. FIRE's executive director, Thor Halvorssen (a former student of Kors), said in 2001 that FIRE receives at least a dozen specific requests for assistance per day. An anonymous e-mail to Halvorssen from a high-level judicial administrator in summer 2001 suggests the considerable extent of the problem in the realm of due process and adjudication:

I spoke with you last week for a while before I got cut off (I was on a pay phone). I am a senior level administrator and director of judicial affairs at a top 10 institution, and have information that I would like to share with you. Believe me, FIRE has barely scratched the surface regarding university/college judicial affairs, and while reading the testimonials on your website is interesting, I notice that none are from

[20] Alan Charles Kors and Harvey Silverglate, *The Shadow University: The Betrayal of Liberty on America's Campuses* (Free Press, 1998), p. 3.

professionals in the field. I believe that information from someone in the field would add greater legitimacy to your good work. Obviously, I don't want to lose my job, but after many years in the field, I believe the public needs to know what really goes on, from a perspective you rarely, if ever, hear from. Can you suggest a next step?[21]

In 2003 FIRE commenced a campaign to challenge speech codes and the suppression of free speech throughout the country. One indicative case dealt with what happened at California Polytechnic Institute in the spring of 2003. A student was found guilty of "disruption" for posting a flier in a public area that offended some students. The poster advertised an upcoming speech by Mason Weaver, author of the 1998 book *It's OK to Leave the Plantation.* Weaver argues in this book that undue reliance upon the government perpetuates a slave mentality in African Americans. During a lengthy hearing, the vice president for student affairs told the student, "You are a young white male member of CPCR [Cal Poly College Republicans]. To students of color, this may be a collision of experience. . . . The chemistry has racial implications, and you are naïve not to acknowledge those." FIRE entered the case in April. After a great deal of jockeying back and forth, the case was finally settled in May 2004, when the university agreed to expunge the conviction from the record and to pay the student $40,000 in legal fees. The case was settled because of the pressure exerted by FIRE on the student's behalf.[22]

Throughout this book we encounter reasons for why this retreat of civil liberty has taken place. The most obvious reason is that the key assumptions undergirding respect for civil liberty – respect for individualism, tolerance of political dissent, and a belief in standards of truth independent of politics and power – have come under suspicion as ostensible obstacles to social justice. But something unexpected happened on the road to a new social justice: a new form of injustice arose.

The Purpose of This Book and My Change of Mind

Much has been written about the proliferation of speech and harassment codes, compromises of due process, and political or ideological indoctrination programs that have assumed prominent roles throughout higher education in recent years. The main concern of this book is to focus on something that has not yet been directly addressed: the politics of resistance and mobilization against the illiberal practices associated with such policies. A successful free speech and civil liberty movement at the University of Wisconsin,

---

[21] E-mail to Thor Halvorssen of FIRE, July 2001. Interview with Thor Halvorssen, July 2001.
[22] "Cal Poly Student Punished for Posting Flier: Public University Gives Veto to Students Who Claim 'Offense,'" on FIRE's website at www.theFIRE.org; "Cal Poly Settles Suit by Student," *Los Angeles Times,* May 6, 2004.

Madison, with which I have been associated has revealed the ways in which an active nonpartisan faculty-student alliance can make a difference when rights are threatened. Such mobilization can protect and promote rights that are essential to the university's most important mission, which is the Socratic pursuit of truth and truthfulness.

The University of Wisconsin and the University of Pennsylvania are two of the few institutions that have witnessed such political mobilization and reversal of restrictions of liberty that were begat in the late 1980s and the 1990s. The situation has probably improved at other institutions as well, if only because the energy behind the suppression of liberty might have lost some of its edge. But Wisconsin and Penn are rare examples of actual reversals at the hands of political action. Under the leadership of Alan Kors, Penn's liberalization movement fits an entrepreneurial model, whereas Wisconsin's movement represents a broader political mobilization. Nonetheless, restrictions on speech and civil liberty continue at other institutions. As of this writing, Wisconsin and Penn remain essentially isolated cases of successful recapturing of liberal principles of freedom.

This book presents and analyzes the three major reasons why this state of affairs has arisen:

1. Key changes in the intellectual, pedagogical, political, and administrative culture.
2. The lack of meaningful political mobilization on the part of faculty and students to protect free speech and liberty interests. This problem represents a failure of *commitment*.
3. The lack of knowledge in the intellectual and public life of universities concerning the nature of basic constitutional rights and the reasons for taking constitutional liberty seriously. This problem is a failure of *education*.

My observations are sharpened by the fact that I was originally a supporter of speech codes and related policies. In fact, as a faculty senator I voted for broadly worded faculty and student speech codes enacted at the University of Wisconsin in 1988. Led by our new chancellor, Donna Shalala, the university assumed the mantle of national leadership in the pro–speech code movement. But events later caused me and others to change our minds about the wisdom of such policies and to question the university's course.

I was hired at Wisconsin in 1985 largely on the basis of my first book, *Nazis in Skokie*, which dealt with the famous Skokie free speech controversy of 1977–78, a case that still echoes in the lore of constitutional law and politics. I maintained that the courts erred in extending First Amendment protection to a Nazi group (the National Socialist Party of America) to hold a rally in Skokie, Illinois, the home of several hundred Holocaust survivors. I argued that "targeted racial vilification" does not merit First Amendment protection because of the trauma and moral harm it inflicts.[23] *Nazis in Skokie* represented an attempt to balance free speech rights with a communitarian concept of justice. Because of this view, I later supported speech codes and related policies, in part because I still trusted university administrators to find a way to strike a reasonable balance.

My ideological turnaround was the culmination of a long process of observing, thinking, and interacting with colleagues and students. As my teaching and writing evolved over time, I became more suspicious of administrative restrictions on speech, especially as I learned about applications of the codes and related policies at Wisconsin and elsewhere to situations they were not supposed to cover. I also began to appreciate the importance of a principle championed by journalist Jonathan Rauch, an eventual ally of the movement at Wisconsin who wrote a small classic book published in 1993 on free speech, *Kindly Inquisitors: The New Attacks on Free Thought*. Rauch argues that a new ethic has won allegiance in many institutions that is inimical to intellectual freedom – the "humanitarian principle," which dictates that one should strive above all not to offend others, especially the oppressed. The West's indifferent reaction to threats by militant Muslims against Salman Rushdie for publishing the book *Satanic Verses* in the late 1980s "showed how readily westerners could be backed away from a fundamental principle of intellectual liberalism, namely that there is nothing whatever wrong with offending – hurting people's feelings – in pursuit of truth."[24] The right not to be offended was now ascendant in many domains of American society, especially its universities, where it was linked to various other causes. The problem is that the pursuit of truth and intellectual engagement wither and die if we grow afraid to offend or anger by presenting our honestly held ideas and beliefs – especially when the antioffense principle is enforced by sanctions backed by administrative power.

By the early 1990s it was becoming evident how the speech codes and the ideologies that they represented had hampered intellectual honesty. Many colleagues and students related that they felt as if they were walking on eggshells in class when talking about racially and sexually sensitive topics – even though these were among the most important social and political topics of our time. In addition, by the early 1990s a small number of faculty had become aware of some very questionable investigations that had taken place under the aegis of the faculty speech code – investigations that had been conducted in a manner suggesting an ideological agenda. These cases gave a human face to the abstract claims that the code compromised civil liberty.

[23] *Nazis in Skokie: Freedom, Community, and the First Amendment* (University of Notre Dame Press, 1985). See *Collin v. Smith*, 578 F. 2d 1197 (7th Cir. 1978); *Skokie v. National Socialist Party of America*, 373 N.E.2d 21 (1978).

[24] Jonathan Rauch, *Kindly Inquisitors: The New Attacks on Free Thought* (University of Chicago Press, 1993), esp. p. 22.

Another major factor that influenced my thinking was my students. Students whom I respected ultimately convinced me that broad speech codes (or any speech codes, for that matter) were a bad idea, especially for *students*. Many code advocates assumed that students needed the administrative apparatus to support their self-esteem, psychological well-being, and identities. This assumption represented a return of in loco parentis to campus in a new, politicized guise after its banishment in the 1960s. Many pro–free speech students – often women and members of minority groups – considered this assumption demeaning. Such students considered themselves responsible young adults who are capable of dealing constructively with the rigors of constitutional citizenship and free speech.

Faculty colleagues who valued intellectual and academic freedom were also influential. These individuals included those who fought back after suffering through some questionable investigations, and those who provided the vehicle for mobilization that ultimately gave civil liberty concerns public voice and a measure of power. Such colleagues in mobilization demonstrated the importance of organizing and being willing to accept the substantial investments of time, effort, and peace of mind that successful political action – especially political action that goes against the grain – demands.

Interactions with such noteworthy students and faculty made me appreciate the liberal republican ethic that holds a special place in First Amendment theory and practice. Liberal republicanism envisions a balance between individualism and active public citizenship, stressing such virtues as self-reliance, public-spiritedness, the willingness to face uncomfortable truths, and intellectual and moral courage. Justice Louis Brandeis championed this concept in his famous concurring opinion in *Whitney v. California* (1927). "To courageous, self-reliant men, with confidence in the power of free and fearless reasoning applied through the processes of popular government, no danger flowing from speech can be deemed clear and present, unless the incidence of the evil apprehended is so imminent that it may befall before there is opportunity for full discussion."[25]

Finally, the illiberal tendencies of many procensorship policies became troubling. In addition to campus incidents, new literature dealing with theories of free speech began moving considerably beyond the balance I had struck in *Nazis in Skokie*. Such thinking as critical race theory and the antipornography movement of Catharine MacKinnon identified as the enemy the principles of individualism, autonomy, and state neutrality in relation to

[25] *Whitney v. California*, 274 U.S. 357 (1927). See Pnina Lahav, "Holmes and Brandeis: Libertarian and Republican Justifications for Free Speech," 4 *Journal of Law and Politics* 451 (1987). Of course, free speech doctrine is predicated on other theories as well, some of which Brandeis also addresses – for example, truth, self-fulfillment, safety valve for society, protecting dissent, self-government, distrust of government, and antithought control.

the content of expression. Such thinking promoted suspicion of individual freedom as a remedy to inequality.[26]

The Importance of a New Kind of Politics

The central thesis of this book is simple and seemingly obvious: the preservation or restoration of free speech and basic civil liberty on campus depends upon political mobilization and commitment that give these principles public presence on campus. Although freedom of inquiry and speech remain deeply entrenched beliefs in most major institutions, these principles will not flourish in the cauldron of modern university politics unless they are backed by the power or presence that only political commitment can bestow.[27] Failure to act surrenders the public realm to movements with other agendas. Academic and intellectual freedom are not manna from heaven. A brief look at recent history suggests the difference that mobilization can make.

Examples

At Penn, the work of Alan Kors, Michael Cohen, and a small cohort of supporters brought about institutional change in the mid-1990s that was virtually unthinkable in the previous decade, in which Penn championed speech codes and related policies designed to foster diversity and civility. But rather than ushering in a new era of harmony and mutual respect envisioned by the administration, the policies often engendered suspicion, acrimony, and compromises of the spirit of intellectual liberty, at least in some telling respects. These trends culminated in a notorious case in 1993, in which the Penn judicial system accused freshman Eden Jacobowitz of violating Penn's speech code. Jacobowitz's transgression lay in calling some African American sorority sisters "water buffalos" for partying loudly outside his dormitory late one night. (Several other students also said disparaging things, but only Jacobowitz admitted shouting something at the women.) Although the term "water buffalo" was widely understood to have a nonracial meaning, Penn proceeded to prosecute the case. Kors became Jacobowitz's adviser and, after much struggle, managed to turn the case into a national cause célèbre. Kors then leveraged the impact of the case to effectuate stunning institutional

---

[26] On how much of critical race and other antiliberal theory in law leads to authoritarianism and other problems, see Daniel A. Farber and Suzanna Sherry, *Beyond All Reason: The Radical Assault on Truth in American Law* (Oxford University Press, 1997). On MacKinnon's antipornography movement, see Donald Alexander Downs, *The New Politics of Pornography* (University of Chicago Press, 1989), and Wendy McElroy, ed., *Liberty for Women: Freedom and Feminism in the Twenty-first Century* (Ivan R. Dee for The Independent Institute, 2002).

[27] On the necessity of power to the actualization of rights, see Stephen Holmes, *Passions and Constraint: On the Theory of Liberal Democracy* (University of Chicago Press, 1995), esp. p. 270. Donald A. Downs, "Human Rights/Civil Liberties," *International Encyclopedia of Social and Behavioral Sciences* (Pergamon/Elsevier, 2001).

change at Penn that included the abolition of the speech code and ideological changes in student orientation programs.

Wisconsin provides a different kind of example. When the faculty senate promulgated a student and a faculty speech code in 1988, no organized opposition arose to challenge or influence the procode movement that had swept the campus. The politics and debate were remarkably one-sided. Timothy Shiell writes about how the lack of opposition led to questionable codes at many schools:

[W]hat happened at Yale (and Michigan and Wisconsin for that matter) was hardly inevitable. . . . things could have turned out differently, and they turned out as they did largely because of political forces. At Michigan and Wisconsin no organized opposition to hate speech regulation with political clout emerged, although it could have. For example, instead of backing down in the face of student pressure, the UW-Madison Chancellor Donna Shalala could have remained resolute in her conviction that the Madison speech incidents were protected by the First Amendment. But she didn't. She became an advocate of regulation, maintaining that "We're talking about harassment here, not impinging free speech."[28]

But as individuals learned about several improper investigations at Wisconsin under the aegis of the codes in the 1990s, they began to scrape together a mobilization movement that culminated in the formation in 1996 of an independent faculty group, the Committee for Academic Freedom and Rights (CAFR). CAFR has served as the home base for several political and legal actions that have brought about Wisconsin's version of surprising change, including abolition of the faculty speech code by a faculty senate vote in 1999, some due process reform in 1999, the dismantling of a system of anonymous complaint boxes in 2000, the legal defense of individuals whose rights have been jeopardized, and the rise of a political environment that is considerably more conducive to civil liberty on campus. In fact, CAFR served as a model for FIRE, as Harvey Silverglate was impressed with its organization and politics when he visited Wisconsin in 1999. When John Wiley became chancellor in 2000, he proved to be noticeably friendlier to civil liberty concerns. The Wiley administration has taken some important civil liberty claims seriously and has striven to find a balance between sensitivity and free speech that takes account of the latter.

The faculty speech code abolition at Wisconsin was the most important victory in terms of setting a new tone for the campus. It also garnered considerable national recognition, receiving coverage in such media as *Wall Street Journal, New York Times, Boston Globe, National Journal,* Associated Press, *Village Voice, Reason, Liberty,* and National Public Radio, as well as the

---

[28] Timothy C. Shiell, *Campus Hate Speech on Trial* (University of Kansas Press, 1998), p. 55. See also Samuel Walker, *Hate Speech: The History of an American Controversy* (University of Nebraska Press, 1994), p. 2.

Chronicle of Higher Education, which published a cover story and several follow-up articles.[29]

The movements at Wisconsin and Penn had to undertake the difficult task of reversing already entrenched policies. The fate of speech codes at Duke University presents an instructive example of political resistance *before* the adoption of codes. Advocates of a speech code were gaining headway when Duke considered adopting a code in 1989, and adoption seemed inevitable until the vice president of student affairs, who had formed a special committee with representatives of various groups, brought a noted constitutional law professor, William Van Alstyne, into the process. The former legal counsel to the American Association of University Professors, Van Alstyne stopped the code movement dead in its tracks when he raised serious questions about its advisability. His prestige on campus gave his claims great weight. According to David P. Redlawsk, "Members of the faculty familiar with the speech code process attributed the lack of a code solely to the efforts of William Van Alstyne.... [At a crucial meeting] Van Alstyne 'was astounded at the hostility' he felt at the meeting, according to [physics professor Lawrence] Evans, so he asked that examples of incidents be supplied. When such incidents were not forthcoming, it became clear that the proposed code could not be justified."[30] It is often far easier to stop a controversial measure while it is evolving than to reverse a policy already enacted. Penn and Wisconsin had to surmount the latter obstacle, whereas Van Alstyne's intervention spared Duke that difficulty.

The literature and debate on speech codes and related policies have focused on the question of constitutional rights enforceable by courts. This approach is important, but it downplays the importance of politics. Court cases are expensive, and courts have limited enforcement powers. More important, reliance on courts can diminish the development of political skills and mobilization dedicated to persuasion and changing minds. Judicial orders might "oblige" one to obey the law, but they do not always make one feel "obligated" to obey. (In the latter case, one obeys because one feels a normative commitment to do so.)[31] Rights won through politics and legislation are more likely to change people's thinking because majorities have to be convinced to agree. In addition, political action and networking encourage

---

[29] See, e.g., "Rethinking Limits on Faculty Speech: U. of Wisconsin Debate Reflects Changing Views of Political Correctness and Academic Freedom," *Chronicle of Higher Education*, October 2, 1998, p. A1.

[30] Redlawsk, "'We Don't Need No Thought Control': The Controversy over Multiculturalism at Duke," in Milton Heumann and Thomas W. Church, eds., *Hate Speech on Campus: Cases, Case Studies, and Commentary* (Northeastern University Press, 1997), p. 217.

[31] Gerald Rosenberg, *The Hollow Hope: Can Courts Bring about Social Change?* (University of Chicago Press, 1991); on the distinction between being obliged and being obligated, see H. L. A. Hart, *The Concept of Law* (Oxford University Press, 1961).

people to build alliances and infrastructures that can endure over time.[32] This is one reason members of the Wisconsin free speech movement were ultimately glad (despite their surprise and initial chagrin) that the Wisconsin Civil Liberties Union turned down their request that it take the faculty speech code to court. Because the movement was forced to fight politically, it had to forge a coalition that changed the complexion of the campus climate for free speech and civil liberty. Members of the movement were not so forgiving about the WCLU's later refusal to even back their case politically, however. This was unfortunate, for the WCLU was the organization that litigated the student speech code at Wisconsin; and its parent, the national American Civil Liberties Union, had a well-earned reputation as a defender of free speech on campus and in other domains.[33]

Counterexamples

Berkeley and Columbia provide two illuminating counterexamples to Penn and Wisconsin in the politics of mobilization. In 2000, for example, the Columbia University senate enacted questionable new procedures for the adjudication of sexual misconduct cases. Although reform was needed, the new policy discarded many essential aspects of due process. When FIRE and its allies made public what Columbia had wrought, public opinion was overwhelmingly negative. In exposing the new policy in October 2000, the *Wall Street Journal* (acting in conjunction with FIRE) editorialized about "silenced faculty" and opined that "The short shrift given due process at one of the nation's most distinguished universities gave rise to no objections from the Columbia faculty, with but one or two exceptions.... It is a policy that mirrors an ominously increasing tendency to devalue due process in the interest of a select category of victims."[34]

I found in my research that the movement toward the policy was remarkably one-sided. Virtually no dissenting voices were heard on any university committee established to deal with the policy, nor did any such voice speak out in the broader political arena. Two professors and one student

---

[32] See Robert McKeever, *Raw Judicial Power? The Supreme Court and American Society* (Manchester University Press, 1993), esp. p. 279; and Mark V. Tushnet, *Taking the Constitution Away from the Courts* (Princeton University Press, 1999). See also Jeremy Waldron's "jurisprudence of legislation" in *Law and Disagreement* (Oxford University Press, 1999), chs. 1–6.

[33] The ACLU's president, Nadine Strossen, has written extensively against speech codes and other restrictions of free speech. See, e.g., Nadine Strossen, *Defending Pornography: Free Speech, and the Fight for Women's Rights* (New York University Press, 1995).

[34] "Due Process at Columbia," *Wall Street Journal*, October 4, 2000, p. A26. The two exceptions were astronomy professor James Applegate and law professor (and now federal judge) Gerard Lynch, who spoke strongly against the policy in the penultimate senate meeting in February 2000. See Columbia Senate Notes, February 5, 2000; interviews with Applegate and Lynch, June 2001.

courageously opposed the policy in the Columbia University senate before the vote, but their opposition was too little too late. A broad coalition of student groups led by a group called SAFER (Students Active for Ending Rape) marshaled a massive campaign in support of the policy that included marches, rallies, and the wearing of red tape by up to 25 percent of the student body, symbolizing the "bureaucratic red tape" that had bedeviled the previous system. It was only after the senate adopted the policy in February 2000 that the campus ACLU entered the fray. Columbia alumnus Lawrence Kaplan of the *New Republic* underscored the failure of resistance and courage on behalf of administrators and faculty in the debate over the due process reforms: "After Columbia's President George Rupp endorsed the new rules, one of the campaign's teenage coordinators boasted, 'There was obviously some fear in the eyes of the administrators.'"[35] Similar problems have beset the status of free speech in the public forum at Berkeley, as I mentioned earlier. No free speech or civil liberty resistance or mobilization exists at either Berkeley or Columbia.

The Return of the Proprietary University

Given their moral charters to promote open discourse and the pursuit of truth, universities should be the last institutions in American society to surrender to a homogeneity of opinion. Yet that is what has happened too often in the drive for diversity, which is one of the motivating forces behind the speech and harassment policies that have come to play such prominent roles in higher education in America.

Ethnic and cultural diversity are among America's greatest strengths, and need to be fostered and respected. A proper education must expose students to the actual diversity of our country; and encountering individuals of different races and backgrounds broadens intellectual horizons and contributes to citizenship. But diversity properly understood also includes numerous categories beyond those of race, gender, and sexual orientation, such as geography, philosophy, aesthetic interests, athletics – one could name a virtually infinite number of things. True diversity respects individual differences in addition to cultural or racial differences and embraces the diversity of ideas and ideologies.[36] Of course, race, ethnicity, sexual orientation, and gender are aspects of identity about which all individuals should be proud. And ascriptive differences are often the basis of discrimination and differentials in power. The problem arises when identity politics uses these categories of

---

[35] Lawrence Kaplan, "Columbia Blues," Washington Diarist, *New Republic*, December 4, 2000, p. 58. On these issues, see SAFER's website at www.columbia.edu/cu/safer, and FIRE's website at www.theFire.org.

[36] My thinking in this regard is similar to that of Peter Wood in his recent book, *Diversity: The Invention of a Concept* (Encounter Books, 2003). Wood distinguishes between "actual" and "imagined" diversity.

difference to marginalize differences *within* identity groups and to thwart the process of individual self-determination and discovery. In other words, diversity works best when it is allied with liberal principles of freedom – not when it conceives of liberal freedom as an enemy.

As presently conceived, however, the diversity movement focuses too obsessively on what divides citizens and on racial and ethnic proportionality and differences. This understanding of diversity has not always been friendly to intellectual diversity and the pursuit of truth. Its practitioners often classify individuals too exclusively according to such ascriptive categories as race, gender, and sexual orientation, thereby downplaying the freedom to define oneself according to one's free self-determination. And for reasons that I elaborate in the next chapter, adherents of the movement have often proved to be surprisingly paternalistic, construing individuals as too weak to withstand the rigors of critical discourse. (Peter H. Schuck argues in a recent book that diversity efforts are more successful and consistent with liberty when they arise from the spontaneous choices of the citizenry rather than being imposed by government or authorities in a top-down manner.)[37] Much of the censorship we encounter in this book has been motivated by the desire to promote diversity as presently understood. In such cases, commitment to the pursuit of truth has taken a back seat to the promotion of ostensible diversity interests. The point is not to abandon diversity for freedom but rather to reconceive of diversity in a manner that is decidedly more consistent with liberal principles of freedom. Schuck is one of a growing list of authors who presents promising alternatives to the present conception. Wisconsin has begun to fashion this type of balance, as the administration and campus community have absorbed some of the principles and lessons promoted by the free speech movement on campus. Rather than opposing diversity as a goal, the movement has striven to broaden the conception of diversity to make it more consistent with traditional liberal norms.

When universities pursue diversity in an unprincipled fashion, they have too often succumbed to dishonesty about such things as their admission practices and their commitment to free speech. In some cases, officials have camouflaged admission policies that conflict with public opinion concerning the proper use of racial preferences. (Many schools have refused to make public relevant nonpersonal information about admissions, for example.)[38]

---

[37] Peter H. Schuck, *Diversity in America: Keeping Government at a Safe Distance* (Harvard University Press, 2003).

[38] At Michigan, it took a lawsuit by philosopher Carl Cohen under the Freedom of Information Act to get the university to make known its criteria for admissions. This led to the Supreme Court case addressing the constitutionality of using racial preferences in admissions. *Gratz v. Bollinger*, 539 u.s. 244 (2003); *Grutter v. Bollinger*, 539 U.S. 306 (2003). The Wisconsin Association of Scholars has filed suit to get the University of Wisconsin to disclose its criteria for admissions, which is pending as I write. *J. Marshall Osborn and Center for Equal Opportunity v. Board of Regents of the University of Wisconsin System*, case no. 99-CV-2958.

In other cases, officials declare their support of free speech, while they endorse censorship of speech deemed politically incorrect. It is hard to contest the claim of sociologist Peter Wood: "Diversity as we have come to know it is seldom a friend of the pursuit of truth. The double standards in admissions tempt colleges and universities into public deception; unwanted disclosures prompt censorship, and campus discussions chill into polite avoidance of some hard and potentially embarrassing topics."[39]

One reason that the diversity movement as presently conceived has too often spawned policies and actions detrimental to the pursuit of truth and intellectual honesty is because the movement has failed to question its own motives, which are often construed as beyond moral reproach. The new administrative elite and campus leadership that have arisen since 1980 consist of persons with similar beliefs and visions concerning the promotion of diversity.[40] This uniformity of opinion is detrimental to universities because the right measure of self-doubt is essential to the Socratic pursuit of truth. The Socratic method consists of a dialectic of continuous questioning among critical thinkers that proceeds in the spirit of the sifting and winnowing of ideas. Dana Villa provides insight into the need for criticism in his book, *Socratic Citizenship*. "The implication of Socratic examination is that virtually every moral belief becomes false and an incitement to injustice the moment it becomes unquestioned or unquestionable." Socrates "suggests that civic virtue and morals, unaccompanied by intellectual hygiene – by a thinking which dissolves opinions rather than solidifying them – are the invariable accomplices of injustice and immorality."[41] This point is consistent with the principle of checks and balances in the Constitution. The framers institutionalized checks and balances not because they feared the clash of different interests but because they feared majority tyranny. The danger to public justice lies not in factional conflict but in the undue homogeneity of opinion.[42]

In its famous 1915 Declaration of Principles on academic freedom, the American Association of University Professors contrasted the mission of the new types of research universities that had grown to prominence with the mission of more traditional colleges and universities. The new research institutions were dedicated to individual freedom in the areas of inquiry and research, teaching, and extramural utterance and action. On the contrary, the older institutions existed to preserve the values – often religious in

---

[39] Wood, *Diversity*, p. 136.

[40] See, e.g., Frederick Lynch, *The Diversity Machine: The Drive to Change the "White Male Workplace"* (Transaction, 2002); Alan Wolfe, "The New Class Comes Home," in Karzweil and Phillips, *Our Country, Our Culture*, pp. 283–91.

[41] Dana Villa, *Socratic Citizenship* (Princeton University Press, 2001), pp. 23, xii.

[42] See Paul Eidelberg, *The Philosophy of the American Constitution: A Reinterpretation of the Intentions of the Founding Fathers* (Free Press, 1968), p. 153.

nature – of their founders and trustees. Such *"proprietary institutions"* were devoted "not to advance knowledge by the unrestricted research and unfettered discussion of impartial investigators, but rather to subsidize the promotion of opinions held by the persons, usually not of the scholar's calling, who provide the funds for their maintenance."[43] The older proprietary university was concerned with preserving a certain vision of the world, not with critical inquiry. It fell into secondary status in the twentieth century after science prevailed in its long struggle with religion to become the primary source of intellectual truth.[44] Today we could be witnessing a new chapter in the politics of higher education, as the tenets of academic freedom compete with the perceived requirements of diversity.

Although it emphasizes societal transformation rather than conservation, in many telling respects the new vision of the university represents a return to the proprietary university of yore. The new version devalues intellectual conflict in favor of an agenda extrinsic to the pursuit of truth and has ushered in new in loco parentis policies that now take the form of speech codes and paternalistic student orientation. Whereas old student conduct codes attempted to reinforce manners, the new codes attempt to influence students' attitudes and thoughts through various kinds of pressure. The new concept of the proprietary university is not necessarily predominant, but it has attained enough status to pose serious challenges to the liberal notion of the university once envisioned by the AAUP.

The Mobilization of Resistance and Change

A comparison of the political contexts at Berkeley, Wisconsin, Penn, and Columbia illustrates the importance of political mobilization to empower checks and balances. It also shows how such mobilization can lead to surprising results if the right circumstances arise. Sociologist-economist Timur Kuran presents a theory of social and political change that is remarkably pertinent to what happened at Wisconsin and Penn. Often radical change is unimaginable for the simple reason that most sympathizers are hesitant to express their true beliefs. Kuran explains in *Private Truths, Public Lies: The Social Consequences of Preference Falsification* that in environments hostile to dissent, large numbers of people feel compelled to keep their true beliefs to themselves and do not speak out because of fear of ostracism or punishment, or because they doubt that their views will be supported by others. They will

---

[43] General Report of the Committee on Academic Freedom and Academic Tenure (1915), American Association of University Professors. In William Van Alstyne, ed., *Freedom and Tenure in the Academy* (Duke University Press, 1993), appendix A.

[44] For an insightful overview of the historic conflict between science and religion in higher education, see George M. Marsden, *The Soul of the American University: From Protestant Establishment to Established Nonbelief* (Oxford University Press, 1994).

speak their truth only if they believe that it is not futile to do so.[45] One of the examples that Kuran discusses is the rise and maintenance of speech codes on college campuses. At Wisconsin, codes persisted for years even though – as we later discovered – many faculty and students opposed them.

Preference falsification means "the act of misrepresenting one's genuine wants under perceived social pressures." Through preference falsification, people suppress their true preferences, thereby compromising their human dignity and the process by which truth and social change are forged. "The status quo, once sustained because people were afraid to challenge it, will thus come to persist because no one understands its flaws or can imagine a better alternative."[46] Kuran's thesis is similar to John Stuart Mill's claim that even absolute truths need to be challenged lest they lose their vitality. It also calls to mind Allan Bloom's penetrating observation that "[f]reedom of mind requires not only, or not even especially, the absence of legal constraints but the presence of alternative thoughts. The most successful tyranny is not the one that uses force to assure uniformity, but the one that removes the awareness of other possibilities."[47]

Kuran paints what at first seems a pessimistic picture of how fear of reprisals and the lack of diverse viewpoints in the public sphere promote living with a lie. But he also portrays how change can suddenly erupt when background opposition is intense and an event or activist group sparks an explosion of change in people's thinking, igniting a chain reaction. The key is passing the critical threshold:

> In the presence of preference falsification, private opposition may spread and intensify indefinitely without any apparent change in support for the status quo. Yet at some point the right event, even an intrinsically minor one, can make a few sufficiently disgruntled individuals reach their thresholds for speaking out against the status quo. Their switches can then impel others to add their own voices to the opposition. Public opposition can grow through a bandwagon process, with each addition generating further additions until much of society stands publicly opposed to the status quo.[48]

Public authority can be a kind of house of cards, sustained by a fragile underlying foundation of support. In such situations, sudden and radical change can happen even in the absence of directed mass mobilization. Seemingly minor events or the activities of small groups can generate a breakthrough. The magnitude of the change can seem almost miraculous. "Political leaders are often amazed to see their efforts bear fruit. When individual decisions are interdependent, small events can have great consequences. . . . It is necessary

[45] Timur Kuran, *Private Truths, Public Lies: The Social Consequences of Preference Falsification* (Harvard University Press, 1995).

[46] Ibid., p. 19.

[47] Allan Bloom, *The Closing of the American Mind: How Higher Education Has Betrayed Democracy and Impoverished the Souls of Today's Students* (Simon and Schuster, 1987), p. 249.

[48] Kuran, *Private Truths, Public Lies*, p. 20.

only for additions to the opposition to trigger further defections from the government's ranks. In other words, the threshold sequence must form a bandwagon that is mobile at the prevailing public opposition."[49]

Although neither Penn nor Wisconsin has witnessed the kind of comprehensive reversals that Kuran portrays in his book, his theory nonetheless fits well with what took place at those schools on their way to abolishing their respective speech codes. The Wisconsin story includes an activist core that was able to generate a bandwagon effect under propitious circumstances. The eventual breakthrough led to the establishment of a new set of public priorities that helped win the code battle, and which remains competitive in the public realm. That said, the Wisconsin case differed from the Kuran model in two respects. First, the administration did not topple (at Penn, the "water buffalo" case did in effect lead to the administration's demise). Second, change came about gradually, rather than all at once. But the movement became credible in circumstances that are otherwise similar to the process that Kuran describes. In reporting in the *National Journal* on the 1991 Richard Long case – the first known example of a questionable investigation at the University of Wisconsin – and the later faculty code abolition, Jonathan Rauch wrote that before 1999, "the speech code and the climate it represented looked as sturdy as the Berlin Wall – which, it turns out, is exactly how sturdy they were. In 1999, Long is rubbing his eyes. 'I thought this would last a thousand years,' says Long. 'I never thought it would change in my lifetime.'"[50]

In the rest of this book, I discuss cases involving the success and failure of pro–civil liberty movements to develop on campus. The case studies highlight how failure to mobilize has left important free speech and civil liberty interests in the lurch.

The Outline of the Book

I address the challenge to freedom that has beset institutions over the course of the later 1980s and the 1990s, and how we could alleviate this challenge through the right kind of political action. This work has implications for the study of higher education, law and politics, and political and legal theory. I hope that it also has something to say about human nature and human action under pressure.

Before I move to the cases, I set the stage in the next chapter by examining the political, cultural, institutional, and legal forces that contributed to the

---

[49] Ibid., pp. 49, 252. This notion is similar to Hannah Arendt's notion of "action" as a product of politics and human effort that cannot be predicted by science or understandings based on scientific cause and effect. Arendt, *The Human Condition* (University of Chicago Press, 1958).

[50] Rauch, "An Earthquake in PC Land," *National Journal*, March 6, 1999.

rise of speech codes and related policies. The new policies were the extension
of interrelated theories that addressed education, race and gender relations,
the distribution of power in society, and the nature and impact of public and
private speech. To understand codes and related policies fully, the reader
must have an understanding of the assumptions from which they arose.

In Part II, I present four case studies that show different forms of the
politics of civil liberty on campus. I discuss the politics of the Columbia
University sexual misconduct policy; the status of free speech in the public
forum at Berkeley and in Boalt Law School during the 1997–98 academic
year; the turnaround that Kors engineered at Penn in the wake of the water
buffalo case; and the politics surrounding the abolition of the faculty speech
code at Wisconsin in 1999, and the institutional consequences of that victory.
In a final chapter in Part III, I draw conclusions from the consideration of
cases. My analysis deals with questions of politics and policy. Here I develop
a model of mobilization for civil liberties on campus and advance some
thoughts about what I consider the proper limits of expression in institutions
of higher education.

My methods and my own role as a participant in the subject of my inquiry
deserve a word of explanation. I interviewed key individuals involved in the
politics of the relevant institutions, and I sifted and winnowed primary and
secondary data. Concerning my own role in the drama of Wisconsin's speech
codes, at appropriate points I discuss my thoughts and experiences when they
serve to illuminate the thought processes and interactions of my allies and
me as we fought this battle. Because I have been a leader of the University
of Wisconsin free speech and civil liberty movement, my observations and
perspectives are part of the story.

Along these lines, the reader will note a change of tone in the two chapters
on the Wisconsin case. Although I sought to be fair and objective, I found
it impossible to divorce completely my own views as a participant from the
chronicling of the story. This fact has both positive and negative aspects. In
my defense, my personal involvement in the case gave me a vantage point
concerning the politics and motivations of key actors that I obviously did
not possess in the other case studies that I present. I ultimately decided that it
would be best to maintain some personal perspective in order to illustrate the
way such cases call forth and impact participants' feelings, motivations, and
thoughts. The drawback, however, is that such an approach can compromise
fairness and objectivity. In the end, I strove to find the right balance by telling
the Wisconsin story as objectively as possible (the reader will note that I am
not wary of criticizing my side) while maintaining the personal angle and
perspective in relevant contexts. I hope that the reader is able to separate any
criticism of me in this regard from his or her evaluation of the case itself.

2

The Rise of Ideologies against Free Speech and Liberty

In this chapter, I provide some background material on the political and ideological culture of universities that gave rise to speech codes and related policies. I make no claim to tracing cause and effect in any definitive sense. My objective is simply to discuss some of the most salient intellectual, legal, and political movements that helped to marginalize such cardinal liberal principles as free speech, academic freedom, due process, and equal status under the law. Nor do I suggest that the ascendance of nonliberal principles and practices has been a monolithic movement, for many institutions have found themselves torn between their commitment to liberal principles and the illiberal aspects of the new agendas.

For example, while Stanford adopted a new undergraduate requirement that moved away from traditional notions of liberal education, many departments have avoided the influence of such norms. The political science department at Stanford, for instance, remains a bastion of high-level methodology that is not affected by many of the trends discussed in this chapter. And while the University of California at San Diego has been afflicted by several free speech crises concerning conservative student publications, the political science department there has remained staunchly empirical and free of ideological bias.[1] But the example of UC San Diego also indicates how the politics of the new campus agendas can affect key domains of even those institutions in which major departments remain committed to more traditional notions of academic freedom. Indeed, we will see that while the crisis of the public forum at Berkeley was mounting, academic freedom and a commitment to scholarship remained the norms within individual departments. The problem lay elsewhere, in such places as the public forum and student politics, where the norms of intellectual freedom that held sway in departments failed to carry over. Problems have often arisen when circumstances caused the politics of the new agendas to collide with traditional norms of freedom,

[1] On the crises at UC San Diego, see the reports on FIRE's website: www.theFIRE.org.

requiring the new class of administrators to choose sides. At Berkeley this collision has occurred in the public forum. At Penn, it took place in the public forum, student orientation practices, and the judicial system. Meanwhile, at the University of Michigan the speech code led to some serious violations of academic freedom in the classroom itself.

What is clear is that liberal principles came under sustained attack on many fronts. Interestingly, many writers have noted that 1987 was the pivotal year in this development; among other things, that year witnessed the launching of speech codes around the country.[2] I begin by presenting an illustrative case at my own school.

The Art Department Wars: A Representative Case

The case of Professor Richard Long and the art department at the University of Wisconsin was eventually instrumental in the drive to abolish the faculty speech code at Madison, which took place eight years after the Long affair ended. The case was also a microcosm of the new world view and politics that were then rising to prominence at the University of Wisconsin and elsewhere.[3]

In mid-November 1990, University of Wisconsin art professor Richard Long said "*Seig heil*, comrades" to two graduate students who had been badgering him for weeks in the hallways because of his perceived "conservative" views. Like millions of Americans before him, Long was simply accusing someone of acting like a fascist. But unbeknownst to Long, one student was part Gypsy, and the other's wife was Jewish. Long soon found himself under investigation by the university's Affirmative Action Office (AAO) and a special committee for possible violation of the faculty speech code. Right away, authorities approached the case from the perspective of a new moral paradigm: rather than being a matter of civility or collegiality, the affair was all about harassment and discrimination. The AAO officer involved in the case began by asking the students who reported the incident if Long – a conservative Catholic – was known as a racist, a sexist, or a homophobe.[4] Long's reputation was dragged through the mud. But at no point during

---

[2] According to Peter Wood, 1987 was "a breakout year for the *diversity* creed." Wood, *Diversity: The Invention of a Concept* (Encounter Books, 1987), p. 12.

[3] My account of the case is based on a manuscript Long wrote about his experience, an interview with a dean who oversaw the investigation of Long's department, and some documents that I received through a public information request. Although I made efforts to contact several people from both sides who had been involved in the dispute, only Dean John R. Palmer of the School of Education replied.

[4] The information is from Richard Long's manuscript, "All That Is Solid Melts into Air: Political Correctness, Speech Codes, and Academic Commissars in the Land of Sifting and Winnowing." This essay was presented at a conference on academic freedom at the University of Wisconsin, February 2002.

the six-month investigation did anyone produce any evidence that Long had ever treated anyone in any way that could be considered biased.

As he walked away from his final encounter with the investigators, Long believed that his reputation was mortally stricken, that "the charges of anti-Semitism, racism, sexism, and all the rest would stick. Or at least the taint of them would stick. Excepting actual assassination or firing nothing worse can happen to a full professor at the top of his form. To prosper or even just get along decently in an institution like the University of Wisconsin–Madison as it is presently constituted, one must be above suspicion – and . . . suspicion [is now] my middle name."[5]

Long's case was part of a broader investigation conducted by the university into the state of affairs in the art department. School of Education dean Palmer wrote in a memo to the art department faculty on January 16, 1991, that "a number of students, both graduate and undergraduate, have raised concerns with the Dean's Office and with the Campus Affirmative Action Compliance Office about their treatment as students in the Department of Art. The students' concerns appear to be varied and the issues raised complex; some concerns relate to discriminatory treatment."[6] In an interview conducted in 2002, Palmer said that students had complained about attitudes, hostile comments about progressive causes, and political bias in grading and admissions. Palmer minimized the harm done to Long in his interview, claiming that Long was only one of many individuals whom investigators interviewed. "He was interviewed . . . but so were fifteen or twenty other faculty members. He had no more cause to come to see me than anyone else."[7]

But Palmer presided over the inquiry from afar and appears to have been unaware of what was transpiring down in the pits of the actual investigation, which was conducted by other people. To be sure, several other faculty members were questioned as well, especially a "Professor X." But within his department, Long became known as the chief target. The two students specifically accused Long of verbal harassment, and his department chair told him that "it was all over the Hill [Bascom Hill, where the administration resides] that Long was being investigated on charges of anti-Semitism, sexism, and 'homophobia.'"[8]

After weeks of damaging innuendo and rumors, a hearing was finally held on March 6, 1991, during which Long was questioned by two faculty members. Law professor Gordon Baldwin accompanied Long, providing his services pro bono. At the beginning of the meeting, Long issued a statement in which he declared that he would answer questions about his potential

[5] Long, "All That Is Solid Melts into Air," p. 26.
[6] John R. Palmer, memo to Department of Art, January 16, 1991.
[7] Interview with John R. Palmer, former dean of School of Education, August 2002.
[8] Long, "All That Is Solid Melts into Air," p. 13.

violation of university rules but not any questions "in regard to my political
or religious views (except to say that I am a Catholic). And I will not answer questions involving motivations, opinions, or actions of others." After
the questioners acknowledged that the accusation of anti-Semitism bore no
credibility, they asked Long to respond to allegations that he had "a lot of
problems in the areas of racism, sexism, and homophobia." Long refused
to answer this and several other questions, but the interrogators persisted.
"Now, Professor Long, have you ever used the word 'feminazi'?" another
asked. At this point, Baldwin put his hand over Long's mouth, clapping it
shut. "He apprised the committee of the fact that he was directing his client
not to answer that question. He went on to inform them that the Constitution of the United States was in effect in the entire United States *including*
the University of Wisconsin and the room in which we were sitting."[9] The
interrogators then adjourned the meeting, conceding that they possessed no
evidence that Long was guilty of any of these sins. The university dropped
the case but refused to grant Long's request that it publicly vindicate him or
even provide him with the documents on the case. In Long's eyes, he was
never really cleared.

The substance and political context of the art department's case resemble
many other investigations that have come to pass on campuses since the
late 1980s.[10] The very content of the charges was a product of the times,
as universities began to be preoccupied with combating racism, sexism, and
related prejudices and developed policies like speech codes to reach this
goal. Of course, instances of racial and sexual harassment take place and
merit serious, even coercive, responses. But the Long case did not appear to
come close to involving such transgression. The application of the speech
code in Long's case, in effect, "criminalized" political differences.[11] Long
suffered a fate that many others have experienced in the new era. First, with
but two or three exceptions, he was abandoned by his colleagues, including
those who believed that he was being scapegoated. Second, Long discovered
the relevance of an old adage: the process is the punishment. Although the
university eventually dropped the investigation, the true damage for Long
came from being submitted to a nerve-wracking process in a context fraught
with emotion. According to Long, many individuals who did not know him
assumed his guilt from the start.

A final theme concerns the political climate in which the case emerged.
The accusation filed against Long arose during a heated debate over objective

---

[9] Ibid., pp. 18–23. Palmer, letter to Department of Art, January 16, 1991.
[10] The case could be called a synecdoche: the single example that represents or reflects the
  whole. On synecdoche, see Kenneth Burke, *A Grammar of Motives* (University of California
  Press, 1969), pp. 507–8.
[11] Such codes were not criminal charges, of course, but they were often punitive and carried
  the potential for expulsion or termination of employment.

standards that riveted the art department in the fall of 1990. Early that term, ten graduate students (including four women, two members of racial minorities) wrote a letter to the department chair calling for a revival of more objective and demanding standards in the evaluation of graduate students' art projects. The students asked Long to sign on, but he declined because he doubted that his involvement would actually help their cause.

The presentation of the letter to the department and chair transformed the climate of the department literally overnight. The letter submitted by the "traditionalists" (Long's term describing this side) publicly galvanized the political tensions that had been simmering just beneath the surface in the department. What Long calls the "radical" faction in the department – also led by graduate students – interpreted the letter as a form of oppression, a direct attack on their ideas of equality and diversity. Within a day, posters and related writings popped up ominously throughout the department, accusing the traditionalists of promoting "oppression," "fascism," "totalitarianism," and furthering racism, sexism, homophobia, and the like. Rather than addressing the traditionalists' request on its merits, the antitraditionalists responded with ad hominem insinuation, accusation, and confrontation. Several efforts to reach a consensus or to heal the deepening wounds through special meetings proved unsuccessful, the casualty of Mau Mau tactics that antitraditionalists deployed in place of meaningful dialogue.

The traditionalists soon grew weary of the ordeal. Long relates, "Even though the Traditionalists had fired the first shot in what they must have known would be a contentious face-off, they were, I think, mystified by the Radicals' immediate politicizing of academic standards. From that point on the Traditionalists were invariably in a defensive position. . . . They quickly wearied of being placed in the unenviable position of explaining that they were not fascists, racists, tormentors of homosexuals, and God knows what else."[12] Soon enough, the department dropped the issue of standards from its agenda.

Rather than being content with their victory, the victors shifted their tactics of harassment, badgering traditionalists when they encountered them in the hallways, classrooms, and other domains. "As time passed, a general atmosphere of incivility, suspicion, and turmoil overtook the department."[13] A group of three graduate students targeted Long, repeatedly greeting him in an insulting way. "Hello, *Professor* Long – How *are* you, *Professor* Long? – *Do* have a nice day, *Professor* Long." Despite Long's entreaties to bury the hatchet, the students persisted in their mockery. One day when he had had enough, Long uttered his "*Seig heil*, comrades" remark to two members of this threesome. The rest is institutional history. Although it was these students and their allies who had engendered an environment hostile to honest

[12] Long, "All That Is Solid Melts into Air," p. 3.
[13] Ibid., p. 9.

intellectual discourse, it was Long and those who thought like him who found themselves scrutinized for their views and for possible harassment.

Key Cases and Assumptions of the New *Episteme*

The art department case is, in the end, quite puzzling. The small group of graduate students' call for stricter standards hardly represented a dominant view in the department, and the antitraditionalists could have surely limited the reach of their foes (at the very least) had they engaged the issue intellectually rather than with coercive and ad hominem tactics. Instead, they acted as if the call for standards were itself an act of discrimination.

The resort to such exaggeration is not unique to the art department at Wisconsin. During the Horowitz affair in the spring of 2001, for example, many activists at Wisconsin, Brown, Berkeley, and elsewhere claimed that the publication of Horowitz's advertisement constituted an assault on their "emotional well-being." In the fall of 2001 the dean of students' office at Wisconsin compared the ad's appearance to criminal physical assaults that had taken place on the campus and insinuated that the psychological impact of the ad was similar to the emotional trauma many people experienced after the terrorist attacks against the United States on September 11.[14] At Brown, twenty-seven faculty members excoriated the interim president for concluding that Horowitz's paid advertisement was legitimate free speech rather than harassment. Quoting from a letter the group sent to the acting president, a reporter in the *Brown Daily Herald* wrote,

The "University, in effect, is actively taking one side of the issue and failing to address the racist attacks on students, faculty and staff of color." The professors urged [President] Blumstein to condemn the ad as a form of harassment, and lamented that no investigations are being conducted against members of *The Herald* staff for publishing the advertisement. The Office of Student Life has begun preliminary inquiries into the theft of nearly the entire press run of *The Herald's* March 16 issue. "Surely, the University has a greater responsibility to its faculty, staff and students of color to 'investigate' those who are publishing such injurious comments, than it does to scapegoat a few students for what was clearly an action undertaken collectively as a symbolic protest against a blatantly racist advertisement that went unchallenged by the University."[15]

As in the Long case, some professors at Brown did not simply want the president to condemn Horowitz and the *Herald*: they also wanted an investigation under the university's harassment policies. They wanted an intellectual and political difference dealt with by coercive rules. But the president refused to

---

[14] "Administration Takes Aim at the *Badger Herald* Again: Dean's Office Comparing Free Speech to Sexual Assault, Campus Violence," editorial, *Badger Herald*, October 3, 2001.

[15] Andy Golodny, "27 Faculty Sign Letter of Concern over Treatment of Coalition, Racism," *Brown Daily Herald*, April 10, 2001.

take this road. Her stance under pressure provides further hope that the tides of campus censorship are starting to recede.

Neil Hamilton, a professor at the William Mitchell College of Law in Minneapolis, was also victimized by new policies in a manner that reflects the "criminalization" of political and moral differences. The college subjected him to ten separate investigations – none of which found probable cause – because of his stance in favor of traditional academic standards in admissions and evaluations. Though he had championed this position for several years while serving on admissions and personnel committees prior to his ordeal, opponents had tolerated his views as within the bounds of acceptable disagreement. Not so after that fateful year, 1987. Hamilton describes what happened in his book, *Zealotry and Academic Freedom*:

All of this changed in the late 1980s. Personnel decisions often became occasions for an inquisition. Beginning in February 1987, I experienced sixty-six months of accusations of moral turpitude and then investigations because of strong support for academic quality in admissions and personnel decisions. All of the accusations were unsupported. Nine investigations were dismissed; one was withdrawn. . . .

Another source of substantial confusion was the absence of significant public collegial support.

The situation feels like living in Ionesco's play, *Rhinoceros*, where even ordinary and normal people start snorting and rampaging about, oblivious to facts and reason. False public accusations of moral turpitude aim at a teacher's soul and spirit. . . . It is like being swept off one's feet and tumbled by a large wave.[16]

Several years ago I had lunch with a professor in the physical sciences who had undergone a similar ordeal in the mid-1990s at another university in the East.[17] One day he advised a woman graduate student of color that her academic record was not promising and that it might be in her best interest to consider other work. (She had gone to him for advice about this very matter.) Distressed, the student filed a discrimination suit, and the professor's life immediately fell into turmoil. He told me that his colleagues abandoned him, that the lead administrator in the case assumed his guilt from the start (the assumption seemed to be that if he had been sufficiently sensitive in the first place, why would the student have reported him?), and that all his previous good works on racial issues and for the university amounted to nothing in the eyes of his accusers. Although he was vindicated in the end, the process was the punishment, and my acquaintance had to take a leave of absence for a year just to escape the cauldron.[18]

---

[16] Neil Hamilton, *Zealotry and Academic Freedom: A Legal and Historical Perspective* (Transaction, 1998), pp. xi, xii, 308. Hamilton's book reports many similar cases; see also, generally, chs. 1 and 2.

[17] The man had an impeccable record for racial justice and was the only professor in his department who lived in a predominantly black neighborhood.

[18] This individual did not give me permission to use his name.

One more example shows how administrators can stretch policies properly designed to prohibit harassment and illegal physical acts in ways that demonize speech that is normally entitled to full constitutional protection. The noted civil liberty and free speech columnist Nat Hentoff writes of the case of Wayne Dick, a conservative Yale student whom the university punished for distributing an anonymous satirical leaflet that made fun of Yale's annual Gay and Lesbian Awareness Days. The leaflet was sarcastic and rude but not threatening in its content. Regardless of this fact, it caused a sensation. After apprehending Dick, the discipline committee gave him two years' probation for violating Yale's regulation against harassment and "physical restriction, assault, coercion, or intimidation." (The punishment was later reversed.) This decision clearly constituted viewpoint discrimination, for had Dick's leaflets praised Awareness Day, the university would not have undertaken punitive action. Hentoff relates, "Because his target had been the gay and lesbian community, Wayne Dick was now regarded by many as a campus pariah. His insufferable views could not be unpunished."[19]

At one time, supporters of the new speech policies at universities accused critics of "cherry picking" bad examples in order to buttress their cases.[20] But that was before an extensive literature developed that has exhaustively furnished examples of transgressions of free speech, due process, and other liberal principles. In addition to the books mentioned in the following footnote, I refer the reader to the website of FIRE (the Foundation for Individual Rights in Education). The cases I have related are but the tip of a large iceberg.[21] Such cases do not disparage properly drafted and applied antiharassment measures. The problem arises when enforcers deploy antiharassment measures to deal coercively with the expression of unpopular views. In their minds, speech and action are not inherently distinct phenomena.

Two aspects of the new *Weltgeist* stand out. First, there is a heightened consciousness of historical oppression based on race, gender, and sexual preference. Through the filter of this consciousness, people who hold this view interpret individual cases as extensions or manifestations of broader societal and historical discrimination. In the more extreme versions

---

[19] Hentoff, *Free Speech for Me, but Not for Thee: How the American Left and Right Relentlessly Censor Each Other* (HarperCollins, 1992), p. 121. See also the discussion of the case in Timothy C. Shiell, *Campus Hate Speech on Trial* (University of Kansas Press, 1998).

[20] See, in general, John K. Wilson, *The Myth of Political Correctness: The Conservative Attack on Higher Education* (Duke University Press, 1995).

[21] See www.theFIRE.org. See the incredible account of a sexual harassment accusation at the University of Hawaii, in Melanie Thernstrom, "Trouble in Paradise," *George*, September 1999, pp. 120–30. See also Alan Charles Kors and Harvey Silverglate, *The Shadow University: The Betrayal of Liberty on America's Campuses* (Free Press, 1998); Hentoff, *Free Speech for Me, but Not for Thee*; Shiell, *Campus Hate Speech on Trial*; Richard Bernstein, *Dictatorship of Virtue: Multiculturalism and the Battle for America's Future* (Knopf, 1994); Hamilton, *Zealotry and Academic Freedom*; David O. Sacks and Peter A. Thiel, *The Diversity Myth: "Multiculturalism" and the Politics of Intolerance at Stanford* (The Independent Institute, 1995).

of this view, racism and sexism are not just serious problems to be dealt with in a serious fashion but revelatory of an inner truth of liberal democracy in America, its sine qua non. Richard Bernstein describes the underlying mind-set:

Hiding behind the innocuous, unobjectionable, entirely praise-worthy goal of eliminating prejudice from the human heart lies a certain ideology, a control of language, a vision of America that, presented as consensual common sense, is actually highly debatable. By its very nature it thrusts the concepts of "racism" and "sexism" and the various other isms to the forefront, turning them from ugly aberrations into the central elements of American life and implicitly branding anyone who does not share that assumption to be guilty of the very isms that he feels do not lie in his heart.[22]

Feminist theorist Catharine MacKinnon's understanding of the political meaning of domestic violence provides a good example of this ideology. MacKinnon views gender relations in a context of systemic male domination: when a man beats a woman, the act is individual to a point but is primarily societal. MacKinnon acknowledges how her group-based theory of justice conflicts with basic assumptions of individual rights and responsibilities but notes, "Feminism tends to collapse the distinction itself [between the individual and universal] by telescoping the universal and the individual into the mediate, group-defined, social dimension of gender. . . . In such a view, a man *never* attacks a woman as an individual, nor does she *ever* respond as such."[23]

This theory is not without merit. Many actions and beliefs are to varying extents the manifestations of broader social and historical forces, and many actions cannot be adequately understood without accounting for these forces. Domestic violence against women is often a part of a larger ideology of male domination that is entrenched in most societies.[24] Nor can one appreciate the meaning of a burning cross without understanding the history of racist violence and unrest in America. The influence of such forces as culture and history in human lives has long been debated, so it is not at all unreasonable to claim that individual actions point to broader societal and historical meanings.[25] (Indeed, I do this in my discussion of the Richard Long case.)

The difficulty with this way of thinking arises when the facts of the actual individual case are ignored or are overshadowed by the broader meaning. Individuals may become scapegoats for the transgressions of others – guilt

[22] Bernstein, *Dictatorship of Virtue*, pp. 36–37. See also Wood, *Diversity*.
[23] MacKinnon, "Toward Feminist Jurisprudence," 34 *Stanford Law Review* 703 (1982), pp. 717–18, n. 73 (emphasis added).
[24] I have addressed this issue in *More Than Victims: Battered Women, the Syndrome Society, and the Law* (University of Chicago Press, 1996).
[25] See, e.g., Marion Smiley, *Moral Responsibility and the Boundaries of Community: Power and Accountability from a Pragmatic Point of View* (University of Chicago Press, 1992).

by ascriptive association. An example of this type of thinking is the infamous 1987 Tawana Brawley case, in which an African American teenager in New York falsely accused several white police officers of rape. Even after it was discovered that Brawley had fabricated her story, some spokespersons claimed that the *actual facts did not ultimately matter*, because many black women who have actually been attacked by white men in the past have been disbelieved, and so we could imagine that the charges were true in some deeper historical sense.[26] The problem is that, however sophisticated a social or legal theory may be in illuminating broader social and historical trends, its application to individual cases can be dangerous and profoundly unjust. Guilt is an individual state. Whether the cause of the accusers be anticommunism or antiracism, if they insist upon an assumption of guilt by association, there will inevitably be miscarriages of justice.

Assuming a link between individuals and broader forces can undermine the presumption of innocence. Neil Hamilton and my scientist acquaintance were presumed guilty because they were charged. Dorothy Rabinowitz, a member of the *Wall Street Journal* editorial board and editorial writer, noted that in the water buffalo case at Penn, defendant Eden Jacobowitz "had yet to learn what they don't teach at the freshman orientation: namely, he had now entered a world where a charge of racism or sexism is as good as a conviction."[27] Once again, I am not claiming that this mind-set exists everywhere. But the evidence strongly suggests that it is too widespread to dismiss.

Now let us look at some background factors that influenced the rise of this mind-set.

New Political Theories and the Rise of Progressive Censorship

As I mentioned in Chapter 1, the seeds that eventually caused the turn away from liberal principles were sown in antiliberal political movements and theories of the 1960s. For example, in place of Martin Luther King's emphasis on integration, individual moral conscience, and universalism, movements beholden to black power that emerged in the later 1960s stressed racial separatism, group-based racial identity, and the abandonment of common standards of right between blacks and whites.[28] The militant branches of black studies programs that mushroomed on campus in the late 1960s built

[26] See, e.g., John McWhorter, *Losing the Race: Self-Sabotage in Black America* (Perennial, HarperCollins, 2000), p. 223; and Jim Sleeper, *Liberal Racism* (Viking, 1997), pp. 26, 29, 39.
[27] "Buffaloed at Penn," *Wall Street Journal*, April 26, 1993.
[28] See, e.g., Stokely Carmichael and Charles Hamilton, *Black Power: The Politics of Liberation in America* (Vintage/Random House, 1967). On King's philosophy, see David J. Garrow, *Bearing the Cross: Martin Luther King, Jr. and the Southern Christian Leadership Conference* (Vintage, 1986).

upon this rationale, in contrast to the more liberal integrationist programs with which they competed.[29]

Students in the 1960s were also influenced by liberation theories that cast a negative light on liberalism and Western civilization. For example, the work of the Algerian psychiatrist and political theorist Frantz Fanon provided a link between student protest in America and unrest elsewhere in the world, as well as a rationale for connecting new ideas of group-based identity, recognition, therapeutic self-esteem, and oppression consciousness. In *The Wretched of the Earth*, Fanon wrote, "A people's victorious fight not only consecrates the triumph of its rights; it also gives to that people consistence, coherence, and homogeneity."[30]

During the transformation of the university in the later 1980s, Fanon's ideas motivated some faculty and administrative activists – often students of the 1960s now risen to positions of influence in universities – to push for change. In 1989, for example, an assistant dean of undergraduate studies at Stanford invoked Fanon's ideas in support of the faculty senate's vote to drop the university's long-running course in Western culture and civilization, a vote that was linked to the passage of Stanford's speech code. The dean questioned the institution's traditional reliance on the principles of liberal democracy, writing that John Locke might have been relevant fifty years ago to answering the question, "what is social justice?" but today "it may be that someone like Frantz Fanon, a black Algerian psychoanalyst, will get us closer to the answer we need."[31]

Paulo Freire's *Pedagogy of the Oppressed*, published in 1970, also had some impact on developments in the 1980s and 1990s. Throughout the 1960s, many student activists denigrated the relevance of traditional studies and accepted understandings of knowledge, calling instead for studies that addressed pressing social problems.[32] In critiquing Hegel, Marx famously wrote, "the purpose of philosophy is not to understand the world. The purpose is to change it." Freire was a Brazilian who fought to teach oppressed minorities to read, a courageous moral act that provoked the repressive ruling regime to exile him for fourteen years. Drawing on a variety of leftist liberation theories, Freire asserted that education should strive to instill the

---

[29] See, generally, Jacob N. Gordon and James M. Rosen, *The Black Studies Debate* (University of Kansas Press, 1974); Donald Alexander Downs, *Cornell '69: Liberalism and the Crisis of the American University* (Cornell University Press, 1999).

[30] Fanon, *The Wretched of the Earth* (Grove Press, 1968), pp. 293–94. On Fanon's impact on the radical student movement of the 1960s, see Todd Gitlin, *The Sixties: Years of Hope, Days of Rage* (Bantam, 1987), p. 263.

[31] Charles Junkerman, letter to the editor, *Wall Street Journal*, January 6, 1989. Quoted in Roger Kimball, *Tenured Radicals* (Harper and Row, 1990), p. 29.

[32] The debate between traditional learning and more pragmatic or relevant pedagogy has characterized educational policy and politics throughout the twentieth century. See Diane Ravitch, *Left Back: A Century of Failed School Reforms* (Simon and Schuster, 2000).

consciousness of liberation in the oppressed. In this pedagogy, the oppressed "unveil the world of oppression and through the *praxis* commit themselves to its transformation."[33]

Activists took a theory that had acute relevance in a desperate undemocratic country and applied it undialectically to a different situation in the United States. Freire's theories of oppression provided a blueprint for some new pedagogies in the 1980s and 1990s. For example, at the 1989 national conference of the National Council of Teachers of English, many speakers alluded to the pedagogy of the oppressed. In a speech entitled "Paulo Freire's Liberation Pedagogy," Anne E. Berthoff of the University of Massachusetts called for writing teachers to "adapt Paulo Freire's theory and practice in their own courses.... We have ways of transforming our society which are neither violent nor millennial."[34] As I show later, Freire's thought has also influenced a major force behind speech codes, critical race theory.

Philosopher Herbert Marcuse merits a special place in our story because he was the first prominent thinker on the left to champion censorship in the name of social justice – what I have elsewhere called "progressive censorship."[35] Progressive censorship is censorship designed to protect and to further progressive causes. Before the 1980s, most censorship had emanated from the right historically, though progressive types did contribute to the antipornography and antismut campaigns that swept America in the first part of the twentieth century.[36]

Marcuse presented his innovative argument in a 1965 article entitled "Repressive Tolerance," in which he argued in the spirit of Hegel and Marx that tolerance and free speech should not be considered abstractly but rather through the lens of historical and social circumstance. Although free speech and tolerance were indispensable to truth and justice during the Enlightenment (which opposed theological and feudal authority), Marcuse believed that modern social and economic conditions had turned this verity on its head. Imperialism, militarism, racism, bureaucracy, corporatism, technology, and mass marketing and media had undermined the possibility of truly rational liberation by systematically inculcating false consciousness and mental conditioning – what Marcuse labeled "totalitarian democracy."[37] Marcuse argued that tolerance in this context would only reinforce the existing domination by irrational forces. There is, he insisted, a fundamental distinction between "true and false tolerance."[38] Marcuse agreed with John Stuart Mill that truth was the ultimate rationale for the system of free speech and the

---

[33] Freire, *Pedagogy of the Oppressed* (1970; Continuum Publishing, 2000), p. 36.
[34] Cited and discussed in Bernstein, *Dictatorship of Virtue*, pp. 314–15.
[35] Downs, *The New Politics of Pornography* (University of Chicago Press, 1989).
[36] See Paul S. Boyer, *Purity in Print: Book Censorship in America from the Gilded Age to the Computer Age*, 2d ed. (University of Wisconsin Press, 2002).
[37] Marcuse, "Repressive Tolerance," in *A Critique of Pure Tolerance* (Beacon Press, 1969), p. 99.
[38] Ibid., p. 105.

marketplace of ideas, and that social progress was the test of truth. But unlike Mill, he believed some enlightened souls were immune to the fallibility
principle and argued that particular forms of censorship were necessary to
achieve the realization of truth:

> Universal tolerance becomes questionable when its rationale no longer prevails, when
> tolerance is administered to manipulated and indoctrinated individuals who par-
> rot, as their own, the opinion of their masters, for whom heteronomy has become
> autonomy. . . .
> [True tolerance] would include the withdrawal of toleration of speech and as-
> sembly from groups and movements which promote aggressive policies, armament,
> chauvinism, discrimination on the grounds of race and religion, or which oppose the
> extension of public services, social security, medical care, etc.[39]

It would be an understatement to say that Marcuse never adequately
addressed the problem of *who* would be the ultimate censor. Unlike the
more realistic Mill, he assumed that repression arises only from the right,
ignoring how the left could also be coercive and authoritarian.[40] This assumption is simply untenable, as the history of communism's gulags sadly
substantiates.[41]

New Legal Theories of Progressive Censorship: Skokie and MacKinnon

The most important sign of a crack in the liberal consensus of the left concerning free speech in the post–World War II era was the famous Skokie
case, which involved the First Amendment right of a Chicago-based neo-
Nazi group to hold a "white power" demonstration in the northern suburb
in May 1977. The city refused to grant the request because of the intense
opposition of Skokie's sizable community of Holocaust survivors, estimated
between eight hundred and twelve hundred. Skokie obtained an injunction
against the rally in state court and passed three ordinances establishing conditions groups must meet in order to obtain a permit, the most important
of which prohibited groups making racial slurs. This ordinance was based
on an old Illinois statute – rescinded sometime before the Skokie affair –
prohibiting "group libel" that the U.S. Supreme Court had upheld in 1952

---

[39] Ibid., pp. 90, 91–92, 100. Marcuse's position reflected Marx's classic argument in his famous
essay, "On the Jewish Question," in which Marx also questioned the efficacy of abstract
liberty principles. See Marx, "On the Jewish Question," in Robert C. Tucker, ed., *The Marx-Engels Reader* (Norton, 1972).

[40] In this respect, Marcuse's slant resembled that of his Frankfurt School colleague, Theodore
Adorno, the lead author of the famous opus of political behavior and psychology. Adorno
et al., *The Authoritarian Personality* (Harper, 1950). On the Frankfurt School, see Martin M.
Jay, *The Dialectical Imagination: A History of the Frankfurt School and the Institute of Social
Research, 1923–1950* (Heineman, 1973).

[41] On the mass murders and crimes of communism, see Stepane Courtois et al., *The Black Book
of Communism: Crimes, Terror, Repression*, consulting editor Mark Kramer, trans. Jonathan
Murphy and Mark Kramer (Harvard University Press, 1999).

(*Beauharnais v. Illinois*), a case that had never been overturned.[42] Considering the case a classic example of censorship, the Illinois branch of the American Civil Liberties Union took the case for the Nazi group. After more than a year of legal and political maneuvering, both state and federal courts upheld the Nazis' rights to rally in Skokie, ignoring the precedence of *Beauharnais*.[43]

Although Skokie may have been an easy case legally, it was complex and difficult in social and human terms. The trauma and pain provoked by what many survivors imagined (at least initially) was the return of the murderous Nazi regime persuaded me to argue against the courts' conclusions in the book I wrote on the subject in 1985. To me and others, the Nazi demonstration constituted a "verbal assault," not speech.[44]

For the first time in memory, a large sector of the progressive left questioned the moral and political validity of liberal free speech doctrine and its essential linchpin of viewpoint neutrality. How could the ideal of free speech – a principle so intimately tied to progressive causes in the past – countenance such a fractious result? The case split such national and local Jewish groups as the Anti-Defamation League, the American Jewish Committee, and the American Jewish Congress. Many members were torn between their long-standing commitments to liberal free speech principles and their sense of loyalty to the Holocaust survivors – their ethnic connection. Some groups, like the ADL, would never again be as dedicated to free speech. Within a few months, up to a third of the members of the American Civil Liberties Union resigned, temporarily throwing the organization's existence into jeopardy. (It eventually recovered after massive membership drives and appeals.)[45] The ideology of progressive censorship had finally arrived.

Meanwhile, a new form of radical, group-identity-based feminism arose during the 1970s that challenged the more liberal thought of the "second wave" feminism of the 1960s. (In this sense, this situation echoed black power's challenge to the liberal civil rights movement in the late 1960s.) The new theories, which found fertile soil in universities nationwide, drew on many of the oppression theories discussed previously to investigate the status of women in society. It was out of this environment that the seeds of new legal policies concerning sexual harassment and pornography germinated and grew.

Although their views are fiercely debated within both liberal and radical feminist circles, legal scholar Catharine MacKinnon and writer Andrea Dworkin are the most important figures in this movement. They developed

---

[42] *Beauharnais v. Illinois*, 343 U.S. 250 (1952).

[43] See *Collin v. Smith*, 578 F. 2d 1197 (7th Cir. 1978); *Skokie v. National Socialist Party of America*, 373 N.E.2d 21 (1978).

[44] Downs, *Nazis in Skokie: Freedom, Community, and the First Amendment* (University of Notre Dame Press, 1985), esp. ch. 8.

[45] On the history of the ACLU and Skokie, see Samuel Walker, *In Defense of American Liberties: A History of the ACLU* (Oxford University Press, 1990), ch. 15.

an innovative argument for the censorship of pornography in the name of civil rights and progressive causes. For a variety of reasons, pornography became an inflammatory domestic issue in America between 1983 and 1984, catapulting MacKinnon and Dworkin to international fame. In a 1983 seminar that MacKinnon and Dworkin held at the University of Minnesota Law School (a class that many participants described as a "transformative experience"), the twosome formulated a new legal approach to pornography and walked it over to the Minneapolis City Council, which adopted the measure to national acclaim later that year. After the liberal mayor, Donald Fraser, vetoed the measure, MacKinnon traveled with the ordinance down to conservative Indianapolis, which passed a somewhat more modest version of the reform in 1984, to similar local acclaim and national attention. Alas, the new law foundered on the shoals of the First Amendment in the federal courts.[46]

Rather than focusing on traditional obscenity doctrine, which deals with sexual morality, MacKinnon and Dworkin targeted "pornography," which they defined as "the sexually explicit subordination of women" in a broad variety of contexts. The Minneapolis and Indianapolis ordinances provided four different types of civil actions that women could take against pornographers: for the "trafficking" of pornography, meaning the sheer presence of pornography in any public area; for exposing people against their will to pornography; for coercing someone into making pornography; and for making pornography that "caused" someone to commit a sexual assault. The ordinance envisioned pornography as a form of group libel of women that expresses sexually the pervasive, systemic inequality and domination of women as a group. Pornography suppresses women's subjectivity and "silences" their voices. MacKinnon and Dworkin relied on both scientific concepts of cause and effect as well as discourse theory to buttress their case. The latter attributes oppression to dominant forms of discursive power. In a seminal law review article based on her Francis Biddle lecture at Harvard Law School, MacKinnon declared that pornography causes a "Skokie-type injury." Later, lawyer Mary Eberts charged that "pornography is our [women's] Skokie."[47]

An important element of the ordinance was the conflation of speech and action, which is consistent with a discursive interpretation of reality. Pornography does not simply "cause" harm (though MacKinnon and Dworkin also

---

[46] *American Booksellers Association v. Hudnut*, 771 F.2d 323 (7th Cir. 1985). The U.S. Supreme Court summarily affirmed the Seventh Circuit, *Hudnut v. American Booksellers Association*, 475 U.S. 1001 (1986). On all the politics, law, and theory surrounding the odyssey of the ordinance, see Downs, *The New Politics of Pornography*.

[47] See MacKinnon, "Pornography, Civil Rights, and Speech," *Harvard Civil Rights–Civil Liberties Law Review* 20 (1984), p. 42; Eberts, quoted in June Callwood, "Feminist Debates and Civil Liberties," in J. Burstyn, ed., *Women against Censorship* (Douglas and McIntyre, 1985), p. 122. Also, see Wendy McElroy, ed., *Liberty for Women: Freedom and Feminism in the Twenty-first Century* (Ivan R. Dee for The Independent Institute, 2002).

made this argument); it also *is* discriminatory by virtue of its very existence. This is one reason that the U.S. Court of Appeals for the Seventh Circuit concluded that the ordinance amounted to "thought control." This conclusion was supported by the fact that the ordinance made no provision for the intellectual value of pornographic works, a tenet that is central to the constitutional doctrine of obscenity.[48]

A similar ideology of significance is espoused by critical race theorists, who oppose liberal free speech principles as detrimental to racial equality. In the introduction to the book, *Words That Wound*, a seminal reader on critical race theory, leading critical race theorists Mari J. Matsuda, Charles R. Lawrence, Richard Delgado, and Kimberle Williams Crenshaw "deconstruct" liberal ideology and pedagogy in favor of "the practice of liberationist pedagogy" (a concept they attribute to Freire), which they hope will contribute to the development of the "postcolonial university." Critical race theory

recognizes that racism is endemic to American life... [and] expresses skepticism toward dominant legal claims of neutrality, objectivity, color blindness, and meritocracy.... Critical race theory measures progress by a yardstick that looks to fundamental social transformation....

Central to the methodology of critical race theory and liberationist pedagogy is an ongoing engagement in political practice. The Brazilian educator and philosopher Paulo Freire has said that liberationist teaching contains two dimensions, "Reflection and action, such radical interaction that if one is sacrificed – even in part – the other immediately suffers."[49]

Although this perspective lies at the more radical end of the spectrum, it has influenced many participants in the campus speech wars, both directly and indirectly. (Some of the authors of *Words That Wound* – including Delgado at the University of Wisconsin and Lawrence at Stanford – played roles in the development of speech codes at their respective institutions.) And in several of the meetings of the official "ad hoc committee" formed at Wisconsin to deliberate what to do about the faculty code in the 1997–98 academic year, liberal members of the committee who were committed to finding a way to balance free speech and sensitivity often referred directly to the writings of critical race theorists for support. For example, they cited Delgado as their primary authority in a crucial part of the "Majority Report" they sent to the faculty senate for consideration in late 1998, in which they presented their case for maintaining a speech code with some teeth.[50]

---

[48] *American Booksellers v. Hudnut*, 771 F.2d 323, pp. 327–28. On obscenity law, see *Miller v. California*, 413 U.S. 15 (1973).

[49] Mari J. Matsuda, Charles R. Lawrence III, Richard Delgado, and Kimberle Williams Crenshaw, *Words That Wound: Critical Race Theory, Assaultive Speech, and the First Amendment* (Westview Press, 1993), introduction, pp. 6–7, 10–11. Quoting Freire, *Pedagogy of the Oppressed*, p. 75.

[50] "Reply to the 'Minority Report,'" Ad Hoc Committee on Prohibited Harassment Legislation, October 29, 1998. Attached as addendum to Report of the Ad Hoc Committee on Prohibited

And in one discussion following a meeting of this committee, a professor who opposed major reform told free speech activists that their concerns about academic freedom were based on "the old understanding of what a university is. The meaning of academic freedom needs to be adapted to the new world." The university and the idea of academic freedom needed to be transformed in order to accommodate the procensorship requirements of oppressed groups.

In critical race theory, racism is endemic in liberal capitalist polities, and censorship of such expression serves the Marcusean purpose of limiting the influence of regressive positions, for "the privilege and power of the racial power structure is wrapped in the rhetoric of politically unpopular speech."[51] Critical race theorists present several grounds for censoring such expression, including preventing emotional and psychic harm to particular individuals and groups (in a racist society, they claim, minorities pay a "psychic tax" for wide-open free speech that the majority does not pay), preventing group or racial libel, limiting the promotion of discriminatory assumptions and myths, and countering the systemic and discursive power of racism.[52] Some of these claims must be taken seriously, especially when hate speech is targeted at individuals. The problem arises when such delimitations are not made.

The rise of these and related theories and assumptions led to a fundamental change in universities' thinking about free speech. Harvey Silverglate told how he and Alan Kors came to the realization that something new was afoot:

[Sometime in the late 1980s] we realized that the cases that we'd handled for students started to morph from charges as to what students *did* to what students *said*. Kors and I started to talk about our respective campus cases. We were puzzled and disturbed at this sudden change – repressing students on campuses of higher education for saying things that were fully protected on Main Street. We agreed that someday we'd write about it. *The Shadow University* later emerged.[53]

New Ideologies of Sensitivity and the New Administrative Elite
Few deny that racism and sexism still haunt American society and that strong and conscientious efforts to deal with these evils are called for. But a new form of addressing these evils has gained headway that is illiberal in inspiration: victimology.[54] The original civil rights movement called for the realization

Harassment Legislation, October 7, 1998 (First Reading), p. 21, n. 10. In Faculty Senate Agenda Materials for December 7, 1998, University of Wisconsin, Madison.

[51] Matsuda et al., *Words That Wound*, p. 15.

[52] See, generally, ibid.

[53] Interview with Harvey Silverglate, civil liberties lawyer and founder, codirector, and treasurer of FIRE, December 2002.

[54] A host of writers have written about victim ideology, including Christopher Lasch, *The Minimal Self: Survival in Troubled Times* (Norton, 1984); Robert Hughes, *Culture of Complaint* (Oxford University Press, 1993); Sally Satel, *P.C. M.D.: How Political Correctness Is Corrupting*

of equal citizenship. This meant not only the enjoyment of equal rights but the assumption of equal capacity on the part of individuals to be responsible for their character and actions. In today's polity, we appear to have forgotten that citizenship and the character virtues it presupposes are the foundations on which meaningful equality is attained, not the other way around.[55] Victimology undermines citizenship by infantilizing its would-be beneficiaries, rather than treating them as responsible adults. Applied to free speech, victim ideology treats individuals as inherently incapable of handling the rigors of open discourse. This assumption is not surprising, given the conflation of speech and action that characterizes much of the free speech theory championed by such ideology. (No one disagrees with punishing targeted expression that is clearly intimidating or threatening. But the advocates of victimology go considerably further than this.) Victimology represents the conjunction of a debilitating form of identity politics and the broader trend that social theorist Philip Rieff identified as the "triumph of the therapeutic."[56]

Berkeley linguist John McWhorter has written one of the most insightful critiques about the new "cult of victimhood" that has distorted the civil rights movement in America. McWhorter maintains that "all too often this [reinforcement of victimhood] is done not with a view toward forging solutions, but to foster and nurture an unfocussed brand of resentment and sense of alienation from the mainstream.... But transforming [injustices] into apocalyptic embroidering does not address victimhood but instead simply celebrates it."[57] Perched between the racist past and the hoped for future, victimology represents a form of transitional justice that needs to be transcended. ACLU president Nadine Strossen has made a similar critique of MacKinnon's and Dworkin's theory of pornography: it treats all women as victims who presumptively lack personal agency and responsibility.[58]

Some maintain that victimhood and the therapeutic conceit have "hijacked" the civil rights movement, influencing many in that movement to turn from promoting principles of liberal citizenship to focus on a mixture of self-esteem and racial identity. A host of "race experts," diversity

---

Medicine (Basic Books, 2000), ch. 7; Shelby Steele, *A Dream Deferred: The Second Betrayal of Black Freedom in America* (HarperCollins, 1998); Joseph A. Amato, *Victims and Values: A History and a Theory of Suffering* (Praeger, 1990).

55 See Hannah Arendt, *The Human Condition* (University of Chicago Press, 1958), p. 215.

56 Philip Rieff, *The Triumph of the Therapeutic: Uses of Faith after Freud* (Harper Torchbacks, 1966).

57 McWhorter, *Losing the Race: Self-Sabotage in Black America* (HarperCollins, 2001), pp. 2, 5. On victimhood in a broader historical perspective, see Joseph A. Amato, *Victims and Values: A History and a Theory of Suffering* (Praeger, 1990).

58 See Nadine Strossen, *Defending Pornography: Free Speech, Sex, and the Fight for Women's Equality* (Scribner, 1995). Also, see McElroy, *Liberty for Women*.

consultants, and sensitivity and etiquette advisers diverted the civil rights movement, causing it to be obsessed instead with "damage imagery," a special form of victimhood.[59] According to Elisabeth Lasch-Quinn, "The desired goal was no longer civic equality and participation, but individual psychic well-being. . . . Racial identity theory, oppression pedagogy, interracial etiquette, ethno-therapy – these are only a few examples of the new ministrations of the self-appointed liberation experts." Unfortunately, this trend has weakened the drive for equality because "sensitivity itself is an inadequate and cynical substitution for civility and democracy."[60]

The brush of victimhood paints much more broadly than in matters of race. One finds its ideas in some schools of feminism, in the spread of "victimization syndromes" as criminal law defenses in the 1980s, in the "recovery" and "trauma" movements of psychiatry and psychology that mushroomed in the 1970s, and even in emerging forms of Christian politics in America.[61] Asserting one's position as a victim is strategically useful as a vehicle for obtaining sympathy and material benefits; and – as Nietzsche understood so incisively – it can weaken the self-confidence of one's opponents. It can also provide emotional satisfaction as a form of redemptive suffering. Alan Wolfe has commented on a similar reveling in victimhood in the university of the early 1990s, which often took on "the character of psychodramas." The clash between radical multiculturalism and its opponents

is also a battle between those who claim that the university should be about ideas and those who believe that the university should be about suffering and redemption. As Henry Louis Gates, Jr. has pointed out, some of the more exotic forms of Afrocenticism resemble twelve-step recovery programs. They do not so much search for new ideas about race and ethnicity as they affirm the pain of racism and the exhilaration involved in recognizing that pain. . . . The period when political correctness achieved its high point was a period of emotion, not one of reason.[62]

Many examples of this phenomenon came to pass at the University of Wisconsin during the 1990s. In one case, a student leader in 2000 responded to a speech on racial issues by the conservative firebrand Dinesh D'Souza by informing the large audience that D'Souza's conservative views on race had inflicted such trauma in him that neither he nor his family would be able to sleep or perform their usual responsibilities for several days.[63]

---

[59] On "damage imagery," see Daryl Michael Scott, *Contempt and Pity: Social Policy and the Image of the Damaged Black Psyche, 1880–1996* (University of North Carolina Press, 1997).

[60] Lasch-Quinn, *Race Experts: How Racial Etiquette, Sensitivity Training, and New Age Therapy Hijacked the Civil Rights Revolution* (Norton, 2001), pp. 81, xiv, xviii.

[61] See Downs, *More Than Victims*, esp. ch. 2.

[62] Wolfe, "The New Class Comes Home," in Edith Kurzweil and William Phillips, eds., *Our Country, Our Culture: The Politics of Political Correctness* (Partisan Review Press, 1994), p. 288. Nietzsche's insights into the psychology of victimhood remains classic. See, e.g., *The Genealogy of Morals*, trans. Walter Kaufman (Vintage, 1967).

[63] Several colleagues and I were eyewitnesses to the Wisconsin episode.

Universities nurtured this way of thinking in the 1990s as the triumph of the therpeutic was embraced by the new type of university leadership, especially those dealing with student affairs. Wolfe maintains that the university of the late 1980s bore "little resemblance to an earlier image of academic life," so "when demands for multiculturalism, speech codes, and diversity hit the campus, a structure was already in place to receive them."[64] "Almost overnight," he writes, sometime in the 1980s, a "new class" of administrative leaders assumed power that personified both the new ethos of diversity and multiculturalism and – even more so – the "therapeutic side of new left politics." Emphasizing the relationship between discourse and oppression, the new leaders cultivated control over communication – for example, speech codes and the marginalization of those not on board – rather than control over production. Many sponsored total quality management, the management theory that was first applied to businesses. TQM envisions the institution as an integrated whole, a community of diverse parts that creative leadership can compel to work as a unit. While the theory is lauded by many business scholars, its application to universities is problematic, for it requires a CEO-style command structure and the inculcation of the rank with a communal purpose that conflicts with individualism and individual academic freedom.

At such places as Berkeley, Penn, Wisconsin, and Michigan, the new chancellors endorsed TQM and made administrative appointments predominantly on the basis of candidates' conformity to the ideal of diversity, which they promoted at every possible opportunity. Although Chancellor Donna Shalala often praised free speech at Wisconsin, she also presided over the rise of speech codes and made sure that her administration was stacked with individuals who supported her new agenda of diversity. Conformity with this message was necessary to administrative advance. Wolfe remarks, "the missionary zeal of university administrators to make the world a better place" was a major aspect of the new era.[65] Shalala expressed this ethic in a widely quoted public statement in 1989. Promoting racial and ethnic harmony through enlightened human relations is not simply a very important objective but *the* most important mission of the university: "Universities must not simply reflect society, but must lead it. Nowhere is this leadership more important than in the area of racial and ethnic relations.... Schools and universities are the most appropriate institutions to recognize the pluralistic nature of our society and to address these needs."[66]

Education theorist Henry Giroux echoed this idea in more utopian language in the early 1990s, proclaiming that education leaders needed to

[64] Wolfe, "The New Class Comes Home," p. 286.
[65] Ibid., p. 291.
[66] Shalala, speech to Board of Regents of the University of Wisconsin, June 8, 1989.

"develop an emancipatory theory of leadership" that speaks to a "sense of utopian purpose.... the real challenge of leadership is to broaden its definition ... to the more vital imperatives of educating students to live in a multicultural world."[67]

At Wisconsin, Shalala maintained that the era of faculty governance had essentially passed, given the complexity of the university and its new responsibilities. But when faculty government is weakened, the balance of power shifts to the administration and its conception of the university. This shift weakens the intellectual mission of the university, as it can entail appointing administrators for reasons other than their academic reputations. The academic credentials of such individuals often do not compare favorably with the faculties they govern. Wolfe observes, "Nearly all college presidents these days govern a faculty far more accomplished than themselves with respect to the business of the university, not a situation conducive to an emphasis on the rewards of merit." And merit is also suspect "among those who advocate the incorporation of a race-class-gender perspective. From this perspective, advancement within the university involves the representation of groups, not the accomplishment of individuals."[68] John Searle observed this process unfold over the past fifteen years at Berkeley:

In Berkeley, in all this there is a subtle change in the atmosphere of the university. When I came here [in the early 1960s], I left a job in Oxford to come here, and what I was told was that the Berkeley administration had made a commitment that Berkeley should be the best in every department. At some point they lost that ambition. Nowadays, they'd like to be good but they value multiculturalism and political correctness and what is called "diversity."

The way it got redefined was that we were going to have "excellence." That was it. And then we were going to have "excellence *and* diversity." And then it became "excellence *through* diversity," and now it's "diversity is excellence."[69]

It should be noted, however, that Searle's comments apply mainly to the administration, not individual departments. The latter remain beholden to an ethos of excellence at Berkeley; and keeping an eye alert to diversity concerns is certainly a justifiable stance. What is important is the shift in the ideologies of administrative appointees at Berkeley and elsewhere, which sets the tone of institutions. And it is such individuals who must decide between academic freedom and sensitivity when these principles come into conflict. As noted earlier, the new administrative elite has often erred on the side of sensitivity, not academic freedom.

---

[67] Giroux, *Living Dangerously: Multiculturalism and the Politics of Difference* (Peter Lang, 1993), pp. 20, 24.
[68] Wolfe, "The New Class Comes Home," p. 290.
[69] Interview with John Searle, August 2001. See also Wood, *Diversity*.

Postmodernism and the Cult of Marginality

Postmodernism has provided a broad philosophical justification for speech codes and related policies. To be sure, the intellectual movement called postmodernism is complex. Some of its ideas can actually be used to argue *against* the institution of codes and other restrictions on liberty and to open the door to fresh insights. Postmodernism has had its greatest impact on those disciplines (mainly in the humanities) in which primary data consist of words rather than empirical phenomena. In fields in which it is unnecessary to deal with real world phenomena it is easier for theorists to conclude that reality consists of talk. Postmodernism encompasses such distinct yet related approaches as contemporary forms of literary criticism, deconstruction, social history, the new cultural studies, structuralism, poststructuralism, critical legal studies, and some forms of critical race and gender studies. Broadly construed, postmodernism challenges such intellectual and moral tenets of the Enlightenment as universal reason, objective truth, empiricism, science, individual autonomy, and rights. Postmodernism proclaims that the Enlightenment's tenets are fictitious social constructions that are morally questionable due to their connection to dehumanizing technology, "scientism," and what Jacques Derrida has labeled "logocentricism" – an emphasis on rational logic as a mode of thinking and experiencing the world that excludes or minimizes other forms of mental experience such as revelation, intuition, and aesthetic sensibility.

Postmodernism assumes that the "ideological system sustaining... Western European civilization is bankrupt."[70] Similarly, critical legal study's critique of liberal law – postmodernist in inspiration – strives to show how such concepts as individualism and the rule of law (which assumes law's autonomy, coherence, consistency, and neutrality) are fundamentally untenable. Law is power.[71] Postmodernism questions the integrity and viability of the ultimate foundation of liberal freedom: the autonomous, self-determining individual. And since free speech is an integral principle of Enlightenment consciousness, some versions of postmodernism question its viability as well. Of course, it would be naive to believe that law is not a form of power in its own right, and that Enlightenment concepts are not subject to the complexities and inner contradictions that characterize all important political and intellectual concepts. It is a question of balance and perspective. Postmodernism works best when it serves as a Socratic challenge to liberal thought, not when it turns into an ideology that rejects liberalism and liberal freedom outright.

Stanford University's elimination of its traditional Western civilization requirement in 1988 in favor of a more relativistic and multicultural program

---

[70] Paul R. Gross and Norman Levitt, *Higher Superstition: The Academic Left and Its Quarrels with Science* (Johns Hopkins University Press, 1998), pp. 4–5.
[71] See Mark Kelman, *A Guide to Critical Legal Studies* (Harvard University Press, 1987).

is one example of the institutionalization of postmodernist logic. Advocates of change opposed the core curriculum of the Western culture requirement for being too "logocentric" and dedicated to "dead white males." The new program "embraced particularism," questioning "the idea of universalism itself." In one course, the materials favorably compared the aboriginal concept of "dream time" as an explanation of cause and effect with the "'logocentric' approach of Western philosophers like Aristotle and Descartes."[72]

Postmodernism also concerns itself with interpretation and discourse. In the *Archeology of Knowledge*, for example, Michel Foucault – perhaps the most influential postmodernist thinker – proclaims the need to "dispense with things" that are "anterior to discourse" and to focus on "the regular formation of objects that emerge only in discourse."[73] Discourse is the fundamental human reality, thus rendering it inherently political. And "if the world is discursive, then it is obviously susceptible to discursive attack. What prevents us from replacing the reigning discourse with another discourse?"[74] Foucault was preoccupied with what lurks in the margins, hidden by the West's obsession with logocentric reason. Marginality harbors hidden truth. Identification with and advocacy of marginal and repressed groups is the most "liberating" form of discursive counterpower. The emphasis on discourse is crucial to the logic behind speech codes: if speech is the ultimate form of power, speech deemed inegalitarian must be suppressed as a form of discursive discriminatory action. Accordingly, postmodern assumptions have been used to promote the case for restricting free speech.

At a forum on academic freedom at Wisconsin in 1994, for example, an English professor challenged the liberal assessment of speech codes by other presenters in terms taken directly from the postmodern handbook:

[A]ll of these speakers sought to ground their proposals on speech codes on the assumptions of liberal humanism – when in fact the debate that has made this issue so hot involves an interrogation of those very founding assumptions. The interrogation was launched... by philosophers of language, history, and knowledge.... The critique of these assumptions goes this way: there is no such thing as the isolated, dispassionate, knowing individual – indeed, the very conception of the self as a discrete entity is an error. Instead, we are embedded in our moment in time and all of the practices that that moment makes available to us. One of those practices is language.[75]

---

72 From Sacks and Theil, *The Diversity Myth*, pp. xx, 2–6.
73 Foucault, *Archeology of Knowledge* (Random House, 1972), pp. 65, 47.
74 Allan Megill, *Prophets of Extremity: Nietzsche, Heidegger, Foucault, Derrida* (University of California Press, 1985), p. 238.
75 Cyrena N. Pondrom, "A Faculty Member's Perspective on Hate Speech Regulation," in W. Lee Hansen, ed., *Academic Freedom on Trial: 100 Years of Sifting and Winnowing at the University of Wisconsin–Madison* (University of Wisconsin–Madison, Office of University Publications, 1998), p. 206.

This statement itself is impaled on a contradiction. In denouncing objectivity and transcendent truth, the speaker presents virtually every claim as an objective, universal truth – "we are embedded in our moment of time"; "there is no such thing as the isolated, dispassionate, knowing individual." The very nature of language inescapably compels us to rely on the assumption that there are objective truths, even when we make statements that there is no such thing.[76] The statement also represents the antiindividualist and antihumanist bias of some postmodernist thinking.

A widely reported example of postmodernist diminution of the individual took place at the University of Pennsylvania in 1989, when an administrator chastised an undergraduate on the university's planning committee for diversity education for using the word "individual" in a memo to the committee. The administrator underlined the transgressive word and sent the memo back to its guilty source along with a note that admonished, "This is a RED FLAG phrase today, which is considered by many to be RACIST. Arguments that champion the individual over the group ultimately privileges [*sic*] the 'individuals' belonging to Penn's largest or dominant group."[77]

Richard Bernstein assesses Foucault's impact more broadly, pointing to the proliferation of postmodernist terms in such bastions of the humanities as the Modern Language Association:

[T]here is "dominant discourse," "marginal subjects," the "victimized subaltern." ... Open up almost any contemporary academic journal and you will find phrases like "colonized bodies," the "vantage point of the subjugated," the "great background terrain of subjugated knowledge," the "marginalized other," which are presented in contrast to ... the "socially produced meaning of the dominant white culture."[78]

Despite the ubiquitous rhetoric, it is *not* inevitable that postmodern tenets lead toward the suppression of liberty. Just as multiculturalism has liberal and authoritarian forms, so does postmodernism. The absence of a transcendent standard for truth can just as readily lead one to the conclusion that there is no basis for claiming that any form of expression is unacceptable. In other words, relativism can just as easily provide a justification for libertarian speech policy and individualism as for censorship in the name of groups. Justice Powell wrote in an important 1974 Supreme Court libel case, "Under the First Amendment there is no such thing as a false idea."[79] Thus, many who favor a linguistic or discourse-oriented theory of truth are often *advocates* of wide-open free speech, for if truth lies in discourse or

---

[76] See Thomas Nagel's excellent deconstruction of deconstruction in *The Last Word* (Oxford University Press, 1997).
[77] Quoted in Bernstein, *Dictatorship of Virtue*, p. 75.
[78] Ibid., p. 227.
[79] *Gertz v. Robert Welch*, 418 U.S. 323 (1974).

language, censorship ultimately biases or cripples the process out of which contingent or consensual truth emerges.[80]

Even Michel Foucault's thinking has a libertarian side that many of his admirers minimize or ignore. Taken with the touch of irony that he may have intended, Foucault's (and other postmodernists') assessments of Western logic and culture can reveal overlooked qualities about the contingency of truths and the ways in which individual meaning is affected by larger forces. His works on madness, sexuality, and the growth of a scientific world view, for example, offer important insights about the limits of rationalism and empiricism. In addition, Foucault's championing of "action groups" does not mean that he abandoned criticism of any group or discourse because of its correct political values. A true Foucaultian might well rebel against the orthodoxies propounded by the contemporary university. Allan Megill portrays Foucault in veritable Socratic terms:

[I]t is not surprising that Foucault's attitude toward the various "action groups" with which he has been associated is precisely double-edged and ironic. He is willing to ally himself with these groups insofar as they are able to mount challenges to the existing order.... But insofar as they are committed to establishing new, allegedly liberating orders, he remains highly suspicious of them. For what Foucault has articulated is an instrument of systemic suspicion toward any order whatsoever.[81]

The Rise of Codes: Racial Incidents on Campus

The speech code movement took off during that pivotal year, 1987, with Michigan, Stanford, and other schools promulgating new measures restricting speech that caused a new type of harm: "discriminatory expression."[82] By 1992 at least three hundred universities had enacted codes of this type.[83]

College leaders rarely called their new codes "speech codes," however, for that designation jeopardizes the policies' legitimacy by linking them with censorship. Instead, supporters often labeled the rules "conduct" or "harassment" codes. Courts permit a much broader regulation of conduct than of speech. For example, Wisconsin bundled its faculty speech code into the section of university rules dealing with sexual harassment and other forms of "prohibited expressive conduct." Labels matter. One of the most

---

[80] See Paul Chevigny, "Philosophy of Language and Free Expression," 55 *N.Y.U. Law Review* 157 (1980).

[81] Megill, *Prophets of Extremity*, p. 239. One insightful biographer has portrayed Foucault as a modern Socratic figure: James Miller, *The Passion of Michel Foucault* (Simon and Schuster, 1993).

[82] See, e.g., Arati Korwar, *War of Words: Speech Codes at Public Colleges and Universities* (Freedom Forum First Amendment Center, 1994, 1995), p. 24.

[83] See Shiell, *Campus Hate Speech on Trial*, p. 3. For the view that many codes were simply updates of established policies, see Wilson, *The Myth of Political Correctness*, p. 92.

difficult tasks that abolition forces confronted in the struggle over the faculty speech code at Wisconsin was winning the battle over definitions, which meant first and foremost getting people to admit that the code was a *speech* code.

It is not always clear that a school has adopted a new code based on the new antidiscrimination logic, for many schools revamped existing rules that addressed civility, intimidation, and harassment. A code is likely to represent the new thinking if it specifies such categories as race, gender, sexual orientation, nationality, and other aspects of identity politics for restriction, and if it prohibits expression that "demeans," "vilifies," or "abuses" individuals or groups on these grounds, or creates a "hostile environment."

Many of the first set of new codes came about in direct response to particular incidents of racism or sexism on campus that reportedly accompanied the growing racial and gender diversity on campus in the 1970s and 1980s. After the initial push, other schools joined the bandwagon whether or not incidents occurred on their campuses. It is hard to tell whether there was an actual increase of such cases, or whether there was simply increased reporting and heightened awareness due to politics and the creation of infrastructures intended to notice abuses. The National Institute against Prejudice and Violence reported 250 incidents of campus bigotry between 1986 and 1989 – a small number given the demographics of higher education.[84]

Clearly, some forms of offense are more severe than others. The worst cases involve highly degrading and even threatening expression, which could be punished under preexisting laws or rules prohibiting so-called fighting words (words likely to trigger a hostile response, thereby causing a breach of peace) or threats. At Wisconsin, for example, an African American freshman woman was vilified by a group of white male students at the entrance of the library; they told her that they did not like "niggers" at their school. At Purdue, someone scratched "Dear Nigger" on a counselor's door. At Smith, a student from Africa discovered a note under the door that said, "African Nigger do you want some bananas. Go back to the jungle."[85] Other reported incidents involved less-targeted, indirect forms of expression, such as skits based on racial or sexual themes and speeches by racist groups. A brief look at the events at Michigan illustrates how a code suddenly emerged in response to incidents of bigotry and how these new ideas were employed to remedy the problems of racism and sexism administratively. This case is important because the Michigan code received as much public attention as

---

[84] National Institute against Prejudice and Violence, *Campus Ethnoviolence ... and the Policy Options* (National Institute, 1990), pp. 41–72.

[85] The Wisconsin case was told to me by the dean of students; the other cases are in Matsuda et al., *Words That Wound*, p. 54.

any code. I examine the events that spawned the speech code movement at Wisconsin in a later chapter.

In January 1987 a group of black female students discovered leaflets in a dormitory lounge announcing "open hunting season" on African Americans, whom the leaflets portrayed as "saucer lips, porch monkeys, and jigaboos." A week later, a campus disc jockey asked listeners to call in racist jokes on the air. When students organized to protest these acts, someone hung a Ku Klux Klan sign from a dorm room window above them. Some of these acts could be interpreted as threats or acts of intimidation that cross a First Amendment line. The U.S. Supreme Court, for example, held in 2003 that cross-burning can be an act of intimidation that is not inherently protected by the First Amendment.[86] The First Amendment protects offensive speech, not threats or intimidations, which can take the form of words or symbols alone if they are targeted at individuals. Under the circumstances, the university had to act to protect the sense of security of affected students. But it had to proceed carefully in a manner that did not open the door to censorship of ideas simply deemed offensive or politically incorrect. News of the incidents swept the country, and state political and campus leaders hurriedly met to discuss the situation. Meanwhile, a campus group threatened to file a lawsuit against the university for "not maintaining or creating a non-racist, non-violent atmosphere" on campus.[87] The university's administrators responded by formulating a six-point antidiscrimination plan that included a harassment policy drafted under the aegis of the new director of the Office of Affirmative Action with the assistance of some law professors. The policy included an "interpretive guide" that significantly expanded the code's reach. The regents unanimously adopted the code on May 1, 1988.

The code exempted the student newspapers and established special public areas where all speech was protected except incitements or threats of physical violence or destruction of property. (Later known across the country as "free speech zones," these policies do more to inhibit free discourse than to facilitate it.)[88] The key provision, which applied to educational and academic centers (classrooms, libraries, study centers, etc.), prohibited sexual harassment and discriminatory speech. The code prohibited

any behavior, verbal or physical, that stigmatizes or victimizes an individual on the basis of race, ethnicity, religion, sex, or sexual orientation, creed, national origin, ancestry, age, marital status, handicap or Vietnam-era veteran status, and that involves an explicit or implied threat, or "has the purpose of interfering with an individual's" academic or non-academic activities, or "creates an intimidating, hostile, or demeaning environment" for campus-related pursuits.[89]

[86] *Virginia v. Black*, 538 U.S. 343 (2003).
[87] See Shiell, *Campus Hate Speech on Trial*, pp. 18–19.
[88] See FIRE's website for a discussion of such zones: www.theFIRE.org.
[89] Michigan Policy, cited in *Doe v. Michigan*, 721 F.Supp. 852 (E.D. Mich. 1989).

Although the incidents that generated the concern at Michigan involved seriously demeaning and even threatening expression, the "interpretive guidelines" that accompanied the code went considerably further in their coverage. The guidelines ventured into territory close to thought control and included such viewpoint-based examples as, "you exclude someone from a study group because of race, sex, or ethnic origin"; "you display a Confederate flag on your dorm room wall"; "you comment in a derogatory way about someone's physical appearance or sexual orientation, or their cultural origin, or religious beliefs."[90] In striking down the Michigan code in 1989, the federal district judge, Avern Cohn, pointed to these guidelines and observed, "The University had no idea what the limits of the Policy were and . . . was essentially making up the rules as it went along."[91]

Three complaints made under the jurisdiction of the code led to formal or informal sanctions against those expressing unpopular, nonthreatening *ideas* in *class* in 1989. First, a graduate student in a social work class was found guilty of sexual harassment for expressing his belief that homosexuality is a disease that could be treated by a plan he had developed (the student also engaged in emotional exchanges with other students over his views). Second, a business student had to write an apology and attend an educational session on gays after he read a limerick during a class public-speaking exercise that made fun of a famous athlete's sexual orientation. Third, a dentistry professor filed a complaint against a student for remarking that, according to his roommate (a black student who had been in the program), minority students were not treated equally in the class; although his comment was made in a small discussion group set up to discuss anticipated problems in the course, the offending student was required to receive counseling about the harassment policy and write an apology.[92] The Michigan experience shows the importance of carefully delineating and honoring the distinction between intimidation and causing offense. Going after the latter ineluctably leads to thought control.

The Motivations, Purposes, and Types of Codes

The new codes vary in terms of content and scope, the types of harm they are intended to address, and the motivations that promoted their passage. Some codes were inspired by liberal concerns about discrimination and harm, whereas others were driven more by the type of postliberal thinking discussed earlier in this chapter. The most limited objective has been to prevent the infliction of substantial emotional harm to particular individuals or groups, arising from the belief that harm can be damaging to individuals' sense of

---

[90] See Shiell, *Campus Hate Speech on Trial*, p. 21.
[91] *Doe v. Michigan*, p. 868.
[92] Shiell, *Campus Hate Speech on Trial*, pp. 21–22. See also Samuel Walker, *Hate Speech: The History of an American Controversy* (University of Nebraska Press, 1994), p. 151.

security and well-being and may unjustifiably interfere with the pursuit of education.[93]

A broader objective arises from the concept of group libel and the motivation to protect the reputation and image of individuals and the groups to which they belong. A liberal version of this argument maintains that the disparagement of racial or gender-defined groups is wrong because it undermines the moral autonomy and individualism of the members of these groups. Race, gender, and sexual orientation are morally irrelevant to an individual's worth.[94] Another version of this objective focuses on the need to protect the reputations of particular groups in a social order characterized by dominant and subordinate classes. A third objective is more traditional: the promotion of civility in the university environment. Civility means treating people with respect and dignity.[95]

A fourth possible objective behind the new codes may well be a classic use of censorship: to promote the new egalitarian orthodoxy by limiting or silencing the discourse of those who disagree with either the ends or (more likely) the means adopted by this movement. Timur Kuran's view on codes emphasizes their censorial *effects*, and no doubt some code advocates intended this as an objective. Kuran writes, "Whatever the purpose of speech regulations, one of their effects is to make students, not to mention faculty and administrators, even more reluctant to speak freely on race-related issues, ever more afraid of using a word or uttering a thought that might be construed as a sign of bigotry. Ironically, this timidity is probably exacerbating racial tensions."[96] This motivation was evident at Wisconsin in 1992, when a member of the university committee (a six-member faculty group that controls the agenda of the faculty senate) asserted during a key moment in the debate over the adoption of a second student speech code that critics' arguments about "a chilling effect on speech" only buttressed the case for codes; after all, this person declared, it would not be bad if speech dealing with race and gender were chilled.[97]

The record of campus politics is replete with examples of this broader censorship objective. A major schism in the ad hoc faculty speech code

---

[93] Writers in Matsuda et al., *Words That Wound*, cite several types of harm, including emotional anxiety, a sense of endangerment, damage to identity, the furtherance of discrimination, and physical reactions.

[94] This was my other logic in *Nazis in Skokie*, although I argued against group libel laws as a means of addressing this concern. See *Nazis in Skokie*, ch. 8. For a more explicit use of this logic, see Hadley Arkes, *The Philosopher in the City* (Princeton University Press, 1981), part 1.

[95] See Hadley Arkes, "Civility and the Restriction of Speech: Rediscovering the Defamation of Groups," in Philip Kurland, ed., *Free Speech and Association: The Supreme Court and the First Amendment* (University of Chicago Press, 1975).

[96] Kuran, *Private Truths, Public Lies: The Social Consequences of Preference Falsification* (Harvard University Press, 1995), p. 227.

[97] Tape of faculty senate meeting, March 2, 1992, University of Wisconsin, Madison.

committee at Wisconsin in 1997–98 formed between those who were concerned with the political and discursive context out of which the codes arose
(and were applied) and those who focused primarily on the actual language
of the measures. In the view of the radical reformers, the most discerning
interpretation in this context required a consideration of the context out of
which the codes emerged, for that background provided the best clues as to
how the codes would be enforced.[98] Similarly, in order to predict the possible
application of codes in particular contexts, one needs to rely on intellectual
and moral instincts (a form of "tacit knowledge") that are honed in actual
political and legal experience. Civil liberties attorney James Weinstein claims
that there is no substitute for experience when it comes to fully fathoming the
First Amendment implications of policies and actions. "Free speech doctrine
is more a product of experience than theory," he wrote.[99]

After his careful consideration of the pros and cons of speech codes, the
author of *Campus Hate Speech on Trial*, Timothy Shiell, concludes that *who*
enforces the rules is often more important than *what* they actually say. Shiell
points to the case of the men's basketball coach at Central Michigan University, who was fired for using the word "nigger" in a locker room speech,
even though the minority players approved of the use of the term in that
particular context. "All they [enforcement officials] needed was a complaint
to convict him. This list of abuses could go on and on.... the apparatus
of the administration and enforcement of speech regulations tends to encourage overzealousness as a means of career advancement." Furthermore,
"even unsuccessful prosecution has a chilling effect on speech."[100] As the
cases discussed previously in this chapter reveal, simply being subjected to
an investigation can be an ordeal.

Addressing the different objectives under discussion, institutions of higher
learning have drafted many different types of codes. Some are limited to direct incitements of harm (such as "fighting words" codes), whereas others
attempt to regulate the broader environment. At the less measured end of
the continuum, the University of Connecticut's code proscribed "inappro-
priately directed laughter" and the "conspicuous exclusion" of individuals
from conversations, while the University of Massachusetts's code sought
to prohibit demeaning not only someone's race, gender, or sexual orientation but also one's "citizenship, culture, HIV status, language, parental

---

[98] Ortega y Gasset has written, "the real meaning of a word appears when the word is uttered
and functions in the human activity called speech. Hence we must know who says it to
whom, when and where.... what we call language forms only one, if a relatively stable,
constituent which must be supplemented by the vital setting." Jose Ortega y Gasset, *Concord
and Liberty* (Norton, 1946), p. 12.

[99] James Weinstein, *Pornography, Hate Speech, and the Radical Assault on Free Speech Doctrine*
(Westview Press, 1999), p. 181. On "tacit knowledge," see, generally, Michael Polanyi,
Personal Knowledge: Towards a Post-Critical Philosophy (University of Chicago Press, 1958).

[100] Shiell, *Campus Hate Speech on Trial*, p. 151.

status, political affiliation or belief, and pregnancy status."[101] In a recent book on campus speech codes, Martin Golding concludes that codes fall into three basic categories, which sometimes overlap: fighting words codes, emotional distress codes, and harassment codes.[102] I would add a fourth type of code, which broadly concerns civility in one form or another.

Although it is arguable how valid the exception is today, the Supreme Court has never overturned *Chaplinsky v. New Hampshire*, a 1942 ruling that "fighting words" are not protected by the First Amendment. The Court defined "fighting words" as words "which by their very utterance inflict injury, or tend to incite an immediate breach of the peace."[103] Modern developments in First Amendment jurisprudence have considerably limited this exception, although lower courts have upheld a few convictions on narrow grounds. For a fighting words code to be constitutional, it must limit its restrictions to words that are likely to trigger a hostile physical reaction of some sort. Fighting words codes are expanded into the broader "harassment codes" when they prohibit fighting words that "create a hostile and intimidating educational environment."[104]

One survey found fighting words codes at 12 percent of public universities and 9 percent of private institutions in 1994. Some fighting words codes specified fighting words involving such categories as race and gender, whereas others applied to all forms of fighting words; some combined both approaches.[105] In 1992 the Supreme Court ruled in *R.A.V. v. St. Paul* that limiting fighting words rules to such categories as race and gender constitutes viewpoint discrimination because such policies only proscribe hostile speech dealing with certain subjects.[106] After *R.A.V.*, all fighting words codes that single out race, gender, and the like for prohibition are probably unconstitutional. Regardless of this, few institutions have revised their codes in the aftermath of *R.A.V.* As Jon B. Gould shows in an innovative and thorough empirical study, the number of speech codes actually *increased* after *R.A.V.* Gould attributes this reaction to several factors, including ideological commitment and institutional political pressures.[107] In fact, Gould probably understates the extent of the resistance to anticensorship court rulings, as he does not deal with institutions' increasing use of harassment codes to limit or investigate free speech.

[101] On Connecticut, see Walker, *Hate Speech*, p. 133. On Massachusetts, see Kors and Silverglate, *The Shadow University*, p. 321.
[102] Martin Golding, *Free Speech on Campus* (Rowman and Littlefield, 2000), ch. 1.
[103] *Chaplinsky v. New Hampshire*, 315 U.S. 568 (1942).
[104] Golding, *Free Speech on Campus*, p. 2.
[105] Korwar, *War of Words*, pp. 25–34.
[106] *R.A.V. v. City of St. Paul*, 505 U.S. 377 (1992).
[107] Jon B. Gould, "The Precedent That Wasn't: College Hate Speech Codes and the Two Faces of Legal Compliance," 35 *Law and Society Review* 345 (2001).

Perhaps the best-known example of a fighting words code that specified such particular categories was Stanford's, which proscribed "harassment by personal vilification" if it (a) is intended to insult or stigmatize an individual or small number of individuals on the basis of their sex, race, color, or national and ethnic origin; and (b) makes use of insulting "fighting words" or nonverbal symbols. A county court of California struck down Stanford's code for being overbroad and viewpoint-based a la *R.A.V.* It was overbroad because it punished speech that "merely hurts the feelings of those who hear it."[108]

The second type of code derives from the civil tort of the intentional infliction of emotional trauma or distress. The University of Texas code restricts racial harassment, defining it as "extreme or outrageous acts or communications that are intended to harass, intimidate or humiliate a student or students on account of race, color or national origin and that reasonably cause them to suffer severe emotional distress." Roughly 13 percent of public institutions and 10 percent of private schools have codes of this nature.[109] General civility codes compose the next category. Most codes of this nature use words other than "civility" to define what is prohibited – such as "threats," "breach of peace," "hazing," or advocacy of outrageously offensive viewpoints – but they tend to address civility or decency in one sense or another.[110]

Harassment Codes: A Special Case

The broadest category of codes addresses "harassment" and its apparent discriminatory effects. The status of harassment codes is the most important question in the speech code debate today, especially after the blows courts have delivered to "fighting words" codes in the *Wisconsin, Michigan, Stanford,* and *R.A.V.* cases.[111] Unfortunately, courts have not adequately drawn the line between harassment and speech, leaving the question open to speculation rather than to precedent. Few people question the necessity of harassment laws that prohibit "quid pro quo" harassment (e.g., job advancement or status in exchange for granting sexual favors) or that ban repeated unwelcome sexual advances. Harassment rules forbidding the creation of a "hostile environment" in the workplace, however, create problems that have yet to be fully thought out. Hostile environments certainly exist and need

---

[108] *Corry et al. v. Stanford University*, Santa Clara County Court, case no. 740309 (February 27, 1995), p. 9. Stanford is a private school, but a California law known as the Leonard Law requires all institutions of higher learning to abide by the principles of the First Amendment. California Education Code, sec. 94367.

[109] Golding, *Free Speech on Campus*, p. 2; Korwar, *War of Words*, pp. 25–34.

[110] See Korwar, *War of Words*, pp. 25–35.

[111] The Wisconsin case is *U.W.M. Post v. Board of Regents of the University of Wisconsin*, 774 F. Supp. (1989).

to be remedied. The problem lies in the extremely elastic contours of the concept and the fact that the law is plaintiff-driven, meaning that the law is made on a case-by-case basis, not according to a clear standard. Accordingly, organizations have an incentive to prohibit a wide range of expression, including expression that is normally entitled to full free speech protection. First Amendment doctrine generally requires harm to be discretely targeted and substantial before expression may be targeted for restriction. But the amorphous concept of hostile environment can apply even to speech with which one seriously disagrees, thereby placing this harassment policy and First Amendment principles at odds.

Antiharassment law arose from a confluence of new theories, from political and legal activism, and from changing relations between men and women as more women entered the workplace.[112] The Equal Employment Opportunity Commission enforces antiharassment law under the authority of Title VII, while the Office of Civil Rights within the Department of Education covers educational institutions under Title IX. (Titles VII and IX prohibit discrimination in employment and in educational institutions receiving public funds, respectively.) Over time, these agencies and courts expanded the scope of harassment laws, until they covered the creation of a "hostile environment" on grounds of gender and race.[113]

The Supreme Court legitimized hostile environment law in 1986 and 1993 decisions that dealt with brutish and unwanted sexual advances.[114] Unfortunately, the Supreme Court did not provide a coherent definition of harassment. Consequently, lower federal courts have issued inconsistent rulings. Many cases have dealt with extreme kinds of sexual advances and innuendo that called out for remedy. Others are more questionable. In one well-known case, University of Nebraska officials ordered a graduate student to remove a five-by-seven-inch picture of his wife in a bikini from his desk. In another case, an employee of a Minnesota public library was required to remove from his cubicle a cartoon that depicted men commenting on the Lorena Bobbit case by using the word "penis"; the offending word was written in small print that could be read only by someone directly in front of the cartoon.[115] Then there are those who make a credible case that women are

---

[112] See Kingsley Browne, "Title VII as Censorship," 52 *Ohio State Law Journal* 481 (1991), p. 529.

[113] See *Rogers v. EEOC*, 454 F. 2d 234 (5th Cir. 1971); *Williams v. Saxbe*, 413 F. Supp. 654 (D.D.C., 1976); EEOC, Final Guidelines on Sexual Harassment in the Workplace, November 10, 1980; *Brady v. Jackson*, 641 F. 2d 934 (1981); Shiell, *Campus Hate Speech on Trial*, p. 101.

[114] *Meritor Savings Bank FSB v. Vinson*, 477 U.S. 57 (1986); *Harris v. Forklift Systems, Inc.*, 510 U.S. 17 (1993).

[115] These and other cases are reported in Walter K. Olson, *The Excuse Factory: How Employment Law Is Paralyzing the American Workplace* (Free Press, 1997), pp. 74–75.

still being subjected to harassment despite all these reforms. Perhaps we are unduly limiting speech without protecting women in any meaningful sense.[116]

The conflict between hostile environment law and free speech law is reflected in the disparate treatment courts have afforded the legal theories of feminist scholar, Catharine MacKinnon. MacKinnon has presented two major legal reforms to alleviate the subordination of women: first, the new theory of pornography discussed earlier in this chapter; and, second, a new theory of sexual harassment in the workplace. Courts forcefully rejected Indianapolis's adoption of MacKinnon's approach to pornography, treating it as a standard case of censorship. On the other hand, her theory of sexual harassment was destined to become the foundation on which contemporary harassment law has grown.

What MacKinnon did was to transform the concept of harassment from one based on liberal, individualist understandings of targeted harm to an identity-politics-oriented concept based on a rationale of group oppression. And she attached this approach to the coercive power of government. The common historical definition of the verb "to harass" is "to fatigue; to exhaust; to tire with repeated exhausting efforts; to weary by importunity; to cause to endure excessive burdens or anxieties."[117] MacKinnon and her allies redefined harassment as a form of *gender class discrimination* rather than as individual harm. In her groundbreaking 1979 book, *Sexual Harassment of Working Women*, MacKinnon labeled her construction the "inequality approach": "[P]ractices which express and reinforce the social inequality of women to men are clear cases of sex-based discrimination in the inequality approach." She defined harassment as "the unwanted imposition of sexual requirements in the context of a relationship of unequal power," and asked: "What if inequality is built into the social conceptions of male and female sexuality, masculinity and femininity, of sexiness and heterosexual attractiveness? Incidents of sexual harassment suggest that male sexual desire itself may be aroused by female vulnerability."[118]

Like critical race theorists, MacKinnon strives to assimilate the First Amendment with the Fourteenth Amendment (equal protection clause) by defining antiegalitarian speech as an actual form of discrimination. The success of this move depends on a crucial step: the elimination of the fundamental distinction between speech and action. MacKinnon aspires to apply her

---

[116] See, e.g., Stephen J. Shulhofer, *Unwanted Sex: The Culture of Intimidation and the Failure of Law* (Harvard University Press, 1998), pp. 41–42. Schulhofer maintains that there has been little or no reduction in workplace harassment, largely due to ineffective remedies.

[117] *Webster's New International Dictionary of the English Language*, 2d ed. unabridged (G.&C. Merriam, 1961).

[118] Catharine A. MacKinnon, *Sexual Harassment of Working Women* (Yale University Press, 1979), pp. 174, 1, 218.

concept of harassment to many realms of society, including those where free speech has traditionally enjoyed the most protection, such as public forums, books, and the press. (Her antipornography ordinance, for instance, did not limit its application to specific contexts.) At the other end of the continuum are those who would apply the same standards to the workplace as apply to domains where the speech right is clearly accepted. Those who support this position believe that the workplace should be governed by First Amendment principles, at least within reason.[119] Another option is maintaining the status quo, which treats the public realm and the workplace differently. Some have argued that it makes sense for speech to be more severely restricted in the workplace than in other contexts because workers are like captive audiences there, and the purpose of the "managerial" workplace is economic efficiency rather than democratic self-governance or the exploration of truth and meaning.[120]

Jeffrey Rosen presents another option that preserves the distinction between the workplace and other forums but attempts to reintroduce traditional liberal norms of liberty and privacy within the workplace. Rosen argues that most harassment is a violation of the *autonomy* and *privacy* of individuals, and that – at least in cases involving hostile environment (not quid pro quo types of harm) – a law or tort addressing violation of privacy should exist in cases that cannot be resolved informally and in which the plaintiff has exercised her autonomy by making known her desire to be left alone. His reform proposal represents an attempt to return harassment law to more traditional liberal, individualist moorings.[121]

Some (including me) argue that universities differ from typical workplaces because universities have the distinctive obligation to pursue the truth. Free speech values, then, should be as strong at institutions of higher education as elsewhere. Of course, the context is important. Departmental offices and other domains differ from student newspapers, public forums, and classrooms. However, some scholars maintain that institutions of higher learning are not special in this regard. Either such institutions are essentially vehicles for later employment, or their predominant agenda should be the dissemination of the values of the new egalitarian sensibility. Mary Ellen Gale, for example, argues for broad antiharassment codes to prohibit the "prejudicial speech" of "dominant" groups everywhere on campus, for such speech is a "[w]eapon to destroy the right to educational equality of blacks, women,

---

[119] See Eugene Volokh, "How Harassment Law Restricts Free Speech," 47 *Rutgers Law Review* 563 (1995). Jonathan Rauch has argued this position in several articles.

[120] See Robert Post, "Racist Speech, Democracy, and the First Amendment," 32 *William and Mary Law Review* 267 (1990).

[121] Rosen, *The Unwanted Gaze: The Destruction of Privacy in America* (Random House, 2000), pp. 117–18, 165.

and other devalued minorities, and to deny them equal access to university dialogue and dispute."[122]

Institutions of higher learning have passed hostile environment or harassment-based codes across the country. Martin Golding believes that such codes are the most prevalent on campuses, and 78 percent of universities in Korwar's survey had enacted such rules (though Korwar did not ask about "hostile environment" specifically).[123]

During the Clinton presidency, the Office of Civil Rights (OCR) in the federal Department of Education threatened to cut off federal funding from institutions of higher learning that had not developed satisfactory harassment policies. At the same time, OCR refused to provide specific notification of what constituted harassment, leading universities to have to guess. Many schools responded by adopting overly broad interpretations in order to stave off federal intervention.[124]

Concerns over the possible loss of federal funds in the event that Wisconsin abolished or weakened its faculty speech code played a significant role in the politics of reform. The leading opponents of radical reform constantly referred to this possibility during many debates in the ad hoc committee and in the three faculty senate hearings in 1998 and 1999. Many faculty took this possibility seriously, for Madison receives more federal research funding than any university in the nation with the exception of Johns Hopkins.[125] Radical reformers' counterargument was threefold: the code was not a harassment code but a speech code; at the very least, the law is unclear about the difference between free speech and hostile environment harassment, so it is worth taking a prudent risk in the name of free speech and academic freedom; and it was not at all obvious how the OCR would react to abolition or serious modification of a code governing speech in the classroom, and cutting off federal funds seemed too extreme. Radical reformers called this claim the "Chicken Little" argument. I discuss this issue more fully in Chapter 7.

Jeffrey Rosen presents an example of how hostile environment rules can restrict speech in educational institutions in a way that normally would be considered intolerably heavy-handed and coercive. At Santa Rosa Junior College, the faculty adviser to the student newspaper set up a virtual computer discussion group for women only, at the request of women on the

---

[122] Gale, "Reimagining the First Amendment: Racist Speech and Equal Liberty," 65 *St. Johns Law Review* 119 (1991), p. 164. See also Lange, "Racist Speech on Campus: A Title VII Solution to a First Amendment Problem," 64 *Southern California Law Review* 105 (1990), p. 127.

[123] Korwar, *War of Words*, p. 32, table 1.

[124] Terence J. Pell, "A More Subtle Activism at the Office of Civil Rights,"10(3) *Academic Questions* 83 (summer 1997), p. 85.

[125] The university achieved this status according to a 2001 study. See University of Wisconsin Alumni Association materials: "An Introduction to UW-Madison."

paper. He then extended the same privilege to the men on the paper in order to provide equal treatment. Trouble arose when some female workers complained about an advertisement the paper ran, showing the derrière of a woman in a bikini. Some of the men posted "anatomically explicit and sexually derogatory" comments about the protesters, assuming that the confidentiality policy that had been established would apply to them. One man posted vulgar things about another staff member who was his ex-girlfriend. Not surprisingly, someone broke confidentiality, and two women convinced the adviser to close down the discussion groups. And with new legal tools at their disposal, they also filed a complaint with the OCR.

Even though the postings were not directly targeted at any women (nor did they constitute repeated expressive acts), the OCR concluded that they probably constituted sexual harassment because the comments were "so severe and pervasive as to create a hostile environment on the basis of sex." The school paid the women fifteen thousand dollars each to ward off legal liability. The OCR also proposed harassment rules particularly for Santa Rosa, prohibiting "Epithets, slurs, *negative stereotyping*, or threatening, intimidating, or hostile acts that relate to race, color, national origin, gender, or disability. . . . This includes acts that purport to be 'jokes,' or 'pranks,' but that are hostile or *demeaning*."[126]

The men's speech was indeed offensive, vulgar, and immature. Rosen maintains that the comments about the ex-girlfriend arguably constituted invasions of privacy as well. But he concludes that it would be a stretch to consider the comments "discriminatory" and that most of the gossip was "a classic example of what should be protected as political speech."[127] I would add two points. First, OCR's tailor-made rule constitutes clear viewpoint discrimination, for one could post "flattering" or "positive" stereotypes but not "negative." What else is this but censorship designed to silence a disfavored opinion? Second, is deploying the coercive arm of the state the best and fairest way to deal with problems such as this?

Now that we have looked at the basic background issues, it is time to present my case studies. The case studies provide detailed looks at the culture and politics of the postliberal university, and how such culture and politics affect liberty and justice. The case studies also show how the right kind of mobilization can protect the status of liberty on campus and reaffirm liberal principles in the public realm.

---

[126] Rosen, *The Unwanted Gaze*, pp. 192–93. I emphasize the broadest language. Rosen drew on Mike Godwin, *Cyber Rights: Defending Free Speech in the Digital Age* (Times Books, 1998), pp. 105–12.

[127] Rosen, *The Unwanted Gaze*, p. 193.

PART II

CASE STUDIES IN THE POLITICS OF CIVIL LIBERTY ON CAMPUS

3

Columbia's Sexual Misconduct Policy

Civil Liberty versus Solidarity

In February 2000 the university senate at Columbia enacted a radically innovative new "Sexual Misconduct Policy" that sought to encourage victims of
sexual assault to be more willing to press formal charges against their attackers. Comparing the number of rape victims being treated by the hospital ad-
joining the campus (St. Luke's) with the small number of incidences reported
by the university, advocates of the new policy came to two conclusions: first,
that the university's administration was covering up an epidemic of rape on
the campus and, second, that the existing university systems of adjudication –
the old "Dean's Discipline," and a new reform adopted in 1995 – were in-
hibiting already traumatized victims from reporting attacks. In addition, certain procedural rights of the defendants – including the rights to be present
during all testimony, to confront the accuser, and to be accompanied by an
attorney – purportedly added to the discomfort of the victim in pursuing a
case through trial.

The activists, claiming that the system's procedures and protections
amounted to mind-boggling bureaucratic "red tape," mobilized a mass political campaign to pressure the university and the university senate to pass
the new sexual misconduct policy. Interestingly, the traditional "Dean's
Discipline" for adjudicating sexual misconduct cases had also failed to
guarantee expressly defendants' procedural rights, a situation that is surprisingly typical of most campus judicial systems.[1] (But deans could provide
such rights on a case-by-case basis.) What is striking about the 2000 enactment is not its failure to provide expressly for these and other procedural
rights but that the new policy *expressly prohibited* them. In addition, the

---

[1] On the widespread lack of specific due process protections in college and university discipline
codes, see Curtis J. Berger and Vivian Berger, "Academic Discipline: A Guide to Fair Process
for the University Student," 99 *Columbia Law Review* 289 (1999). A Columbia law professor,
Vivian Berger, played an important role in the critique of the Columbia sexual misconduct
policy once it became a public issue.

new policy set up special tribunals to adjudicate only sexual misconduct cases, staffed by adjudicators trained to be especially sensitive to the needs of victims.

Although there were valid concerns about how Columbia was handling sexual misconduct cases, the new system's severe tilt toward the accuser unavoidably raised serious questions about due process, fundamental fairness, and the independence of the judicial system. When the public learned about what Columbia had produced, it greeted the news with strong criticism. Just how could such a one-sided policy have emerged from such a distinguished institution of higher learning? The Columbia story is an example of how a probably valid critique of existing procedures led to a new policy that swung way too far in the opposite direction. Only when outside forces (led by the Foundation for Individual Rights in Education) entered the fray was Columbia compelled to address the need to balance concern for accusers with the basic rights of the accused. The Columbia case also displays how the university community can become insular and cut off from the constitutional values of the American polity.

Before I turn to Columbia's tale, I must say that during my visit there in June 2001 and April 2002, no administrator would talk with me about the case; and the one administrator who at least agreed to meet with me was under strict orders to say not a word about the case in any form. My first visit took place several months after the case had exploded on the national scene (to Columbia's chagrin) and at the same time that Andrew Brownstein, a reporter for the *Chronicle of Higher Education*, published an article about the policy and its politics in that journal. Although Brownstein tried to be balanced, the essay did not exhibit Columbia in its best light. Fortunately, because many student leaders and some key faculty members did speak with me, I was able to gather meaningful data. I would like to take this opportunity to say that, although I disagree with what the student leaders did, I admire them for doing what they thought was right. Many of them will be leaders of constructive social change one day. Unfortunately, they simply had not had enough exposure to the principles of due process and constitutionalism. In this respect, they suffered from a failure of liberal education. Such exposure might have provided them with the intellectual tools to evaluate intelligently and critically the strong moral claims for reform with which they were confronted. The need for more meaningful exposure to such principles in higher education is one lesson that emerges from this chapter.

The Issue of Sexual Assault

Sexual assault is a serious crime that continues to pose vexing problems of prosecution. Although debate rages over the actual frequency of attacks, no one contests that sexual assault profoundly affects women's sense of security.

According to two researchers, "Most women experience fear of rape as a nagging, gnawing sense that something awful could happen, an angst that keeps them from doing things they want or need to do."[2] One recent survey by the federal government found that 870 of 100,000 women eighteen years old or older had been victimized each year, while about 18 percent had been victims of rape or attempted rape during their lifetimes.[3] Some contend that underreporting camouflages the true extent of abuse. Others maintain that the problem is especially acute on college campuses, where both sexes live closely together and social life is suffused with alcohol and drugs. In a 1999 survey by the U.S. Department of Justice, 2.8 percent of college women reported being victimized by rape or attempted rape the previous six months – an annual rate of 5,600 per 100,000. Some argue that these figures are too low. In a famous study conducted in the late 1980s, Mary P. Koss and her associates concluded that 27 percent of college women had been so victimized since the age of fourteen.[4]

Campus counselors and activists at Columbia and elsewhere began citing the Koss study as evidence that an epidemic of rape and "date rape" plagued American campuses. (Date rape is understood as a rape that takes place between acquaintances on a date or similar situation; it is often linked to consumption of alcohol or drugs.) Some scholars, however, contest such figures as representing "advocacy" rather than objective fact.[5] For example, in its assessment of cases, Koss's study concluded that rape took place in almost three-fourths of the cases in which the women themselves denied having been raped. Columbia law professor Gerard Lynch, a federal judge in New York appointed by Bill Clinton and one of the very few faculty members who opposed the new policy in the university senate, told me that the Koss study is a "bad study." He agrees that underreporting is widespread but has seen no evidence that the Koss figure is correct or that the number of assaults has increased over the years. Astronomy professor James Applegate, the other major foe of the policy in the senate, also questioned the validity of the Koss study. "I did the math on that once – that's one rape on this campus a day," he remarked.[6]

[2] Margaret T. Gordon and Stephanie Riger, *The Female Fear: The Social Cost of Rape* (University of Illinois Press, 1991), p. 2.

[3] Patricia Tjaden and Nancy Thoennes, *Prevalence, Incidence, and Consequences of Violence against Women: Findings from the National Violence against Women Survey* (National Institute of Justice, 1998).

[4] The former study is Bonnie S. Fisher et al., *Extent and Nature of the Sexual Victimization of College Women: A National-Level Analysis* (National Institute of Justice, 1999). The second is Mary P. Koss et al., "The Scope of Rape: Incidence and Prevalence of Sexual Aggression and Victimization in a National Sample of Higher Education Students," 55 *Journal of Consulting and Clinical Psychology* 162 (1987).

[5] Neil Gilbert, "The Phantom Epidemic of Sexual Assault," *Public Interest* (Spring 1991), pp. 54, 60, 63.

[6] Interviews with Gerard Lynch and James Applegate, June 2001.

Skepticism aside, even the lower estimates of national researchers reveal "an enormous amount of abuse – at least 150,000 cases a year."[7] In addition, prosecuting rape cases has always proved to be exceedingly difficult because of the nature of the evidence, often involving issues of "he said, she said," and because of the difficulty of determining the *mens rea* (the mental element of culpability) necessary for the offense. In the past, the law required substantial proof of nonconsent by the complainant, often asking for evidence of physical resistance to the sexual advance. The rules of evidence also allowed the defense to question the victim about her sexual past, making it even more humiliating and traumatic to press charges. Two major reform movements have attempted to alleviate these problems. In the 1960s, the members of the Model Penal Code redefined rape by focusing more on the conduct of the defendant than on the actions and remarks of the accuser. The code did away with the resistance requirement, did not mention lack of consent as an element of the crime, and created four degrees of rape. Although many states followed these recommendations, conviction rates remained unaffected, as appeals courts persisted in requiring the prosecution to show some evidence of physical force to uphold convictions.

In the 1970s and 1980s, legislatures passed rape shield laws that prohibited questioning the accuser about her relations with men other than the defendant, except in limited circumstances. While these latter reforms have made testifying less humiliating for many women, convictions remained as elusive as ever.[8] According to Stephen Schulhofer, "Disappointing results such as these have convinced large numbers of antirape activists of the need for new and far more ambitious reforms."[9]

Columbia's experiment is a prominent example of "more ambitious reforms" after repeated failures with previous efforts. In this sense, the politics and aspirations of those who campaigned for the policy resembled the tenor of the interest generated by Catharine MacKinnon's antipornography ordinance in the 1980s. The ordinance promised a new way to fight pornography that would empower women and bring success where previous approaches had failed. Both measures ultimately portrayed victimized women as weak-willed and emotionally unstable, and both posed serious challenges to traditional liberal concepts of freedom and rights.[10]

---

[7] Sanford H. Kadish and Stephen J. Schulhofer, *Criminal Law and Its Processes: Cases and Materials* (Aspen Publisher's, 2001), pp. 315–16.

[8] See, e.g., Cassia Spohn and Julia Horney, *Rape Law Reform: A Grassroots Revolution and Its Impact* (Plenum Press, 1992), pp. 86, 159–73.

[9] Schulhofer, *Unwanted Sex: The Culture of Intimidation and the Failure of Law* (Harvard University Press, 1999), p. 46. My discussion of rape law reforms is based in general on this book. Kadish and Schulhofer, *Criminal Law*, pp. 361–62, n. 13.

[10] On MacKinnon's ordinance, see Donald Alexander Downs, *The New Politics of Pornography* (University of Chicago Press, 1989).

The Politics of Solidarity

Columbia has its share of notable public intellectual professors, but people I interviewed corroborated the widespread belief that faculty involvement at Columbia is slack. Faculty members do play an important role in the university senate, a body of around seventy-five members. (The senate was established in 1968 in response to the student upheavals of that year. Its mix of students, faculty, and staff was a manifestation of the belief in shared governance that emerged in that era.)[11] However, only a few faculty members are active in the senate, and even fewer concern themselves with general campus affairs. When asked if there is a "sense of campus citizenship," Lance Liebman, former dean of Columbia Law School, quickly replied, "No. None." Karl Ward, a student who identifies himself as a civil libertarian, agreed, "Columbia is seriously lacking a sense of community at most levels. There are few ties between professors and the students." Applegate said that faculty members are active in matters pertaining to the faculty but eschew broader campus engagement. "Most tend not to involve themselves in student politics. One of the things that occurred to me thinking about this interview this morning is that I can only think of about three or four articles that have been written by faculty in the student newspaper [the *Spectator*]. And I wrote one of them."[12] When I asked the students I interviewed – who were among the activist elite and supremely aware of campus affairs – if they knew of any faculty members who had earned notable reputations on campus for teaching or defending the fundamental principles of civil liberty and free speech, no one could think of a single example.

A prominent minority is very active in campus politics at Columbia. Campus groups are varied and range from the International Socialist Organization on the far left to the Columbia College Conservative Club on the far right. Between these poles, scores of groups are registered, including such names as: National Abortion Rights Action League, Columbia Students United against Sweatshops, College Republicans, College Democrats, American Civil Liberties Union, Amnesty International, Columbia Men against Violence, Chiapas, International Deconstruction Workers United, Student Labor Action, Take Back the Night, Students for Economic and Environmental Justice, the Federalist Society, Campus Crusade for Christ, Cantonese Christian Fellowship, Libertarians, and more.[13] A few years ago, a group of College Republicans, College Democrats, and libertarians formed

---

[11] On the famous 1968 Columbia upheaval, see Jerry L. Avorn and the Staff of the *Columbia Daily Spectator, Up against the Ivy Wall: A History of the Columbia Crisis* (Atheneum, 1968); Cox Commission Report, *Crisis at Columbia: Report of the Finding Commission Appointed to Investigate the Disturbances at Columbia University in April and May 1968* (Vintage, 1968).

[12] Interviews with Lance Liebman and James Applegate, June 2001; and Columbia student Karl Ward, June 2001.

[13] See the groups on the Columbia University website: www.columbia.edu/cu/groups.html.

the Campus Political Union to sponsor speakers and political issues on a non-partisan basis. According to one student leader, this group has had a very positive effect on the campus.[14]

Despite the apparent ideological diversity, campus politics tilts hard to the left. Student politics is dominated by Columbia Students Solidarity Network (CSSN), an influential umbrella organization that strives to unite the various liberal-leftist and radical groups on campus in common pursuit of social justice. Established in the 1980s to show solidarity with the Sandinistas in Nicaragua, CSSN envisions itself as more than simply an umbrella organization that strives to create communities among leftist groups on the campus. CSSN's major goal is *solidarity*, which means that its members must avoid severely criticizing other members. After a leader of the newly reinvigorated campus branch of the American Civil Liberties Union attacked an advocate of the sexual misconduct policy by name in 2000, CSSN passed a bylaw that made it illegal for any group in CSSN to publicly defame another member of the group. CSSN leader Ginger Gentile described the political scene at Columbia as "extremely liberal." (Sofia Berger, a more moderate liberal student leader, said, "It's a very political campus. There's almost no Republicans on campus.")[15] Lynch observed that students on both the right and left at Columbia are suspicious of questions or discourse that challenge their sense of community. "To the right, it's all about 'community.' To the left, it's about solidarity," Lynch said.[16]

Overall, free speech has probably been less undermined at Columbia than at many other schools, as groups of various stripes have presented their ideas in the public forum. Conservatives are vilified, but student leaders tend to value political responsibility, which includes protecting public discourse. Perhaps Columbia's exceptional commitment to liberal education – exemplified by the core curriculum requirement that features the great minds of Western and other cultures – instills an appreciation of intellectual give-and-take. (Several faculty and student interviewees made this connection.) But some exceptions to this apparent intellectual tolerance have reared their heads. One prominent recent example is the reception students gave a two-day conference held by Accuracy in Academia and College Republicans in 1998, which featured speeches by nationally known conservatives, including the author Dinesh D'Souza, the syndicated columnist John Leo, University of California regent Ward Connerly (who led the fight against race-based affirmative action in California), and conservative author David Horowitz. After several hundred protesters threatened disorder the first evening by attempting to storm the building (they were held at bay by security), university representatives told the conference organizers that they would have to meet

---

[14] Interview with Columbia student Sofia Berger, April 2002.
[15] Interview with Columbia student Ginger Gentile, April 2002. Interview with Sofia Berger, April 2002.
[16] Interview with Gerard Lynch.

off campus the next night, and that no one could attend the meeting who was not a member of the Columbia community – even though many who attended from outside the university had paid to attend the conference, and despite the fact that many of the protesters were outsiders themselves. It was not Columbia's finest hour. John Leo blamed the administration for backing down in the face of student militancy. "We wound up giving our talks off campus, with protesters shouting things like 'Ha, ha, you're outside' and carrying signs that said "Access denied – we win.' Columbia was, of course, teaching its students to deal with dissent by suppressing it."[17] This episode provoked student Ron Lewenberg to form the Columbia College Conservative Club as a militant right alternative to College Republicans. Lewenberg commented that the Republican leaders "were like a 'deer in headlights' through the whole thing. They were in utter disbelief. They didn't know what the hell happened.... We literally had to walk through the protesters to get in – they blocked the court.... The university caves to opposition by the left, all the time."[18]

The effort that activists put into progressive solidarity played an important role in the politics of the sexual misconduct policy. Although students had recently won victories in hard-fought battles in the antisweatshops movement, as well as the movement to force the university to divest itself of involvement in South Africa in the 1980s, student activist alienation from the administrative establishment remained strong. In fact, the sexual misconduct policy became a litmus test of the administration's willingness to listen to students' concerns. Rohit Aggarwala, a business history graduate student who headed the student caucus in the senate, was struck by this larger significance of the policy's acceptance. As he walked out of Uris Hall after the senate enacted the policy in February of 2000, he relates that a leading activist

came over and shook my hand, and said, "You know, Rit. It's amazing. It turns out the system can work." So in the end, insofar as this massive activist group working an issue through with the administration, this was a great success. The system worked.... We are desperately trying to recover from the scars of 1968 and build that level of trust and build that sense that students really are a part of the university.... It was a phenomenal process, to get so many people who assumed themselves to be disenfranchised, to have them have such an impact.[19]

The *Columbia Daily Spectator* reported, "The activists saw the adoption of the policy as a turning point in the relationship between students and the Administration."[20]

---

[17] John Leo, "A Gaggle of Gag Orders," *U.S. News and World Report*, February 25, 2002; interview with John Leo, June 2001. See also interview with Sofia Berger, April 2002.
[18] Interview with Columbia student Ron Lewenberg, June 2001.
[19] Interview with Rit Aggarwala, June 2001.
[20] James Thompson, "Senate, Activists Craft Sexual Misconduct Policy," *Spectator*, May 10, 2000.

Previous Incarnations of the Policy

The 1970s witnessed the rise of the national victims' rights movement in reaction to the rise of crime in the 1960s and to the Supreme Court rulings that expanded the constitutional protections of criminal defendants.[21] For their part, women's groups campaigned to increase public awareness of the prevalence of rape and to reform rape laws. By the end of that decade, the Take Back the Night movement was born on campuses, uniting concern about rape and violence with the new ideology against pornography. The movement held annual protest marches in major cities and college towns, placing Columbia and Barnard College (the women's college connected with Columbia) in the spotlight after Barnard hosted a ground-breaking conference on feminism and pornography in 1982. A few hundred people marched when Take Back the Night launched its campaigns at Columbia and Barnard in 1988; by 2000 the number had swelled to more than a thousand.[22] In 1992 the Barnard-Columbia Rape Crisis Center (RCC) opened its doors, counseling victims and providing information about sexual assault. A movement was in place that began to question the adequacy of the existing system of reporting and trying sexual assault complaints.

The system that had operated since the 1950s bore the dubious name, "Dean's Discipline." Dean's Discipline was highly informal, leaving it up to the dean of the defendant's school to decide whether to pursue a case and what procedural rules to apply. Under pressure in the early 1990s, the Provost's Advisory Committee on Sexual Assault called for the establishment of a special committee to investigate reform of the system.[23] On the basis of this report, the senate formed a Task Force on Sexual Assault consisting of a dozen students, administrators, and faculty members. The task force met for over a year and issued its recommendations in April 1995, after laborious deliberation and campus outreach. The committee proffered a new definition of "sexual misconduct" that took into consideration the problem of intimidation: "non-consensual, intentional physical contact of a sexual nature which includes, but is not limited to, unwelcome physical contact with a person's genitals, buttocks, or breasts. Lack of consent may be inferred from the use of force, coercion, or physical intimidation, or advantage gained by the victim's mental or physical incapacity or impairment of which the perpetrator was aware or should have been aware." The report also called for new "volunteer advocates" and the establishment of an "Alternative Form of Dean's Discipline" that included special hearing panels for sexual misconduct cases.

---

[21] See George P. Fletcher, *With Justice for Some: Victims' Rights in Criminal Trials* (Addison-Wesley, 1995).

[22] See "Take Back the Night Draws More Than 300," *Spectator*, April 3, 1995.

[23] "Recommendations for Adjudication of Sexual Assault Complaints," Provost's Advisory Committee on Sexual Assault, May 23, 1993.

The task force also presented recommendations concerning the procedural rights of the participants, including the right of both parties to receive a list of witnesses; the right of the accuser and the accused to be accompanied in the hearing by an adviser (who could be an attorney) to offer them "support, guidance, consultation, and advice." The adviser, however, was not allowed to question panel members, witnesses, or the opposing party directly or to make statements on behalf of his or her client. Nor could either party or his or her adviser directly question the other side.

Finally, the task force recommended tape-recording adjudications for use in appeal and addressed basic rules of evidence: the accuser bore the ultimate burden of proof, and guilty verdicts had to be unanimous and establish guilt by "clear and convincing evidence," which means that guilt is "highly probable." The prior sexual conduct of either party was inadmissible, with the exception of relations between the two parties themselves. The task force also recommended disciplining students who brought false charges.[24]

The recommendations represented an honest attempt to be accommodating to accusers without sacrificing basic fairness to the accused. The new definition of misconduct was a legitimate broadening of protection for women; and, by formally calling for the right of the accused to be present, to have an attorney present, and to cross-examine witnesses (but not the opposing party), the reforms provided more explicit support for due process than had Dean's Discipline. The reforms established a fairly high standard of proof and called for protections against false charges.

One reason for the balance of this policy was the presence on the task force of law professor Eben Moglen, a brilliant and sometimes irascible teacher of international law and human rights who was a stickler for the rights of the defendant. At Columbia, each school maintained the right to "opt out" of the system and adopt its own policy, and befitting its calling, the Law School had its own much more formalized policy.[25] Moglen understood that normal university procedures need not be as formal as in the Law School or civil courts but maintained that certain fundamentals must always be observed. Minutes of the task force reveal that the group conducted many debates over what was fundamental, in particular over Moglen's *causa summa*, the right to have an attorney who would actively participate in the proceedings. In a "Confidential Memorandum" presented on October 5, 1994, Moglen challenged those who opposed the right to counsel on the grounds that the hearing was meant to be "nonadversarial" – a phrase heard constantly throughout the policy debates of the 1990s. In Moglen's eyes, *any* proceeding

[24] University Senate, "Sexual Assault Task Force, Resolutions," proposed April 28, 1995.
[25] Interview with Lance Liebman; "Law School Upholds Own Assault Policy: University Policy Is Rejected," *Spectator*, November 21, 1995.

dealing with serious charges is *inherently* adversarial and ridden with tension regardless of its ostensible purpose:

> The present code embodies a profoundly misguided belief in the possibility of effective self-representation. I have never represented anyone even potentially subject of a criminal prosecution who did not experience profound psychological disorientation. . . . The subjective experience of having one's community explicitly engaged against one . . . is often literally paralyzing. . . . Much of the task of the lawyer in criminal defense practice is to counteract those absolutely predictable disabilities.[26]

Conflict over the presence and role of attorneys in the hearings bedeviled the task force right up to a month before the senate vote in April 1995, when the panel settled on a compromise position: attorneys could give advice to clients but not otherwise actively participate in the proceedings. A Columbia student member of the task force said, "We want the panel to hear the truth while making the complainant as comfortable as possible."[27]

Moglen also expressed a concern that would reappear five years later: the effect of setting up a special tribunal to try only sexual misconduct cases "is to strengthen the impression of a biased process devised for the purpose of disadvantaging defendants." One thinks of the history of "special courts" designed to attack specific crimes and of the problems associated with the federal independent counsel law that Congress allowed to expire after the impeachment of President Clinton. Moglen chose not to belabor this point, focusing instead on the issue of counsel.[28]

In the end, Moglen did not prevail, but his stance contributed to the compromise position. The administration also received advice from law professor Barbara Schatz, who joined a special group of advisers to the task force. Lance Liebman participated as Law School dean in a group of deans that included President George Rupp and Provost Jonathan Cole, which met every few weeks. Like Moglen and Schatz, Liebman believed that the task force was moving too far in favor of the accuser. At a pivotal meeting, he expressed his concerns about the lack of due process protections. "I just assumed, 'we'll fix that,'" Liebman said. "They just kept looking at me funny." Liebman surmised that Rupp (who also declined to be interviewed) wanted to avoid being "criticized as being hostile to the cause of women. I can't believe there was anything else."

---

[26] Moglen, "Confidential Memorandum" to Task Force, October 5, 1994, p. 5. Also, interview with Columbia law professor Eben Moglen, June 2001. The Supreme Court ruled in *Miranda v. Arizona*, 384 U.S. 436 (1966), that custodial interrogation is inherently coercive, thereby requiring special warnings.

[27] "Task Force Debates Legal Representation: Sexual Assault Committee May Submit Two Drafts to Senate," *Spectator*, March 9, 1995.

[28] Moglen, "Confidential Memorandum," p. 6, n. 8. On how the independent counsel law distorted the sense of balance in investigations, see Justice Scalia's dissent in *Morrison v. Olson*, 487 U.S. 654 (1988).

Liebman attended several meetings and "thought they were hearing what I was saying, but then I'd come back three weeks later and the same draft would be in front of me." Eventually, Rupp turned to Liebman at a meeting and said, "Lance, I tell you what. We'll leave the Law School out." In April 1995 the Law School decided to adhere to its own policy by a unanimous faculty vote.[29] Liebman remained concerned about the rest of the campus, so he showed up at the next meeting of the deans' group. There he was informed that he was no longer welcome as a participant because the Law School was going to opt out of the university-wide policy. Liebman said that he was "stunned" at what passed. "I was surprised that when they did it, there wasn't more complaint or criticism."[30]

One reason for the lack of discussion was that most of the campus remained uninvolved and apparently uninterested in the entire issue. This is also one reason why the task force's recommendations prevailed in the senate without serious amendments. In an article reporting a rally supporting the policy published soon after the senate vote, the *Spectator* described a campus with other things on its mind. Only thirty students attended the April 28, 1995, rally on the famous steps of Low Library, leading Columbia College Student Council president Allison Baker to complain about the "apathy of students and administrators." "We're here to wake you up!" she yelled to the crowd. "We're here to let you know that Columbia needs a sexual assault policy now!" At one point during the demonstration a woman addressed the students sitting on the steps, asking them to yell or clap if they supported the policy. Not one person responded. "Sorry to disturb you with this unpleasant reality," Baker replied to the silence.[31]

In late April the senate passed the task force's recommendations with only one amendment recommended by the Rape Crisis Center, which extended the statute of limitations from three months to six. The new policy contained the provision that it be reexamined in three years. When that time arrived, silence is the last word one would use to describe the university's posture toward the policy.

More Reform

Unfortunately, the new policy fared no better than previous efforts. Despite a supposedly more hospitable process, "hardly anyone used it," according to Andrew Brownstein of the *Chronicle of Higher Education*. At a task force meeting in March 1999, the new chair of the committee, Patricia Catapano, pointed out that only two students had used the Alternative Procedure, while students had used the traditional

[29] "Law School Upholds Own Assault Policy: University Policy Is Rejected."
[30] Interview with Lance Liebman.
[31] "Students Rally for Policy," *Spectator*, April 28, 1995, pp. 1, 7.

Dean's Discipline "more than twice."[32] According to Judge Gerard Lynch, "we passed a new, elaborate system in 1995. Not surprisingly, there was no increase in the number of complaints. Because it is an article of faith that there is vast under-reporting, the *procedures* are seen as the problem."[33] Although members of the administration defended the gatekeepers – the deans and their aides who initially dealt with accusations – as conscientious and able, many students considered them to be purveyors of red tape and obstruction.[34] Sarah Richardson, the most important activist in the new reform movement, made serious criticisms. "The gatekeepers were poorly trained. They would ask complainants to meet in public restaurants not long after the incidents were supposed to have occurred. They would ask them what they were wearing at the time. They asked students about their sexual history. The students were often told to take a breather and think about it or to go on leave."[35]

So the senate appointed a new task force in early 1998 to study the policy and report back to the senate in November 1999. Lynch (who volunteered for the task force but was not selected) related, "the task force members from the administration were molded in response to the student demands, so you get people on the task force whom you want. What emerges is preordained."[36] But Sofia Berger, a leading student on the task force, maintained that the group strove hard to do the right thing. The problem would prove to be the one-sided nature of the input it received.[37] After intense debate and inquiry, the new task force called for change, citing the "procedurally dense and bureaucratic nature of the Alternative Procedure."[38]

The task force consisted of twelve members. There were three administrators: Patricia (Patsy) Catapano, who was also the university general counsel; Karen Blank, dean in Barnard; and Richard Ferraro, dean in General Studies; four professors: Dental School professor Carol Kunzel; Social Work professor Edward Mullen; English and comparative literature professor Guari Viswanathan; and journalism professor Wayne Swoboda (the first chair of the committee until he yielded the post to Catapano in

[32] Arthur Harris, "Senate Sexual Misconduct Task Force to Meet in Low," *Spectator*, March 26, 1999.

[33] Andrew Brownstein, "A Battle of Wills, Rights, and P.R. at Columbia," *Chronicle of Higher Education*, July 2001; interview with Gerard Lynch.

[34] In defense of gatekeepers, see letter of Beth Wilson, assistant provost, Office of Equal Opportunity and Affirmative Action, June 8, 1998.

[35] In Brownstein, "A Battle of Wills, Rights, and P.R. at Columbia."

[36] Interview with Gerard Lynch. Such stacking of commissions is typical. On how the 1986 Attorney General's Commission on Pornography was stacked by conservatives, see Donald A. Downs, "The Attorney General's Commission and the New Politics of Pornography," 1987 *American Bar Foundation Research Journal*, p. 641.

[37] Interview with Sofia Berger, October 2001, April 2002.

[38] Report of the University Senate Task Force to Review the Sexual Misconduct Policy and Procedure, November 3, 1999, p. 4.

1999); and five students: Columbia students Sofia Berger, Necva Kazimov, and Matthew Matlack; law student Natalie Edwards; and Lili Wright (whose affiliation I could not find). According to sources, the major figures on the task force were Catapano, Berger, Blank, and Ferraro. Catapano was crucial for showing the administration's goodwill, and for her organization and leadership, while Blank and Ferraro brought experience in adjudication to the group.

The key figure was Berger. A 2002 graduate of the School of Engineering and Applied Science, Berger was probably the most important undergraduate establishment political figure on campus. In addition to being a senator during this episode, she had served on such important committees as the Student Activities Board (president), the Committee for Socially Responsible Investing, and the search committee for a university president to replace Rupp in 2002. Like Aggarwala – the other student on the Presidential Search Committee – Berger was equally at home with administrators and student activists, all of whom spoke of her in glowing terms. Applegate, who opposed the new reforms, said that Berger is "the sweetest thing in the world. She's bright as hell, but tough as nails."[39]

A review committee of the task force began meeting in the fall of 1998, receiving information from a number of groups. At a meeting in early 1998, a member of the Rape Crisis Center asserted the need for fairness in the procedures. "RCC understands very well there are stakes for the accused, that lives and reputations are precious. [The advisory board] has also experienced Columbia as a place that cares for fair play."[40] In 1999 the task force solicited commentary from the larger community, which began to arrive in March. One student sent a letter discussed at the crucial March 26 meeting that expressed fear that changes would railroad the accused, while another criticized the conflicts of interest and lack of training of deans and panelists.

Between March and May 1999, the task force dealt with the question of adversarial rights, focusing on cross-examination and the presence of attorneys. Ferraro stated that they needed to get away from adversarial procedures. "At the heart of the matter is the need to free things out, to make this as easy [as it] can be under very difficult circumstances, trying to get away from an adversarial posture." One member asked why anyone would even need an attorney if the whole format was meant to avoid confrontation between the two parties. Members also debated the pros and cons of confrontation.

---

[39] Interview with James Applegate. See also a portrayal of her in "Berger Appointed to Search Committee," *Spectator*, April 30, 2001.

[40] Minutes of the review committee of the Task Force, February 1998. The quotations may not be exact, but I write them as they were read to me by a source.

The Task Force Speaks: The Return to Dean's Discipline

The task force published a draft proposal on November 3, 1999, which the senate was to consider at its November 12 meeting. Without the perspective that could be provided by someone like Moglen or Schatz on the task force (and with the Law School now even less involved than it had been in 1995, having opted out right away), the recommendations gravitated toward a pro-prosecution position. According to Sofia Berger, "Basically, we created a version of Dean's Discipline that was focused on sexual misconduct. The old officers were not trained to know how to ask the right questions. When we finally had to decide what to do, there was consensus about the need for major change. The equal opportunity and affirmative action officer said that there were so many details that the system was a nightmare to administer. So we tried not to make it too specific."[41]

Part of the report stressed the need for enhanced education and information, while another part recommended keeping the 1995 policy's "progressive" definition of sexual misconduct. In regard to procedures, the task force suggested giving complainants three options: to proceed under the regular disciplinary procedures of Dean's Discipline; to go to "mediation"; to proceed through a special "Alternative Dean's Discipline" designed for sexual misconduct cases only. Columbia's various colleges still maintained their own separate systems of Dean's Discipline for other cases. Such schools as Columbia College, the School of Engineering and Applied Science, and Barnard utilized relatively informal procedures, whereas such schools as General Studies, Law, and other graduate schools relied on more formal rules.

To ensure greater informality and to encourage complaints, the task force also eliminated some important due process protections. It "specifically recommends that the requirement of both parties being present at the hearing at all times be eliminated, that lawyers not be permitted to represent students in such hearings, and that the deans be free to question any witness whom they believe to have relevant or probative evidence to offer."[42] The task force also recommended stretching the statute of limitations to eighteen months. Surprisingly, it made no reference to the standards or burden of proof.

Although the task force had heard concerns about fairness, it proposed eliminating the right that is one of the most fundamental to fair hearings: the right simply to be present to hear testimony and evidence against you. (Equally fundamental is the right to an impartial jury and judge – which the new policy also compromised.)[43] One reason for this omission was the lack

---

[41] Interview with Sofia Berger, October 2001.

[42] Report of the University Senate Task Force to Review the Sexual Misconduct Policy and Procedure, p. 8.

[43] On the fundamental nature of both of these rights, see Charles H. Whitebread and Christopher Slobogon, *Criminal Procedure: An Analysis of Cases and Concepts* (Foundation Press, 2000), ch. 27, and pp. 765–76. See *Illinois v. Allen*, 397 U.S. 337 (1970).

of civil liberty representation on the panel. Another was the almost total lack of such a perspective among those involved in the politics surrounding the policy reform on campus.

Rejection

Despite the task force's sincere efforts, many activists greeted its long-awaited report with scorn. Almost immediately, the panel found itself under relentless attack, especially by a new group that had only recently entered the scene: Student Advocates for Ending Rape (SAFER). Sofia Berger related,

SAFER hated Dean's Discipline. Once we called it "Alternative Dean's Discipline," it's a problem. It's like putting red in front of a bull. A lot of pressure was put on the task force, especially by SAFER. . . . They hated it without talking to anyone to figure out why we did what we did. They set up posters that said, "We got fucked by the task force!" They put us on a huge defensive right away. They set up a forum in Lerner Hall right away [in early November] to rail against the policy and didn't even invite me or talk to us. They immediately went on the offensive in the public forum. . . . Then they started to overtake the [more moderate] Policy Research Organization, and they were demanding stuff from the task force. Sometimes they'd call Patsy [Catapano] and say, "We want you to do this." Then she'd respond, "I can't just be at your beck and call."[44]

The new mobilization steeply escalated the pressure on the task force and the university. Critics' main objection concerned the alleged dearth of student contributions to the new system, the lack of a sitting body to review the program and improve information, and the retention of Dean's Discipline.[45] The main groups leading the attacks were the Policy Research Organization (PRO) and SAFER. Activists established PRO as part of the Rape Crisis Center in September 1998 in response to Columbia's alleged mishandling of rape cases. Its major objective was to provide education and information to the Columbia student body. One of its founders, Ashley Burczak (Barnard, 2000), was motivated to form a new organization after hearing rape victims tell wrenching stories at a Take Back the Night Speak-Out in April 1997. The next day Burczak and her allies attended a senate meeting on the subject and were put off by what they perceived as community indifference. "It was so obvious they didn't care," she told the *Spectator*.[46]

SAFER and PRO operated separately. PRO did more policy work, while SAFER led the mass mobilization and the grilling of administrators. Several people I interviewed reported that tensions developed between SAFER and PRO (as well as between SAFER and other groups, such as the RCC and the Columbia Men against Violence) for several reasons, including SAFER's confrontational style and its penchant for grabbing the publicity. Sofia Berger,

---

[44] Interview with Sofia Berger, October 2001, April 2002.
[45] Revisions to the Task Force Report on the Sexual Misconduct Policy and Procedure, December 9, 1999.
[46] "Senior Profile: Ashley Burczak," *Spectator*, May 17, 2000.

the target of much of SAFER's wrath, clearly favored PRO to SAFER. Before it presented its first report in November 1999, the task force had many dealings with PRO but hardly any with SAFER. "We dealt with PRO first, four or five people," Berger related. "They totally know their stuff; they are really on the ball.... Columbia Men against Violence were also very active.... They made their case very well."[47]

SAFER became a major player after the task force presented its report in November 1999. Burczak and others realized that a broader political front would be needed if truly radical reform were to pass and that PRO would not fill the bill because the framework and resources of the Rape Crisis Center limited its membership. Enter SAFER. Burczak and Sarah Richardson founded it as an offshoot of PRO in September 1999, just before the task force released its first report. SAFER's most prominent leader, Richardson was poised to become the most important figure in the politics of the Columbia sexual misconduct policy.[48]

The road to Richardson's involvement began in her freshman year, 1999, when she filed a sexual harassment complaint against two men in her dorm who, according to the *Boston Globe*, had been "hounding her." Someone I interviewed claimed that the men (one was a friend) had made Richardson watch a sexually explicit video. The *Globe* reported that Richardson was very unsatisfied with how her dean handled the case.[49] Regardless of the motives, Richardson and her allies were now ready to pressure for more radical change.

It was only after the release of the task force report in November that the issue became incendiary at Columbia. According to Michelle Bertagna, editor in chief of the *Spectator* in 2000–1, the issue "didn't emerge until late October. Then it became huge."[50] But when the task force released its report in November, SAFER was ready to enter the fray. Richardson (who refused to be interviewed) was described as driven and mercurial by those I interviewed. But it was her emotion and dedication – with the efforts of her colleagues – that galvanized the campus. As a CSSN leader related, "SAFER was really the one leading the way."[51]

The November 12 Meeting: Solidarity and Student Power
Early that fall, SAFER activists had struck upon an ingenious tactic: posting provocative posters around campus attached by red tape that symbolized "bureaucratic red tape." Thousands of students began wearing red tape on

[47] Interview with Sofia Berger, October 2001.
[48] See SAFER's website for information about the organization and its positions: www.columbia.edu/cu/safer.
[49] Patrick Healy, "College's Discipline Policy a New Flash Point," *Boston Globe*, November 20, 2000.
[50] Interview with *Spectator* editor Michelle Bertagna, July 2001.
[51] Interview with Ginger Gentile.

their bodies, backpacks, bicycles, and other items, and activists placed red tape on various objects across the campus. By early November, Columbia was awash in red tape and a sense of urgency. Posters proclaimed such things as: "We got fucked by the task force," "We're screwed," and "Where will you be on November 12?" They even ventured into the poetic: "Fess up, George Rupp! How many rapes did you cover up?!" A week before the senate vote on November 12, *Spectator* contributing writer, Danielle Dileo, wrote a two-page article entitled "Peeling Off the Red Tape: The Battle to Reform the Sexual Misconduct Policy." The article dealt at length with the history of the issue at Columbia, discussed the upcoming senate meeting, and included a copy of a PRO petition and statistics of sexual violence.[52] SAFER's website provided a "summary in bullet form" of the activities it sponsored during the 1999–2000 academic year, which included: "Tens of Thousands of posters covering the Columbia and Barnard campuses from September 99 through February 2000 . . . Dormstorming every student residence hall with flyers . . . Organizing a 4000 person rally and march on the University Senate on November 12 to protest the initial recommendations for 'reform' . . . Over 40 residence hall Floor Raps informing students . . . Over 30 presentations to campus student organizations . . . Four, week-long tabling marathons on both the Barnard and Columbia campuses distributing information . . . Dozens of articles in campus newspapers, articles in major newspapers such as Newsday, AP news coverage as well as by NPR, 1010 WINS, NBC, NY1 and others."[53] In addition, other student and campus groups held numerous meetings around the campus to discuss the policy.

Resistance brought quick results, as the senate immediately decided to postpone the vote until February and to discuss further change on November 12. Expecting a large turnout to discuss the next step, it moved the November meeting to an auditorium in the Law School. On November 12, all eyes at Columbia were on the senate. The *Spectator* published three front-page articles and a lengthy analysis of the policy choices and the politics involved.[54] The problem of civil liberties was not mentioned in the extensive coverage. That morning, more than three hundred protesters held a vigil rally at the gates of Barnard, after which they marched across the Columbia campus to the Law School for the 1:15 P.M. meeting, wearing red tape (many over their mouths), carrying signs, and singing or chanting slogans. The protesters, now between two and three hundred, then entered the auditorium and took seats across the back of the room. Although they

---

[52] Danielle Dileo, "Peeling Off the Red Tape: The Battle to Reform the Sexual Misconduct Policy," *Spectator*. My copy of this article did not provide a date, and the article predated the paper's on-line version, so I cannot provide the exact date. But it was the week before the week of November 8–12.

[53] SAFER, "Sexual Assault Policy Activity; Achieving a New Policy 1999–2000," available at SAFER website: www.columbia.edu/cu/safer/safer9900.html.

[54] See, generally, *Spectator*, November 12, 1998.

were an intimidating sight, the protesters were respectful. Ben Casselman's and James Thompson's observations in the *Spectator* matched those of the students I interviewed, "Despite the chants of 'University silence perpetuates the violence' and the red tape covering the mouths of student protesters inside the chamber, the meeting's tone of reconciliation and reform surprised many."[55] Sofia Berger said the scene was "extremely dramatic."[56]

After some preliminary discussions, Patricia Catapano told the senate that the task force would be submitting a new report based on the information it had received. Three faculty members raised questions about due process – gutsy acts considering the hundreds of protesters staring down on them. When Senator Ralph Holloway (faculty, Arts and Sciences) asked her about the elimination of the defendant's right to be present and the expansion of the statute of limitations, Catapano replied that even the traditional Dean's Discipline did not include such rights and that the hearing was not intended to be adversarial. (She did not mention that Dean's Discipline did not expressly exclude this right, however.) Conceding that provisions of due process vary with different contexts, Gerard Lynch said that there are certain fundamental components of due process that are universal to justice. While fairness is conceivably consistent with not having an attorney present, the rights to hear the evidence and to challenge witnesses are indispensable. The edited notes of the meeting reported Lynch as saying, "no proceeding under any legal system in the world would find someone guilty of a criminal act punishable by a long [sentence] without allowing him to hear the evidence against him or even propose questions for cross-examination. He [Lynch] said he did not see how to conduct a serious fact-finding without these provisions." In his interview, Lynch added that the key to questioning is to be able to ask follow-up questions after the witness responds.[57] Catapano replied once again that such rights pertain only to adversarial procedures, not to Columbia's policy. Applegate then raised questions about the reliability of the statistics upon which reform relied, sparking discussion about the need for better record keeping.

The climactic point of the meeting arose when Sofia Berger asked for speaking privileges for a nonsenator, Jennifer Glasser, a co-coordinator of PRO. Glasser read a statement based on PRO's petition criticizing the task force's original report and then presented it to the senate. Then four activists picked up all eighteen hundred signed petitions and dropped them at the table in front of Rupp, to "thunderous applause," according to the *Spectator*. The senate then ordered the task force to come up with a new proposal, including expanding the force's mandate to collect statistics.[58]

---

[55] Casselman and Thompson, "Senate Hears Task Force Resolutions," *Spectator*, November 15, 1998.

[56] Interview with Sofia Berger, April 2002.

[57] Senate Notes, November 12, 1998, edited, p. 4. Interview with Gerard Lynch.

[58] James Thompson, *Spectator*, May 10, 2000.

Although the protesters behaved well at the meeting, their intensity and sheer presence created an intimidating scene. Sarah Richardson said, "All our screaming and yelling and red tape and postering has obviously had an impact." She also gloated that, "There was obviously some fear in the eyes of the administrators when they saw that."[59]

Rohit Aggarwala emphasized the positive aspects of the protesters' presence: "The room was packed. No question they are great organizers. They got a lot of people out there, and I also think they did themselves a very good service by being well behaved. They did not disrupt anything, their leadership was in control, their leadership was eloquent, and the university was listening." When I asked Applegate if the atmosphere in the room made it hard to oppose the activists, he answered, "I think it did. Didn't scare me. They came in. It was about three hundred students. I think the students were very well behaved. They came in as spectators. They did not attempt to disrupt the meeting... on the other hand, if there's three hundred people over there obviously supporting one side of an issue, that's intimidating."[60]

Solidarity triumphed. From this point on, the task force would respond primarily to SAFER and its allies, the only constituency that had made its presence felt. After the senate enacted a new policy the following February, Richardson claimed the credit for SAFER: "Almost every word, every phrase, every clause came from the students." In his *Spectator* article summing up the movement at the end of the school year, James Thompson wrote, "The movement left the November 12 meeting stronger and more energized, prepared to take a new, 'less confrontational style,' according to CMAV [Columbia Men against Violence] co-president Darien Meyer, CC '00. The next few months saw the Task Force release a series of new resolutions, revising them each time in accordance with student criticism."[61]

On November 17, an op-ed piece in the *Spectator* entitled "University Comes Together on Sexual Misconduct Policy" appeared. The next day an open forum was held on the policy, sponsored by the task force, Columbia College Student Council (also chaired by Sofia Berger), the Engineering Student Council, and Barnard's Student Government Association. At one point fifteen members of SAFER stood in line to fire questions at the panelists.[62] By now, members of the task force were tired and exasperated. Two sources whom I may not identify told me that Catapano had by this time reached the end of her endurance and was becoming emotionally strung out. Berger

[59] The first quotation is from the *Spectator's* report of the meeting, November 15, 1998, in Casselman and Thompson, "Senate Hears Task Force Resolutions." The second quotation is from James Thompson's summary of the politics in the *Spectator*, May 10, 2000.

[60] Interviews with Rit Aggarwala and James Applegate.

[61] Thompson, *Spectator*, May 10, 2000.

[62] Ariel Neuman, op-ed, *Spectator*, November 17, 1999; Ben Casselman, "Misconduct Task Force Hosts Forum," *Spectator*, November 22, 1999.

also seemed distraught over the abuse she began receiving at the hands of SAFER, criticizing the group in her interview.

A New Special Tribunal for Sexual Misconduct

On December 9 the task force presented a revised proposal that gave the activists virtually everything they wanted. The new proposal called for improved oversight and replaced the Alternative Dean's Discipline with a new process that added a student to the hearing panels who would not have a vote but whose opinion would be a matter of record. The most important provision was the establishment of what amounted to a special administrative head who would be responsive to the antirape network on campus. This "coordinator of sexual misconduct and education" would deal exclusively with sexual cases and oversee education, prevention, data collection, *and adjudication.* In the proposed system, cases would be "handled by specially trained deans, student affairs administrators, and students to be administered by the Coordinator. . . . These deans and students must be provided with extensive training, reported to annually, in the psychological, social, including cultural and racial, and legal issues involved in sexual misconduct, as well as in procedures appropriate for hearing such cases, and in 'First Responder' procedures. Legal issues to be covered would include training in the evaluation of evidence, standards of proof, and the irrelevance of prior sexual history."[63]

The new version maintained the previous proposal's limitation of due process, such as the exclusion of lawyers and the right to be present throughout the hearing, but recommended that each side be allowed to be accompanied by a "silent supporter," who could not be a lawyer. The accused was permitted to "consult" with a lawyer outside the proceedings if criminal charges were possible. (Any evidence from such a proceeding would be subject to subpoena in a subsequent criminal trial.) It also stipulated that the hearing panel must provide the accused with "an opportunity to hear the accusations, and the opportunity to answer all allegations and to provide witnesses or other evidence."[64] Finally, the proposal's "exhibit B" called for "confidentiality" on the part of all participants; however, exhibit B placed virtually all the responsibility for confidentiality on the accused, revealing the unbalanced nature of the deliberations.

The only part of the proposal that distressed activists was a clause that allowed the dean of the defendant's school to be informed of the verdict before it was released. This provision was quickly dropped. The new proposal represented what was tantamount to a complete victory for SAFER and its allies. It set off alarm bells for a handful of critics, however. In an age so

---

[63] Revised Report of the University Task Force to Review the Sexual Misconduct Policy and Procedure, December 9, 1999, pp. 12–23.
[64] Ibid., p. 23.

fraught with the pressures of identity politics and the resulting groupthink on campus, the new policy seemed to be a platform for promoting an agenda rather than for seeking the truth. Although Lynch and Applegate had criticized the first incarnation of the task force at the November meeting, they were now ready to be more forceful.

Dissent Begins to Stir

On December 2 Jaime Schneider, a Columbia College sophomore who had received an advance copy of the new task force report, mounted the first attack in print of the policy in his "Rationality Syndrome" op-ed column in the *Spectator*. One of the few public conservatives at Columbia, Schneider cast a jaundiced eye toward student politics and seemed to enjoy the distress he initiated by challenging the solidarity many student activists held dear. Pointing to the lack of procedural protections, Schneider charged, "The sweeping changes to the Sexual Misconduct Policy overwhelmingly demanded by members of the student body pose a great threat to liberty on campus."[65]

As Catapano presented the task force's latest effort at the senate meeting on December 17, Applegate noted two things: nobody was saying anything, and Rupp started looking his way. "I must have had this incredulous look on my face," he observed.[66] An affable, fiery astronomy professor in his late forties who has served on the university's Commission on the Status of Women and takes his role as a senator seriously, Applegate believes strongly in the concepts of personal freedom and responsibility that he learned in the 1960s. "If you had taken this policy and waived it in front of me as a seventeen-year-old college freshman, I would have gone ballistic," he remarked. "Pretty much everyone else would have, too."[67]

Applegate rose to speak at the senate meeting. As reported in the notes of the meeting, he notified the crowd that, if his children were charged under this system, "he would advise [them] to hire an attorney, and refuse to participate in the internal proceeding. He said that he feels strongly that the whole proceeding is a violation of due process. He said he could not imagine suspending court proceedings and resolving any criminal cases among the adult members of the community in this way."[68] Applegate said that the edited versions of the senate meeting were "sanitized" and proceeded to report his unedited opinion. He repeatedly called the policy "misguided compassion":

The thing is riddled with the assumption of guilt. There's no discussion of burden of proof. The deans can do anything they want in this kangaroo court that operates

---

[65] Schneider, "Sexual Misconduct Policy Circumvents Due Process," *Spectator*, December 2, 1999.
[66] Interview with James Applegate.
[67] Ibid.
[68] Senate Notes, December 17, 1999, edited, p. 3.

in secret. The report that the task force produced is the image of a woman being weak, incapable of defending herself, incapable of testifying.... The single greatest problem is that the accused does not hear the testimony. You're not even allowed to hear it, or cross-examine. You don't even get a transcript of it. You can't even talk about it [to anyone].

He also questioned the "special training" provisions of the special system overseen by a coordinator who controls both advocacy and adjudication. "When you start bringing in special training, you're basically rigging the jury."[69]

A woman senator, Professor Anne Prescott (Barnard), who often sat by Applegate, also questioned the procedures. "Many would find them morally repugnant, and a violation of traditions going back many centuries.... it's appalling to show students that they can be accused without these protections."[70]

Highly regarded on campus for his insight and frankness, Gerard Lynch was poignant in his criticism. He "said it is remarkable that students are pushing for a procedure that allows students to be expelled after what is literally a Star Chamber proceeding, in which they do not have the right to be present to hear evidence against them. Hearing officers hear the evidence, and the defendants hear only what hearing officers choose to tell them. They then must construct a defense without being able to challenge directly what's said about them." In his interview with me, Lynch stressed the importance of questioning one's accuser. He cited the tendency of those charged to be influenced by the person who tells the first story. "It can shift the burden of proof psychologically," he said. "Once you have heard from one side, you are already forming opinions, making assumptions."[71] One cannot help wondering why such criticism by a noted liberal legal scholar, about to become a federal judge, did not influence the administration more. In his interview with me, Lynch offered two reasons: "A rational administrator wants whatever gives [him or her] more power. And there was no organized civil liberties constituency at the time."[72]

The Final Vote

During the first several weeks of the spring term, the task force and advocates prepared for the final vote on February 25.[73] Two days before the vote, the *Spectator* published an editorial denouncing the new policy, charging

---

[69] Interview with James Applegate.
[70] Senate Notes, December 17, 1999, p. 4.
[71] Ibid.; interview with Gerard Lynch.
[72] Interview with Gerard Lynch.
[73] See Resolutions with Respect to the University Misconduct Policy and Procedure, February 22, 2000.

that it "has no means of protecting the innocent and adequately punishing the guilty."[74] The editorial shocked the university community, which had assumed that the *Spectator* supported what appeared to be a virtual consensus of opinion. The new editor of the editorial page, the indefatigable Jaime Schneider, wrote the piece and cajoled the editorial board into supporting it. This move sparked controversy among the newspaper's staff and angered members of the Solidarity Network, who considered it almost treasonous. An article in the *Spectator* by Ben Casselman appeared the next day, entitled "Misconduct Policy Consensus Finally Reached." In it, Ashley Burczak was quoted as saying that the policy was "the best policy in America." A board member of Take Back the Night praised the new policy as "one of the best we've ever seen."[75]

By then, the result of the vote was a foregone conclusion. On February 25 fifty-three out of the seventy-six or so senators were present, making it one of the most highly attended meetings in years. Although the atmosphere was less charged than it had been in November, the *Spectator* reported that "every section of 301 Uris Hall was filled."[76] Early on, Jennifer Glasser of the PRO spoke and thanked the coalition movement, declaring, "the issue of sexual misconduct had brought a rebirth of student activism at Columbia."[77] Catapano then introduced five resolutions encapsulating the task force's revisions:

1. Continuing the policy.
2. Education, training, and oversight of the policy.
3. Creation of the new special coordinator.
4. Creation of the new alternative procedure.
5. The establishment of the new, specially trained hearing panels.

Senators introduced several amendments. The first four resolutions passed unanimously with an amendment providing that one-third of the oversight committee must be students.

Lynch introduced an amendment supported by Applegate to clarify the confidentiality rule. Lynch said that it amounted to a "gag rule." After much debate, Sarah Richardson was given permission to speak and offered wording that Lynch said he could live with. It required confidentiality only of "identifying information regarding the participants."[78]

The most heated debate concerned due process. Lynch led the way, followed by Applegate. Lynch presented a motion that would allow the accused to be present throughout the hearing and to be able to pose questions for the

[74] "Preserving Due Process," editorial, *Spectator*, February 23, 2000.
[75] *Spectator*, February 24, 2000.
[76] Ben Casselman, "Senate Passes Sexual Misconduct Policy," *Spectator*, February 28, 2000.
[77] Senate Notes, February 25, 2000, p. 4.
[78] Ibid., p. 8.

deans to ask. To much applause, Dean Karen Blank (a member of the task force) countered that the "traumatic consequences" of sexual misconduct means "compelling a victim to face the person accused of sexually mistreating her has the effect of victimizing her again."[79] Securing permission to speak, Richardson backed Blank's point to more applause.

Two senators agreed with Lynch's amendment. Professor Lars Tragardh of Barnard said it was an effective way of balancing the concerns of the accuser and the accused. Applegate was more militant, saying it "is preposterous" to maintain that such proceedings were not inherently adversarial. And he raised a vital point that few had dared broach: that the *accuser* has certain *responsibilities* in addition to rights. Senate minutes noted, "He said that the accuser under the proposed procedure has no particular rights and responsibilities. This is not non-adversarial, but juvenile."[80]

That moment presented the one window of opportunity for opponents of the proposed policy to make themselves heard. With the creation of special training and a special coordinator, the issue addressed by Lynch's amendment – the right to be present throughout the hearing and to pose questions in the presence of one's accuser – cut to the core of the differences between the two sides. Casselman observed in his *Spectator* coverage, "At one point the passage of all the resolutions during the session looked far from certain."[81]

At that point, two students saved the day for the forces of radical reform. Sarah Richardson won yet more applause when she defended the new procedures on the grounds that they made the process "more accessible" to accusers.[82] Then Rit Aggarwala spoke. Sensing the turning of opinion – that Lynch's amendment would gain enough votes to spoil the solidarity that activists so ardently desired – Aggarwala elicited more applause when he told the senate that it should make a leap of faith:

He said students, after discussion, have made the judgment that it is in their best interest to sacrifice a measure of due process, to take a risk, relying on the fact that any serious guilty verdict is subject to appeal by the dean of the accused's school.... The point, he said, is to encourage more complaints, even if they don't lead to guilty findings, because one of the goals of the policy is education.... If the policy goes too far, he said, significant defects can be addressed through the provisions for continuing oversight and a two-year review.[83]

Rupp soon called for a vote, and Lynch's amendment lost to thunderous applause.

---

[79] Ibid., p. 11.
[80] Ibid., p. 12.
[81] Casselman, "Senate Passes Sexual Misconduct Policy."
[82] Senate Notes, February 25, 2000, p. 12.
[83] Ibid., p. 12.

Aggarwala told me, "I don't think we made a mistake. . . . We were taking a calculated risk. . . . I had some concerns, about getting rid of due process. I think anybody should have these concerns. But at the same time there are competing concerns, and the people we are trusting were the deans, and if we're always going to be suspicious of the deans, the whole university doesn't work."[84] The problem was that under the sway of the new system, one side would be institutionalized to influence the deans in their deliberations: SAFER and its allies.

Applegate believed that Aggarwala's speech was the coup de grace for the few civil libertarians:

Aggarwala, at a key moment, may have knocked a dozen people off the fence. It was just before the final vote was taken. He got up and – this is a guy who was in the senate as an undergraduate, in the senate as a graduate student. The level of respect for him in the community was that he was on the presidential search committee, along with Sofia Berger. He got up and said . . . "It's a calculated risk. But it's a risk we're willing to take." I knew we were going to lose the vote, it was clear this was going to pass by a large margin. But as soon as he said that . . .[85]

The senate adopted the new reform and sent it on to the trustees, who gave it their approval.

Victory with Little Dissent

Flush with victory, SAFER and its allies made two vows: to be the foremost "watchdog" group "supervising the policy's implementation"; and to "take its advocacy to other schools, having applied for federal nonprofit status."[86] Six weeks after the vote, Casselman reported that "prominent activists" had played key roles in appointing students to the three major subcommittees established by the policy (one-third of each group was to be students): education, intercampus relations, and oversight. Each appointee had to take special training in the field. Activists Jennifer Glasser and Adrien Brown helped choose the undergraduate members from a group of twenty applicants. Four of the five undergrad appointees had been major movers in the mobilization, including SAFER's Jeff Sentor (intercampus relations) and Kate Fillin-Yeh of PRO (education). Sofia Berger and Sarah Richardson received appointments to the crucial committee on oversight chaired by Catapano, which dealt with the disciplinary aspect of the policy. The fact that such strong advocates as Richardson and Sentor assumed key roles in implementation did not allay the concerns of libertarians, who believed the program was being directed by

[84] Interview with Rit Aggarwala.
[85] Interview with James Applegate.
[86] Thompson, "Senate Activists Craft Sexual Misconduct Policy," *Spectator*, May 10, 2000.

those least concerned with due process. Schneider called such appointments a classic "conflict of interest."[87]

One fact regarding the vote stands out in stark relief: the complete absence of an organized civil libertarian perspective. However courageous and frank they may have been, Schneider, Lynch, Applegate, and a few less conspicuous critics in the senate were lone wolves who had not sought out anything resembling an opposition movement. A surge of largely uncontested moral urgency had overtaken Columbia, sweeping concerns about civil liberties into the dust bin. Moreover, SAFER activists then captured the key mechanisms of implementation.

To some, the lack of an opposition merely reflected the inherent wisdom of the policy. In responding to Schneider's critique of the policy, SAFER's Jeff Sentor emphasized the campus consensus and derided the idea that anyone could interpret things differently. "The few critics of the newly-adopted Sexual Misconduct Policy spout reactionary rhetoric condemning the new policy for its supposed violation of the rights of the accused," he proclaimed.[88] In the eyes of some policy advocates, concerns about due process were "reactionary."

A second point of view parallels Timur Kuran's analysis of how fears of rejection or ridicule can silence dissent and the expression of one's honest opinion.[89] Ginger Gentile, who displayed a keen understanding of the obligations of political action, had little patience for those who slipped into the shadows out of fear. "A few people posted anonymous posters around campus [in violation of campus rules] ... two sets of two posters. They tried to claim that it was a mob mentality. But I never got the sense that it was a mob mentality.... It's their fault for not speaking out. I feel that they were cowards."[90] Sofia Berger also regretted the lack of civil libertarian input:

One thing that made me so mad all this time was that I was getting all this information, all those phone calls and e-mails that I got, the open forum – no civil liberty group ever said anything. There was barely anyone ever who said anything against it, anything along the lines of what FIRE ended up fighting for.... I feel like we paid attention to everyone's concerns. I wish there had been someone fighting against SAFER. That would have made it so much more raucous on campus, but then it wouldn't have been one overwhelming voice. SAFER was not representing every single student, and there's no way it could.[91]

Others were more sympathetic to those silenced by the campus environment. Nick Singer, who had helped start up a campus ACLU group in fall

[87] Interview with Jaime Schneider, June 2001.

[88] Sentor, "Sexual Misconduct Policy Promotes Fairness," *Spectator*, March 6, 2000.

[89] Timur Kuran, *Private Truths, Public Lies: The Social Consequences of Preference Falsification* (Harvard University Press, 1995).

[90] Interview with Ginger Gentile.

[91] Interview with Sofia Berger, April 2002.

1999, told me, "I think nobody wanted to speak out against the SAFER movement. I'm thinking specifically of the senators, people who voted for the policy perhaps against their conscience or despite it. I think when you have hundreds of supporters marching and organized, it's hard to resist. Despite objections, it got railroaded through because of the support of students. I don't think the deans were ready to resist that."[92]

Student Karl Ward pointed out that opponents ran the risk of being the recipients of the most dreaded label, "You can't be *conservative*. If you are, you automatically get notoriety or infamy. A lot of people know who Jaime Schneider is who probably never met him. Friends of his don't talk to him anymore. I had to fight tooth and nail [to prove] I'm not a conservative, and I'll bet you people still think I am." (Schneider confirmed the loss of friends to me.)[93]

Every single person I interviewed described the politics as extremely one-sided. Sofia Berger said that the task force was short-changed by the lack of exposure to the civil liberty viewpoint. (The fact that the task force had no such members was also a factor: recall that Lynch failed to be selected.) "No one said anything [to the task force] during the whole debate over the policy from the civil liberty side. They never came forward when the proposed revisions came out. I can understand how SAFER made it very intimidating to disagree."[94] Michelle Bertagna, editor in chief of the *Spectator*, observed that "anyone who opposed SAFER was demonized. By getting all those groups involved, SAFER made it virtually impossible to criticize them. If you criticize the policy, you are anti-SAFER and against those who oppose violence against women. The administration caved in to the activists. They appear to have made no attempt to find out what non-SAFER students felt. They took SAFER as the student opinion."[95] Bertagna told me that the administration had worked hard to gather a broad range of student opinion on other campuswide matters, such as the issue of whether students should be allowed to enter the student center only by swiping an identification card.

Rit Aggarwala also noted the lack of conflict. "In general, and particularly from the student body, the civil libertarian critique was really not that prominent in any way. . . . I think your main story is going to be the absence of an organized voice from the other side." Rather than blaming the beleaguered task force for giving short shrift to civil liberty, Aggarwala pointed his finger at those who had an obligation to promote that view. "I blame those who were silent. 'Bad things happen when good people are silent.' At the same time, I don't think we made a mistake."[96] Enter FIRE.

[92] Interview with Nick Singer, June 2001.
[93] Interviews with Karl Ward and Jaime Schneider.
[94] Interview with Sofia Berger, June 2001.
[95] Interview with Michelle Bertagna.
[96] Interview with Rit Aggarwala.

Two major tasks faced the university following the senate vote. First, it had to hire the new coordinator of the Office of Sexual Misconduct Prevention and Education (OSMPE) to implement what everyone was now calling the "landmark policy." Second, within a few months it would have to deal with something that caught everyone by surprise: the rise of virulent criticism of the policy from outside academe.

During the summer of 2000, Columbia named J. J. Haywood, director of budget and planning, as the interim coordinator. Then, after an extensive search that considered eighty candidates, the search committee of five administrators and four students made a unanimous choice for permanent coordinator: Charlene Allen, the director of the Boston Area Rape Crisis Center. Allen impressed everyone with her personality, commitment, and, as it was reported in the *Spectator*, extensive "experience as a lawyer, fundraiser, lobbyist, lecturer, and program director within the field of sexual assault and relationship violence." The energetic Allen looked forward to the challenge, declaring she was "'excited' by the number of students who were already involved in the policy process."[97] The job began on October 16.

But trouble was brewing. Harvey Silverglate, cofounder and vice president of the Foundation for Individual Rights in Education, came to campus over the summer to visit his undergraduate son, and he chanced upon a poster advertising the new policy. Alarmed by what he read, Silverglate looked into the matter and quickly decided that something had to be done. He contacted his colleagues at FIRE, the president, Alan Kors, and the executive director, Thor Halvorssen. The new organization decided to take on Columbia. Although it was almost buried in the avalanche of cases already coming its way, Columbia would be the case that put FIRE on the national map.

FIRE's membership includes many individuals who have attained positions of influence in education, law, and journalism. The organization is also well connected to major media institutions and other leaders. Founded in 2000 by Kors and Silverglate as a political vehicle modeled on the Committee for Academic Freedom and Rights (Wisconsin) to carry out the vision presented in their book, *The Shadow University*, FIRE has adopted an uncompromising approach to the protection of civil liberty on campus. It is committed to protecting liberty on campus and is willing to take on any institution.

FIRE's executive director, Thor Halvorssen, is a brilliant former student of Alan Kors who participated in the campus wars at the University of Pennsylvania in the mid-1990s (see Chapter 5). Ward observed, "He's a good counterpart to Sarah Richardson – hard core in a weird way. You have to have someone on the other side."[98] After FIRE attacked Columbia, the university

---

[97] Casselman, "First Sexual Misconduct Administrator Hired," *Spectator*, September 8, 2000.
[98] Interview with Karl Ward.

hired Brett A. Sokolow, president of the National Center for Higher Education Risk Management, a Philadelphia-based organization that advises colleges on issues of health and safety. When Sokolow asked Halvorssen at a lunch in March 2001 what kind of deal FIRE could live with, Halvorssen answered without hesitation "complete capitulation."[99] Sofia Berger did not appreciate the intensity with which FIRE attacked Columbia, accusing the organization of hyperbole. "I thought FIRE was so ridiculous by associating [the policy] with Star Chamber . . . etc."[100]

But FIRE's first strategy was to work quietly behind the scenes. Meanwhile, Columbia circled the wagons. Halvorssen told me:

> We are not interested in the publicity that this case will garner us. The record speaks very clearly as to how hard we tried not to have this case go public, appealing to the trustees time and again. Saying please step in and please put an end to this. We wrote to the trustees weeks and weeks before this came about. We wrote individual letters to each and every one of them at their businesses. They did not even have the courtesy to respond. Not a single one of them.[101]

FIRE first wrote a letter to all of Columbia's twenty trustees on August 1, 2000. The letter stated, in part, "The Trustees of an institution of higher learning have a solemn fiduciary obligation to pass along to the next generation a university at least as free, humane, and decent as the institution it inherited from its predecessors." The letter charged that the new policy failed to provide "even the most fundamental principles of fairness," including the lack of a clear right of notice of the charges, the right to be accompanied by an attorney, the right to know the opposing evidence and who the witnesses are, the lack of a presumption of innocence, and the lack of standards of proof. The letter also attacked the special training and tribunals for sexual offenses: "We should have learned from witchcraft trials, courts of Star Chamber, and various inquisitions that justice suffers under tribunals with special moral missions."[102] FIRE also launched a petition on its website that collected numerous names of scholars and experts.

When the trustees failed to reply to FIRE, the organization decided it had to increase the pressure. Kors and Silverglate had learned how to use outside publicity to pressure universities to respect free speech and due process.[103] (They learned this lesson during the famous 1993 water buffalo case at Penn.) FIRE has a loyal and important ally in Dorothy Rabinowitz, editorial writer for the *Wall Street Journal*, who worked with Kors and Silverglate

[99] Brownstein, "A Battle of Wills, Rights, and P.R. at Columbia."

[100] Interview with Sofia Berger, April 2002.

[101] Interview with FIRE executive director Thor Halvorssen, July 2001.

[102] FIRE, letter to Columbia Trustees, August 1, 2000, available at FIRE's website: www.theFIRE.org.

[103] Interviews with Alan Kors and Harvey Silverglate, July 2001.

on several issues over the years. For example, Rabinowitz and Silverglate had long been involved in trying to correct the highly questionable conviction of Gerald, Violet, and Cheryl Amirault in the famous Fells Acres Day School sexual abuse case in Massachusetts in the 1980s. (Silverglate was one of the Amiraults' appellate attorneys, while Rabinowitz has been their major defender in the press.)[104] FIRE contacted the *Journal* about the policy, as well as the *New York Times* and the noted *Village Voice* columnist, Nat Hentoff.

On October 4, the *Journal* published a long editorial authored by Rabinowitz titled, "Due Process at Columbia." The editorial charged that the policy treated female victims "as having the same capacities as four and five year olds," and that "[i]t is a policy that mirrors an ominously increasing tendency to devalue due process in the interest of a select category of victims." Rabinowitz wrote that Columbia and SAFER "wanted to put an end to the 'bureaucratic red tape' of the old campus policy. The red tape they had in mind, apparently, were such precepts as the right to confront one's accuser, to confront and examine witnesses, to have an attorney present – the basic rights of due process.... students accused under the new policy won't have the right to be present when the accuser testifies, nor during the testimony of witnesses."[105]

The *Journal* editorial shocked all of Columbia. The *Spectator*'s Ben Casselman told me, "all hell broke loose" upon its publication.[106] The next day, a factual presentation of the policy appeared in the *New York Times*, drawing further attention to the issue.[107] On October 5, the *Spectator* ran a front-page article chronicling the attacks by FIRE and the *Journal*, quoting FIRE's letter to the trustees and Halvorssen, who declared, "There is no compromise. If the trustees don't listen, we are going to take this to the alumni. And if the alumni don't listen, we will go to the parents. Do not rule out mass mailings by FIRE."[108] True to Halvorssen's word, FIRE eventually sent out about eight thousand letters to parents, alumni, and friends of Columbia.[109]

Over the course of the next few weeks, the opposition swelled, including organizations that could not be dismissed as "reactionary": the national ACLU, the New York Civil Liberties Union, Feminists for Free Expression, the *Village Voice* (widely read at Columbia: Applegate related that a surprisingly large number of colleagues contacted him after columnist Nat Hentoff wrote about him in the *Voice*), and others. Between October 25 and the end

[104] See Rabinowitz's book on this and related cases, *No Crueler Tyrannies: Accusation, False Witness, and Other Terrors of Our Time* (Wall Street Journal Books, Free Press, 2003).
[105] "Due Process at Columbia," *Wall Street Journal*, October 4, 2000.
[106] Phone conversation with Columbia student Ben Casselman, May 2002.
[107] Karen W. Arenson, "New Procedure for Handling Sexual Misconduct Charges at Columbia University Is Challenged," *New York Times*, October 5, 2000.
[108] Nick Shifria, "Outside Groups Attack New Misconduct Policy," *Spectator*, October 5, 2000.
[109] Interview with Thor Halvorssen.

of November, the *Voice* published four prominent front-page pieces ripping into the policy. The first, written by Norah Vincent, said that the policy represented the second of two kinds of tyranny: "Fascism, which appeals to the bully in all of us ... and identity politics, which appeals to the groupie in all of us [and] has degenerated into the latter." Hentoff followed with three attacks, the first entitled "Orwellian Justice on Campus: Columbia Star Chamber."[110]

Norah Vincent was only one of several feminists repulsed by the policy. On November 16, Feminists for Free Expression (whose board includes Betty Friedan, Erica Jong, and Nadine Strossen) charged in a letter to Columbia that the policy was "arbitrary" and that it "infantilized" students by "streamlining away" the "accountability of the accuser."[111] A few days later, Columbia law professor Vivian Berger – who is a member of the board of the national ACLU, noted feminist, and the leading national scholar on due process in education – wrote an op-ed piece in the *Spectator* criticizing the policy. Although she was a longtime friend of Silverglate, Berger was not comfortable with what she called the "shrill tone of some outside critics"; she was also somewhat less alarmed by the policy, possibly because she knew better than anyone that most campus discipline codes are not paragons of due process in the first place. Berger pointed out that Columbia had subordinated the means to the ends and that the policy, "though well-intended, is profoundly flawed," and "patronizes complainants – usually women – by treating them like children."[112]

The attacks launched on October 4 bore quick results beyond the walls of Columbia. Following Columbia's lead, New York University had begun considering amending its own policy on sexual misconduct to match Columbia's new measure. (The existing policy gave the accused the right to confront and cross-examine the accuser, and to have a friend, parent, or attorney present.) But one week after the October 4 attacks, Beth Morningstar, NYU's assistant to the president for student affairs, announced that the school would not follow Columbia's lead. "NYU decided that in the interest of fundamental fairness, we are not going to change our policy. ... it is a fundamental right for an accused person to face his or her accuser. Our policy is aimed at preserving the rights of both the accuser and the accused."[113] A short while later, Rensselaer Polytechnic Institute also decided to abandon its consideration of following in Columbia's footsteps.

[110] Vincent, "Higher Education: Columbia's Sexual Misconduct Policy the Accused," *Village Voice*, October 25–31, 2000; Hentoff, *Village Voice*, November 8–14, 2000.
[111] Feminists for Free Expression, letter to Alan J. Stone, Columbia University Vice President for Public Affairs, November 16, 2000.
[112] Vivian Berger, "Sexual Misconduct Policy: No Due Process at CU," *Spectator*, November 21, 2000; interview with Vivian Berger, May 2001.
[113] Dawn Santoli, "NYU Rejects Columbia-like Sexual Misconduct Policy," *Washington Square News*, October 12, 2000.

Columbia's Reaction

The October 4 attacks "blindsided administrators," according to Andrew Brownstein of the *Chronicle of Higher Education*.[114] The university rushed to defend itself, with Alan J. Stone, vice president for public affairs, composing a letter that was sent to everyone who contacted the university concerning the controversy. Stone challenged the accuracy of the *Journal's* allegations and asserted that the policy was similar to those of "peer institutions." FIRE immediately attacked this letter on its website in a lengthy statement.[115]

Meanwhile, student activists reacted with outrage. Sarah Richardson and her associates wrote letters and op-eds defending the policy. Defenders' counterattacks were based on three major claims: the critiques were exaggerations; FIRE and its ilk were conservatives; the attackers lacked legitimacy because they were outsiders who were not part of the Columbia community. Jeff Sentor defended "the enormously popular Sexual Misconduct Policy" and castigated the *Spectator* for breaking solidarity by publishing a front-page article on the October 4 attack and also for printing Jaime Schneider's critique the previous February. In response, Silverglate accused Sentor of demonizing students for their "refusal to fall in line with the latest campus orthodoxy."[116]

Organized Dissent from Within

The activists' indignation was intensified by the first appearance of organized opposition within Columbia soon after the October 4 attacks. On October 5, senior Karl Ward read the account of the attacks in the *Spectator* as he sat in a lecture in the library. "I was sitting there and chuckling. It was a realization that I wasn't the only person in the world who saw how ridiculous all of this was. It was the first time that I ever heard of FIRE." A drama major from Texas whose father is a former labor organizer, Ward described himself as decidedly liberal with a strong civil libertarian bent. But unlike many Columbia liberals, Ward had no patience for the precept of solidarity and its norms of collegiality and consensus. Ward believes that a large minority (possibly even a majority) of Columbia students had serious misgivings about the policy, but that the climate of mobilization had cowed them into silence. "If you raised an argument against a group that's active for ending rape," he said, "then you are automatically active for rape or a potential rapist. Most people I talked to [about fifty people] thought that this was so ridiculous that it would never be passed, that the faculty would

---

[114] Brownstein, "A Battle of Wills, Rights, and P.R. at Columbia."

[115] Stone, letter on Sexual Misconduct Policy; FIRE, "Columbia Public Relations Official Makes False Claims to Defend a Factually Flawed Procedure," available at www.theFIRE.org.

[116] Jeff Sentor, "*Spectator's* Action Was Irresponsible," *Spectator*, October 9, 2000; Silverglate, letter, *Spectator*, October 12, 2000.

never let it happen." Ward did take some individual action before the senate vote, but he felt ineffective because of the lack of connection to others. He appreciated reading the critical articles in the *Journal*, FIRE, and such papers as the *Detroit News* because it showed him "there was someone out there who agreed with me."[117]

Like his ally, Jaime Schneider, Ward was not afraid to be criticized by members of the majority. Each appeared to have a congenital disdain for conformity and groupthink and were uncompromising about fundamentals. When I asked him what inner reason drove him to throw himself into the maelstrom, Ward replied, "I felt compelled. I knew that no one else would do it. I realized that my position as a liberal with libertarian bent was almost as good as a woman criticizing the sexual misconduct policy because I'm not a conservative. So I realized that not only was I one of the only people who had been courageous enough to say anything about it, but my position as a nonconservative gave me more credibility."[118]

In early December, Ward wrote an op-ed article in the *Spectator* entitled "Sexual Misconduct Policy Will Ruin Lives," in which he cited the litany of procedural shortcomings in the policy. (It was also in December that FIRE sent a more aggressive letter to the trustees, calling their continued silence "obtuse" and a "model of oppression.")[119] Ward's attack brought down an avalanche of reproach. CSSN reviled the breach of collegiality in correspondence with the Solidarity Network, while Richardson and SAFER attacked the piece in its entirety.[120]

Ward decided to get more organized and started by sending e-mails to several acquaintances. One recipient passed the message along to the leaders of the campus chapter of the ACLU, just recently formed in the spring of 1999 by Nick Singer and David Annuncio. Although the sexual misconduct policy had been the most newsworthy item at Columbia in years, the campus civil liberties group had avoided addressing it because they were not yet organized enough to tackle the inflammatory issue. But after the October attack from the outside, Singer and Annuncio decided it was time to act and brought Ward in to lead its committee on disciplinary procedures. Ward spent three days setting up a website that included material that media groups and individuals from around the country had gathered.

Although SAFER leaders had greeted Ward's initiatives with scorn, in December 2000 they shifted tactics, claiming that the sexual misconduct policy was still a work in progress and open to further reform. Both the

---

[117] Interview with Karl Ward.
[118] Ibid.
[119] Brownstein, "A Battle of Wills, Rights, and P.R. at Columbia."
[120] Ward, *Spectator*, December 5, 2000; letters to the editor, December 7, 2000; December 8, 2000; interview with Ginger Gentile.

campus ACLU and SAFER had expressed interest in reforming the rest of the university's disciplinary procedures, so Richardson, Sentor, and Burczak agreed to hold a meeting with Singer, Annuncio, and Ward in the café of the student center to see if an agreement could be reached.[121] SAFER attached three conditions to the formulation of a coalition: the relationship would have to be nonadversarial, no "personal attacks"; the ACLU group must publicly disavow any connection to FIRE; and the group must tell FIRE to take down its link to the ACLU website. It was clear the SAFER people hated FIRE. "They despise them. It's definitely personal," Ward observed. Singer concurred. "They said FIRE had misrepresented facts and bad-mouthed their organization, mentioning 'feminist hysteria.' Their objection to FIRE was also that it was not a 'campus group.'"[122]

Although Singer did not like the condition of severing ties to FIRE, Ward said he could live with it but would not sever website ties. "Do you realize how strange this is, to ask a civil liberties group to deny the free speech rights of another civil liberties group?" he asked.[123] Thus ended the attempt to reconcile SAFER and the ACLU. With the possibility of a student movement compromise dead, the question became how the administration would respond to the growing crisis.

The Forum

After the winter break, things heated up again in February 2001 when Ward organized a campuswide round table talk to discuss and debate the policy. He acted as moderator. Silverglate and Vivian Berger agreed to be panelists, and Ward also invited SAFER and the new coordinator of the sexual misconduct policy, Charlene Allen, to participate. Saying they would participate only if the forum were run by a coalition of student groups, the SAFER people turned down the invitation. Ward believed that Charlene Allen had agreed to take part, but he was mistaken, as she, too, chose not to join the gathering on the grounds that Ward's role as moderator meant that the forum would be too one-sided, not a "chance for meaningful dialogue." She and Kaya Tretjak of SAFER recoiled from dealing with "outsiders," especially FIRE. "Ultimately, FIRE's approach isn't compatible with a desire to establish fair disciplinary procedures," they told the *Spectator*.[124]

Regardless of their reasons, Allen's and SAFER's refusals to participate could not have helped their cause in the eyes of the undecided, as they appeared unwilling or unable to engage in the rigors of genuine debate.

---

[121] Ward told me that these were the individuals present at this meeting. Singer said that Ward was not there. I was unable to reconcile the differences, but went with Ward's account because it is more likely that he would remember being there.

[122] Interviews with Karl Ward and Nick Singer, June 2001.

[123] Interview with Karl Ward.

[124] Felice Bajoras, "Panel on Misconduct Will Lack Opposition," *Spectator*, February 22, 2001.

Although a *Spectator* editorial chastised Ward and the ACLU for not presenting an impartial moderator (a fair critique), it praised Silverglate and Berger – who presented strong criticism of the policy in the forum on February 25 – as "a pair of distinguished civil libertarians."[125] Later, Silverglate criticized Columbia and SAFER for not appearing and alleged that SAFER activists had pulled down posters announcing the event.[126]

Perhaps in response to the publicity, SAFER opened the door to some procedural modifications. Richardson called for greater student cooperation, writing in the student paper that the policy "can always benefit from further reform."[127]

The Trustees Start to Move

Meanwhile, the trustees had begun to push behind the scenes for modification of the policy.[128] Sometime in April, Allen called a meeting with Patricia Catapano, J. J. Haywood, Sofia Berger, Nick Singer, Karl Ward, and some members of the Rape Crisis Center. There she expressed her frustration with the job. The tensions between the educational and disciplinary aspects of the policy were increasingly apparent, and the trustees had begun pressuring the administration in secret meetings to make changes in the policy without what Allen considered adequate student participation. There was debate over whether trustees were "suggesting" or "mandating" changes.[129] According to one interview source involved in administrative politics at Columbia (who asked to remain anonymous concerning this point), the trustees were divided and deeply distressed at all the publicity. (No trustee would talk with me about the policy, although one trustee did tell me that the group had agreed not to discuss the matter with outsiders.)

On April 26 Columbia was shaken by an announcement: Charlene Allen resigned as policy coordinator due to "irreconcilable differences of opinion with the Board of Trustees and the Office of General Counsel, according to student leaders." Catapano was "stunned" by the announcement and denied that the trustees had ordered changes. Columbia College senior Erica Levi, a member of the oversight committee, summed up the problem from the activists' perspective. "The way in which the policy was developed last year involved a really powerful dialogue between students and administrators and staff.... Her resignation had brought to light that this process completely ceased to exist."[130] Allen "went into hiding" according to many sources and

---

[125] Staff editorial, *Spectator*, February 26, 2001.
[126] FIRE, "Columbia University Unable to Defend Policy in Public," available at www.theFIRE.org.
[127] "Student Groups Must Act," *Spectator*, February 28, 2001.
[128] No trustee has spoken to anyone, so I rely on other sources. I made two futile attempts to speak with someone.
[129] Interview with Karl Ward.
[130] Tallie Liberman, "Allen Resignation Met with Surprise," *Spectator*, April 30, 2001.

has given no interviews about what happened. J. J. Haywood reluctantly returned as interim coordinator.

In response, activists forged a new "Policy Coalition" and distributed a pamphlet entitled "Behind Closed Doors," which condemned the secrecy of the trustees' pressure tactics. The administration was now undermining the solidarity that had reigned the previous fall. "The whole campus joined together to show support for student involvement in university decisions," the pamphlet stated. Vice president for student services, Gene Awakuni, commented, "if Allen lost control, it was in part due to the attack by the Foundation for Individual Rights (FIRE)." *Spectator* reporter Ben Casselman reported that Allen grew frustrated in part because the trustees had met only with Catapano. Awakuni also said that Allen opposed some of the pending reforms, such as allowing the accused to view the proceedings on closed-circuit television, "which Awakuni said Allen thought might 'have a chilling effect on students coming forth.'" [131] (Courts have ruled that defendants in child sex abuse cases have a right to watch the testimony of children on closed-circuit television.) According to Jaime Schneider, who reported the Columbia story in the *National Review*, still another reason Allen resigned was because she was told she could not speak publicly about the issue. [132]

Toward the Final Product

By the summer of 2001 Columbia's administrative leaders had decided that some revision of the sexual misconduct policy was necessary. Catapano called such changes "clarifications" rather than "changes" or "amendments," which would have to be resubmitted to the senate. Critics charged that the distinction was contrived; but the university officials clearly wanted to get the changes adopted as quietly as possible before students returned in September.

In early July Andrew Brownstein published his lengthy article on the policy in the *Chronicle of Higher Education*. Although he strove to be balanced, Brownstein's article embarrassed Columbia simply by reporting the facts. The article's appearance corresponded to my own first visit to the campus, and no administrator other than J. J. Haywood would meet with me. Even Haywood spoke with me only on the condition that we not address anything even touching on the policy. [133]

In order to keep student representatives in the loop, OSMPE selected six summer "interns" from the policy coalition to meet and discuss the development of outreach and education, the structure of the OSMPE, and the

---

[131] Casselman, "Columbia Struggles to Launch a New Policy," *Spectator*, May 2, 2001.

[132] Jaime Schneider, "Columbia's Summer Vacation: Changing Policy behind Closed Doors," *National Review*, July 10, 2001.

[133] Interview with interim Sexual Misconduct Policy coordinator J. J. Haywood, June 2001.

hiring of a new coordinator. I interviewed one intern, but she, too, would not discuss the policy with me.[134] Schneider quoted a student from the Rape Crisis Center expressing the concern that the university might hire "someone with a different kind of politics."[135]

On September 1 Haywood left the turmoil of Columbia to pursue a business opportunity back in Minnesota, her home state. Columbia replaced her with another interim coordinator, assistant director of administrative planning, Richard Welch.[136] Finally, in early October, the university hired Misumbo Byrd as the new coordinator. An M.A. student in public administration at NYU at the time, Byrd had the same political orientation as Allen and had extensive experience working with survivors of domestic violence and in the prosecution of sexual violence cases.[137]

The OSMPE had already written new procedures for cases by September 28 that incorporated what the trustees wanted. The key "clarifications" included, first, a definite standard of proof, "clear and convincing evidence"; and, second, rules that clarified to whom the parties (accuser and accused) could speak about the case outside the process: family members, potential witnesses, a "counselor or legal advisor" – including a lawyer – and a "supporter." According to the procedures, supporters were not allowed to pose questions or intervene in the proceedings, but could talk quietly to the party or pass notes. It is not clear if a lawyer could accompany the accused to the hearing as a supporter; however, the regulations stated clearly that the accused had a right to consult a lawyer outside the process of the hearing, which implied that a lawyer would not be welcome in the actual hearing. Third, the accused had a clear right to receive "written notice" of the complaint and a copy of the complainant's written statement. Fourth, a verbatim transcript was to be provided to each party. Fifth, neither party would be allowed to be present while the other testified, unless they mutually agreed that each would be present. Sixth, both parties could watch a "simultaneous transmission" of all testimony on closed-circuit television. Seventh, neither party could directly confront or cross-examine witnesses, but each could "submit questions to the hearing panel to be asked of the other party and of potential witnesses, at the discretion of the hearing panel." Eighth, each party could make a closing statement summarizing his or her case before the hearing panel.[138]

---

134 Schneider, "Columbia's Summer Vacation"; interview with Columbia student Anharad Coates, June 2001.

135 Schneider, "Columbia's Summer Vacation."

136 Casselman, "Misconduct Turmoil Continues as Interim Coordinator Quits," *Spectator*, September 4, 2001.

137 Katherine Isokawa, "New Coordinator Hired for Office of Sexual Misconduct," *Spectator*, October 3, 2001.

138 Office of Sexual Misconduct Prevention and Education, *Status Report to the University Senate*, March 25, 2002. Appendix C, *Procedural Regulations for the Sexual Misconduct Disciplinary Procedure* (September 28, 2001).

Although the changes were less unfavorable to the accused, FIRE was not satisfied with the compromise. Key problems still remained, especially the absence of a right to be present and confront one's accuser, the right to cross-examine and ask follow-up questions, and the right to be tried by a neutral tribunal, not one specially trained in a manner oriented toward the accuser.

In many respects, the clarifications appeared to represent an accommodation to political pressures rather than a considered judgment based on any informed conviction. Applegate perhaps said it best. Although he praised the presidency of George Rupp in general (which ended after the spring semester in 2002), Applegate lamented the administration's lack of vision concerning civil liberties, and how it allowed itself to be bullied by the mobilization of activists. "On this issue, he [Rupp] had an opportunity to teach students something about the balance between civil liberties and security, and he didn't do it."[139]

Two days before the OSMPE adopted the clarifications, Columbia student David Sauvage of the *Spectator* presented his final observations about the pending changes and the problems that continued to linger. After asking how acceptable legislation could come from groups such as SAFER and their allies, groups "which by their very names [are] the least qualified to frame legislation that must deal fairly with those accused of violence and rape," he asked the most cogent question: "Just imagine you face trial by a panel of administrators headed by someone whose principal function is to 'educate students about the problem' . . . and you can't have a lawyer."[140]

Conclusions

As of the spring of 2002, the new system had adjudicated only one case, exonerating the accused.[141] Although one could not draw definitive conclusions about the policy as of the time of this writing, the Columbia story does raise some important points about the status of civil liberty in academe. First, the extremely one-sided policy was an example of what can happen in the absence of organized checks and balances. Along the lines of the theory of "interest group liberalism," organized opposition could have provided a pressure group whose views had to be taken into consideration.[142] Such opposition could also have provided information that could have enlightened

---

[139] Interview with James Applegate, April 2002.

[140] David Sauvage, "Misconduct Policy Blues," *Spectator*, September 26, 2001.

[141] Interview with James Applegate, April 2002.

[142] For a defense of interest group liberalism as policy, see Robert Dahl's classic, *Who Governs?* (Yale University Press, 1961). For a critical perspective on interest group liberalism as lacking substantive justice, see Theodore Lowi, *Interest Group Liberalism: The Second Republic of the United States* (Norton, 1979).

the task force and others who dealt with policy. Research in political science has supported the commonsense view of how important information is to good policy and to the exercise of power. Groups with relevant information possess more power than those who do not, and institutions need relevant information in order to perform their duties well.[143] The two leading student members of the task force at Columbia said that they would have had to take the civil liberty perspective into consideration had it been presented, but it simply was not presented.

The Columbia story also supports Timur Kuran's theory of preference falsification and mobilization. Until FIRE and its allies entered the debate from outside the university, few spoke out against the new policy, even though many people I interviewed believed that there was widespread concern about it. FIRE's entry made such individuals as Karl Ward realize that they were not alone, and a meaningful opposition developed. Although those who opposed the policy did not succeed in overturning it completely (in Kuran's case studies, the opposition turns things decidedly around), they did succeed in exposing the policy's weaknesses and in forcing the reluctant trustees to act. FIRE's intervention also meant that the SAFER-endorsed policy did not spread to other campuses. The case also shows the veracity of Kors and Silverglate's point that "sunlight is the best disinfectant."[144]

Most important, the case reveals the failure of professors and university administrators to teach the basic principles of due process, civil liberties, and freedom. The administration allowed the activists to control the process and did little to balance their claims with counterclaims that were clearly needed. The process was marked by a failure of education and a lack of courage in the administration and faculty, two qualities whose presence is necessary for the protection of fundamental rights. Recall how Sarah Richardson gloated about the administrators who had "fear in their eyes." The case also reveals an important point: accusers have responsibilities as well as rights. Fundamental rights of the accused must not be sacrificed despite sympathy for victims who cry out for justice. As James Applegate remarked at a senate meeting, "the accuser under the proposed procedure has no particular rights and responsibilities. This is not non-adversarial, but juvenile." We do not honor victims by treating them like helpless children incapable of withstanding the requirements of fundamental fairness.

Finally, the story of "solidarity" at Columbia reveals the dangers of unquestioned moral sentiment. As Dana Villa has written, "The implication of

---

[143] See, e.g., T. W. Gilligan and K. Krehbiel, "Organization of Information Committees by a Rational Legislature," 34 *American Journal of Political Science* (1990), pp. 531–64.

[144] See Kuran, *Private Truths, Public Lies*; Alan Charles Kors and Harvey A. Silverglate, *The Shadow University: The Betrayal of Liberty on America's Campuses* (Free Press, 1998), ch. 15.

Socratic examination is that virtually every moral belief becomes false and an incitement to injustice the moment it becomes unquestioned or unquestionable."[145] Columbia activists were so convinced of their own moral virtue that they considered any word of dissent to be immoral. Their righteousness blinded them to the importance of due process to the scales of justice.

[145] Dana Villa, *Socratic Citizenship* (Princeton University Press, 2001), p. 23.

4

Berkeley and the Rise of the Anti–Free Speech Movement

As seen in Chapter 1, the Berkeley campus teems with student groups. In this sense, the legacy of the free speech movement is alive and well. But the variety and vibrancy of the many student groups belie the actual state of free speech at Berkeley. Based on a variety of data and interviews with over thirty professors and politically prominent students, I came to some conclusions about the status of free speech on campus. First, with some exceptions I address later, basic academic freedom thrives in the classroom. Second, the administration has not engaged in progressive censorship; indeed, Berkeley has remained surprisingly free of speech code conflicts.[1] Third, the real threat to free speech that has arisen takes the form of "progressive social censorship" in the public forum – meaning pressure from individuals or groups outside of government or official institutions in the name of progressive causes, such as the shouting down of speakers, intimidation, threats, the theft of publications, and even burglary.[2] Every person I interviewed agreed with this assessment. Fourth, until 2002, neither the administration nor the faculty had made any meaningful effort to safeguard free speech in the public forum. No political organization promoting free speech exists.

With the exception of those in the Law School, and of a few incidents I discuss, no students I interviewed recalled any significant restriction of free speech in the classroom. Overall, professors were conscientious about fostering a climate that supported free intellectual dialogue. The linguistics

---

[1] Neither the head of the Student Judicial Advocates office (the body that gives advice to students charged with misconduct) nor a leading judicial advocate could recall a speech code being invoked. Interviews with Berkeley Student Judicial Advocates officers Alex Kipnis and Kevin Deliban, November 2001. Law professors Jesse Choper and Robert Post – both First Amendment scholars – told me the same thing.

[2] Both John Stuart Mill and Alexis de Tocqueville were aware of how social censorship can be as oppressive as government censorship. See Mill, introduction to volume 2 of Tocqueville, *Democracy in America*, trans. H. Reeves (Schocken, 1961).

professor, John McWhorter, for example, said that he has never encountered pressure by students or colleagues to make his views more palatable, even though he is now a lightning rod as author of the best-selling book, *Losing the Race*, in which he attacks the theory and practice of contemporary racial politics. Another example is political science professor Jack Citrin, one of the most outspoken critics of race-based affirmative action on campus, and a former – usually dissenting – member of the admissions committee. Citrin conceded that he has encountered some social heat for taking his unpopular stands, but he maintained that no one has disrupted his classes and that no colleagues questioned his right to express his views.[3] Then there is business and political science professor Alan Ross, who has gained a campuswide reputation for teaching a class of several hundred students that tackles controversial public issues by regularly presenting prominent speakers from across the political spectrum. Ross works hard at the beginning of the course to create an environment that respects ideological disagreement. He has not shirked from bringing many controversial conservative people to speak to the class, including Ward Connerly, the member of the board of regents who led the successful fight to pass Proposition 209, the statewide initiative that eliminated race-based affirmative action in admissions and government hiring. Despite these controversial speakers, Ross's class has never suffered disruption. The class is the closest thing to a free public forum that Berkeley has to offer.[4]

William Ker Muir, emeritus political science professor, offered a similar perspective. Although he agreed that the public forum at Berkeley is a problem, he could recall only two instances in over thirty years of students confronting professors in class. According to Muir, one of the professors – anthropologist Vincent Sarich – was "aggressive and I think he reveled in it. I think you ought to have people like that." Muir appreciates the activism that infuses so much energy into Berkeley, especially compared with other schools. "What strikes me as I go out [to other schools] is that it is so quiet. There is nothing to upset. It has given me a greater appreciation of just how wonderful Berkeley is."[5]

Despite these positives, Ross did point out that McWhorter had recently declined to speak to his class because of his concerns about hostility. While McWhorter has presented his arguments about race in a wide variety of venues in the national media, he refrains from speaking on this topic at Berkeley itself, where he has encountered what he considers character assassination in forums. And Ross conceded that the freedom in his class does not transfer to the public sphere of the campus. In that domain, he laments the tactics of disrupters and the lack of intellectual diversity and freedom,

[3] Interview with Berkeley political science professor Jack Citrin, August 2001.
[4] Interview with Berkeley business and political science professor Alan Ross, January 2002.
[5] Interview with Berkeley political science professor William Ker Muir, July 2002.

stating that it is "not possible" for certain viewpoints to be entertained in the public forum.[6]

All students I interviewed agreed that the state of free speech is healthier in the classroom than in the public forum. Referring to David Horowitz's 2001 advertisement on reparations and how students treated Horowitz when he came to campus a couple of weeks later, Anka Lee, a political science major who rebuilt the College Democrats into a viable organization, said,

> After a year or two [at Berkeley], I really came to a realization that free speech is not as respected here as I thought. The conservatives are really shot down when they want to express their views. I disagree with just about everything that they say, but I think that they have a right to say it. [But] professors always allow students of different political beliefs to speak in class – virtually all of the professors I have had. I have never seen shouting down of speech in class.[7]

Muir also conceded that troubled times had come to the public forum at Berkeley: "Pete Wilson never spoke here, and he was [Republican] governor and a graduate of Boalt. So in a sense there is a censorship or a censoring already at one level that is covert and unknown. Ed Meese [California and U.S. Attorney General under Ronald Reagan] would have trouble coming to campus, but he would also have trouble being invited. I think the public forum problem has a left bias."[8]

Both pro- and antiwar public discourse did indeed flourish at Berkeley after the terrorist attacks of September 11, 2001. It was during this time that the *Daily Cal* acted to reaffirm its free speech credentials; but before this time, it was often very hard for conservative views to be expressed publicly. According to McWhorter, one reason for the one-sidedness of public discourse at Berkeley is the inability or reluctance of those whose views predominate in the public sphere to imagine that dissent might have substantive merit. The spirit of John Stuart Mill does not flourish on campus. McWhorter depicted this problem in language similar to Timur Kuran's and Allan Bloom's descriptions of the "unthinkable": "I have been given the thumbs-up from the chancellor [Robert Berdahl] and the dean of social sciences. Academic freedom is very secure here. In general, what is difficult is the level of appropriateness.... [Intolerance of dissent] is not deliberate. It's the fact that people just cannot imagine another way."[9]

---

[6] Interview with Berkeley linguistics professor John McWhorter, August 2001; interview with Alan Ross.

[7] Interview with Anka Lee, November 2001.

[8] Interview with William Ker Muir.

[9] Interview with John McWhorter. See Timur Kuran, *Private Truths, Public Lies: The Social Consequences of Preference Falsification* (Harvard University Press, 1995); Allan Bloom, *The Closing of the American Mind: How Higher Education Has Betrayed Democracy and Impoverished the Souls of Today's Students* (Simon and Schuster, 1987), p. 249.

The Berkeley scene includes several identity groups, some of whom have challenged the speech rights of those whose views they find abhorrent. The Muslim Student Association tried unsuccessfully in the fall of 2001 to force the *Daily Cal* to apologize for a cartoon; and MEChA, a militant Chicano identity group that has reviled whites and called for the return of vast areas of the American southwest to Mexico, has opposed the *Cal Patriot* – a hard-hitting conservative publication – in vehement terms. But the most important proponent of progressive censorship is the Berkeley chapter of the national group BAMN. BAMN stands for "By Any Means Necessary," the famous title of one of Malcolm X's books. Formed in 1995 in reaction to the elimination of race-based affirmative action at the university, BAMN combines the ideology of critical race theory with the tactics of direct confrontation. It disparages the notion of objective standards of merit and individualism, and believes in a system of equality of results and proportional racial representation in admissions. BAMN stridently challenges the right of free speech of anyone who holds what it considers racist views. It led the assault on the *Daily Cal* when it published David Horowitz's ad.

During the year after the passage of Prop 209 in late 1996, BAMN led the anti-209 attack by conducting a series of dramatic demonstrations and occupations on campus designed to force the administration of then chancellor Chang-Lin Tien to defy the will of the voters of the state. A BAMN poster declared the goals:

[W]e must force Chancellor Tien to publicly state that the Berkeley campus will defy 209! We must continue and expand the mass actions such as the Campanile occupation and marches through buildings on campus. We must demonstrate that this campus will be ungovernable unless Tien accepts our demands. So far, he has been acting as though he has no choice but to follow orders and implement 209, while merely looking for "loopholes" to soften the blow of destroying affirmative action.... Tien must choose equality now!

According to students I interviewed, BAMN is a "huge group" that is the force behind many major protests against rollbacks of affirmative action, the war on terrorism (which BAMN considers racist), and policies that BAMN considers contrary to its causes. In targeting the *Daily Cal* in the Horowitz affair, BAMN openly accused the paper of being racist, even though the *Daily Cal*'s leadership is decidedly multicultural in background. *Daily Cal* photographer Ben Miller explained, "It was very easy for them to brand us as racist. It is such an easy term to throw around, it has such a punch. Then when you try to argue something, they call you racist. I was really upset at BAMN's tactics at that time." Anka Lee had a similar observation about BAMN students who shouted Horowitz down during his question-and-answer period. "They would not let him make his case. That is sad and hypocritical in many ways. These are the same students who ask for freedom of speech, rights, and civil liberties, and there they were, screaming and shouting down other peoples' point of view. Nothing was really done about it, either, and as a result, nobody learned a thing [about free speech]."[10]

In the early 2000s, the Berkeley BAMN has been led by Hoku Jeffries, who did not respond to my request for an interview. BAMN has striven to rid the Berkeley campus of all vestiges of racism, including ideas BAMN considers detrimental to the cause. In the debate in the student senate (the Associated Students of the University of California, or ASUC) in February 2002 that addressed the newspaper thefts and burglary of the *Patriot* after it published an article criticizing MEChA, Jeffries and an ally blamed the *Patriot* for provoking the crimes. According to the senate notes, "They [the student movement] should demand equality now. He understood that copies of the *Patriot* were stolen.... It happened, and it was outrageous. But they should have seen it coming, to be truthful." A woman named Nicole followed Jeffries to the podium and charged that the *Patriot*'s words constituted "an act of terrorism. The David Horowitz incident was an act of terrorism."[11]

Interestingly, applause followed speeches by both defenders and critics of the *Patriot* at the ASUC meeting. In an intriguing interview, Troy Duster, a Berkeley sociologist, argued that the contentious debates over curriculum and free speech are the inevitable effects of expanding diversity and political viewpoints. He cautioned against applying abstract principles to evaluate the predicament of higher education, preferring a pluralistic approach that pays close attention to intergroup tensions and particular situations.[12] In 1990 Duster led a team commissioned by Chancellor Tien that studied race relations on the campus. The "Diversity Project" concluded that minority students perceived widespread subtle and institutional racism and felt "ignored or excluded." At the same time, white students considered themselves unjustly accused and felt like they were walking on eggshells, always afraid of being called "racist" or "oppressors."[13] Other commentators have observed the spread of a questionable trend: the rise of victim ideology on the right in response to its "success" on the left.[14] In an essay on his report, Duster

---

[10] Interview with Ben Miller, November 2001; interview with Anka Lee. See also interviews with Berkeley student senators Anand Upadhye and James Gallagher, November 2001. For the national chapter's positions, see BAMN *Liberator, Journal for the Emerging New Civil Rights Movement*, and a statement of purpose on its website: www.BAMN.com. See Malcolm X, *By Any Means Necessary* (Pathfinder Press, 1970).

[11] Notes of ASUC Meeting, February 27, 2002.

[12] Interview with Berkeley sociologist Troy Duster, November 2001. For a similar idea derived from Hannah Arendt and similar thinkers, see Richard Bernstein, *Beyond Objectivity and Relativism: Science, Hermeneutics, and Praxis* (University of Pennsylvania Press, 1983). Duster's thinking incorporates race more fully than Bernstein's does.

[13] Duster et al., "The Diversity Project: An Interim Report to the Chancellor," Institute for the Study of Social Change, University of California, Berkeley, 1990.

[14] See the illuminating article by Michel Feher, "Empowerment Hazards: Affirmative Action, Recovery Psychology, and Identity Politics," in Robert Post and Michael Rogin, eds., *Race and Representation: Affirmative Action* (Zone Books, 1998), pp. 175–84.

maintained that the tensions could be part of the birth pains that accompany a developing dialogue about race and the growth of cultural pluralism: "If our students learn even a small bit of this, they will be better prepared than students tucked safely away in anachronistic single-culture enclaves. And what they learn may make a difference not just for their personal futures, but for a world struggling with the issues of nationalism, race, and ethnicity."[15] Duster's perspective in the report is illuminating and hopeful. But more than ten years after his study, race relations at Berkeley had hardly improved, at least in terms of public discourse. In the absence of a university-wide insistence on mutual equal respect for the rights of all students – including those who hold dissenting views – group conflict continued unabated, with little apparent attempt by any group to find common ground.

The Crisis of the Public Forum

The crisis of the public forum at Berkeley has intensified in recent years as the commitment of some groups to certain moral and political causes has superseded respect for the principles of free speech. In the midst of the renewed turmoil in the Middle East in 2002, for example, Jewish students have been victimized by hostility while engaging in pro-Israeli demonstrations at Berkeley and San Francisco State University. During the outbreak of suicide bombings in Israel in the spring of 2002, someone threw a concrete block through a window of UC Berkeley's Hillel building, and two Orthodox Jews were brutally beaten one block off campus. On April 9 pro-Palestinian protesters shouted prayers in memory of suicide bombers to drown out Jewish students who were reciting the Kaddish for the dead.[16] According to Karen Alexander of the *New Republic*, these and other incidents at Berkeley are the products of an alliance between campus groups and "the Bay Area's preexisting, off-campus lefty groups. The pro-Palestinian organization at UC Berkeley, for instance, receives assistance from Left Turn (a socialist group), the Revolutionary Communist Party, and the International Socialists Organization (ISO)."[17]

The number of censorship efforts by the militant Berkeley left has gained legendary status at the school. In the fall of 1996, for example, someone stole more than twenty thousand copies of the *Daily Cal* from its distribution racks when it printed an editorial approving of Prop 209.[18] There were also thefts

---

[15] Duster, "They're Taking Over! – Myths about Multiculturalism," *Mother Jones*, September–October 1991.

[16] See Karen Alexander, "'West Bank': San Francisco Dispatch," *New Republic*, June 24, 2002, pp. 17–18.

[17] Ibid., p. 18.

[18] Ward Connerly, *Creating Equal: My Fight against Race Preferences* (Encounter Books, 2000), p. 192.

of many copies of the *Daily Cal* and the *Patriot* after the publication of the Horowitz ad and the critique of MEChA.

Several well-publicized incidents on or near campus in which speakers were shouted down have tarnished Berkeley's free speech legacy over the years. In 1983, for example, hecklers opposed to the U.S. policy in El Salvador forced the United Nations ambassador, Jeane Kirpatrick, to leave the stage during a lecture on campus. In April 1985, protesters disrupted a speech by Clarence Pendleton, the first black commissioner of the Commission on Civil Rights, because of his expressed doubt about racial quotas in hiring and education. In January 1990 activists interrupted the speech of U.S. Supreme Court Justice Sandra Day O'Connor because they objected to her decisions concerning abortion and sodomy. Then, in November 1990, more than fifty protesters disrupted the class of anthropology professor Vincent Sarich, who had argued that affirmative action discriminates against whites. In October 1994 protesters stormed an off-campus talk by David Irving, who has notoriously denied that the Holocaust was nearly as extensive as many more credible historians claim. According to the *San Francisco Chronicle*, "[r]ocks and bottles were thrown and three people were injured." Then, in February 1995, the university had to stop a lecture by Irving on campus after fights broke out in the audience.

At a May graduation ceremony in 2000, protesters opposed to U.S. sanctions against Iraq repeatedly interrupted and eventually brought to a halt a commencement address by U.S. secretary of state Madeline Albright. In September 2000, BAMN activists repeatedly hassled Dan Flynn, executive director of Accuracy in Academia, when he challenged the belief of many activists by arguing that Mumia Aba Inma was guilty of murdering a police officer. A month later, protesters disrupted a speech by former NATO commander General Wesley Clark, calling him a "war criminal."[19]

Then an event took place in November 2000 that forced the Berkeley community to face up to the censorship gorilla that had taken up residence in the public forum. The Marin Peninsula-Berkeley Lecture Series, a prestigious Bay Area society that had only recently added Berkeley to its rotation, brought Benjamin Netanyahu, former Israeli prime minister, to the Berkeley Community Theatre for an address. He was met by two hundred opponents of his policies toward Palestine, who "broke through a police barricade and blocked the entrance" to the theater. As the *San Francisco Chronicle* reported, "Some also taunted the 2000 waiting ticket-holders who were trapped outside." One ticket holder assailed the display: "Never in America have I waited and been turned away from a paid lecture that was unofficially cancelled by a mob shouting accusations at me. Harassed, hassled, with accusations shouted at me and my friend, as though we were Uzi-carrying slayers of

[19] On all the incidents that I mention here, see Charles Burrer, "Infringing on Free Speech: Debate Rages on Cancelled Talk in Berkeley," *San Francisco Chronicle*, December 10, 2000.

children, we, two quiet ladies from Moraga ... wanted to hear both sides of the issue." One protester presented his or her version of the other side: "I don't believe in free speech for war criminals."[20]

The disruption was so troubling that a group representing some original free speech movement members wrote a joint letter condemning the incident as "a serious violation of the principles for which thousands of students struggled in 1964." In its coverage of the affair, the *Chronicle* wrote that Berkeley had to admit that it was in the grips of a crisis of activist-inspired progressive censorship. "The uproar is fueled by a cumulative frustration over several years of leftist demonstrators, particularly at the UC campus, disrupting the speeches of those they view as criminal in one form or another." The disruption also caused the "acclaimed" lecture series to reconsider its inclusion of Berkeley as a site for the series.[21]

Background Issues

One reason for the lack of attention to the problem of the public forum could be that the right of free speech has lost status to the university's drive for diversity: when certain forms of discourse are deemed harmful for equality and diversity, the institutional commitment to free speech falters. As discussed in Chapter 1, diversity is an important value, but it should not trump the institutional commitment to free speech. Indeed, during the 1980s the diversity objective became as entrenched at Berkeley as anywhere. The Law School paved the way in the late 1960s, adopting an aggressive affirmative action policy that quickly achieved close to proportional racial representation in the school.[22] Although some unsuccessful faculty resistance arose in the 1970s, over time an operational consensus on affirmative action in admissions prevailed in the Law School. (Faculty diversity has, however, consistently been a touchier issue.)[23] It took longer for the rest of the campus to get up to speed, but undergraduate admissions managed to match the Law School in the 1980s. In 1988 the legislature revised the state's Master Plan for Higher Education, declaring that "each segment of Californian higher education shall strive to approximate by the year 2000 the general

[20] Ibid.

[21] Ibid.

[22] Interviews with Berkeley law professors Herma Hill Kay, Robert H. Cole, and Sanford Kadish, August and November 2001. On the evolution of Boalt Hall policy on affirmative action, including the reaction to Prop 209, see the essay of Herma Hill Kay, "The Challenge to Diversity in Legal Education," 34 *Indiana Law Review* 55 (2000), pp. 58–60; and a report led by law student Kaaryn Gustafson et al., "New Directions in Diversity: Charting Law School Admissions Policy in a Post–Affirmative Action Era," Report of Boalt Hall, May 9, 1997.

[23] Interviews with Robert H. Cole and Sanford Kadish; interview with former Boalt student and activist William Kidder, July 2002.

ethnic, sexual, and economic composition of the recent high school gradu-ates."[24] According to Berkeley political scientist Jack Citrin, the state legis-lature joined hands with the Berkeley administration to adopt the diversity cause:

So you had these organized interest groups. It became much more difficult to speak openly about these things because you would be insulting someone who was a col-league or a student. It shows the weakness of the commitment to free discourse. And then you had political pressure from the legislature.... Liberal Democrats in particular controlled the key positions [from 1983 to 1998].... Now it's the Latino caucus which has completely displaced them. They viewed affirmative action as [an imperative]....

The university's budget negotiations are always muddied by "we have to do this or else we won't get money."... In the case of the Latino caucus just this past year, the threat was quite explicit.[25]

The institutionalization of diversity at Berkeley involved a process simi-lar to what has taken place at many universities: the creation of diversity-oriented offices and programs staffed by advocates throughout administra-tive hierarchies.[26] Commenting on the attitude of admissions officers toward the passage of Special Policy 1 and Prop 209 in 1995 and 1997 (which out-lawed race as a criterion in admissions in California public higher education), an admissions officer told researcher Daniel Lipson, "almost everybody in the admissions office shares frustration with the anti-affirmative action cli-mate." At one point in 1995, admissions staff wore sweatshirts to work with "I Support Affirmative Action" emblazoned in front.[27]

In instituting the diversity policy, the seven schools in the University of California system covertly adopted the so-called Karabel matrix, named after Jerome Karabel, the sociology professor whose report was the basis for the policy. Under the sway of "the matrix," admissions officers assigned different points to applicants according to the race of each applicant. The university did not publicly acknowledge the matrix's existence until it was unveiled by an outside investigation under the aegis of regent Ward Connerly. In his autobiography, Connerly wrote that his discovery of the matrix constituted a turning point in his drive against race-based admissions:

The crucial document that came to me that spring [1995] – also arriving anony-mously – was something called the Karabel Matrix.... Its existence and contents had

---

[24] Joint Committee for Review of Master Plan for Higher Education, 1988, p. 19.
[25] Interview with Jack Citrin; see also interview with Tom Wood, president of California As-sociation of Scholars, August 2001.
[26] See Frederick Lynch, *The Diversity Machine: The Drive to Change the "White Male Marketplace"* (Transaction, 2002); John David Skrentny, *The Ironies of Affirmative Action: Politics, Culture, and Justice in America* (University of Chicago Press, 1996).
[27] Daniel Lipson, "Affirmative Action as We Don't Know It" (Ph.D. dissertation, University of Wisconsin, Madison, 2003).

never been made public, and as I read it, I realized why. The Matrix proposed a sliding scale for assigning points for admissions. There were 8,000 points possible. Whites and Asians had to have over 7,100 to be admitted. "People of color" could be below 6,000 and still get admitted. This was one of the smoking guns that showed race was not one among many factors, but *the* factor.[28]

Whatever one thinks of the diversity rationale as presently conceived, the issue here is *how* diversity is reached – the means employed to achieve the end. A wrongheaded approach to diversity can compromise discourse and the pursuit of truth. Concerns about the sensitivities considered necessary to attain and sustain diversity can lead to measures that restrict free discussion about race, gender, and the like. Such thinking has motivated the propagation of many questionable speech codes and similar policies over the past fifteen years. And the issue of truthfulness and intellectual honesty persists. As Connerly's experience reveals, the University of California system was simply not forthright about its reliance on the matrix. A similarly dishonest policy was applied in the mid-1980s, when the university adopted a new minimal verbal SAT requirement in order to *limit* the growth of Asian undergraduate admittees. After several years of publicly denying the motive for the new standard, the university administrators were compelled to admit it was true after a secret "SAT 400 memo" was leaked to a State Assembly committee holding a hearing on Asian admissions.[29] Likewise, it took a lawsuit to compel the University of Michigan to divulge such information.

The chilling of discourse about affirmative action is symptomatic of the shortchanging of the truth mission. Affirmative action is an important, inherently controversial issue, and honest debate on all sides of the issue can be found in countless domains in society. But it is often very difficult to discuss it on university campuses. Three of the most noted faculty critics of racial preferences at Berkeley – Jack Citrin, John Searle, and Martin Trow – told me that colleagues often inform them that they agree with their views on racial classifications but are reluctant to speak out publicly.[30] In fact, a 1995 Roper Center random survey of one thousand voting members of the University of California Academic Senate – sponsored by the generally conservative California Association of Scholars – found that only 31

---

[28] Connerly, *Creating Equal*, p. 134. See also Jerome Karabel, "No Alternative: The Effects of Color-Blind Admissions in California," in G. Orfield, E. Miller, and Harvard Civil Rights Project, eds., *Chilling Admissions: The Affirmative Action Crisis and the Search for Alternatives* (Harvard Education Publishing Group, 1998), pp. 33–50.

[29] See Andrea Guerrero, *Silence at Boalt: The Dismantling of Affirmative Action* (University of California Press, 2002), pp. 38–42.

[30] Interviews with John Searle and Jack Citrin, August 2001; interview with Martin Trow, Berkeley Graduate School of Public Policy and the Center for Studies in Higher Education, August 2001. See also Trow, "Reflections on 'Affirmative Action' in Higher Education," in Abigail Thernstrom and Stephan Thernstrom, eds., *Beyond the Color Line: New Perspectives on Race and Ethnicity* (Hoover Institution Press, 2001).

percent of respondents supported racial and gender preferences, whereas 48 percent supported color-blind and gender-blind policies.[31] And it is likely that the chilling of discourse on this important, controversial issue spills over into other areas of controversy concerning race. Rather than leading the country in opening up honest, civil discourse about race, universities appear to be doing a better job of providing models of how to chill discourse. For example, in the fall of 2003, conservative students at the University of Washington, Seattle, and the University of California, Irvine, were forced by their respective universities to stop conducting "affirmative action cookie sales," in which the students offered cookies at different prices based on the race of the purchaser. The sales were classic symbolic protests of public policy; and women's groups have held such sales for years to protest the "wage gap" between men and women. At Seattle, the protesters posted a sign that said, "Affirmative Action Is Racism." But opponents could not brook such an offense to campus orthodoxy. The police report stated that those who successfully opposed the symbolic speech "felt it was outrageous for the UW to let an organization promote such an event when cultural diversity should be celebrated and not looked down upon."[32]

The situation mirrors Timur Kuran's theory of self-censorship of true preferences: many people are intimidated to speak their minds because the penalty is too high.[33] Berkeley philosopher John Searle remarked, "In any university, though we're supposed to be committed to the free exchange of ideas, there are certain views that are really forbidden. You run into outrage if you even express those views. You can now attack the most extreme forms of affirmative action. I do all the time, but a lot of my colleagues are afraid to do so."[34]

Gunfights at the *Daily Cal*: The Lessons of Freedom

A series of extraordinary events beset the Berkeley student paper, the *Daily Californian*, in 2001 and 2002. The paper is independent of the school, receiving its funding from advertisers, although the student government (ASUC) does give it a discount on its rent for the entire fifth floor of Eshelman Hall, the student government building. Although it competes with a myriad of other student publications representing a wide range of perspectives, the *Daily Cal* – like most student newspapers – remains the main barometer of

---

[31] Roper Center Survey, reported on website of CAS: www.calscholars.org/roper/exsam.html. A similar nationwide Roper poll of faculty sponsored by the National Association of Scholars found that two-thirds supported color-blind policies. See www.nas.org/reports/roper/exsam.htm.

[32] Bruce Ramsey, "When Does Free Speech Become 'Fighting Words'?" *Seattle Times*, November 5, 2003, available at seattletimes.nwsource.com/html/opinion/2001783037.ramso5.html.

[33] Kuran, *Private Truths, Public Lies*.

[34] Interview with John Searle.

Darrin Bell's cartoon in the *Daily Californian*, September 19, 2001. Reproduced with permission.

campus opinion. (The free speech status of student papers is, therefore, often the most reliable indicator of the status of free speech on campus.)

Despite several incidences of censorship, the university handled the aftermath of the terrorist attacks on September 11, 2001, admirably. Arguments for and against the war on terrorism clashed vigorously in the pages of the *Daily Cal*, and advocates of both positions held demonstrations in the public forum that were not marred by hostile incidents.[35] I also attended a student forum on the war with Afghanistan in November 2001, at which the audience listened civilly to the views of both sides. Professor Alan Ross's presence on stage and the ground-clearing remarks of the moderator helped maintain the integrity of this particular public forum.

Nevertheless, the university did not escape this period without a major incident. On Tuesday, September 19, the *Daily Cal* published a cartoon by syndicated cartoonist Darrin Bell, depicting two long-bearded men dressed in robes and turbans, standing on a large hand, engulfed by flames. A "flight manual" drops from one man's hand while the other speaks: "We made it

[35] Interview with Berkeley history professor Reginald Zelnik, November 2001. Zelnik was one of the four faculty founders of FSM. See also Zelnik's comments along with political science professor Laura Stoker's in "UC Berkeley's Anti-War Stance Likely to Continue," *Daily Californian*, September 18, 2001.

to paradise! Now we will meet Allah, and be fed grapes, and be serviced by 70 virgin women, and...." Bell defended himself by maintaining that the men were caricatures of Osama bin Laden and that he merely meant to show that under the tenets of traditional Islam, they were destined for hell, not heaven.[36]

Bell's cartoon did not differ from many other cartoons that appeared across the country during that time, none of which is known to have incited hostility. Indeed, Bell's cartoon itself appeared elsewhere without incident. One reason controversy arose at Berkeley was that Berkeley's rather sizable Middle Eastern and Muslim community had been victimized by harassment, hate speech, threats, and even a few assaults in the days following 9/11. Muslim students felt endangered by these vicious acts, and the administration had to increase security to protect their safety. Even though the publication of the cartoon could in no way be construed as an incitement to violence against Muslims, the students nonetheless accused the *Daily Cal* of doing precisely that.[37] Citing the paper's immediate apology a few months earlier for publishing David Horowitz's paid editorial against the idea of monetary reparations for slavery, the students demanded similar treatment. But this time, the paper's staff was prepared to take a different stand. In order to understand the meaning of this stand, we need to look first at the Horowitz incident.

The Horowitz Incident

David Horowitz's paid advertisement listed ten reasons why monetary reparations for slavery are a bad idea (its text is reproduced in the Appendix). Published in 2001 at the end of Black History Month (February) and in a provocative style, the piece caused an uproar on campuses across the country, especially where student papers published it. Though hard-hitting and no doubt meant to provoke, the piece itself was not inherently racist. The virulent reactions that erupted on many campuses starkly exposed the gulf that lies between academe and the informed public regarding the range and importance of open discourse. About nine months earlier, the Internet journal, *Salon.com*, had published a similar version of Horowitz's advertisement along with a proreparations piece by another author. In follow-up letters, a vibrant joust ensued between the two sides. In an extraordinary article in *Salon.com* entitled "Who's Afraid of the Big Bad Horowitz?" written during the brouhaha nine months later, editor Joan Walsh wrote, "The debate was lively, argument on all sides got thoroughly aired, and a good time was had

---

[36] "Crowd Decries..." cites this, and the September 18 article. Darrin Bell, "You've Misunderstood My Cartoon," *Daily Californian*, September 20, 2001.

[37] See "UC Berkeley Arabs, Muslims Face Harassment," *Daily Californian*, September 13, 2001. Under the relevant First Amendment law, the cartoon fell way short of being an illegal incitement. See *Brandenburg v. Ohio*, 395 U.S. 444 (1969).

by all. Nobody picketed our offices. Nobody came to *Salon* with a list of grievances to be addressed. Nobody sought or was given an apology. Nobody called us racist."[38] But when Horowitz sent his opinion piece to student newspapers nine months later, it was greeted by a different mentality entirely.

The ad appeared in the *Daily Cal* on Wednesday, February 28. As at the *Badger Herald* at Madison, the *Daily Cal* published the ad without consulting with its advertising department, which had received the piece and had not fully considered its possible impact. As soon as the paper containing the advertisement hit the stands, thousands of copies disappeared before the public could get a copy. BAMN immediately denounced the paper as "racist." By midmorning, a group of about one hundred students showed up at the paper's offices, demanding an apology. Janny Hu was a member of the *Daily Cal* board at the time; the next academic year, she became the paper's editor in chief, replacing Daniel Hernandez, the editor in chief during the Horowitz affair. Hu related, "There was so much anger and hurt on the part of the protesters. They really thought that we were trying to hurt them. They just felt wounded."[39] The board was simply overwhelmed not only by the reproaches of BAMN and its allies but also by its own staff. (Meanwhile, at the *Badger Herald* in Wisconsin, the editors made a point of explaining the situation and getting the staff's opinion and consent, thereby purchasing room to maneuver in defense of free speech.) Hu described the staff as utterly unprepared to deal with the onslaught:

I was crying. It was very emotional.... It was a situation that none of us had gone through before and nobody expected that kind of reaction. Our staffers were really affected. Some of the staffers came to me afterwards and said things like, "How in the hell could we have run such an ad?" and so on. No one understood the process. And we did not have the answers at that time. So it was not just the protesters outside of the office, but we had staffers yelling at us as well.[40]

The beleaguered board met and immediately decided to apologize. The protesters even suggested the content of the apology letter. When asked if she and her colleagues thought they did the right thing in retrospect, Hu replied without hesitation, "Looking at it twenty/twenty hindsight, obviously not. I don't think we really understood what that meant. At the time we thought we were doing the right thing."[41]

In the unsigned apology for the whole paper that appeared the next day on the front page, the *Daily Cal* editors confessed that the paper had allowed itself "to become an inadvertent vehicle for bigotry." Hernandez wrote a longer apology as editor in chief. While conceding that the ad was racist, he partially blamed the ineffectiveness of the paper's review process. Ignoring

[38] Joan Walsh, "Who's Afraid of the Big Bad Horowitz?" *www.Salon.com*, March 9, 2001.
[39] Interview with Janny Hu, November 2001.
[40] Ibid.
[41] Ibid.

the fact that many historically important political and moral statements have appeared as paid advertisements, Hernandez also justified the decision to apologize by drawing a distinction between paid advertising and opinions expressed on the editorial and news pages. "Freedom of speech is compromised when it is *bought*."[42]

That same day BAMN and a coalition of groups held a rally and circulated a flier accusing the *Daily Cal* of racism. There was support for the paper's right to freedom of speech on campus – several letters to the editor published the next week showed this. But the *Daily Cal*'s apology left its potential supporters in the lurch, creating a strange public discourse in which the champions of free speech were not able to attach their allegiance to a concrete institution. The hapless paper found itself under attack from both sides, as the apology failed to assuage the wrath of the ad's objectors, and alienated the friends of free speech. Photographer Ben Miller recalled, "we got it from both sides. Nobody was happy with us at all."[43]

During this episode, no faculty members or administrators spoke up in support of the First Amendment or free speech, either in the press or in public.[44] In addition, the campus ACLU, which had just been revived, was barely visible. Several people I interviewed were distressed at the ACLU's lack of presence in this and other free speech issues. At the monthly ACLU meeting that I attended in November 2001, it was evident that libertarian free speech issues took a back seat to issues concerning identity politics. And in the debate in the fall of 2001 over what sort of actions the student government should take against the *Daily Cal* concerning Darrin Bell's cartoon, the ACLU recommended sensitivity training as a compromise.[45]

In the summer of 2000, the journalist Jonathan Rauch gave an address at a gathering of several college newspaper editors in Washington, D.C. Playing devil's advocate, he presented hypothetical situations to prod the students into conceding that not publishing an inflammatory article might be advisable in certain circumstances. As his "what-if" situations strove to convince more student editors, Daniel Hernandez and most others remained holdouts, refusing to compromise their positions. Rather than judging Hernandez for being hypocritical for his apology several months later, Rauch – who had no doubt that Horowitz's advertisement should be allowed into the marketplace of ideas – pointed to the lack of support at Berkeley as one potential reason for Hernandez's capitulation in the face of mob anger. At Madison, the

---

[42] "To Our Readers"; and "Holding Ourselves Accountable," letter from the editor, *Daily Californian*, March 1, 2001 (emphasis in original). See, e.g., *New York Times v. Sullivan*, 376 U.S. 254 (1964).

[43] Interview with Ben Miller.

[44] See, e.g., interviews with Anand Upadhye, James Gallagher, Janny Hu, and Ben Miller. No such letters appeared in the *Daily Californian*, for example.

[45] UC Berkeley ACLU meeting, Friday, November 9, 2001; interviews with Berkeley students Anand Upadhye and James Gallagher.

Committee for Academic Freedom and Rights gave its unequivocal support to the *Badger Herald* even before it published its editorial refusing to apologize. "Hernandez and the *Daily Cal*, by contrast, dangled in the wind."[46]

Rauch's portrayal also highlights the difference between rhetorical commitment and actual commitment under pressure. For example, when the leadership of the *Badger Herald* apologized for a cartoon in 1998 under circumstances that closely resembled the controversy swirling around the *Daily Cal* (see Chapter 7), an editor who resigned in disgust the next day observed that those who had previously been the most vociferous advocates of free speech were among the first ones to run for cover. As Kristin R. Monroe has insightfully shown, individuals often have to decide quickly what to do in high-pressure situations, for the "window of moral opportunity" is usually very limited. Monroe's most memorable examples are Germans' decisions whether to help Jews escape from Nazis during the Holocaust. One may fail to make the right decision because of cowardice, or simply because one is not prepared to act decisively in the moment of crisis.[47]

Hit from the Other Side

According to Ben Miller, "the real trouble started when we apologized for [the Horowitz ad]."[48] Letters that poured in to the editor were evenly split between those who denounced publication of the advertisement and those who disdained the paper's apology. I can provide only a sample of letters. One alumnus who refused to accept the apology compared publication of the ad to slavery itself: "There are no words that can accommodate your act nor the holocaust of enslavement." A student expressed "shock and outrage," while another was "extremely upset, offended, and appalled by the complete disregard of the black community." Another proclaimed, "Never again should an ad be published in a paper that is connected to such an institution of high statutes [*sic*] where students of all ethnic backgrounds study to earn degrees."[49]

Several of the letters on the other side came from alumni and individuals outside the university (though certainly not all), including one from alumnus David Horowitz himself, who criticized both the decision to apologize and the paper's interpretation of the ad's content. Again, I provide a representative sample. One writer exclaimed, "The *Daily Cal*'s response to David

---

[46] Rauch, "A College Newspaper Messes Up, and So Might You," *National Journal*, March 24, 2001. I also discussed this matter on the phone with Rauch in March 2001.

[47] See Benjamin Thompson, "Paper of Protest: A Short History of Free Speech Disputes at the *Badger Herald*" (Senior thesis, University of Wisconsin, Madison, May 2002); Kristin R. Monroe, *The Heart of Altruism: Perceptions of a Common Humanity* (Princeton University Press, 1996).

[48] Interview with Ben Miller.

[49] "Ad's Publication Disgraces University," letter to the editor, *Daily Californian*, March 6, 2001.

Horowitz's ad is outrageous. This is censorship at its worst and at – of all places – Berkeley, the so-called purveyor of free speech." The editor of the *Cal Patriot* asked, "Why is the *Daily Cal* apologizing for inadvertently exposing its readers to an alternative viewpoint?" Another alumnus mocked the paper: "Apologize! Of course! Grovel at the feet of the whining campus black wounded by the truth. Display the *Daily Cal's* 'tolerance' and 'compassion' with shriveling *mea culpas*. Whatever happened to brave *Daily Cal* editors who had the cajones to proudly buck the establishment?"[50]

These samples barely indicate the mountain of criticism thrust upon the *Daily Californian* from outside the university. In a world connected by e-mail and the Internet, any locale can find itself the center – and target – of national and international attention; during the Horowitz controversy the student papers at Brown, Berkeley, and Wisconsin were deluged with e-mails and hits on their websites. The hapless Hernandez bore the brunt of the criticism, receiving hundreds of e-mails calling him and the paper "gutless cowards."[51] But it was the avalanche of national criticism from their peers in the media that had the greatest impact on the paper's leaders. "Had we not had that national media backlash, I don't know that any of us would have thought twice about it being wrong to apologize," Hu stated. "I know that I started to self-educate myself on the First Amendment afterwards."[52] Stories appeared in the local and national media, including the *Los Angeles Times*, *Wall Street Journal*, *New York Times*, *U.S.A. Today*, *New York Daily News*, and national television. Perhaps the most hard-hitting commentary came from the seasoned journalist, Jonathan Yardley, in the *Washington Post*, who also turned his sights on the weak character of the contemporary university:

Crying racism or any other ism – sexism, ageism, imperialism, homophobia, you name it – is the easy way out. Instead of coming to grips with the case made by one's opponents, just smear them with the tar of bigotry.... It's an old trick that's been employed by just about every special interest group in today's hothouse of competing grievances, and by now most Americans are probably wise to it. But the American college campus is a foreign country; they do things differently there.[53]

Horowitz's Forum

Just when people sighed in relief that the *Daily Cal's* apology had defused the situation, College Republicans and the conservative student publication the *Patriot* invited Horowitz to give a speech on March 15. The student slated to introduce Horowitz was the event's organizer, Ben Carrasco, whose parents – like Hernandez's – were Mexican immigrants who had risen through hard

[50] "Apology Undermines Freedom of Speech," letter to the editor, *Daily Californian*, March 6, 2001.

[51] Interview with Janny Hu.

[52] Ibid.

[53] Jonathan Yardley, "Politically Corrected," *Washington Post*, March 5, 2001.

work. A conservative, Carrasco had little patience for those who "complain about stupid comments that generally mean nothing except stupidity."[54] Carrasco asked someone from College Democrats and the ACLU to debate Horowitz, but they declined the invitation.

Two days before Horowitz's arrival, seventy-five students from such groups as Bridges, the Black Recruitment and Retention Center, the Black Board, and the African-American Student Development Office held well-organized demonstrations on campus, which they called "Black Out" to symbolize the lack of visibility of African American interests on campus. Dressed in black and wearing black bandanas over their mouths as masks, groups of demonstrators entered random classrooms at various times and stood silently in the background for several minutes before leaving. At noon, demonstrators locked arms and blocked the path between Sproul Plaza and Sather Gate while distributing fliers to students in Sproul. The fliers listed several complaints, including lack of office space and staffing for the groups, the presence of such "racist" publications as the *Patriot*, and the *Daily Cal's* publication of Horowitz's ad.

One physiology professor considered the demonstration in his class improperly disruptive and "startling" but conceded that "it was well behaved." Demonstrators also entered the class of public policy professor David Kirp, who that day happened to be dealing with the free speech rights of white hate groups. Although he and his students were initially intimidated, Kirp turned the situation to his pedagogical advantage by discussing the First Amendment rights of protesters in such situations. Kirp remarked that many students "had enough confidence in one another to risk putting their own ideas on the line."[55]

But free speech at Berkeley often takes one step up, two steps back. The week of the event began inauspiciously with the response that Horowitz received to his letter asking Chancellor Berdahl to introduce him at his talk. It was a chance for the chancellor to take a strong, public stand in favor of open and vibrant discourse in a tense situation that mattered. Replying on behalf of the chancellor, Assistant Chancellor John Cummins chided Horowitz for even raising the issue of reparations on the campus, as the administration had detected "no active discussion of such claims on this campus." (Horowitz wrote that his student hosts had informed him that there had been a "Reparations Awareness Day" on campus during Black History Month, and that several professors had spoken in favor of reparations in class.) Claiming that Berkeley needed no dialogue when it came to this erstwhile most contentious of issues, Cummins in effect derided Horowitz for having the gall to take the wrong side in such a public fashion: "You indicate that in response to

---

[54] Carrasco, quoted in David Horowitz, *Uncivil Wars: The Controversy over Reparations for Slavery* (Encounter Books, 2002), pp. 23–24.

[55] David Kirp, "When a Classroom Becomes the Lesson," *California Monthly*, June 2001.

the 'swift and hostile' reaction to the advertisement, other voices from the community have spoken up, demonstrating the desire for a genuine dialogue on this subject. No demand for 'dialogue' existed prior to your effort to provoke it." Cummins concluded by informing Horowitz that the university could not guarantee that he would not be shouted down, "because the right of free expression also belongs to those who disagree with you."[56]

Security at the actual event was high. The three hundred attendees had to pass through metal detectors and police inspections before filing into the lecture hall in the Life Sciences Building, while members of the Spartacist Youth League rallied outside, denouncing the speaker as an offspring of the Ku Klux Klan. (Racial groups did not show up, choosing a boycott over confrontation.) Uniformed officers lined the hallways, and armed guards even checked the stalls before Horowitz entered the bathroom. In an editorial, the *Daily Cal* chastised College Republicans for excessive security, charging that the precautions were designed to "demonize the opposition." "Thankfully," the editorial continued, "the opposition just didn't show up. Despite the misplaced presence of a socialist picket-line, we applaud the campus groups who boycotted Horowitz's speech to avoid dignifying it with a response."[57]

Despite the fuss, Horowitz's speech itself actually went better than might have been expected. He began by speaking about his own past involvement with the Black Panthers and other leftist causes, McCarthyism on the left, the new "sensitivity," and the problems that arise when the feeling of being offended engenders censorship. He then addressed the failure of the university administrators to foster and support free speech principles, at one point singling out Cummins in the audience. Then he dealt with the issue of reparations. He was able to finish his talk. "Until then, the crowd had been fairly well-behaved."[58] The problem arose with the question-and-answer session. Members of the audience began making speeches and baiting Horowitz, calling him a "racist" point blank. As catcalls and shouts rained down upon the speaker, campus police asked Carrasco to shut off the microphones, an act that only incited accusations of "censorship" from the audience. With tension escalating, Horowitz no longer felt safe and exited the stage. Cummins gave the *Daily Cal* his assessment of the event: "The event, in a sense, symbolized the argument that [Horowitz] was putting forward about the 'PC' nature of Berkeley and the difficulty of free speech on this campus. I completely disagree with his argument, and the event itself illustrated that our students do not need someone like David Horowitz to tell them to speak freely – they do it all the time."[59]

[56] Cummins letter, reported in Horowitz, *Uncivil Wars*, pp. 32–33.
[57] "Pulling the Plug on (Contrived) Free Speech," editorial, *Daily Californian*, March 20, 2001.
[58] Horowitz, *Uncivil Wars*, p. 40.
[59] Steve Sexton, *Daily Californian*, March 16, 2001.

In the event's aftermath, the *Daily Californian* and others blamed Horowitz and College Republicans for not giving opponents a chance to express their criticisms. "Instead of debate, Horowitz retreated," the paper editorialized. Horowitz defended his quick exit by pointing out that it was his – not the critics – whose safety was at risk.[60] Whether danger loomed or not, the event had a surreal quality. As a fitting end to the festivities, a member of College Republicans made an unusual citizen's arrest of a graduate student whom he had allegedly overheard telling a friend about a bomb he was going to place in the Life Sciences Building. Police made the arrest and set bail at $20,000. The next morning, the authorities dropped all charges when the arrested graduate student charged racial profiling.[61]

Cummins's cryptic remarks notwithstanding, troubled times had come for free speech at Berkeley. And with the exception of a few intrepid activists on the right, no voice with broader appeal or respect appeared to champion free speech.

Renewal

As one would expect, when President George W. Bush began the war in Afghanistan, strong antiwar sentiment reigned in the Berkeley area. The Berkeley Stop the War Coalition and other groups that considered the war racist and imperialist held rallies decrying U.S. action. Outside the campus, Congresswoman Barbara Lee, who represents the Oakland-Berkeley area, was the only member of Congress to vote against authorizing the Bush administration to conduct the war – an act praised by the Berkeley City Council and the *Daily Californian*.[62] But war supporters also filled the public square, with such groups as Pro-America and others holding rallies. A lively debate erupted in the letters and op-ed columns of the *Daily Cal*; by early 2002 the *Daily Cal* was even reporting that the antiwar movement on campus had run out of steam, causing dismay among those committed to Berkeley's radical legacy.[63]

If the *Daily Cal*'s refusal to apologize for Darrin Bell's cartoon did not contribute to the pro–free speech climate in a major way, it certainly helped to set the tone for the campus. Aggrieved students interpreted the cartoon as an offensive stereotype and a potentially dangerous incitement in already tense

---

[60] "Pulling the Plug"; Horowitz, *Uncivil Wars*, p. 41.
[61] Erin Gallagher, "Alleged Threat Pits One Student against Another: Citizen's Arrest Takes Place at Horowitz Speech," *Daily Californian*, March 20, 2001.
[62] See Eve Lotter, "A New Movement Emerges against War: Violence: Anti-War Coalitions Form at College Campuses across U.S.," *Daily Californian*, September 18, 2001; "Barbara Lee: A Voice of Reason, a True Patriot," editorial, *Daily Californian*, September 18, 2001.
[63] See K. C. Crain, "Demonstrators Support War on Terror," *Daily Californian*, September 25, 2001; "Pro-War, Pro-Peace Lures Campus into Debate," letter to the editor, *Daily Californian*, September 27, 2001; Nate Tabak, "Anti-War Protests Lose Steam, Lack Vigor of Campus's Past," *Daily Californian*, January 22, 2002.

circumstances. As it had with the Horowitz affair, the *Daily Cal* published dozens of letters representing both sides of the free speech issue. Here are a few representative examples. A Boalt Law School student who belonged to a group called Justice for Palestine excoriated the cartoon for being "the most vile form of ethnic characterization because it comes during a time when many people are suffering a severe backlash." Another student lashed out at the *Daily Californian's* inclination to be a lightning rod for controversy: "In my four years at Cal, I have seen much criticism of the *Daily Californian's* continuous use of the excuse 'fair content' and 'free speech' to justify offensive, hate-filled, powerful advertisements, columns and cartoons that aggravate nearly all at this hallowed university. At times I wonder why the paper is even distributed on this campus." The president of the Muslim Student Association stated, "The cartoon says Muslims – not crazy people – Muslims did it. [It makes people think that] anyone who has a beard is a terrorist."[64] Kevin Deliban, a student judicial advocate and a keen observer of the student scene, writes a weekly journal on the Web addressing student issues. He was critical but less shrill. "I am part Arab myself, [but] I personally did not find [the cartoon] super offensive. It was like, 'I can't believe they did this,' almost laughingly. [But] I *was* offended that something like this would be printed. . . . They should have been more sensitive."[65]

When the *Daily Cal* refused to apologize, the political reaction was swift. Large groups of students held demonstrations and carried signs calling the paper "racist" and proclaiming that it was guilty of "hate crimes." Once again, an entire print of newspapers vanished from stands in the early morning dawn. Campus police undertook an investigation that yielded the usual nothing.

The big event was the demonstration by one hundred students who demanded an apology at the *Daily Cal* offices at 7 P.M. on the day the cartoon appeared. They remained until midnight, yelling, chanting, crying, and pounding on the doors. The situation resembled the protest over Horowitz, and students expected a similar result. But this time the leaders of the *Daily Cal* neither allowed the group to enter its headquarters nor apologized. The only real debate on the editorial board had been over the original decision to run the cartoon. The ten members of the board took only fifteen minutes to decide not to apologize when the demonstrators issued their demands, and the rest of the staff agreed. But they did not inform the demonstrators of their decision that night. Instead, they asked the campus police to remove the demonstrators at midnight and waited to announce their decision in the paper the next day. The new editor in chief, Janny Hu, said that the staff

---

[64] "Free Speech Comes with Responsibility," letter to the editor, *Daily Californian*, September 20, 2001; Eric Ostrum, "Crowd Decries Lack of Apology," *Daily Californian*, September 20, 2001.

[65] Interview with Kevin Deliban, November 2001.

had learned both normative and strategic lessons from the Horowitz de-
bacle the previous spring: "It was an easy conclusion, not highly debated.
We knew what the consequences would be if we [apologized] from experience. Protesters and their emotions cannot persuade us. . . . The consensus
was pretty immediate among us that we would not apologize. . . . We felt that
this was our opportunity to maybe right a wrong judgment last year."[66] Ben
Miller's perspective paralleled Hu's: "After the Horowitz thing, it was very
clear that we were not going to apologize this time around. They decided the
day it was published that they were not going to apologize and they decided
they were not going to tell the demonstrators that they were not going to
apologize until they got the paper out and the UC Police Department had
more people there."[67]

The next day the *Daily Californian* published an editorial entitled "Campus
Must Foster Open Discussion." The editorial decried attacks on Muslim
citizens on and off campus, yet asserted that the cartoon was not linked to
such loathsome acts. (In contrast, Muslim Student Association leader Sajid
Khan asserted in the ASUC senate that there was "not direct causation,
but direct correlation" between the cartoon and violence against Muslim
students.)[68] The editorial then linked the paper's predicament to the broader
threat against civil liberties – a concern shared by Muslims and many other
erstwhile critics of the paper – and reminded readers that the paper had
been the campus's most prominent counselor of caution and thoughtfulness
in the midst of September 11 anxieties. The editorial affirmed the paper's
institutional obligations as a protector and promoter of free speech:

The cartoon falls within the realm of free speech. It was printed on the Opinion page
of our paper, a section that has housed many other controversial cartoons and letters
that we do not always agree with, but print because they represent our readership's
opinions. . . . There is a quote commonly attributed to Voltaire that reads, "I may not
agree with what you say, but I will defend to the death, your right to say it." . . . It
is only through a civil dialogue that we can ever hope to undertake the first steps in
rebuilding this country.[69]

The editorial sparked further anger and provoked some people to hack
into the paper's website to post a fake apology. Some student senators then
dragged the paper's rental arrangement before the ASUC's legislative body,
advocating a rent increase. (Such action would probably have been unconstitutional, as the Supreme Court has invalidated taxes that are targeted at

---

[66] Interview with Janny Hu.
[67] Interview with Ben Miller. See also Eric Ostrum, "Crowd Occupies Daily Californian Office
over Controversial Cartoon: Editors Decide against Printing Apology in Today's Edition,"
Daily Californian, September 19, 2001.
[68] ASUC Senate Notes, October 10, 2001.
[69] "Campus Must Foster Open Discussion," editorial, *Daily Californian*, September 20, 2001.

the press, per se.)[70] But when the smoke cleared, the *Daily Cal*'s strong stand won a pivotal victory for free speech in the public forum. Principled strength speaks for itself, energizing supporters while attracting the undecided. The *Daily Cal*'s decision was the first example in memory at Berkeley of an institution with a campuswide constituency and responsibility taking a firm and eloquent public stand under formidable pressure in favor of free speech. When the staff of the *Daily Cal* drew this line in the sand, it established a precedent that might have influenced the emergence of more public support for free speech on campus that academic year.

This was also a lesson that Hasdai Westbrook learned as the editor of the editorial page of the *Badger Herald* at Wisconsin in the fall of 2000. During that semester, student groups threatened to take over the paper's offices to protest the publication of articles that had criticized "white power analysis" that Westbrook had printed in the op-ed section. (Each article was clearly within the bounds of legitimate discourse.) Westbrook published them because he had a strong commitment to robust discourse about controversial issues. His adversaries alluded to what had happened in the fall of 1998, when a group representing the multicultural coalition on campus, outraged over a cartoon, had coerced the *Herald* into publishing an apology that the group had dictated (see Chapter 7). Westbrook's response was clear and strong: "I will not issue an apology and I will not stop publishing what I see as fit. What I will do is give you space to have your say, which I hope you do." Westbrook said that he had come to realize that the only way to deal with such pressure is through strength, as weakness is inherently wrong and only begets more pressure. (He also contacted the faculty group, the Committee for Academic Freedom and Rights, to enlist broader campus support. CAFR gave him the support right away.) The editors of the *Herald* acted through a similar understanding of the relationship between power and principle in the battle over Horowitz's advertisement in their paper. Like Janny Hu and the board of the *Daily Californian*, Julie Bosman, Alex Conant, Ben Thompson, Katie Harbath, Jay Senter, and their allies used the 1998 humiliation as a model of what not to do.

When the *Daily Cal* took its stand in September 2001, its institutional support was no stronger than it had been during the Horowitz affair. One faculty member did send it a private supportive e-mail, but no one in a position of pedagogical or administrative responsibility spoke out on the paper's behalf. But the paper did receive some meaningful support in the ASUC senate in the debate over its rent.

The debate over Senate Bill 67 encapsulated the conflict between the model of free speech citizenship and the model of sensitivity and victimology.

---

[70] See, e.g., *Arkansas Writer's Project, Inc. v. Ragland*, 481 U.S. 221 (1987); *Minnesota Star and Tribune v. Minnesota Commission of Review*, 460 U.S. 575 (1983); *Grosjean v. American Press Co.*, 297 U.S. 233 (1936).

The minutes of the debate reveal deep disillusionment with constitutional freedoms on the part of most senators, as well as a lack of understanding of its basic principles – even on the part of some of the *Daily Cal*'s supporters. However, a few senators demonstrated both understanding and courage.

Originally, the purpose of the bill was to raise the rent on the *Daily Cal* in Eshelman Hall in retaliation for its refusal to apologize for Bell's cartoon. Many senators pointed to the *Daily Cal*'s history of causing offense, saying that the recent cartoon represented the last straw. Many thought that something had to be done to illustrate that the cartoon amounted to an offense to community values and to dissociate the student government from the paper. Senator Khan, who originally pressed this position, considered the cartoon "one of the most extremely offensive things he's seen come out in a long time." According to the minutes, Kahn said that "His concern was that the ASUC was basically, in some way, supporting the hate speech that appeared on Tuesday, by having the *Daily Cal* in the building."[71]

By the time of the vote, on October 10, the bill had been amended to drop the rent provision in favor of a proposal that "requested" the *Daily Cal* to apologize and have its staff undergo "sensitivity training." The change came about because some senators and even the campus ACLU realized that the original bill bordered on censorship. Spectators packed the ASUC chamber for the first time in anyone's memory to witness the tense debate. Most senators supported the sensitivity training provision, but a few defended the paper. Richard Schulman declared that a paper has an obligation to be honest about its views and referred to how senate condemnation of a magazine he had worked at the previous year – the *Heuristic Squelch Magazine* – had made the staff "afraid to publish sometimes what they wanted to say." Schulman also pointed out that he had received e-mails from many advocates of free speech nationwide, including the American Cartoonists Society, "saying the bill was a joke," and that the senate would "be a national embarrassment" if it passed the measure. In response, someone identified only as Michelle drew applause when she announced that she "felt papers *should* [my italics] be in fear."

Others who spoke ably against the bill were Anand Upadhye, Jesse Gabrail, Joanne Liu, and James Gallagher (also of the *Patriot*). Pointing to the universality of free speech principles, Upadhye talked about how free speech principles empowered the rights of all students, including those who disdained the *Daily Cal*. Gallagher spoke about the dangers of playing the victimology card: "As to whether it [*Daily Californian*] was insensitive, he could name a million political cartoons he's been really offended by, but he wouldn't beg the papers to apologize and condemn them. . . . For the David

---

[71] ASUC Notes, September 19, 2001.

Horowitz ad, the paper did apologize for that, but Cal was the laughing stock of the national media after that."[72]

Senate Bill 67 passed, 11-7, with one abstention. In the end, the bill had merely symbolic value, as the *Daily Cal* simply ignored it without encountering any reprisal. It is interesting to note that immediately after this vote, the senate passed Senate Bill 65, which called on the university not to cooperate with the government in spying or providing information on foreign students. This vote was animated by a concern for civil liberties.

The "Thieves of Liberty": New Critiques of Progressive Censorship

Yet another skirmish broke out on February 26, 2002, when the monthly publication, the *Cal Patriot*, published an article critical of MEChA, the militant Chicano activist group. Entitled "MEChA: Student Funded Bigotry and Hate," the article criticized MEChA for impeding "advances in civil rights toward a colorblind society," "fomenting anti-American hate," and promoting a "mentality that leads its adherents to believe anyone who is white and male is to blame for any historical injustice."[73]

Considering the article in the *Patriot* to be an unprovoked assault, MEChA and supporters surrounded and harassed *Patriot* and College Republican staff members as they distributed the publication on Sproul Plaza. Someone also circulated fliers falsely accusing the College Republicans of opposing an investigation of Enron. The *Patriot* staff received death threats from unidentified sources. Finally, unknown individuals burglarized the *Patriot*'s offices in the dead of night and stole three thousand copies of the magazine – the entire remaining run, worth between $1,500 and $2,000.[74]

As a hard-hitting conservative publication, the *Patriot* is considerably more controversial than the *Daily Cal*. Not surprisingly, it received its share of criticism for publishing the article. But the offenses against the publication provoked widespread campus condemnation and concern for the state of free speech. (Everyone was careful in public not to accuse MEChA of the crimes, as the culprits remained unidentified.) Perhaps sensing a possible shift in campus opinion, the *Daily Cal* editors built on the foundation they had laid the previous semester and wrote an editorial entitled "Thieves of Liberty," which invoked Berkeley's heritage of free speech. That heritage,

---

[72] All speakers in ASUC Senate Notes, October 10, 2001.

[73] See the *Patriot*'s report of the incident on the World Net News website: www.worldnetdaily.com/news/article.asp?ARTICLE_ID=26652. For the Berkeley MEChA website, see http://berkeleymecha.org/main/.

[74] See John Cise, "Copies of *California Patriot* Stolen: Publication Staff Allegedly Harassed. Break-In May Be Reaction to Article in February Issue," *Daily Californian*, February 27, 2002.

they wrote, was being betrayed not by the administration but by students in the name of their own moral agendas:

Back in the 1960s when thousands of UC Berkeley students rallied on Sproul Plaza demanding free speech, they wanted protection from an administration bent on suppression of opinion.

But that was then. Now, sadly enough, free speech needs protection not from administration or government, but from UC Berkeley students. . . .

Those behind the theft think themselves noble. The rest of the world knows they are criminal, and striking at one of the roots of American, and civil, society.[75]

The editorial included a quotation from a letter Chancellor Berdahl had written to the *Daily Cal* that also appeared that day. In the previous fall, the chancellor had made a public statement shortly after September 11 calling for tolerance of ideas and disagreement in an environment gripped by fear. It was a necessary stance, but many on the right gave it short shrift because it was easy to take such a stand in the wake of the events of September 11, when speech on the left was thrown into jeopardy. This time around, there was no equivocating. Berdahl clearly linked the *Patriot's* free speech rights to the broader institutional mission. The mission of the university and the rights of the most unpopular publication on campus are indivisible, he wrote. Berdahl also promised that the university would investigate the crimes and bring criminal charges if the culprits were apprehended:

Thefts of publications or any interference with the access of individuals or groups to freedom of expression is unconscionable behavior. Such actions are completely antithetical to the values that form the foundation of our democracy, and such actions are particularly egregious in an educational setting. Over the past few years, there have been several instances of this behavior. These acts diminish our community.[76]

Several letters to the editor bemoaned the theft of liberty, while no one wrote on behalf of the other side. The president of College Republicans and the publisher of the *Patriot* also wrote an op-ed piece that appeared that day, calling on the university to take action to reverse free speech's long slide at Berkeley. "If the university truly supports free speech it must act to defend it. If there is to be a free exchange of ideas on this campus, the university cannot sit idly by as thousands of publications are stolen year after year."[77]

At long last, the advocates of free speech appeared to be gaining, at least for a time, while the proponents and practitioners of social censorship and sensitivity lost ground. Even the debate in the ASUC senate reflected the shift, however haltingly. Although a few senators chastised the *Patriot* and supported the members of MEChA who spoke to register the pain they suffered

---

[75] "Thieves of Liberty," editorial, *Daily Californian*, February 28, 2002.

[76] Robert M. Berdahl, letter to the editor, *Daily Californian*, February 28, 2002.

[77] Robb McFadden and Kelso G. Barnett, "It's Time, Once Again, to Defend Free Speech," *Daily Californian*, February 28, 2002.

for being severely criticized, only one speaker seemed to excuse the crimes against the *Patriot*. BAMN's leader Hoku Jeffries stated that, while he deplored the transgressions, the *Patriot* was more or less asking for it.[78] Though it was a rare free speech moment in the sun, one must remain somewhat circumspect about rushing to conclusions. The university never discovered who the "thieves of liberty" were, and the matter receded into the shadows as time went on.

Lepawsky's Prophecy

The struggles between 2001 and 2002 held the promise of a turning point for free speech at Berkeley. For the first time in memory, overwhelming student and campus opinion supported the free speech rights of a conservative publication that was perhaps the most opposed publication on campus. The *Daily Californian* – which had recently raised its own free speech stature by taking a strong stand under pressure – led the way, and the chancellor defended the *Patriot*'s rights in unusually firm and unqualified language. Supporters of free inquiry and discourse were finally finding more support against those who considered sensitivity to be paramount. Segments of the university community had revivified the priorities that Professor Albert Lepawsky had called for in his prescient essay written at the height of the free speech movement (see Chapter 1): "The main task we face is preserving the university not merely as a free political community but primarily as an institution which is privileged to be an intellectual sanctuary within a greater society that is now in political flux. . . . any conflict between the intellectual and political way of life must be resolved in favor of the primacy of the intellectual over the political."[79]

We can draw a few conclusions from the experiences just chronicled. First, it seems clear that those whose free speech has been violated or jeopardized must stand up for their rights. If they do not, they will probably not attract broader support. The marketplace of ideas is kept open and vibrant by unpopular individuals and groups claiming and battling for their own rights. The First Amendment has been built through the words of dissenters and outsiders.[80]

Outsiders can gain credibility when they link themselves to more transcendent principles, such as the mission of the institution and the rights

---

[78] ASUC Senate Notes, February 27, 2002.
[79] Albert Lepawsky, "Intellectual Responsibility and Political Conduct," in Seymour Martin Lipset and Sheldon S. Wolin, eds., *The Berkeley Student Revolt: Facts and Interpretations* (Doubleday Anchor, 1965), p. 272.
[80] See, e.g., Shawn Francis Peters, *Judging Jehovah's Witnesses: Religious Persecution and the Dawn of Rights Revolution* (University of Kansas Press, 2000).

of others.[81] (One questions, therefore, the wisdom of groups calling for exemptions from the rigors of free speech's effects rather than declaring their equal capacity to deal constructively with criticism. The former approach divides and eviscerates, whereas the latter approach establishes common ground, and inner strength upon which differences can then flourish.)[82] This result can be achieved through public persuasion, as well as through winning the support of those whose audience includes a broader, more universal constituency – such as the chancellor or president of a university, or the student newspaper. In the *Patriot* case, all these factors came together, as the publication's spokespersons were strong and eloquent defenders of their own rights, rights backed by the chancellor, the *Daily Californian*, and general campus opinion. The letters to the editor of the *Daily Cal* were unanimously opposed to the violations against the *Patriot*.

The importance of leadership is undeniable, among student organizations and in the university administration. Berkeley political scientist William Muir told me that even universities tend to reflect the character of their administrative leader, and Berkeley is no exception. It remained to be seen if Berdahl's renewed faith in free speech would persist and make a difference.[83] Still notably absent from the Berkeley scene is any organized faculty involvement.

It is also important to expose what is happening to free speech inside the university to the outside world. The world outside academe has reacted swiftly and negatively to universities' adoptions of policies that unduly restrict liberty. (Recall Jonathan Yardley's depiction earlier in this chapter of the university as a "foreign" country within America. The world outside the university's gates is less stricken by aggressive identity politics and more respectful of free speech.) When the *Daily Cal*'s apology over the Horowitz advertisement hit national media opinion, the chastened editors were taught to take the First Amendment and free speech seriously. Even the administration at Columbia University was compelled – however reluctantly – to revise the sexual misconduct policy. The one major difference that distinguishes the situations at Berkeley and Columbia from Wisconsin and Penn was that the faculty at the first two schools remained inattentive to the threats against civil liberty. At Berkeley, student supporters of free speech in the public forum and press were left to fight the battle on their own with their own guile. Indeed, no one bears a greater obligation to protect free speech values than faculty. Students can be indispensable in building institutional legacies, as I discuss in the chapters on Wisconsin. But in the end, they come and go. The faculty embody the institutional memory and bedrock of the institution.

---

[81] This is the logic of what Tocqueville called "self-interest rightly understood." *Democracy in America*, vol. 2, bk. 2, chs. 8 and 9.

[82] See, e.g., Jose Ortega y Gasset, *Concord and Liberty*, trans. H. Wryl (Norton, 1946).

[83] Interview with William Ker Muir.

Meaningful faculty support at Berkeley could have given a real boost to the fledgling renewal of free speech.

Let us now turn to the debates over free speech and inquiry that animated Boalt Hall during the 1997–98 academic year, when the Law School was thrown into turmoil by student reactions to the dramatic drop in minority enrollment in the first entering class after Proposition 209, ending race-based enrollments, had passed into law.

Social Censorship at Boalt Hall

The decline in minority enrollment at Boalt had a profound effect on the school, and some critics of Proposition 209 made good arguments that dwindling diversity would compromise the quality of discussion and debate. At the same time, however, those opposed to 209 created their own form of *social* censorship that itself compromised discourse in class and out. The Boalt experience during this tense period poignantly illustrates how the lack of an institutional and public commitment to the principles of open discourse creates a vacuum into which other agendas can pour. The free speech voices that emerged lacked an organized public dimension, thereby assuming the posture of an alienated protest rather than a plausible political movement. What happened during the 1997–98 academic year is a story of how a silent majority was left stranded by the failure of a leadership group to step forward. Private truths did not become public truths.

I was able to interview a number of faculty and students who were at Boalt during the 1997–98 year. Unfortunately, only one student involved in the anti-209 movement responded to my letters by granting me an interview, and she eventually declined to sign a consent form. But I am able to draw upon the writings of several students from this movement who published their thoughts on the events of that year.

Background

Boalt Hall was a national pioneer in diversity, having instituted an aggressive affirmative action program in the late 1960s that lasted until the passage of Special Policies 1 and 2 (SP 1 & 2) and Proposition 209 in 1995 and 1996. For thirty years, Boalt was the scene of student strikes and activism over a host of issues involving diversity, including the famous campuswide "Third World Strike" of the late 1960s and periodic pressure to increase minority enrollment and faculty hires at the Law School.[84] These pressures helped to produce results, as more than 30 percent of new Boalt students were

---

[84] Interview with Boalt law professor and former dean Herma Hill Kay, August 2001; interview with Robert H. Cole, November 2001. See also Sumi Cho and Robert Westley, "Critical Race Coalitions: Key Movements That Performed the Theory," 33 *U.C. Davis Law Review* 1377 (2000), p. 1382.

classified as minority (blacks, Asians, Native Americans, Hispanics) by the early 1970s. Boalt maintained high levels of minority enrollment over the years by setting goals derived from ranges of percentages for different racial and ethnic groups based on their distribution within the population.[85] After the federal Office for Civil Rights initiated an investigation of reverse discrimination in the early 1990s, Boalt abandoned the use of separate admissions committees or groups and of overt goals in 1993 in favor of a policy that relied less on direct quotas but still enabled it to maintain a roughly proportional racial representation until the strict requirements of SP 1 & 2 and Prop 209 brought such policies to a halt.[86] Sanford Kadish, a noted criminal law and jurisprudence scholar, who served as dean during the controversies of the early 1970s, said that affirmative action was "actively debated" for a long time but had become "institutionalized" by the 1980s.[87] Faculty and student advocates sat on the key committees at Boalt, and the students who occupied the most important political positions (e.g., president of the class or student body) were usually committed to diversity efforts. Professor Robert H. Cole, a faculty ally of the FSM in the 1960s and a longtime supporter of diversity and student power at Boalt, related:

What just happened is that the activist students, mostly minority students, got a lock on all the key officerships in student government, the Boalt Hall Student Association, and over time nobody seemed to run for it except pro–affirmative action, civil rights, minority-driven left-wingers. Probably by the late seventies they captured the student organization. There was a student newspaper, and they more or less captured that. I don't mean "captured" in a bad sense, and I am not using "left-winger" in a pejorative sense.

Cole also incisively depicted how dissent was marginalized over the years by a subtle process:

People played to this left-wing audience, and I think those students who really disagreed definitely felt silenced. If they talked, nobody would shut them down or anything, but I think they just felt awkward, they didn't want to swim against the stream. So in effect there was a lot of silencing. But meanwhile, a large number of faculty members were quite conservative and spoke up, even in class, so there was a certain amount of public conflict. Mainly people tried to avoid that conflict, so that the outspoken left-wingers have by and large dominated public discourse.[88]

[85] Interview with Herma Hill Kay, August 2001; interview with Boalt law professor and former dean Jesse Choper, November 2001.

[86] Cho and Westley, "Critical Race Coalitions," pp. 1382–95. On the history of affirmative action and policy at Boalt, with a special focus on the post-209 period, see Guerrero, *Silence at Boalt Hall*. For a broader history of Boalt, see Susan Epstein, *Law at Berkeley* (Berkeley, Institute of Governmental Studies, 1997).

[87] Interview with Sanford Kadish.

[88] Interview with Robert H. Cole.

Despite the consensus, debate over such inherently controversial terms as liberty, equality, free speech, and identity kept bubbling to the surface. Many students and faculty had reservations about the legitimacy of affirmative action in its more aggressive varieties. Furthermore, many on the faculty were politically and ideologically to the right of the student leadership, including the few conservatives and the liberal majority; both groups believed that truths and rights possess legitimacy beyond power relations and that egalitarianism should be balanced with liberal freedom. (Cole, for example, embraces a strong dose of John Stuart Mill.) But the faculty is not very involved in the public arena or student life at Boalt. Most students are too busy to be very active, leaving the public arena to activists on the left and a few conservatives who make up the outspoken Federalist Society.

The intellectual climate at Boalt in the last half of the 1990s resembled a Tower of Babel – students of all political persuasions felt alienated for different reasons. Talking past each other, each group felt different slights and nursed different grievances. Dean Kay's administration also found itself in difficult straits. A longtime champion of affirmative action, which she believes is a moral and social imperative, Kay nonetheless felt constrained by the clear terms of Prop 209 to cut back on race-based enrollment. Accordingly, she believed that Boalt had to proceed deliberatively in creating a new policy that could retrieve at least some of what had been lost when the voters of the state chose Prop 209.[89] But this approach angered diversity activists, who wanted stronger resistance. The administration's actions and omissions also upset many student conservatives and moderate liberals, who accused it of acquiescing to the silencing of discourse that accompanied the activists' drive to resist Prop 209 in the 1997–98 academic year. While many liberal and conservative students lamented what they believed was a lack of open discourse, anti-209 students bemoaned what they saw as the indifference of most students to their plight and the lack of a genuine racial diversity and a diversity of views on racial issues. Andrea Guerrero, a leader of the anti-209 coalition, wrote in *Silence at Boalt Hall*, a book on the impact of Prop 209 at Boalt, that "the few underrepresented minorities at the law school continue to share their views with their colleagues and to bring up the other perspective in class, but they're less comfortable doing so. They are so few, that their every move is noticed. If they speak, their voices are scrutinized and their contribution sometimes ignored."[90]

Critical race scholars Sumi Cho and Robert Westley also illustrate an important intellectual and political change that began in the late 1980s at Boalt and other law schools: the rise of critical race theory, which radicalized the diversity movement and created tensions between liberals who

[89] Interview with Herma Hill Kay.
[90] Guerrero, *Silence at Boalt Hall*, pp. 164–65.

supported a more moderate affirmative action and those who translated such moderation as but another manifestation of white privilege. "Critical race theory offered theoretical tools that proved useful to organizers during this time.... [It strove] (1) to undertake race intervention into Left [Critical Legal Studies] discourse, and (2) to undertake a left intervention into liberal civil rights discourse."[91] In 1987 the linchpin journal, the *Harvard Civil Rights–Civil Liberties Law Review,* dedicated an entire volume to the movement, entitled "Minority Critiques of Legal Academia."[92] The antiliberal, confrontational nature of the new approach was off-putting to many students who did not share this ideology, especially in 1997–98. An otherwise sympathetic writer in the *San Francisco Daily* put his finger on the problem: although he agreed with the activists' lament about the radical decline of diversity, he criticized those who "chant obscenities,... yell racism... play smash-mouth politics as a lark... and... never consider how their actions turn off their allies."[93]

Racial tensions were high at Boalt even before SP 1 and Prop 209. On the first day of final examinations in December 1994, for example, an unidentified source placed fliers in the mailboxes of minority students that on one side exclaimed, "AFFIRMATIVE ACTION SUCKS!!!! DON'T FLUNK OUT!!!!" On the other side was a photocopy of an article about the recent resignation of U.S. surgeon general Jocelyn Elders (an African American), accompanied by the wording, "CLINTON AND TIEN [the Berkeley chancellor] AGREE: MONKEES BELONG IN THE JUNGLE HASTA VISTA SAYARA SANS BLAGUE SIL VOUS PLAIT." This venomous act shocked Boalt, leading to a town hall meeting for members of the Boalt community to air their thoughts on Berkeley's racial climate. A second flier distributed in February 1995 responded to the meeting with yet more virulent racism: "Rejoice you crybaby Niggers it's affirmative action month. A town hall meeting will not save you wetbacks or the chinks."[94]

Post-209 Politics at Boalt

In the fall of 1997 the class of 2000 had one African American student, compared with twenty in the entering class of 1999. Latino or Chicano and Native American entrants dropped precipitously to four and zero, respectively.[95] For the first time since the late 1960s, the entering class was overwhelmingly white. Boalt would eventually increase the minority numbers somewhat by devising a new admissions policy that deemphasized such

---

[91] Cho and Westley, "Critical Race Coalitions," p. 1394.

[92] 22 *Harvard Civil Rights–Civil Liberties Law Review* 301 (1987).

[93] Jonathan S. Shapiro, "Nuts and Boalts: UC Protesters May Offend, but They're Right about Diversity," *San Francisco Daily,* January 8, 1998, p. 4.

[94] Fliers quoted in Garner K. Weng, "How Stella Got Her Character," 13 *Berkeley Women's Law Journal* 1 (1998), p. 21.

[95] *Berkeleyan,* August 20, 1997, at www.berkeleyan.com.

traditional indicators of merit as grades and the Law School Admissions Test (LSAT) scores, stressing instead such factors as experience, leadership, and socioeconomic disadvantage. Guerrero, the leader of the Coalition for a Diversified Faculty and Student Body (CDFSB), considered the main problem to be the lack of a "critical mass" of black, Latino, and Native American students who could provide meaningful fellowship for students of color and alternative viewpoints.[96]

Students and former students reported their reactions to the situation in a series of short essays in the 1998 *Berkeley Women's Law Journal*. The journal published the essays because "the emotion, pain, and conflict that remains deep inside the halls at Boalt never made the headlines."[97] Kaaryn Gustafson, the leading coauthor of an extensive student-generated 1997 report on how diversity could be achieved by new means that did not run afoul of Prop 209's strictures, also spoke of the "critical mass" problem. "I woke up the first day of school this year with knots in my stomach. I was numb when I left my house, and on the verge of tears when I arrived at school."[98] Jessica Marie Delgado wrote that the "re-segregation of Boalt Hall . . . felt like spirit murder."[99] Another student spoke of the "lack of desire on the part of many whites to recognize and disavow white skin privilege."[100] Diversity activists, therefore, sought to preserve racial representation in every venue possible. Sources told me that when some students and faculty sought to eliminate race as a criterion of law review selection in the belief that the continuation of the existing policy of racial quotas violated 209, they were called "racists" by many who wanted to preserve the race-conscious approach.

"Admitted Students Day" in spring 1997 was a dress rehearsal for what lay ahead in the fall, as protesters transferred their antipathy toward Prop 209 to the new students themselves. Posters urged the incoming students to "Stop the Hate," and asked them pointedly, "Why Do You Hate Me?" Other posters labeled 209 a "Klan Approved" initiative, and rechristened Boalt Hall "Jim Crow University." Jeff Bishop (class of 2000), who claimed that Boalt students were generally tolerant of conservative and dissenting views except when it came to 209, wrote, "Students wore red armbands reminiscent of East Germany. A crowd gathered like a lynch mob, cheering while one destroyed a piñata named 'diversity.' Several first-year law students noted that had they seen such a spectacle the year before, they would not have

---

[96] See Guerrero, *Silence at Boalt Hall*, chs. 3, 4.

[97] "Commentary," 13 *Berkeley Women's Law Journal* 1 (1998), p. 2.

[98] Kaaryn Gustafson, "Broken Promises," 13 *Berkeley Women's Law Journal* 1 (1998), p. 5.

[99] Jessica Marie Delgado, "The Courage I Know," 13 *Berkeley Women's Law Journal* 1 (1998), pp. 7–8.

[100] Marcie Neff, "The Elephant in the Room," 13 *Berkeley Women's Law Journal* 1 (1998), p. 17.

attended Boalt."[101] It must be stressed, however, that such demonstrations are classic examples of protest and free speech.

When students arrived at Boalt in the fall of 1997, they encountered further protests and demonstrations; it seemed that everywhere one looked, posters, flyers, and writings loomed denouncing Prop 209. The prodiversity movement consisted of a loose coalition of CDFSB, the Latino group La Raza, the Black Students Law Association, and some progressive white groups. The coalition's primary objective was to pressure the administration to adopt the policies embodied in the 1997 report written by Gustafson and several other students, entitled "New Directions in Diversity." The report advocated deemphasizing the LSAT, looking more "holistically" at applicants' credentials and contributions, and employing more aggressive forms of recruitment. In response to the report and pressures exerted by activists, Boalt established a faculty committee led by Robert H. Cole to formulate an official policy (the "Cole Report").[102] The conscientious Cole carried most of the load, so the report was delayed, which the activists interpreted as foot-dragging by the administration. To speed things up, activists deployed several strategies, including contacting alumni, members of the bar associations, and local and national media; holding rallies and press conferences; conducting symbolic "walk-ins" of two large first-year classes on Columbus Day (October 13), to be followed by a takeover of the dean's or registrar's office; and placing anti-209 posters and fliers in a variety of spots around the school. On the first day of class, major media people captured the image of the one African American student entering the building.

Students Speak Out

According to many students, the manner and attitude with which activists dramatized the negative effects of 209 created a climate hostile to the open exchange of ideas, denying students the pursuit of a meaningful legal education. Protests in favor of *racial and ethnic* diversity undermined *intellectual* diversity. To others, Prop 209 had already rendered such an education a moot point by omitting minority voices that are an indispensable ingredient of a valid education. And, of course, demonstrations are an honored part of free speech, especially for the disempowered.

In 1999 Boalt student David Wienir (class of 2000) coedited an explosive book with Marc Berley, *The Diversity Hoax: Law Students Report from Berkeley*.[103] Berley is a lecturer in English and comparative literature at Columbia,

---

[101] Jeff Bishop, "Disorientation Day," in David Wienir and Marc Berley, eds., *The Diversity Hoax: Law Students Report from Berkeley* (Foundation for Academic Standards and Tradition, 1999), pp. 98–99.

[102] See Kaaryn Gustafson et al., "New Directions in Diversity," Boalt Hall Report, April 1997; Robert H. Cole, chair, "Report of an Ad Hoc Task Force on Boalt Diversity in Admissions," Boalt Hall, October 14, 1997.

[103] Wienir and Berley, *Diversity Hoax*.

and president of the Foundation for Academic Standards and Tradition (FAST), a small conservative New York organization that champions academic freedom, free speech, and traditional notions of merit and truth. *The Diversity Hoax* consists of twenty-five essays written by Boalt students from across the ideological spectrum; all but two lament how the politics of affirmative action inhibited meaningful dialogue and debate in and outside the classroom. Berley and a radio talk show host wrote a separate introduction and conclusion, which several faculty I interviewed found excessive.

Wienir bristled at the ostracism he encountered at Boalt due to his conservatism. But his dismay also seemed a product of disappointed educational expectations. "The university setting is different [from elsewhere]. It is where the ideas of equality and liberty in a certain sense came from and are nourished and allowed to grow and develop."[104] Wienir anticipated similar stimulation in learning the law at Boalt, especially given Berkeley's reputation for championing free speech that challenges all orthodoxies. What he found did not meet this expectation: "Many Boalt students act as if their education is threatened whenever any conservative view is expressed.... almost any time a lone conservative tried to raise his or her voice during my years at Boalt, things got ugly. Fists, rather than hands, were raised. Eyes rolled. Glares flashed. Intolerance radiated. Diversity of mind was declared dangerous and unwanted."[105]

According to most of the writers in *Diversity Hoax*, a majority of Boalt students were actually tolerant of opposing viewpoints, even conservative ones. The problem lay in the censure exerted by a small number of students who created an environment that inhibited the majority from speaking with intellectual honesty and from openly defending free speech and debate. One conservative student described the problem in terms that echo Timur Kuran's thesis of the spiral of silence: "Most of my fellow students are perfectly tolerant of conservative views and differences of opinions. Unfortunately, a very small group of students who are unwilling to allow free debate to flourish have seized the agenda at Boalt. Most of the discussion in class and in the hallways is dominated by this small contingent of students. In my opinion, they have ruined a large part of the law school experience."[106]

On the other side, some anti-209 activists cloaked their arguments in the name of free speech itself, asserting that the absence of racial and ethnic diversity limited the range of opinion essential for meaningful debate and the exchange of ideas. Andrea Guerrero argued that Prop 209 had "silenced" minority voices, thereby undermining free speech values.[107] This argument

---

[104] Interview with Boalt law student David Wienir, June 2001.

[105] Wienir, "The History," in Wienir and Berley, *The Diversity Hoax*, pp. 19, 34.

[106] Anthony Patel, "The Great Buzzword," in Wienir and Berley, *Diversity Hoax*, p. 45.

[107] Guerrero, *Silence at Boalt Hall*. See also Gustafson, "Broken Promises," p. 5; Chancellor David Berdahl, *The Berkeleyan*, August 20, 1997; *L.A. Times*, August 19, 1997, p. A3.

amounted to an endorsement of progressive social censorship: social censure of expression deemed detrimental to the cause of diversity in order to even the scales.

Encounters outside the Classroom

Soon after they arrived in the fall of 1997, prodiversity advocates within Boalt composed an open letter declaring students' "grave disappointment in the lack of diversity" in the class of 2000, which has "compromised our legal education. The pool of background experiences and perspectives we are exposed to has diminished significantly, limiting opportunities for intellectual growth."[108] The letter's advocates asked members of the student body to sign a petition supporting the letter's claims. Many of those who did not sign considered the letter to be tantamount to a loyalty oath. Seventy-one percent of the student body signed, and those who refused, according to Wienir, "were – I speak from experience – scorned and disparaged.... My decision not to sign the open letter to the dean resulted in unfounded allegations that I was a racist."[109] On October 13, Columbus Day, students from several Bay Area law schools held a large "solidarity" rally at Boalt calling for the adoption of the *New Directions in Diversity* report.[110] Demonstrators also engaged in two dramatic class disruptions.

Anti-209 students employed several tactics over the course of the year to promote their cause, some of which were surprising for young adults studying to become practitioners of the law. For example, public postings of conservative events and meetings were sometimes removed at various times during the year. In February, unknown sources repeatedly took down announcements of events of the conservative Federalist Society. It got so bad that the beleaguered Dean Kay had to write a memorandum to the Boalt community, condemning the furtive acts as an assault on free and open discourse. The society's director of publicity called the actions "cowardly."[111]

Several students also described how relationships that formed among them reinforced the chilling of discourse. The first year of law school can be psychologically regressive, oddly reviving the clique psychology of high school, as nervous students spend a lot of time together, take the same courses, and form cliques and groups that compete with one another. Daryl Singhi, an Asian American in the class of 2000, described

[108] *San Francisco Examiner*, September 13, 1997, p. A3.
[109] Wienir, "The History," pp. 18–19. On the letter, see Guerrero, *Silence at Boalt Hall*, pp. 124–25.
[110] "Boalt Students Rally for Affirmative Action," *Daily Californian*, October 13, 1997.
[111] See Catharine Baily, "Of Vandals and Cowards," in Wienir and Berley, *Diversity Hoax*, pp. 78–81.

how group dynamics at Boalt were sometimes influenced by political ideology:

Quickly, whom you associated with became more indicative of your opinions than what you actually said.... It is fine to castigate somebody for having an opinion that stands in the face of yours, but it is another matter to lob personal attacks to debase the person instead of their thoughts. Rumors and innuendo pervaded the campus. "Terrorist," "sexist," "white supremacist," and "racist" were all terms used as commentary on various individuals.[112]

Another student recounted how this process sometimes resembled a version of the old punishment of shunning: "Students who individually challenge the dominant paradigm with their own thoughts are ostracized by many other students at the law school.... In my experience, other people at Boalt choose to penalize you when you speak up, by choosing to ostracize you. And at Berkeley – once the great home of the free speech movement – that is an odd result that I did not expect."[113] Megan Elizabeth Murray – whose piece was, she stated, "written from the heart" – describes her participation in a secret exchange of views over affirmative action scrawled on the hallowed walls of the bathroom stalls. The exchange ended with her unknown adversary accusing her of being "a fucking idiot." To Murray, the bathroom exchanges were a kind of epiphany. "My bathroom experience sums up my frustration with the lack of true diversity at Boalt. How can we call the school diverse when a segment of the population speaks out only in the bathroom stalls? ... How can a school claim to be one of the best when no meaningful discourse takes place?"[114]

The classroom disruptions on Columbus Day were followed by a sit-in in the registrar's office that led to fifty-four arrests for trespassing, and twenty for resisting arrest.[115] The faculty then released the Cole Report – the faculty's response to the previous report authored by Gustafson and her coauthors – which it formally adopted in December. The report called for adjustments in how grade averages and LSAT scores were weighed in admissions decisions, enhanced recruitment and workshops, consideration of socioeconomic status in admissions, and encouragement of applicants to discuss their racial backgrounds in their statements of purpose.[116]

Two days after the Columbus Day demonstrations, fire alarms were set off during classes. The Law School had to be cleared, and a disabled student suffered a seizure during one episode. Unable to identify the culprits, Boalt authorities had to deactivate the alarm system and assign patrolmen to keep

---

[112] Singhi, "Vanishing Diversity," in Wienir and Berley, *Diversity Hoax*, pp. 72–73.
[113] Nick-Anthony Burford, "What Ever Happened to John Stuart Mill?" in Wienir and Berley, *Diversity Hoax*, pp. 90–91.
[114] Murray, "New from the Ladies Room," in Wienir and Berley, *Diversity Hoax*, pp. 82–85.
[115] Lisa Nishimoto, "Boalt Promises Outreach Report," *Daily Californian*, October 14, 1997.
[116] Cole Report. See also Guerrero, *Silence at Boalt Hall*, pp. 135–36.

watch. The *Daily Cal* reported that the situation had become "highly disruptive." One first-year student said, "I have great sympathy for the protest. But I get the feeling that people are getting pissed off in class."[117]

The Classroom

Students cited two major class-related problems during the 1997–98 academic year: the freedom of class debate per se, and the October disruptions that set the tone for the whole academic year. (By the next year, anti-209 forces had exhausted themselves. A member of the class of 2001 said that discussion about controversial issues by that time was moribund.)[118] Student interventions in classrooms and administrators' offices for expressive political purposes are nothing new at Boalt. They were commonplace during the Vietnam War era, and former dean Jesse Choper related that he had had up to fifteen sit-ins in his office during the last five years of his deanship (1987–92) over faculty hiring policy. Professor Stephen Barnett recalled that "quite a few students" came into his tort class in April 1996 to protest Prop 209. They came "marching in the classroom and banging pots on the walls. It made it impossible to teach the class. The dean considered calling the police but did not."[119]

Regent Ward Connerly, attempting to point out what he considered the hypocrisy of some affirmative action supporters, had publicly stated that most anti-209 white supporters would be unwilling to give up their own spots to a minority applicant who had been denied admission.[120] The protests of October 1997 were a symbolic response to Connerly's claim. Because they were large classes taught at advantageous times of the day, leaders targeted two first-year classes that happened to be taught by two visiting professors: the criminal law class of Joshua Dressler, then of McGeorge Law School in Sacramento (now at Ohio State), and the torts class of John Diamond of Hastings Law School in San Francisco. A small group consisting largely of minority students would enter the classroom during the lecture and ask white students to give up their seats. Members of the group would take seats offered them, or take an empty seat on the side or toward the back of the room. Coalition leaders planned to hold walk-in demonstrations on only one day, but two days later, a separate group came back to Dressler's class on its own initiative. "The students tried very hard to prevent us from finding out about it," Kay said. "We caught wind of it because one of my fellow deans at USF... called me and told me a day before, but we did not know what

[117] Alexa Capeloto, "Boalt Hall Disables Several Fire Alarms," *Daily Californian*, October 17 or 18, 1997.
[118] Interview with William Kidder.
[119] Interview with Robert H. Cole; interview with Jesse Choper; interview with Boalt law professor Stephen Barnett, August 2001.
[120] Annie Nakao, "Entering Boalt Students Chafe at Homogeneity," *San Francisco Chronicle*, September 13, 1997.

they were going to do."[121] Dressler granted me an interview, but Diamond did not respond to my request.

Diversity Hoax does not say much about Diamond's class beyond a brief description by Richard Welch: "Several white students abandoned their seats, enabling 'students of color' . . . to share 'their experiences' with the class." Welch related that the protesters "even launched a personal attack against Professor Diamond himself." In an interview, Welch said, "It took over the class. One person got up in front of the class and started reading a piece of paper, a speech . . . then stormed out of class chanting with others. It seemed like [it lasted] for the whole class. A lot of people were sympathetic to affirmative action, but would not give up their seats out of principle."[122]

Unlike Diamond, Dressler had to deal with two incidents. The noted criminal law scholar agreed with the claim of the coalition that the lack of minority voices undercut the diversity of ideas in class. "The arguments for diversity in terms of students who have different viewpoints is absolutely right when it comes to criminal law. You do want to have African Americans in class." Dressler describes himself as a "Socratic" teacher. "I very much push the idea of critical thinking. I tell students day one that I want them to question everything they hear, everything they read, hear from fellow students and me. All I want is that it be done in a civil manner."[123]

Kay notified Dressler in advance that something was brewing, so he was prepared when several students entered the room midway into the lecture and asked white students to surrender their seats. Dressler gave a speech about the dangers of morally browbeating people, and then let the anti-209 leader give his speech. Overall, Dressler, Kay, and others were pleased with how well it had gone.[124]

Two days later, Dressler was discussing the famous controversial self-defense case of Bernard Goetz, the white man who had shot at four young black toughs (hitting two) on a New York subway train in 1984. Although the facts presented a poor case for self-defense, a crime-obsessed jury that included two African Americans essentially exonerated Goetz, convicting him of only a minor possession offense.[125] Dressler has taught the case for years and knew that he would have to work hard to ensure open debate, especially given the institutional climate that semester. Having taught at several law schools in recent years – Berkeley, McGeorge, UCLA, Michigan, and now Ohio State – Dressler had the experience that allowed him to compare institutional climates. He found Boalt the least hospitable environment for

---

[121] Interview with Herma Hill Kay, August 2001.
[122] Welch, "An Institutionalized Problem," in Wienir and Berley, *Diversity Hoax*, p. 102; interview with Richard Welch, August 2001.
[123] Interview with Boalt visiting law professor Joshua Dressler, August 2001.
[124] Ibid.
[125] For an excellent account of the case, see George P. Fletcher, *A Crime of Self-Defense: Bernard Goetz and the Law* (University of Chicago Press, 1988).

intellectual freedom in class. For example, compared with Michigan, "which has students of roughly comparable quality, I found a much broader openness in the discussion of all perspectives; found it just a more pleasant experience with the students, with each other in class, than at Berkeley, where I did feel both years that it seemed that they had a grudge almost from day one. It seemed as if a lot of students very early on had agendas, and they wanted to get those agendas dealt with, day in and day out, in the classroom in a way that I had not seen at any other law school." The main agenda Dressler noticed embraced a blend of critical race and white power theories, seasoned with the assumptions of postmodernism and radical multiculturalism, which consider "justice" and "law" to be fundamentally masks for power and privilege. "Their view was virtually that everything we were learning in the law – in all classes, but more clearly in criminal law – was based on cultural values, bias, and power, and that everything needed to be seen that way."[126] Dressler noted that this slant was endorsed by a minority of students but that they often dominated debate or made it difficult for critics to confront the agenda.

Dressler was already nervous going into the *Goetz* class because he was to be interviewed by ABC national news right after the class for a job as a commentator on the Unabomber case that was in the courts at that time. About fifteen minutes into the class, a group of about six students who were not enrolled in the class entered through the two doors on either side of the front and took seats on the left and right sides of the room. Tension swept through the hall. Unprepared for the encounter, Dressler made the hurried decision to ignore the unanticipated visitors. As he struggled to promote class discussion, the visitors kept silent with their hands raised. The discussion went from bad to "terrible," so Dressler dismissed the class. "Anonymous" in *Diversity Hoax* reported that "Many of these 'new' faces sneered at the professor."[127] Dressler believes that this incident poisoned the class for the rest of the semester – a conclusion corroborated by Wienir. After the class, one of his best students called him a "racist" – an act for which the student later apologized.[128]

Dressler praised the way that Dean Kay handled the case, and he was confident that she would back his decision and the idea of academic freedom. But other than Kay, no one contacted Dressler or made any public statement of support – even though the case became a cause célèbre at Boalt.

Though his class was not disrupted, Sanford Kadish also had a trying experience teaching the *Goetz* case. Jim Culp's recounting does not mention the professor's name, but his description of the instructor leaves little room for doubt: "a rather small, elderly man...somewhat larger than life. His

---

[126] Interview with Joshua Dressler.
[127] Anonymous, "Truly Anonymous," in Wienir and Berley, *Diversity Hoax*, pp. 154–55.
[128] Interview with Joshua Dressler; interview with David Wienir.

wisdom (he has won many national awards, was a former dean of Boalt Hall, and authored the textbook used in our class) and his respectful, caring, and gentle manner reminded me each class why I wanted to become a lawyer."[129]

In teaching the issue of self-defense presented by the *Goetz* case, Kadish typically posed a question that cuts to the heart of the case, which concerns the relationships among race, stereotyping, and the "reasonable fear" that is needed to justify self-defense: "If all murders are committed by 'purple' people, may a person's 'reasonable fear' be based partly on the fact that she finds herself in the midst of 'purple people'?" Rather than taking the question as a useful Socratic prod, some students leapt to a moralistic judgment that stopped critical debate cold:

What happened next disgusts me to this day.... he [the professor] was verbally attacked by several minority students. In ugly tones they called him, among other things, a "racist," and characterized his behavior as everything that is evil.... I believe tears welled up in his eyes, and then he simply replied that he didn't think he would share such experiences with students in the future.... it was simply the worst example of disrespect and ignorance I had ever witnessed. I will never forgive myself for not saying as much on the spot.[130]

Students I interviewed and essayists in *Diversity Hoax* provided several examples of similar behavior in class. Heather McCormick, a self-professed "moderate Democrat" who now works for a major law firm in Los Angeles, presented a more balanced and less adversarial account than many essayists, yet her conclusions were no less critical. She went out of her way to praise the way in which many professors fostered engaging debate or discussion in class. For example, she called constitutional law expert Jesse Choper a "wonderful professor," a "master" of the art of facilitating dialectical and critical thought. Like Wienir, her disappointment with Boalt derived from her esteem for liberal education, which she had gained as an undergraduate at Penn. She had hoped that Boalt would continue the Penn experience, only "at a much higher, intense level." Liberal legal education should cultivate the ability to wrestle constructively with unsettling arguments and claims: "Is [Boalt] an environment in which all viewpoints are welcome and considered an important part of the discussion? In some classes, that was not the case at all. I mean, some people would actually *hiss* – can you imagine grown adults hissing at an idea that they do not like? The extreme behavior was not a large number of individuals, yet that behavior was still tolerated by a large number of people because of the climate."[131]

---

[129] I use Kadish's text in my own course on criminal law and jurisprudence. Sanford H. Kadish and Stephen J. Schulhofer, *Criminal Law and Its Processes: Cases and Materials* (Aspen Publisher's, 2001).

[130] Jim Culp, "A Call for Respect," in Wienir and Berley, *Diversity Hoax*, pp. 61–66.

[131] Interview with Boalt law student Heather McCormick, August 2001.

McCormick's essay in *Diversity Hoax* describes a visiting professor who showed a video about discrimination in housing and then called for "open dialogue" among the students. When a classmate asked a question about "reverse discrimination" in this context, the instructor shot back, "How could you even bring that up? It just belittles everything you've seen here!" McCormick continued, "Her tirade went on for a good two minutes while my classmate sunk down into his chair, lowered his eyes, and said nothing." In her essay and interview, McCormick spotted the root of the problem in the guilt of white students after Prop 209, and the absence of true *political diversity* at Boalt. She wrote, "many Boalt students who lean toward liberalism nevertheless would like to see a more balanced dialogue." In McCormick's eyes, many students were afraid to be intellectually honest and to push the limits of accepted thought. The result was too often a tepid, uninteresting discussion that was sometimes more beholden to half-truths and dogma than to the kind of dynamic Socratic inquiry that inspires and challenges young minds. Fear of mistakes was also a problem among the students, for making mistakes – and being exposed to criticism that corrects or challenges one's mistakes – is one of the key intellectual processes by which provisional truth is acquired.[132] McCormick's words also bring to mind the classic tributes to free speech by Milton, Mill, Brandeis, and others who envisioned vibrant free speech as a catalyst of human exploration and growth:

> This lack of exchange is not only boring, it is antithetical to the educational mission of a university. . . . Most of us at law school are relatively young, still trying out new ideas and testing the bounds of our beliefs. Yet this type of development requires a tolerant, forgiving atmosphere, one that allows for the full exploration of ideas, including directness, exaggeration, and even mistakes. But because no such atmosphere exists at Boalt, students are rarely willing to put their necks on the line. . . . They cautiously state just enough to get a point across, lest any passionate over-stepping forever be ascribed to their belief system, rather than viewed as what it was meant to be – an exploration. . . . We have "debate-lite." . . . our behavior is more like that of polite dinner than that of law students.[133]

One student who signed his or her essay as "Anonymous" wrote about Dressler's class, concluding, "I have witnessed the death of the individual."[134]

Students and Faculty Critiques and Assessments
Some of the professors whom I interviewed questioned the accounts in *Diversity Hoax* for being overwrought. This charge might indeed have merit. One should also consider the negative impact on debate because of the exclusion

---

[132] See Karl Popper, *The Logic of Scientific Discovery* (Harper and Row, 1968).
[133] Heather McCormick, "The Unprofitable Monopoly," in Wienir and Berley, *Diversity Hoax*, pp. 52–53.
[134] Anonymous, "Truly Anonymous," p. 155.

of minority voices – a claim that Dressler himself supported. Nonetheless, the negative assessments of *Diversity Hoax* need to be placed into perspective.

First, the two dissenting essays in *Diversity Hoax* did not challenge critics' assessments of the suffocated state of discourse but rather made another claim: conservatives and free speech liberals were blameworthy for not vigorously supporting their own views. The otherwise champions of free speech apparently suffered a failure of nerve. Student Lesley R. Knapp, for example, had little patience for the "whiners": "[If] you haven't learned to speak up for your own ideas, what have you been doing?" Even David Wienir conceded that this was a valid point in an interview.[135]

Second, as for the faculty's dismissal of the book, many of the unsettling incidents reported in *Diversity Hoax* took place outside of the classrooms, beyond the notice of faculty. Nor were faculty members generally privy to many of the classroom incidents discussed in the book. The best teachers are normally able to maintain open forums in their own classes. Noted constitutional scholars Jesse Choper, Robert Post, and others are famous at Boalt for generating critical thinking and open discourse in their classes. Choper said that the two most sensitive issues in his courses were affirmative action and abortion, and that the conservative view had actually grown stronger over the past decade or so because of the influence of the Federalist Society. "There has grown in the last fifteen years a much more articulate conservative point of view. The Federalist side has become a very articulate force. . . . I don't know that in my classes I would notice a strong difference in terms of rational discourse, open dialogue. I think there are more people speaking out on the conservative side."[136]

Third, even anti-209 leaders did not deny the charge that discourse had been stifled in the school. Rather, they justified the suppression with a rationale: given the profound lack of ethnic diversity in the first-year class, they were simply creating a special space for their view to be heard. In a sense, they implied that intellectual diversity at Boalt would have to be sacrificed in the name of empowering a viewpoint that had been crushed by majority power outside the university. Jessica Marie Delgado observed that the Prop 209 cutbacks created a vacuum of silence in class. "For the most part, students and professors proceeded as though there had been no change – in spite of an enormous amount of media attention and community scrutiny. I know of only a few professors who talked about the change in their classes. More importantly, hardly any faculty members attended town hall meetings or other events planned to foster community dialogue."[137]

---

[135] Knapp, "Stop the Whining," in Wienir and Berley, *Diversity Hoax*, pp. 114–15; interview with David Wiener.

[136] Interview with Jesse Choper; interview with Boalt law professor Robert Post, August 2001.

[137] Delgado, "The Courage I Know," 13 *Berkeley Women's Law Journal* 1 (1998), p. 8. See also Guerrero, *Silence at Boalt Hall*, ch. 4; Gustafson, "Broken Promises," p. 5.

Fourth, no individual or group has published on the record anything resembling a refutation of the book. Guerrero does not mention or discuss *The Diversity Hoax* in the main text of her detailed history of affirmative action politics at Boalt, though she does quote, without comment, a couple of its authors' essays.[138] Anti-209 activists were angered by the book and held a demonstration at a local bookstore during Wienir's book signing ceremony. However, no one has publicly refuted the book's claims.

Fifth, even some of the strongest critics of the book on the Berkeley faculty made statements that suggest that the book has some merit. For example, some of the faculty critics of the book limited their critiques to certain parts of the book, especially the introduction and the afterword, which were written by nonstudents who made broader charges about the ways Boalt reflected the wider state of higher education in America. The exceptionally thoughtful and fair-minded Robert H. Cole stated, "I read only the introduction, which I thought was outrageous. It was totally unfair, it was biased. It was just unimaginative. It was just a one-sided hatchet job." But Cole did not read beyond the introduction, which means that he did not expose himself to the numerous facts presented by many essayists, some of which he may have known, of course.[139] Cole also believed that the class disruptions surrounding Columbus Day were more serious than previous disruptions at Boalt, and he remarked that the climate for dissent was not ideal: "The other theme is the political correctness, intimidation theme that you asked me about. That is a big free speech theme and it needs to be talked about."[140]

Like Cole, Joshua Dressler reserved his strongest critique of the book for the introduction and afterword, but his assessment was more balanced for other parts of the book. "I found the book a little over the top, certain of the things in there I thought were more over the top than others. There was one in there that I liked a lot and nodded my head." (His comments suggest that this may have been McCormick's essay, but I did not ask him directly.)

---

[138] Guerrero, *Silence at Boalt.*
[139] Cole became a faculty adviser to some FSM leaders in December 1964. Other interviewees, Reginald Zelnik and John Searle, had been actively advising the FSM more or less from the beginning. Cole was part of the small group, which included Zelnik and Searle, that drafted the famous December 8 faculty resolution. He was also one of the coauthors of the December 1964 report adopted by the UC Berkeley Academic Freedom Committee on the scope and limits of free speech at the university. The other authors were future University of Wisconsin system and University of Virginia president, Robert M. O'Neil, who now heads the Freedom Forum at the University of Virginia, and Hans Linde, who went on to become a Justice of the Oregon Supreme Court. See R. H. Cole, H. A. Linde, and R. M. O'Neil, "To: The Committee on Academic Freedom of the Berkeley Division," in Lipset and Wolin, *The Berkeley Student Revolt*, pp. 273–80.
[140] Interview with Robert H. Cole.

Two other assessments of *Diversity Hoax* were also ambivalent. Former dean Sanford Kadish told me:

I've read the book. Terrible title. Some of the essays are pretty sensible, others aren't. There is no doubt that it is a very sensitive subject. One can say what he wants about it, but there is a lot of pressure not to. For many of our students, it [affirmative action] is a fundamental moral issue. It's not a matter of "well, some people can think this way, some people can think that way." For many people, there really aren't two sides. It's a matter of rectifying brute injustices in American society. If you're opposed to that, you're suspect.[141]

Professor Stephen Barnett said, "that book is overdone and exaggerated, but there is some truth to it. . . . I think that Dean Kay recognized that there was a problem here in that classes were broken up. She was always hesitant to criticize students or anyone else."[142]

A final revealing point concerning the credibility of *Diversity Hoax* is that not all the student contributors are white males or conservatives. Some of the most effective essays were written by women, by Asian Americans, by liberals who believed in open discourse, and even by individuals who wrote that they agree with affirmative action.

Boalt Conclusions

A system of free speech cannot be sustained if offended individuals and groups do not learn to deal with their offense constructively and respond to unsettling arguments with their own counterarguments, not with silence or the censor's hammer.[143] As seen here, free speech requires those who are intimidated by social pressure to gather their courage in the face of it and stand up for their rights and their views. It was the responsibility of students who disagreed with the moral politics at Boalt during 1997 and 1998 to stand up for their desire for an intellectually diverse public forum and education, as they were the ones on the line, the ones who witnessed the nature and extent of the problem. More important, it was their responsibility to give counterviews a meaningful presence in the public arena, thereby providing intellectual and moral support for others. Sanford Kadish – himself the target of much censure from the Boalt Student majority – remarked in words that seem to step right out of the pages of Justice Brandeis: "Freedom of speech is not for sissies. It takes courage to present a dissenting view – [especially] when the majority view is held on the basis not of personal gain but on the basis of a certain moral position."[144]

[141] Interview with Sanford Kadish.
[142] Interview with Stephen Barnett.
[143] See Jonathan Rauch, *Kindly Inquisitors: The New Attacks on Free Thought* (University of Chicago Press, 1993).
[144] Interview with Sanford Kadish.

The Diversity Hoax was a step in this direction. Published a year before the class of 2000 matriculated, the authors intended to unleash debate and encourage change. But the book was not accompanied by the type of organized effort that could institute change. In the absence of organization and mobilization, this unusual book failed to turn private truths into public truths.

Neither did the faculty nor the administration appear to have worked collectively to foster an environment conducive to open discourse. Alienated students had some quiet allies, but neither group took action to change what was happening. The transformation that Timur Kuran describes in *Private Truths, Public Lies*, through which privately held grievances concerning freedom become transformed into public questions, did not materialize.[145] I had the good fortune to interview some extraordinary faculty members whose intellectual acumen and commitment to their fields left a powerful impression with me. Boalt Law School is clearly intellectually committed to free speech. During the year, Kay reportedly listened earnestly to the complaints of students about the state of free discourse. But most members of the faculty were dismissive of the claims of *The Diversity Hoax*, despite the varied background of its authors and the consistency of their complaints. Wienir's assessment of the broader institutional problem is perhaps exaggerated, but others agreed with it to some extent:

Nobody cared.... The book was published in April 1999, and for the first couple of months it generated enough media attention to get people talking. There was no mention of it at the Law School, though. The university is afraid to engage in this sort of dialogue. [Professor] Barnett sent an e-mail to the law school student body and faculty, basically stating that this publication has come out and it is important to diversity issues in this Law School. He said that this is something we should be discussing, and that if this book was published from the liberal perspective, it would have been trumpeted.[146]

Things could have been different. Several observers pointed out that many, perhaps most, students and faculty were not sympathetic to the censuring of dissenting thought. Several propitious conditions were present at Boalt that could have sparked the type of shift that Kuran describes. First, the number of alienated students constituted a critical mass, so outspoken students would not have been alone; a countermovement existed *in potentia*. Second, a considerable number of students (including many who were anti-209) opposed what was happening. Third, free speech is an important institutional cause that appeals to interests beyond the political and is clearly held in high regard by the Boalt faculty and, no doubt, by most students. Properly presented, free

145 Kuran, *Private Truths, Public Lies.*
146 Interview with David Wienir.

speech claims support the interests of both liberal and conservative students – they cannot simply be dismissed as a mask for conservative self-interest.

Opponents of Prop 209 had every right to criticize the effects of that measure on diversity and education and to challenge those who disagreed or remained indifferent to what was taking place. But many students at Boalt observed a process that is inimical to healthy debate: turning *political* disagreements into *personal* attacks. Such thinking encourages personal attitudes that are not conducive to constructive democratic politics. (Hence, parliamentary etiquette discourages such rhetoric and tactics.) Perhaps this tendency is the natural outcome of a philosophy that invariably considers *ideas* the mere masks of *power*. If ideas are primarily derived from power, then bad ideas are seen as the products of bad people. And there is no reason to grant credence to the idea of a marketplace of ideas, which is premised on Justice Holmes's famous maxim that freedom of speech means freedom "for the thought that we hate."[147]

A final issue at Boalt concerns the anti–Prop 209 coalition. However understandable the coalition's lament, two facts remain. First, Boalt was utterly blameless for the enactment of Prop 209, so making the school a target of criticism for its existence was unfair. Second, the ideology and tactics of the coalition alienated potential allies by treating those who disagreed (or were uncertain) as enemies when they might have been persuaded, rendering impossible a genuine debate about what was going on and what should be done. Although law schools and law study inculcate respect for intellectual diversity and speech, and law students form a rather cohesive community with common interests, somehow in spite of this professional common core, inadequate common ground – an inadequate social contract – existed that could make serious moral disagreement tolerable. Perhaps a separable, divisive political tradition was entrenched at Boalt that could not be transcended. Perhaps the coalition acted out of panic that no minority students would be at Boalt in the future. In any event, tied to the tenets of critical race theory, anti-209 activists worked from the foundation of confrontation and alienation, rather than one of universal human rights, which would have provided a more productive basis for building a broader movement and fostering a tolerance of other opinions. The result was both an alienated movement and compromised public discourse.

---

[147] *United States v. Schwimmer*, 279 U.S. 644 (1929), Justice Holmes, dissenting.

5

Undue Process at Penn

The famous water buffalo case at the University of Pennsylvania in 1993 cat-apulted the issue of political correctness into the national media's spotlight. The case involved the Penn judicial administration's pursuit of formal charges against a student for calling some noisy African American sorority women "water buffalos" – a term that most observers would not consider racist. The affair became an example of questionable, politically biased "due pro-cess" and led to the discrediting of the administration of Sheldon Hackney. Many have written about the case, including Hackney and his primary chal-lenger in the case, Professor Alan Kors.[1] What this chapter offers is an exam-ination of the political strategies that Kors learned in this ground-breaking case that can serve as a blueprint for the protection of civil liberty on cam-pus. As with the case at Columbia, no administrator would talk with me. But the events were well documented, and I spoke with all the leaders of the civil liberty movement at Penn, as well as with others. I also took advantage of the exceptional publication, the *Almanac*, the official newspaper of record for Penn.

The Penn story differs in one major respect from the Wisconsin story: it depends on the extraordinary political entrepreneurialism of Alan Kors. Although he had some allies, Kors was the key in the pivotal mid-1990s. While the change at Wisconsin was based on an organization with an official name and access to outside funds (the Committee for Academic Freedom and Rights), the smaller group at Penn consciously avoided such organization. Kors's political mentor, Michael Cohen, a physics professor, related, "We had no official group status, but we were all friends. We were asked to organize and become a coherent political entity on campus, and I said that was the

[1] Sheldon Hackney, *The Politics of Presidential Appointment: A Memoir of the Culture War* (New South Books, 2002), pp. 96–97; Alan Charles Kors and Harvey S. Silverglate, *The Shadow University: The Betrayal of Liberty on America's Campuses* (Free Press, 1998), esp. ch. 1.

worst thing that we could do. I said I will not do that because then we would become identified as a right-wing group."[2]

Kors came to Penn in 1968 as a professor of modern European intellectual history. He is also known as the editor of the *Encyclopedia of the Enlightenment* and as a lecturer for two courses on the Enlightenment in a nationally syndicated taped lecture series (for The Teaching Company). Kors quickly established a reputation at Penn as a formidable lecturer and campus citizen. Some of Kors's foes today portray him as overly doctrinaire and insensitive. (One professor who has been both ally and foe, told me, "Alan is a simple principle ideologue, who is also a bit of a rhetorical scenery chewer.")[3] But his admirers point to his integrity and his many students. While many describe him as a congenial gentleman, he can also be intractable when he believes an important principle is at stake.

In 1971 Kors cofounded Penn's first "College House," which housed 180 undergraduates, 8 graduate fellows, and 4 resident faculty. "I was untenured, and a lot of my colleagues thought I was crazy, living with undergraduates," he related. But the house quickly gained fame at Penn for its intellectual vitality and diversity. "It got the reputation as a place to be an individual," said Kors. At the same time, it was home to such strange bedfellows as the campus's first wave of gay activists, members of Campus Crusade for Christ, activists in the fledgling feminist movement, and affiliates of the conservative Newman Center board. While African Americans composed only 2 to 3 percent of the student body in the 1970s, Kors's house was 20 percent black. Students came on board, said Kors, "because it was a place *not* to be a representative of a group. We had College Republicans and Maoist revolutionaries. And that for me was a university."[4]

In 1972 Penn established Du Bois House for African American students, paving the way for numerous other residences defined more narrowly by race, ethnicity, and subject matter or theme – a trend that spelled the beginning of the end for Kors's house, which closed as a residence sometime during the 1980s. To Kors, it was the "end of the dream."

Some Background

During the 1980s the Hackney administration instituted a number of programs and policies designed to make Penn more racially and sexually "sensitive." At Penn, the president holds the ultimate power over most important

[2] Interview with University of Pennsylvania professor Michael Cohen, July 2001.
[3] Interview with University of Pennsylvania professor Larry Gross, April 2002. See also the comment in response to a Kors speech by the author of Stanford's now defunct speech code, Thomas C. Grey: "Slogans have their place. I have put them on my car from time to time, recognizing that they can't treat the full complexity of an issue." Grey, "Slogans, Amens, and Speeches," 10 *Academic Questions* 18 (summer 1997), p. 18.
[4] Interview with University of Pennsylvania professor Alan Kors, July 2001.

decisions, including whether to adopt speech and antiharassment codes. Penn has a faculty senate and a university council consisting of elected representatives of major groups on campus, including students. These bodies influenced important decisions in the 1960s and 1970s, but today they possess only advisory power. Kors explained, "The senate and university council are both like Renaissance parliaments: you gather the notables, you largely talk *to* them, you let them vent if they need to vent, and then go out and explain your policies."[5] When the trustees appointed Hackney to replace Martin Meyerson as president of the university in 1980, they passed over the popular provost, Vartan Gregorian. In reaction, the senate held a special meeting and voted overwhelmingly for Gregorian, only to be ignored. According to Larry Gross, a communications arts professor, "It meant, among other things, that Hackney came in under something of a cloud."[6]

One reason that Gregorian was so well regarded was because he was instrumental in transforming Penn from a relative academic backwater in 1960 to the forefront of American higher education in 1980.[7] He also had the human touch, earning campuswide respect for his dedication to higher learning. Calling his snub a "tragic turn," one bereaved admirer wrote in the *Almanac*: "Gregorian drew to himself a degree of personal affection and loyalty from students and colleagues rarely, if ever, witnessed or experienced in academia.... Vartan's quality of presence was the flowering of an institutional aliveness, an openness, an adventuresomeness which began at Penn around 1960."[8]

Hackney's ascension from the outside was perhaps a harbinger of the coming culture wars. Though a fair, competent, and conscientious man, Hackney did not possess Gregorian's level of charisma and vision, perhaps making it all the harder for him to hold the pieces together when new political forces began tearing Penn apart at the seams. Hackney came to Penn from the presidency of Tulane; prior to that, he had served as provost at Princeton, where he had earned plaudits for pioneering the development of black studies, and won a national award for his book, *Populism to Progressivism in Alabama*.[9]

To serve as provost, Hackney brought in the energetic Tom Erlich, a professor and former dean of Stanford Law School – Penn's first provost from outside the university in over a century. Before going to Stanford, Erlich had served as the first president of the Legal Services Corporation, the nonprofit

[5] Ibid.
[6] Interview with Larry Gross.
[7] Interview with University of Pennsylvania professor Henry Teune, July 2001.
[8] George Rochberg, Annenberg Professor of the Humanities, "Speaking Out," *Almanac*, November 18, 1980.
[9] Hackney, *Populism to Progressivism in Alabama* (Princeton University Press, 1969); "Hackney at Tulane," *Almanac*, September 23, 1980.

government organization established to provide civil legal services to the poor.[10] Hackney portrayed Erlich as "a creative person, with educational vision and a sense of social responsibility." Anthony Tomanzinis, former chair of the faculty senate in the early 1980s, described Erlich as an engineer of institutional change: "He came over here and started establishing priorities on the national level. He introduced a number of things," including updating the undergraduate curriculum to be more multicultural and influencing the composition of the senate and key committees. "He was one of the first people who talked about 'dead white males.' ... he felt we needed to update and enlarge [the curriculum]."[11]

Part of this change was what political scientist Henry Teune calls "the expansion of the creature comforts of students," which means students demanding a more agreeable emotional and material environment. Carolyn Marvin, a communications arts professor who teaches courses dealing with freedom of speech, bemoaned the "expansion of creature comforts":

At a certain point, universities decided that students should not have ordeals. They should be coddled because their parents are paying these outrageous sums of money. ... The university has become a corporation and they have to ask, "are the customers satisfied? If the student has a complaint, then there must be something to that." And to satisfy the student population means that nobody will ever be mad at each other – and this particularly applies to ideas.[12]

Such is one prominent rationale for speech codes. Over what Kors and Silverglate call the "strenuous objection of a handful of professors," Hackney fashioned a speech code in that fateful year, 1987. Arguing against the code along with a few others, Cohen pointed to another reason for the code's emergence: "The common point of view on this issue was that the same thing was happening everywhere, and there was a certain evolution that had to occur."[13]

The Diversity Agenda at Penn

According to Michael Cohen, "when Hackney came in the climate really changed. Hackney really introduced the nonacademic part of the administration."[14] (The same thing happened at Wisconsin when Hackney's friend, Donna Shalala, took over as chancellor in late 1987.) By the end of the 1980s, Penn was bristling with racial and gender awareness workshops, freshman orientation sensitivity sessions, official denunciations of racism and sexism, and two of the broadest codes regulating speech and harassment

[10] See "For Provost: Tom Erlich of Stanford," *Almanac*, May 19, 1981.
[11] Interview with University of Pennsylvania professor Anthony Tomanzinis, July 2001.
[12] Interview with Henry Teune; interview with Carolyn Marvin, University of Pennsylvania, July 2001.
[13] Kors and Silverglate, *The Shadow University*, p. 10; interview with Michael Cohen.
[14] Interview with Michael Cohen.

in the country. Even before the water buffalo case, Penn was known as the school at which an undergraduate woman was chastised by an administrator in the university's planning committee for diversity because she wrote about her "deep regard for the individual and my desire to protect the freedom of all members of society." The administrator wrote back, "This is a RED FLAG phrase today, which is considered by many to be RACIST."[15] Despite such trends, students still reported that they attained quality education (see Heather McCormick's comment in Chapter 4).

Racial tensions erupted in 1981 when unknown sources made threatening phone calls to Du Bois House. Later racial altercations included conflict over divestment from South Africa (the university did divest later in the decade) and the reaction to classroom comments by an adjunct professor, Murray Dolfman. But according to Gross, gender was an even bigger issue in the 1980s at Penn than race. Encouraged by the famous antipornography conference at Barnard in 1982, feminist activists campaigned to limit pornography and harassment at Penn. Some of the leading activists, in particular Elena DiLapi, who took over as head of the Women's Center in 1985, shared Catharine MacKinnon's interpretation of gender relations, which stress the systemic presence of male domination.

An event in early 1985 signaled the move toward a more radical form of institutional feminism at Penn. Three articles in the student newspaper, the *Daily Pennsylvanian* (*DP*), reported controversy engulfing the new director of the Women's Center, Ximena Bunster, who had replaced the center's legendary founder, Carol Tracy. Activists attacked Bunster for not being responsive enough to their interests and visions and accused her of anti-Semitism, racism, and homophobia – charges she vigorously denied in a letter to the *Almanac*. Bunster claims that her alleged sin lay in expanding the center's agenda to include the needs of those who were not activists. A defender wrote, "it is clear that she has not been able to serve effectively the needs of activist women students at Penn. . . . However, there are other constituencies among university women whose needs, in spite of Carol's [Tracy] efforts, have not been adequately addressed."[16]

Bunster was replaced by DiLapi, a former social worker and counselor, and author of what the *Almanac* called a "publication" entitled *Between a Rock and a Hard Place: When Racism and Sexism Intersect in Post-Secondary Education.*[17] DiLapi soon implemented a proactivist agenda at the center. When Richard Bernstein visited Penn in the early 1990s to research his book,

---

[15] Richard Bernstein, *Dictatorship of Virtue: Multiculturalism and the Battle for America's Future* (Alfred E. Knopf, 1994), p. 75.

[16] Letters from Ximena Bunster and Jean A. Crockett, finance professor, *Almanac*, February 26, 1985.

[17] "Women's Center: Ellie DiLapi," *Almanac*, October 8, 1985. This publication is not listed as a holding in any library at the University of Wisconsin.

Dictatorship of Virtue, he asked about the center's refusal to hand out literature dealing with the pro-life side of the abortion debate. DiLapi replied, "my position is that the pro-choice position is the middle ground." Bernstein also quoted a form letter sent from the center to a male student accused of violating the school's sexual harassment policy: the letter essentially assumed guilt before the investigation.[18]

About the same time that DiLapi took over as the head of the Women's Center, Penn released a major report on the prevalence of sexual harassment and assault on campus. Part of an ongoing project addressing racial and sexual harassment, the report dealt not only with quid pro quo harassment and unwanted advances but also such things as "jokes," "sexually suggestive looks," and "leaning over" someone.[19] Hackney, Erlich, and other administrators acknowledged in a statement, "we underscore that the term 'sexual harassment' as used in the Report is substantially broader than the term as defined in the current University policy," as the term now included offensiveness, teasing, jokes, looks, and the like, and applied to "all relationships among peers, some of which are not covered by current University policy." The survey found there to be widespread harassment at Penn, but critics claimed that the report failed to adequately distinguish between minor and major incidents.[20] Regardless of this weakness, the survey helped set the stage for the new sexual harassment policy that Hackney developed in 1987.

Racial Issues

The explosion over Murray Dolfman's class comments in November 1984 was a pivotal event at Penn. The ordeal was foreshadowed in the early 1970s, when students disrupted the classes of the conservative urbanologist, Edward Banfield, renowned for attributing some of the problems of the inner city to the shortcomings of inner city residents.[21] Kors recalled a student – now "a professor somewhere" – who used to follow Banfield home, "shouting, on the Philadelphia streets, 'racist...racist...racist.' [President] Martin [Meyerson] had been Banfield's dear friend, and had brought him to Penn. I once asked Banfield why he didn't call on President Meyerson for an appropriate response. 'Why should I have to?' he replied."[22]

In 1984 Murray Dolfman was an adjunct lecturer in the Wharton School's Legal Studies Department. Overall, Dolfman was an enormously popular

---

[18] Bernstein, *Dictatorship of Virtue,* pp. 74, 82.

[19] See "Release of Survey on Sexual Harassment," and "Conduct and Misconduct on Campus," *Almanac,* September 24, 1985; "On the Sexual Harassment Survey Report," *Almanac,* suppl., September 24, 1985.

[20] Interview with Michael Cohen. See also criticisms in "Debate on Sexual Harassment Survey," *Almanac,* October 15, 1985.

[21] See Edward Banfield, *The Unheavenly City: The Nature and Future of Our Urban Crisis* (Little, Brown, 1970).

[22] Interview with Alan Kors; interview with Larry Gross.

teacher whose classes were always oversubscribed, with students repeatedly giving him among the highest evaluations in the school. But under the sway of the politics and tenor of the times, he was destined to be a pariah.

During a discussion in class on November 12, 1984, about the role of specific promises in contracts, Dolfman raised the issue of the legal status of involuntary servitude. Frustrated by the lack of student knowledge of slavery and law, he asked black students individually and as a group if they knew the meaning of the Thirteenth Amendment, which prohibits slavery and involuntary servitude. None did. The irrepressible Dolfman then singled out one black student, and twice had him stand and read the amendment out loud. According to the official report on the incident (the "Wharton Report"), "Mr. Dolfman then expressed surprise that while he, as a Jew and a 'former slave,' celebrated the end of his slavery at Passover, the black students, who he likewise called 'former slaves' or 'ex-slaves,' did not celebrate the passage of the 13th Amendment."[23] Even Dolfman's supporters admit that singling out a student in this way was very poor pedagogy. After the class, three black students went to Dolfman's office and demanded an apology, which he quickly gave. But they were not satisfied.

Activists waited until the end of February – Black History Month – to make their views public. They wanted to make the incident a prominent example of racism on the campus. They held several large rallies on campus and in front of Hackney's home, and sent angry letters to the campus papers. In addition, two hundred students took over Dolfman's class, forcing him to move the class to another room, which they promptly took over as well – acts that clearly violated Penn's "Open Expression" policy. One hundred nine professors signed a petition denouncing Dolfman and demanding his dismissal. The Black Student League issued three demands: Dolfman's dismissal; an increase in the number of black faculty; and the institutionalization of mandatory racism awareness workshops.[24]

Within a week of the protests, Hackney and Erlich issued a "Response on Racism," which declared, "We will immediately initiate, in consultation with faculty, students, and staff, the development of a strong University Policy on Racial Harassment." Erlich convened a special meeting of deans to discuss the need "to make racial awareness sessions for Department Chairs, faculty members, and teaching assistants." In this statement, the president and provost also thanked the protesters: "You have brought forward sharply and clearly a number of real concerns on this campus, and we are grateful."[25] They did not mention the lack of civility of the protesters, who had

---

[23] "Report of the Wharton Committee on Academic Freedom and Responsibility," *Almanac*, April 9, 1985. Most of the basic facts related here are from this report, unless stated otherwise.

[24] "A Week of Protests Charging Racism," "Open Letter on Racism," and "Statement of BSL," all in *Almanac*, February 26, 1985.

[25] Hackney and Erlich, "Response on Racism," *Almanac*, February 21, 1985.

physically taken over two classes. Kors and Silverglate report that the Black Student League issued several press statements warning that the takeover of Dolfman's class and the protest at Hackney's house were mere preludes to what Penn could expect if their demands were not met: "Doubters 'should brace yourselves for a very rude awakening.' Penn was being offered a 'final chance.' It would be folly to 'believe that our fury will subside. . . . We are Dead Serious. . . . THE FIRE NEXT TIME!!!!!!!!!!!!"[26]

Professors also made hostile remarks. At one rally, a faculty member excoriated Dolfman. According to the *Almanac*, he "delivered and expanded on BFA's [Black Faculty Association's] February 20 statement, charging insensitivity among University leaders." Richard Bernstein contends that the *Almanac* "bowdlerized" this statement. According to Bernstein, the professor actually said, "This is no longer just a black struggle. We are in the forefront because some asshole decided that his classroom is going to be turned into a cesspool."[27]

In the end, Dolfman was given a one-semester suspension, with his return to teaching conditioned upon a public apology and his successfully completing sensitivity and racial awareness sessions, and his agreeing to be continuously monitored by the university. The usual handful of faculty – especially Michael Cohen – worked behind the scenes on Dolfman's behalf, but their efforts were handicapped by the fact that, according to Kors, "It was hard to fight for Dolfman because he accepted the terms offered."[28]

The Dolfman case was a defining moment at Penn. It energized the drive toward a speech code and showed how traumatized the entire institution could become over an act that was very ill-considered, yet hardly a racist insult when placed in context. Dolfman was an "old school" instructor who was well known for putting students on the spot, often criticizing them for such flaws as poor grammar, sloppy speech, and lack of precision in thought. Yet he was among the most popular instructors at the school. He singled out the students on November 12, 1984, *in order to stress the historical and moral importance of antislavery enactments.* Even if one agrees with the assessment of the Wharton Report that his tactics were "deplorable," it is difficult to justify the response that he received.

Furthermore, nothing was done about the takeover of Dolfman's classes by the mob of students that invaded the inner sanctuary of education. The political scientist Henry Teune wrote in the *Almanac*, "no explanation" for such actions is justified, "except when life and health are in danger. Many struggled long for the privileged position of the class as essential to academic freedom. Students have classroom rights; faculty have rights to be able to

---

[26] Kors and Silverglate, *The Shadow University*, pp. 334–35.
[27] Bernstein, *Dictatorship of Virtue*, p. 112.
[28] Interview with Alan Kors.

discuss in a protected setting."[29] In April the Committee on Open Expression issued its report on the class disruptions, concluding unanimously that the actions violated Penn's Guidelines on Open Expression.[30] They sent their conclusions and evidence to the relevant judicial officers, and the matter died. In Bernstein's assessment, the situation resembled a "lynch mob," and he noted that in this era "the charge of racism, unsubstantiated but accompanied by a few demonstrations and angry rhetorical perorations, suffices to paralyze a campus, to destroy a reputation, and to compel an administration into submission."[31] Civil liberties columnist Nat Hentoff, who interviewed Dolfman, wrote that the "sensitivity and racial awareness session" was like "a Vietnamese reeducation camp" and that Dolfman was "exiled from the campus for a year." Hentoff also wrote that, "as far as I can find out, none of the law school professors, including those specializing in civil liberties, defended Dolfman. Nor did the liberals elsewhere on the faculty."[32] (Recall that Kors said it was hard to support Dolfman because he had made a deal before support could consolidate on his behalf.) That said, Michael Cohen did work energetically behind the scenes to help the beleaguered teacher.[33] It is not hard to imagine how the affair might have chilled honest discourse about race in class and on campus.

A few years later, the incident reappeared as an example of racial harassment in Penn's official "Facilitators Guide," a manual that assisted faculty in conducting discussion sessions with freshmen on racism and sexism. The guide included examples from other incidents, including a striptease party at ZBT fraternity and a white student's punching a black student in an elevator. The faculty facilitators were supposed to read about the incidents to freshmen, and then ask, "what is happening here, and why?" In talking about the Dolfman case, the guide said that the instructor "continuously referred to African-American students in his class as 'ex-slaves.'" It did not mention the context, making it appear that the instructor's comments were motivated simply to demean the students. Michael Cohen knew that the guide exaggerated that case and conducted some research on the other cases. He discovered that the guide exaggerated them as well. In fact, the incident on the elevator

[29] Teune, "Classroom Rights," *Almanac*, February 26, 1985.

[30] "Report of the Committee on Open Expression, on Demonstration in a Classroom on February 13, 1985," *Almanac*, April 23, 1985.

[31] Bernstein, *Dictatorship of Virtue*, pp. 114–15. The Dolfman affair – like many of the instances I discuss in Chapter 2 – must be read through the lens of social psychology and scapegoat literature. See, e.g., Rene Girard, "The Plague in Literature and Myth," in Girard, *To Double Business Bound: Essays on Literature, Mimesis, and Anthropology* (Johns Hopkins University Press, 1978); Paul S. Boyer and Stephen Nissenbaum, *Salem Possessed* (Harvard University Press, 1976).

[32] Nat Hentoff, *Free Speech for Me, Not for Thee: How the American Left and Right Relentlessly Censor Each Other* (HarperCollins, 1992), p. 191; see, generally, pp. 188–92.

[33] Interview with Alan Kors.

never even happened. Administrators defended the guide by saying that the examples were "composites" of various cases, not factual accounts.[34] The guide was one example of the widespread network of sensitivity workshops, freshman orientation sessions, and literature that permeated Penn by the end of the decade. After spending time there in the early 1990s, Bernstein found that "The themes of struggle and oppression saturate freshman orientation, and much else of freshmen life. Students are encouraged to believe that if they do not feel racism and oppression, it is because they have engaged in internalized repression."[35]

Finally, in April 1985, the chair of the senate committee on academic freedom and responsibility issued the report on the status of academic freedom at Penn after the Dolfman incident. Rather than holding out the promise of a new sense of community at Penn, he said, the "racial and sexual awareness workshops" that the administration now planned forebode the rise of deep conflict and tension, whether they were voluntary or mandatory. But the die was cast. "The genie is out of the bottle and will not be put back easily or perhaps at all."[36]

Two Codes for All Seasons

After a year of extensive consultation and campus discussion, in the spring of 1987 Hackney introduced the expanded sexual harassment code and a new "Racial and Ethnic Harassment" code. One aspect of the debate over the latter code involved the name: if the code only covered prohibited harassing *conduct*, it was not a *speech* code; if it were actually a *speech* code in disguise, however, its legitimacy would be more questionable. As at other schools, supporters at Penn tried to divert attention from the free speech implications by contending that the code covered harassing *conduct*, not speech. Kors and Silverglate, however, said the measure constituted "the university's first modern-era restrictions on speech."[37] The new policy defined racial and ethnic harassment as "any behavior, verbal or physical, that stigmatizes or victimizes individuals on the basis of race, ethnic or national origin, and that: a) involves a stated or implicit threat to the victim's academic or employment status; b) has the purpose or effect of interfering with an individual's academic or work performance; and/or c) creates an intimidating or offensive academic, living, or work environment."[38]

---

[34] Interview with Michael Cohen; Bernstein, *Dictatorship of Virtue*, p. 67. Bernstein is the source of this particular episode.

[35] Bernstein, *Dictatorship of Virtue*, pp. 64–65, 71.

[36] "Chair's Report, Senate Committee on Academic Freedom and Responsibility, 1984–85," *Almanac*, April 23, 1985.

[37] Kors and Silverglate, *The Shadow University*, p. 10.

[38] Harassment Policy, reported in *Almanac*, June 2, 1987.

Only a few professors opposed the new code.[39] Although Larry Gross has found himself on the opposite side of Kors on several issues over the years, when it comes to free speech, Gross and Kors ultimately ended up on the same page. "The speech code issue was discussed in various forums, including the university council.... Alan Kors and I were saying exactly the same thing: 'You can't do this.' It's a bit like the standard argument for democracy, which is the worst system of government except for all the others. You have no alternative to free speech, at least in this society. Yes, you pay the price from time to time, as with some offensive event or another. But the alternative is much worse."[40] It was during the debate over the speech code that Kors rose to prominence on campus. "I started fighting this stuff in the 1980s. I wrote to Hackney against his first proposed harassment policy. Then the president promulgated a horrific first harassment policy. Totally partisan."[41]

Hackney defended the code as consistent with the First Amendment. (Even though Penn is not subject to constitutional strictures as a private school, the administration knew that it would look bad for a leading academic institution to be in conflict with national free speech norms.) But this contention took a blow when a federal court ruled Michigan's less expansive code unconstitutional in 1989.[42] (The plaintiff brought the case at Michigan after listening to a speech Kors gave at the 1989 national meeting of the National Association of Scholars.) After this ruling, Kors and his allies badgered Hackney "at every occasion," Kors related. So Hackney appointed law professor Edwin Baker, a noted First Amendment theorist, to revise the code. Though skeptical that any such code could pass First Amendment muster, Baker told Hackney that limiting the code to the "fighting words" standard was the only possibility. The narrower revised code, drafted in 1990, prohibited "verbal or symbolic" behavior that is directed at "an identifiable person or persons," and which "insults or demeans" such person or persons. In addition, the expression must be "intended by the speaker or actor to inflict direct injury."[43] The intent standard was meant to limit significantly the code's reach to only the most extreme cases of hostile expression.

The Road to the Water Buffalo

Although no major cases occurred in 1991 and 1992, it seemed just a matter of time before a major conflict would erupt. In the spring term of 1993, a confluence of controversial events thrust Penn and its new code into the

---

[39] Kors and Silverglate, *The Shadow University*, p. 10.
[40] Interview with Larry Gross.
[41] Interview with Alan Kors.
[42] *Doe v. University of Michigan*, 721 F. Supp. 852 (E. D. Mich. 1989).
[43] University of Pennsylvania, Policies and Procedures, 1990–91; Kors and Silverglate, *The Shadow University*, p. 11; interview with Alan Kors. See C. Edwin Baker, *Human Liberty and Freedom of Speech* (Oxford University Press, 1989).

national spotlight. It was also during this semester that President Clinton nominated Sheldon Hackney to be the new chair of the National Endowment for the Humanities, focusing even more national attention on Penn.[44]

The first event involved the student paper, the *Daily Pennsylvanian*. As the only student paper on a racially tense campus, the *DP* had often found itself embroiled in controversy concerning racial issues. The fact that its staff was overwhelmingly white did little to alleviate the problem. The trouble began when the *DP* published the columns of its lone archconservative voice, Greg Pavlik. Though soft-spoken and reticent in demeanor, Pavlik's pen was a political Howitzer. Pavlik wrote two columns in early 1993 that many considered to reach the heights of political incorrectness. In "Rethinking the King Holiday," written on Martin Luther King Day, he chastised the civil rights movement for undermining property and liberty and criticized King for his personal moral lapses. Then, in "Not as Clear as Black and White," Pavlik took a shot at Penn's double standard in dealing with race, pointing to a recent incident in which the university punished the whites involved but not the blacks, whom Pavlik considered equally culpable.[45]

The columns provoked an uproar. On March 19, 202 African American students and faculty published a response accusing Pavlik of being a "racist" and charging that the very publication of his columns constituted outright discrimination. Tailoring their words to fit the speech code, they admonished those "hiding beyond the delicate laws of freedom of speech," which they said should not be allowed to protect the right "to slander, demean, harass, and incite violence in those who don't share a Eurocentric upbringing."[46]

The Pavlik affair could not have arisen at a less propitious moment. The university was under attack from the minority community for its handling of a lawsuit over its allocation of "Mayor's Scholarships," an important source of funding that was intended to improve local minority access to Penn. According to Kors and Silverglate, "Hackney was accused of racism. It was the tenth year of his presidency, and he obsessed throughout on race relations.... Hackney was a captive of the very perception of endemic racism that Penn had encouraged and of the expectation that had been created that all 'disadvantaged' groups had a right not to be 'offended.'"[47]

In January 1993 Hackney had reenergized the "Minority Permanence" campaign at Penn. In a letter in the *Almanac*, he linked the renewal of the campaign to eliminate racism at Penn with the arrival of the newly elected President Clinton in Washington. It was "the beginning of a new era of

[44] "The White House Call: Dr. Hackney for NEH," *Almanac*, April 13, 1993.

[45] Pavlik, "Rethinking the King Holiday," *Daily Pennsylvanian*, January 14, 1993; "Not as Clear as Black and White," *Daily Pennsylvanian*, January 25, 1993. See Kors and Silverglate, *The Shadow University*, pp. 19–20.

[46] *Daily Pennsylvanian*, March 19, 1993. I could not find this statement in the *Daily Pennsylvanian*'s Internet archive. For more, see Kors and Silverglate, *The Shadow University*, p. 21.

[47] Kors and Silverglate, *The Shadow University*, pp. 19–20.

change and renewal for our nation." A meeting with faculty and staff of color had taught Hackney that "we had not yet achieved the kind of caring community that we want to be. We were told that students, faculty, and staff members of the University of Pennsylvania community still feel frustrated and oppressed by what they experience as a hostile environment." Hackney then declared war against harassment in all its forms: "This is the time to tell all members of our community again, *but this time in a way that must be heard*, that we will not tolerate acts that demean students, faculty and staff – not in the classroom, not in support offices, not on the campuses, not in our residences. *We will find means to ensure that such acts have important consequences.*"[48]

A week later, the new provost, Michael Aiken, and acting executive vice president, John Wells Gould, presented "Action Steps Regarding Minority Permanence," which amounted to a call to arms at Penn regarding harassment and "intolerant behavior." The steps included more awareness sessions, consultations, brochures, and information, to be accompanied by more rigorous enforcement of antiharassment norms. The statement asserted, "The Provost will inform all Deans of incidents of intolerant behavior reported by students, faculty, and staff. Deans will be asked to take immediate action with department chairs and faculty regarding specific incidents ... *to assure that all available institutional, commonwealth, and federal remedies are used and these behaviors cease at Penn.*"[49]

The judicial inquiry officer's (JIO) first response to the furor over Pavlik's articles was to notify him on the phone early one morning that on the basis of no less than thirty-five complaints, he was under investigation for having violated Penn's racial harassment code. A "terrified" Pavlik spent a week trying to find someone who would stand up for him and help. He asked his minister what he should do and found out about Kors. He got hold of Kors, who in turn contacted Hackney, reminding the president that a wrong step could sabotage his hopes of an NEH nomination. Hackney told Kors that the charges "aren't going anywhere," and the JIO dropped the case the next day.[50]

Kors was also involved in another case about the same time that the Pavlik case riveted Penn. Tim Monaco, a political science graduate student and residential assistant – and one of the only openly Republican students in the RA program – cursed at a female undergraduate desk worker who had just sworn at him for criticizing her job performance. Although he apologized, he found himself under "informal" investigation for sexual harassment. The inquiry proceeded without regard for such basic procedural norms as putting

[48] From the President, "On Minority Permanence at Penn," *Almanac*, January 26, 1993 (emphasis added).

[49] "Action Steps Regarding Minority Permanence," *Almanac*, February 2, 1993 (emphasis added).

[50] Kors and Silverglate, *The Shadow University*, pp. 21–22; interview with Alan Kors.

the charges in writing, so Monaco contacted Kors. The administration was informed that Monaco would sue top administrators as individuals if he were found guilty by a "kangaroo court." Within a week, Monaco received a letter from the director of the program informing him that they had dropped the case.[51]

Meanwhile, the Pavlik affair continued to haunt Penn. On April 15, the *DP* published his final column, which addressed the lack of meaningful debate on the sensitivity-obsessed campus. Angered at the vindication of Pavlik, a group of students stole an entire run of papers – some 14,000 copies – from several distribution points on campus. Members of the *DP* staff caught the thieves in the act at six locations and were subjected to threats and racial epithets when they attempted to thwart their escape. A University Museum officer managed to apprehend some individuals as they ran out of the building with bundles of papers in a garbage bag and then took them to the university police headquarters for questioning.[52]

Theft and destruction of student newspapers have plagued the nation's universities in recent years. Usually, administrations excuse such acts on the grounds that the papers are free or that such acts represent counterspeech against the papers. But taking or destroying many more papers than is one's due is a form of theft of advertisers' money, as it deprives them of the advertising for which they paid. Furthermore, publishing a student paper costs labor and money (sometimes in the form of student fees), so large-scale confiscation or destruction robs many people of the fruits of their labors and of financial contributions. And, of course, confiscating or destroying large numbers of papers substantially limits the flow of public discourse. Destroying newspapers is no different in principle from shouting down an unpopular speaker. There is a clear difference between the symbolic destruction of a few papers to demonstrate a point – such acts are clearly protected by basic free speech principles – and the theft or destruction of large numbers of papers.

The theft of the *DP* on April 15, 1993, was clearly illegitimate, and provoked a great deal of commentary on the Penn campus and in the press. The JIO did charge the nine students and a faculty member who had been apprehended with violating the Open Expression Guidelines. However, in September, the JIO concluded that the defendants were guilty of the lesser violation of the university's Policy of Confiscation of Publications and recommended that the university take no further action against them. Interim President Claire Fagin then accepted this recommendation.[53] The Public

---

[51] See Kors and Silverglate, *The Shadow University*, pp. 302–5, on which I base this narrative of the case. Also, interview with Alan Kors.

[52] See "Individual Incidents on April 15, 1993 [Re: The Removal of *DP*s]. Report of Public Safety Task Force," *Almanac*, July 13, 1993.

[53] "Report of the Special Judicial Inquiry Officer Regarding the Confiscation of the *Daily Pennsylvanian* on April 15, 1993," *Almanac*, September 14, 1993.

Safety Task Force wrote that one reason that the group had not violated the Open Expression Guidelines was because university police should have recognized that the removal of the *DP*s from at least three different locations was "a form of student protest and not an indicator of criminal behavior."[54]

Accentuating the "pain and anger" that had provoked the thefts, Hackney maintained that the case boiled down to a difference of values: "diversity and open expression," and the free speech rights of the *DP* and the "protesters." He also chastised the campus police for overreacting and announced the creation of yet two more committees to "address the serious problems now existing in relations between the minority community at Penn and the University Police."[55]

Penn's Waterloo: The Water Buffalo Case

The Monaco, Pavlik, and *DP* cases thrust more controversy Penn's way than any beleaguered administration should have to suffer. But these incidents were mere trial runs compared with the water buffalo case.

The case simmered in the background over the course of the already tumultuous semester, bursting into the public realm only in April, when the New York Jewish magazine the *Forward* published an account of the case after hearing about it from a friend of Kors.[56] This article was the first rock in an avalanche. As of July 2001 Kors had personally counted 700 articles on the case. The administration's stance was the product of at least three things: racial politics; a reluctance to drop yet another case after dropping the Pavlik and Monaco cases; and what Larry Gross described as an escalation of legal formalism and punitiveness in the actual adjudication of cases. "It was a typically overblown example where, once the mechanism starts, it has its own momentum."[57] It is also important to note that the president possessed more authority to intervene in the Pavlik case because formal charges had not yet been brought.

Although Kors had had important differences with Hackney over the years, he said that the water buffalo case was the first time that matters went over the top. Kors and Cohen had often been able to get Hackney to modify a policy pushed by the advocates of sensitivity. "The extraordinary use Cohen and I were to Hackney was to give him a middle ground to occupy. The faculty would say, 'Let's censor all offensive speech,' and we'd get him to say, 'only the most offensive.'"[58]

---

54 "Report of Public Safety Task Force."
55 Hackney, "On the Campus Controversy of April 15–16: Narrowing the Difference," *Almanac*, April 20, 1993.
56 "Pennsylvania Preparing to Buffalo a Yeshiva Boy," *Forward*, April 23, 1993. See Kors and Silverglate, *The Shadow University*, pp. 24–25.
57 Interview with Larry Gross.
58 Interview with Alan Kors.

So what happened? Most of the facts are pretty clear. What is in dispute is whether Eden Jacobowitz, an orthodox Jewish freshman from New York City who had attended Yeshiva school, intentionally shouted a racist epithet at a group of African American women. The evidence strongly suggests that he did not.

Late at night on January 13, 1993, a group of fifteen to twenty sorority women celebrating their group's Founders Day sang and chanted loudly outside High Rise East, a freshman dorm, as students were studying or trying to sleep. Some students were disturbed and started shouting racist words at the revelers, such as "black bitches" and "black asses." In a final statement on the case in May, the five women who filed complaints said that they "were subjected to a barrage of racial epithets and slurs."[59] Regardless of one's view about the advisability of prosecuting on the basis of actual racial epithets, it is clear that such expression would run afoul of Penn's code.

The problem is that none of the students who made such remarks was charged. Only Jacobowitz was charged, for a simple reason: only he admitted that he had shouted something out the window. Several sorority sisters stormed into the dorm and made their way to the floor from which the shouting had emanated. When they asked who had made the offending remarks, the dorm residents they encountered, some of whom had made their own contributions to the verbal barrage, pointed down the hall toward Jacobowitz's room. When the sisters entered Jacobowitz's doorway, his roommate – who had himself contributed to the ill-advised chorus – declared his innocence and pointed to the hapless Jacobowitz.

According to Jacobowitz and an eyewitness I interviewed, the scene was raucous. Tina Besian, whose parents came to America from Syria and whose roommate was African American, said that Jacobowitz was not likely to have used epithets. "They counted up the windows to figure out what room it was. I also feel responsible because I kind of directed them to his room. They came to our room and asked if there were any guys in the room. They were very irate. They just kind of walked into our room and started making accusations, and I said, 'If you are looking for the guys, they are down the hall.'"[60] On September 9, 1993, the *DP* published an article in which Jacobowitz's roommate – who had also been investigated by the university until charges were dropped – admitted that he had deflected blame from himself and onto Jacobowitz.[61] The roommate was also critical of how the university handled his case. When the police came and then questioned

---

[59] "Statements Made Monday, May 24, Concluding the 'Water Buffalo' Case," *Almanac*, May 25, 1993.

[60] Interview with Penn student Tina Besian, July 2001. I fortuitously met Besian in the office where copies of the *Almanac* are shelved.

[61] Christopher Pryor, "The Other Water Buffalo," *Daily Pennsylvanian*, guest column, September 9, 1993.

students at the station, once again only Jacobowitz admitted that he had shouted out the window.

Just what *did* he holler? Everyone agrees that he said the following: "Shut up, you water buffalo! If you want a party, there's a zoo a mile from here!"[62] Those with an interest in the case would later learn that "water buffalo" translates to "behemoth" in Hebrew, a language in which Jacobowitz was steeped at home and in earlier schooling. The five women who filed the complaint claimed that he had added a pernicious word: "Shut up, you *black* water buffalo!" Jacobowitz steadfastly denied that he used the word "black," and many other sources supported this claim. A second, much more exhaustive police report also exonerated him, but the relevant office of the administration never showed the report to the defense or made it part of the proceedings. Although the complainants continued to insist that Jacobowitz used the forbidden word, the case proceeded, more or less, on the assumption that the term "water buffalo" was in itself racist when directed at African Americans.

But is it racist? Over the next months, a stunning array of scholars from various fields checked in with their own interpretations. The consensus view was that it referred to a large Chinese cow. The most authoritative interpretation was presented by a noted Israeli scholar of African folklore, who concluded that the term meant "behemoth" in Hebrew, which denotes a "thoughtless or rowdy person." According to Kors and Silverglate, this interpretation should have settled the case, for Jacobowitz recalled that he and his friends had often used the Hebrew term "beheme" in Yeshiva school to refer to rude or rowdy people.[63] Not everyone was convinced that Jacobowitz's use of the term was so innocent. The reference to the "zoo" was suspicious, as was the context. Larry Gross and some others felt that Kors made Jacobowitz too much a paragon of virtue. Though he admitted that the case was marked by "bureaucratic stupidity," Gross did not let Jacobowitz off so lightly:

I grew up in Jerusalem, and people do not call each other behemoth, no matter what he wants to say. If it is the case, what he said was, "There's a zoo down the road," it becomes a little harder to say that this was somebody translating from the Hebrew that you called each other water buffalo. It's just silly. On the other side, the fact is that the notion that these members of a sorority should be doing their singing and dancing routines late at night and right in front of these dormitories is ridiculous also. And this is exactly where it calls for the old-fashioned call them in, tell them to cut it out, and stop escalating it to legalisms.[64]

---

[62] Kors and Silverglate, *The Shadow University*, p. 9; interview with Penn student Eden Jacobowitz, November 2001.
[63] Kors and Silverglate, *The Shadow University*, p. 15; interview with Alan Kors.
[64] Interview with Larry Gross.

According to Kors, however, Jacobowitz's rabbi in New York City was willing to testify that he and the teachers at Jacobowitz's school called students "behema" all the time.[65]

Two of the sorority sisters also contended that Jacobowitz's comments were demeaning. A year after the case was settled, Ayanna Taylor commented in the *Almanac* that "Mr. Jacobowitz considers calling black women 'Black Water Buffalo' and telling them to go 'back to the zoo' a 'harmless almost humorous' thing. That is a sick, perverted sense of humor." In the same forum, Nikki Taylor claimed that Jacobowitz's refusal to apologize right away compelled the sisters to report the incident to the police: "When we went up to talk to Eden about why he yelled those words to us, he refused to speak to us. He had the opportunity to explain that he was 'joking' and 'did not mean to demean' us. Instead, he chose to hide and refuse to face up to his actions. His refusal to talk to us is why we decided to go to the police."[66] Jacobowitz did offer to apologize several times after the police got involved; but he refused to apologize for saying "*black* water buffalos," because, he said, he did not utter that word. And he was the only resident of the dorm to admit to police right away that he had shouted something. Above and beyond such points, the larger issue is whether even calling students "black water buffalos" who should go to the local zoo merits the punitive intervention of university police and judicial process, however demeaning and offensive. Is this the best way to promote racial understanding?

Robin Read, the JIO assigned to the case, decided that there was "reasonable cause" to believe that Jacobowitz had violated the racial harassment code. Jacobowitz then chose an adviser from an official list, Fran Walker, the director of student life, who told him that he would have to appear for several interviews. For several weeks Jacobowitz complied with everything the authorities requested, including confidentiality. "I thought honesty and justice would prevail," he said. "I don't have trouble getting my side across in a normal environment."[67] Jacobowitz did not even tell his parents about what was happening until April. Believing the affair was a monumental misunderstanding, he repeatedly asked if he could just meet with the complainants and apologize for unintentionally offending them. But his requests were not honored.

Read eventually stipulated in a meeting with Jacobowitz and Walker that Jacobowitz had only used the words "water buffaloes" and "zoo," not any racial terms. According to Kors and Silverglate, Walker was willing to testify at the final hearing in May that this stipulation took place but was told by the university general counsel's office "that I am not permitted to testify about

[65] Interview with Alan Kors.
[66] Ayanna Taylor, "From the Mountaintop," and Nikki Taylor, "Response of Nikki Taylor," "Speaking Out" section, *Almanac*, May 3, 1994.
[67] Interview with Eden Jacobowitz.

that meeting."[68] Read informed Jacobowitz in mid-March that sufficient evidence existed to prosecute him formally on the grounds that "water buffalo" referred to an *African* animal. She set the trial for March 22 – four days after Hackney's statement in the *Almanac* calling for extraordinary measures to combat harassment and "intolerant behavior" on campus. Jacobowitz was stunned. Kors and Silverglate wrote, "The entire weight of the university was coming down on a frightened freshman." In Jacobowitz's own words, "That was the first time I actually cried in her presence. They told me I can agree to a settlement or we can go to a hearing. This was the first time I got really scared that I was dealing with psychopaths. I was dealing with a court that was an obvious joke."[69]

The settlement – which his adviser recommended he accept – required four things: writing a letter of apology to the complainants, admitting wrongdoing; planning and developing a program on enhancing the environment for diversity for the High Rise East resident hall; being placed on "residential probation" for a year; and having a statement placed on his transcript for one year that said, "Violation of the Code of Conduct and Racial Harassment Policy." The terms of the "settlement" were actually harsher than the set of sanctions Jacobowitz had originally faced. The university's official report that came out a year later admitted that this "upping the ante" violated fundamental fairness.[70]

Although he felt overwhelmed, something inside Jacobowitz told him not to accept the deal. "I was never going to agree with that," he told me. "I didn't want anything ever on paper that said I had violated the racial harassment policy. They were asking me to agree to a lie."[71] He refused the offer and dismissed his adviser.

Enter Kors

But no one agreed to become his new adviser. "I couldn't find anyone who was willing to take on the university." At this point he felt "completely alone." Then he came across an article in the *DP* on Kors and free speech. The article said "that Kors was a fighter, not afraid to take on the administration, he really believes in these rights." When Jacobowitz called him, Kors's first reaction was disbelief. He told the freshman that he should find someone with less political baggage on campus. "I told him that I didn't care," Jacobowitz said. "I just wanted someone who believes in free speech and will actually do something to take on the administration." He told Kors, "If they're afraid

---

[68] Kors and Silverglate, *The Shadow University*, p. 33; see also pp. 10–12. Also, interview with Alan Kors.

[69] Kors and Silverglate, *The Shadow University*, p. 14; interview with Eden Jacobowitz.

[70] "Inquiry into the Procedural Aspects of a Case of Alleged Racial Harassment in the Spring of 1993" (Abel Report), *Almanac*, April 5, 1994.

[71] Interview with Eden Jacobowitz; Kors and Silverglate, *The Shadow University*, pp. 12–13.

of you, that's even better." He was "convinced that Kors was the real thing. "I [now] felt like everything was going to be okay. I felt ten times better and will be forever in debt to him for that. I had seen many of the things I believed in crumble before my eyes at an Ivy League school. Kors saved the day but also helped me piece my faith in humanity back together."[72]

The alliance between Kors and Jacobowitz would make academic history, leading to the single most prominent example of institutional reversal on the civil liberty front. Kors used the case to effect significant change. Some critics, including those who wrote the official university report on the case, accused Kors of being an opportunist: he used Jacobowitz as a pawn in the battle against the forces of political correctness, and he used the case for his own glorification. Kors insists these charges are without merit.

The facts strongly support Kors. First, though Kors was the first one to tell the outside press about the water buffalo case, he waited until it was clear that the university would not back off the case. Second, Jacobowitz himself strongly disagrees with such charges. He said, "Kors warned me at every point because the wrong person could have taken advantage of the situation. I'm not saying he wasn't fighting for the greater good, but he realized that I was involved, that a student's life was involved."[73] Finally, concrete proof is provided in an e-mail entitled "Sanity" that Kors sent to the new provost, Michael Aiken. On May 4, three weeks before the final showdown, Kors pleaded with Aiken to intervene to end the case and save the university from the humiliation that he knew Penn would suffer:

Confidential to Michael Aiken: You may remember that almost a month ago now, I stopped you in the corridor and suggested that there was a case you would wish to intervene in before it involved the university in unnecessary shame and embarrassment. I wish profoundly that you had taken me more seriously. . . . you referred me to Kim [Morrison, the Judicial Administrator]. . . . I BEGGED Kim, Larry, and Robin Read and the President's office to stop this preposterous case from going forward. No one even tried to understand. I spent two weeks pleading with people to spare Eden the pain of this case and to spare the University the humiliation and damages of this case, unsuccessfully.

I should also mention that when I interviewed Thor Halvorssen, the director of FIRE – the national organization Kors and Silverglate set up to carry out the agenda raised by *The Shadow University* – he showed me several cases that FIRE would have loved to publicize in order to demonstrate its prowess but which remained secret to honor the wishes of the client. (Recall also that FIRE pleaded with Columbia trustees for weeks in 2000 before taking the school's sexual misconduct policy to the press.) Halvorssen emphasized that FIRE's first obligation is always to the client, not the political agenda,

---

[72] Interview with Eden Jacobowitz.
[73] Ibid.

although it is more than happy to engage in the case's political aspect if given the green light. Kors took Jacobowitz's case for two simple reasons: "I don't like bullies. And I think students are young adults" who have the capacity to deal constructively with the rigors of constitutional citizenship.[74]

Questionable Process

The first thing Kors did was to implore Hackney and his assistants to do what they had recently done with Pavlik and Monaco: drop the case. He called Hackney and said, "This violates everything. Drop the charges! If I were tactical, this is the case I would want. It will bring down the whole speech code and the whole regime at Penn. But I don't want to be tactical. I just want this kid restored to his life." Altogether, Kors spoke with the president or his assistant at least eight times. Jacobowitz related that he and Kors talked with many people behind the scenes, begging them to just drop the case. But Hackney would not budge. He had alienated the pro–speech code crowd in the Pavlik case and was still concerned about charges of insensitivity because of his handling of the Mayor's Scholarships. (The *DP* thefts had not yet taken place.) "He made a calculation. Over one shoulder are militant blacks, over the other shoulder you have a professor of history. You make the call," Kors recalled.[75]

Hackney explained his decision in his own words in a recent book. He said that he agreed with Jacobowitz at the time that the JIO was sending the case on for a hearing because "the JIO did not want to take personal responsibility for ruling that the charges of the women did not amount to a violation of the racial harassment policy." (This provides a good interpretation of the JIO's motivations: she might have felt indebted to the student complainants.) Furthermore, Hackney believed Jacobowitz was clearly innocent of the charges. In passing on a letter from Jacobowitz to his assistant, Steven Steinberg, Hackney scribbled this note: "If this guy gets convicted it will be a horrible miscarriage of justice." But Hackney believed that adherence to university rules required that the process continue to its end once the JIO had officially referred the case to the hearing panel. (This fact distinguished the case from Pavlik and Monaco. In those cases, Hackney acted before formal charges were brought.) Thus, his note to Steinberg continued: "[B]ut I suppose there is nothing to do but let the process play out and hope for the best from the Panel." In his book, Hackney also said that "I felt certain that no faculty-student panel would punish Jacobowitz."

Hackney also took a shot at Kors for insisting on intervention at this point. "It struck me as ironic that one so punctilious as Kors was about the principle of due process was pressuring me to throw due process out the

---

[74] Kors e-mail to Provost Michael Aiken, May 4, 1993, "Sanity"; interview with Alan Kors; interview with director of FIRE Thor Halvorssen, July 2001.

[75] Interview with Alan Kors; interview with Eden Jacobowitz.

window."[76] But to Kors, the entire process was a sham in the first place, as the missing police report and the apparent political pressures revealed. In addition, Hackney's note itself conceded that the JIO's motivation for bringing the case had less to do with a proper interpretation of the code than a personal commitment to the complainants and the cause they represented – not normally a legitimate basis for the exercise of coercive legal power.

Kors knew right away that the case was important and dedicated all his time to it for several months. He had honed his instincts for combat and was now ready for action:

I just decided to outthink them. I knew how to present this case. I knew where to present this case. I knew how absurd it was. . . . I knew their assumption that the left would find it reasonable to prosecute an Israeli kid for saying "water buffalo" to people who are chanting and stomp-dancing at 2 A.M. [was wrong]. . . . I've always known that they can't defend in public what they believe and do in private. So I would just wake up and figure how to outsmart them – everyday. That was my life for a couple of months.[77]

Kors and Silverglate explain in *The Shadow University*, "the issue now was not the speech code itself, but Eden's innocence even assuming the speech code's legitimacy." Perhaps the best statement in support of this point was the commentary in the *Almanac* by Will Harris, a noted expert on constitutional law and theory in Penn's political science department and an advocate of the code. An exacting, sophisticated legal theorist, Harris wrote an exhaustive analysis of the purposes and scope of the revised racial harassment policy. His conclusion: Jacobowitz's expression fell well outside the sphere of its prohibitions. "The Policy is clearly not aimed at curtailing what is 'offensive,' for the University here commits itself to 'protect expression of ideas, opinions, information, and knowledge that may be deemed objectionable and insulting to some members of the community.' . . . That means that the benefit of any doubt about its application in a fact situation should be resolved in favor of the accused."[78]

But the administration was committed to the case. The judicial administrator at Penn, John Brobeck, attempted to set up a formal hearing. Before a date could be set, Kors and Jacobowitz asked judicial administrators to contact Jacobowitz's many witnesses in order to assess the wisdom of pursuing the case. They agreed to do so, but when the judicial office contacted Jacobowitz two weeks later to set a time, they informed him that no

---

76 Sheldon Hackney, *The Politics of Presidential Appointment: A Memoir of the Culture War* (New South Books, 2002), pp. 96–97.

77 Interview with Alan Kors.

78 Kors and Silverglate, *The Shadow University*, p. 14; Will Harris, letter, "Interpreting Racial Harassment," *Almanac*, May 11, 1993, p. 5. See William F. Harris II, *The Interpretable Constitution* (Johns Hopkins University Press, 1993).

witnesses had been contacted.[79] According to Brobeck, "Professor Kors insisted that I dismiss the charges. There was nothing in the guidelines for the judicial system that permitted dismissal."[80]

Brobeck then set the hearing for April 26, a day when Kors was slated to attend a major scholarly conference. Kors asked for a hearing on another date: April 12. Brobeck replied, "The hearing will be held on April 26, period. If you can make it, wonderful. If you can't, then Eden will have to be there without his advisor. There is no possible change of the April 26 date." It was at this point that Kors and Jacobowitz decided that they would take the case to the court of public opinion. According to Kors and Silverglate, at this point, "Neither Eden nor Kors knew how to bring the water buffalo case to the public."[81]

The first publicity break occurred almost by accident. A friend to whom Kors had related the case on April 20 informed the important Jewish newspaper, the *Forward*, which published an article on the case three days later entitled, "Pennsylvania Preparing to Buffalo a Yeshiva Boy." The editors of the *Wall Street Journal* read the story, and editorial board member Dorothy Rabinowitz – a future Pulitzer Prize winner for commentary – wrote a scathing editorial on April 26 that turned the case into a national sensation. Entitled "Buffaloed at Penn," the editorial excoriated Penn's judicial system as "Kafkaesque" and made a point that would become Rabinowitz's trademark critique of political correctness. Jacobowitz "had yet to learn what they don't teach at the freshman orientation: namely, he had now entered a world where a charge of racism or sexism is as good as a conviction."[82] The Rabinowitz contact would prove useful in future years, as in the Columbia case discussed in Chapter 3, which the *Journal* broke open with a strategic editorial. Rabinowitz also wrote an editorial on the speech code abolition victory at Wisconsin.[83]

The *Journal* would write further editorials about the case, and Hackney spoke with Rabinowitz on the phone after the publication of the first editorial. He was put off by Rabinowitz's position, which he considered extremist. As for the editorial page of the *Journal* in general, it was "messianically ideological."[84] Then again, the vast majority of the hundreds of commentators on the case came to conclusions similar to that of the *Journal*.

---

[79] See Kors and Silverglate, *The Shadow University*, pp. 18, 22; Kors e-mail to Aiken, May 4, 1993; Kors e-mail to Jacob Abel, April 1, 1994.

[80] Written correspondence from University of Pennsylvania judicial administrator John Brobeck to Donald Downs, December 30, 2002.

[81] Brobeck telephone message to Kors, in Kors and Silverglate, *The Shadow University*, p. 18.

[82] "Pennsylvania Preparing to Buffalo a Yeshiva Boy"; "Buffaloed at Penn," *Wall Street Journal*, April 26, 1993.

[83] See "Due Process at Columbia," *Wall Street Journal*, October 4, 2000; "A Speech Code Dies," editorial, *Wall Street Journal*, July 16, 1999, p. A14.

[84] Hackney, *The Politics of Presidential Appointment*, p. 104.

Suddenly, the case exploded into the media, with Kors acting as the central figure. Recognizing the possibilities, Kors leapt to take full advantage of the situation, making the most of every opportunity to contact the media, or to respond to their inquiries. The movement was not just what Timur Kuran calls a "bandwagon": it was a rocket. Kors and Silverglate remark, "The effect of the *Forward*'s article and the *Wall Street Journal*'s editorial – in the wake of Hackney's nomination and his equivocation on the theft of the *DP* – was electric. Eden was interviewed on television by Tom Snyder and John McLaughlin. George Will devoted his syndicated column in the *Washington Post* to Eden and to the theft of the *DP*s. Within short order, the international media settled in at Penn. . . . The case had turned over a rock at Penn."[85] Over the course of the next month, scores of major national newspapers, magazines, television shows, and radio shows covered or addressed the case – most of which were critical of the administration. The case was exactly the kind of case that the media adores: a conflict between good and evil that pits the hapless individual against the bureaucratic machine, with a heroic intervener who attempts to save the day.[86] A partial list of media that covered the story includes the *Philadelphia Daily News*, *Philadelphia Inquirer*, *Los Angeles Times*, *New York Times*, *International Herald Tribune*, *Washington Post*, *Washington Times*, *Financial Times* (London), *Toronto Star*, *Spectator* (UK), *Village Voice*, *Rolling Stone*, *New Republic*, *Time*, *Newsweek*, *U.S. News and World Report*, *NBC Nightly News*, National Public Radio, and even a mocking *Doonesbury* cartoon by Gary Trudeau.[87]

Although Brobeck had told Kors that the April 26 meeting was cast in stone, it seemed the stone was not exactly unbreakable. On Friday, April 23, Brobeck called Kors and said that the meeting had to be postponed. At first he attributed postponement to the publicity, but then confided the real reason: the complainants' adviser had withdrawn from the case. "We can't have the hearing without their advisor," Brobeck said.[88] Brobeck told me, "In two letters the women asked me to postpone the hearing until fall because they could not find an appropriate advisor."[89] Thus, although Penn was quite prepared to hold the hearing without the *defendant's* adviser, it would not allow the hearing to take place without the *complainants'* adviser. The scales of justice, which are normally supposed to err in favor of the defense, functioned differently at Penn.

[85] Kors and Silverglate, *The Shadow University*, pp. 24–28; Timur Kuran, *Private Truths, Public Lies: The Social Consequences of Preference Falsification* (Harvard University Press, 1995).

[86] On how the media thrive on such dichotomous conflicts, see Edward J. Epstein, *News From Nowhere: Television and the News* (Random House, 1973), pp. 173, 262–63.

[87] For this list, see Kors and Silverglate, *The Shadow University*, pp. 27–28; interview with Alan Kors.

[88] Kors and Silverglate, *The Shadow University*, p. 25; see also Kors e-mail to Abel, May 8, 1994, "Your Stupidity."

[89] Correspondence with John Brobeck.

Doonesbury cartoon depicting the water buffalo case at Penn. Doonesbury © 1983 G. B. Trudeau. Reprinted with permission of Universal Press Syndicate. All rights reserved.

Brobeck – whom Kors and Silverglate described as "a decent man caught up in an absurd situation" – proposed to postpone the hearing indefinitely, which meant that the case would hang over Jacobowitz through the summer and into the fall term. Kors and Jacobowitz intensified their efforts to get Penn to drop the case, but the administration claimed that it would be improper to intervene in a case once formal charges had been brought. Intervention could compromise the independence of the system. As Aiken e-mailed Kors on May 6, "It is vitally important to the integrity of that system that it be allowed to work without interference from the Administration."[90]

But one day in early May, Brobeck appeared unannounced at Kors's house outside Philadelphia and informed him that a hearing now had to take place on May 14 – even though virtually all of Jacobowitz's witnesses had left for the summer. Kors beseeched Brobeck to limit the hearing to one consideration: whether to drop all the charges. Given the lack of witnesses and time to prepare, the only fair hearing would deal with the prima facie question of law, not an adjudication of the facts: was Jacobowitz's language sufficiently close to violating the code to justify continuing the case? Brobeck related, "Professor Kors and I agreed that I would arrange a hearing solely to consider dismissal of the charges. If the panel said 'No,' the full hearing was to be postponed until fall."[91]

But late in the evening of May 12, Brobeck called Kors at home to inform him that his "superiors" had ordered him to hold a hearing to determine innocence or guilt on May 14. Thus, Jacobowitz would have to prepare a defense without witnesses and with less than two days to prepare. Kors and Silverglate reported that Brobeck felt terrible about what his higher-ups had decided: "Until today, I would have thought that I [as a judicial administrator] was independent, too, but I have bosses, and they've ordered me to do this. . . . I have no choice. I have superiors. Please be gentle with me."[92]

In Jacobowitz's eyes, the process now represented "a witch-hunt mentality in the administration." The fact that someone had buried the second, more exhaustive, police report that exonerated Jacobowitz was also a major problem. Kors and Silverglate maintain that a major objective of the administration was to "salvage Penn's reputation." Kors told me:

When the university defended itself in the Jacobowitz case, they took the position that the judicial system was not a contract with students, and that they were under no obligation to hand over exculpatory evidence to someone in their judicial system. No one even tried to get to the bottom of that awful scandal of the suppressed police

---

[90] Aiken e-mail to Kors, May 6, 1993.
[91] Correspondence with John Brobeck.
[92] Kors and Silverglate, *The Shadow University*, pp. 28–29.

report and the coming of the false one. No one paid a price for that. No one involved on the other side will take on this case.[93]

If nothing else, this act of omission suggested that the roles of prosecution and adjudication were now hopelessly intertwined, rendering judicial independence a chimera.

Resolution

It was at this point that Kors and Jacobowitz went to court. They attained the services of local attorneys Arnie and Sonya Silverstein, as well as Stefan Presser of the Pennsylvania branch of the American Civil Liberties Union. Citing the Monaco precedent, they filed a lawsuit against Hackney, Aiken, Morrison, and Brobeck as individuals. Almost immediately upon receiving notice of the suit, the university informed Kors and the lawyers that the May 14 hearing would consider only dismissal of the case.

Kors and Silverglate describe the scene at the hearing as "surreal." The university's official report of its investigation of the case, the Abel Report, was presented a year later. It criticized the fact that the hearing considered only dismissal. The report asserted, "The initiative for this extraordinary and ill-conceived meeting lay with the J.A. [judicial administrator], and its certain impact on the perceived fairness of the process was not appreciated by him."[94] Hordes of reporters and media crowded outside as Kors and Jacobowitz confronted a panel of five adjudicators who were upset that the hearing would consider only dismissal of the case. One administrator reportedly wept as the complainants told their story after Jacobowitz related his side. The panel stated that it would render a decision within ten days. According to Brobeck, "the panel recommended that I be dismissed from the case, and that the hearing be postponed until fall." He also noted, "At the hearing to consider dismissal, Kors and the women's advisor got things turned around so that I was the one on trial."[95] Kors and Jacobowitz were sternly warned that things would go "very hard on Eden Jacobowitz" if either of them uttered a word about the case to the press outside. Kors tried to obey the "order" for a few minutes but relented when Dorothy Rabinowitz gave him "an awesome three-minute lecture on a free country, a free press, and his own lack of testosterone." Kors then "broke his silence and told her everything."[96]

---

93 Interview with Alan Kors; e-mail exchanges between Kors and Abel, April 1994; Kors, "More on 'Water Buffalo,'" and Abel, "Response of Dr. Abel," *Almanac*, April 12, 1994. See also other letters by Kors and others in *Almanac*'s "Speaking Out" section, April 26, May 3, May 24, and July 12, 1994.
94 Kors and Silverglate, *The Shadow University*, p. 30; "Inquiry into the Procedural Aspects of a Case of Alleged Racial Harassment in the Spring of 1993" (Abel Report).
95 Correspondence with John Brobeck.
96 Kors and Silverglate, *The Shadow University*, p. 31.

Meanwhile, Hackney was in Washington, preparing for his NEH nomination hearing before the Senate Labor Relations Committee. Key people in the Senate and the new Clinton administration were closely following the events at Penn. Hackney called Kors and offered a deal: at a press conference on May 24, the complainants would drop the charges if Jacobowitz apologized for "rudeness," which was exactly what Jacobowitz had begged for all along. Jacobowitz quickly agreed. On May 25, the *Almanac* published the press statements of Hackney, the complainants, Jacobowitz, and Kors, accepting the conclusion while presenting their sides of the case. Anthropologist Peggy Sanday also made remarks, dismissing the claim that the case raised issues of "political correctness." She contended, "From my perspective as an anthropologist, calling African American women 'black water buffalo' reduces them to work animals and beasts of burden." Deborah Leavy, executive director of the Pennsylvania chapter of the ACLU, had a different view: "We are grateful that the case against Eden has been dropped. But the case involving the University of Pennsylvania remains and now we call upon the University to repeal its hate codes, its hate speech code."[97]

The Abel Report

The official university report on the case appeared almost a year later. The Abel Report – named after the chair of the investigating committee, Jacob Abel, a professor of engineering – drew three conclusions: first, the process had treated Jacobowitz unfairly by the way it "upped the ante" early on; second, the university's rules did not provide for dismissing the case once the JIO made formal charges and, consequently, the May 24 meeting's consideration of dismissal was highly improper; and third, the external intervention by the attorneys was improper, as the university should have been able to adjudicate the case to its conclusion without outside influence.[98] Kors had hoped that the Abel Report would provide a definitive public record of what actually happened and strove assiduously to provide the committee with substantial information.

Hackney had gone on to the NEH after a surprisingly tough confirmation battle, due entirely to the publicity surrounding the water buffalo case. Though some of his critics were liberals (e.g., Lieberman, Hentoff, Silverglate), Hackney attributed the opposition to the "consistent right-wing critique of higher education that has been developed and elaborated over the past fifteen years."[99] (Senator Joseph Lieberman and others had made strong speeches against Hackney's candidacy. He received twenty-seven negative

---

[97] "Statements Made Monday, May 24, Concluding the 'Water Buffalo' Case."
[98] "Inquiry into the Procedural Aspects of a Case of Alleged Racial Harassment in the Spring of 1993" (Abel Report).
[99] Hackney, *The Politics of Presidential Appointment*, p. 56, and generally.

votes in the Senate.) Under interim president Claire Fagin, Penn began actively considering reform or abolition of the code. An honest report on what had happened was not only important for the record and to the prospects of change at Penn: it was also important to the compromised intellectual integrity of the institution.

But the committee gave Kors only limited opportunity to supply information. Kors considered its conclusion to be a whitewash. In response, he wrote a lengthy, hard-hitting critique of the report that appeared in the *Almanac*'s "Speaking Out" section on April 12. Kors's letter represented his first official statement outlining the procedural and substantive problems with the case. He concluded with scathing words:

The Abel Committee may prefer a set of mechanisms in which powerless innocent people must defend themselves against Kafkaesque charges in the shadows of collusive injustice, but, universities in their self-image excepted, this is America... to judge from their behavior, [Abel] and his committee could not have cared less. Three of them talked briefly to Eden! Three of them talked briefly to me! That they don't even discuss the matter of Eden's first advisor is already astonishing! That they don't even know about the suppression of the police reports speaks volumes about the vile, repugnant, wicked dishonesty of this affair, and, since I know of that report, about their catastrophic incompetence.

In a letter of response in the *Almanac*, Jacob Abel claimed that the committee's mandate did not authorize it to look into issues beyond whether the procedures were followed. He accused Kors of illegitimately asking the administration to intervene in a judicial matter, citing even the Pavlik case as an example of improper interference. Abel concluded by charging that Kors had done both the university and Jacobowitz a disservice: "I think that he [Kors] chose the wrong strategy to defend Mr. Jacobowitz, one that did not bring the real issues into the sunlight but rather brought Mr. Kors into the limelight. Mr. Jacobowitz was a victim of that error as well."[100] Further debate flared in subsequent editions of the "Speaking Out" pages of the *Almanac*, including further commentary by Kors and Abel, and letters from Michael Cohen, Jacobowitz, and two of the complainants (quoted earlier in this chapter).[101]

Kors had worked hard to make the Abel Committee cognizant of the problems that he saw with the case. In an e-mail on April 1 – a few days before the report's release – Kors continued to plead with Abel, whom he addressed as "Dear Jake." "I doubt very much that you have been given an accurate picture.... CENTRAL to your report... YOU'VE BEEN DECEIVED" through the omission of information about the missing police report, the JIO's failure to interview defense witnesses, and the judicial adviser's lack

---

[100] Kors, "More on 'Water Buffalo'"; Abel, "Response of Dr. Abel."
[101] See "Speaking Out" sections of *Almanac*, April 26, May 3, May 24, and July 12, 1994.

of independence. "Do you know the General Counsel's involvement in the 'independent' judiciary?" He signed the message, "Warmest, Alan." Abel replied that the commission's charge was to examine only the procedures, not the substantive issues. Kors e-mailed back that it was precisely the procedures that were at fault, and that the committee was not performing its duty to unearth the truth. The missing police report alone "reveals the corrupted nature of every PROCEDURE associated with this case.... Doesn't that shock you and raise the most serious questions in your mind?"[102]

When the Abel committee presented its report the next day, Kors was disconsolate. He wrote his critique for the *Almanac*. Over a month later, and after exchanges of letters in the *Almanac* and other correspondence, he sent an e-mail to Abel that is remarkable for its hostility toward a colleague:

I do not know if you are merely stupid or wicked, or some sad combination of the two, but I do know that you are cynically misinformed after one year of inquiry... you mendacious soul who had the opportunity to hear EVERYTHING from me about the ACLU interactions in this case but CHOSE NOT TO SCHEDULE THE HEARING ON THE VERY SUBJECT AT ISSUE.... As you know, you mendacious, tendentious, poseur, 18 hours before that hearing the JA, allegedly "independent" and mandated to secure "substantive justice" telephoned me to inform me that "I cannot keep my word – my superiors have instructed me to make this a dispositive hearing on the issue of guilt or innocence. I know I told you not to bring witnesses, but do your best." THAT, you moral mountebank, is when the ACLU entered the case. You, unconscionably, didn't even seek to interview either Deborah Leavy or Stefan Presser of the ACLU.... What gall! I shall write about this and you as often as I can until the day I die.[103]

The book, *The Shadow University*, which was published in 1998, represents Kors and Silverglate's attempt to make a definitive public record of the case. In a *DP* review of the book, Hackney disagreed strongly with the book's assessment of the water buffalo case. "This is a polemic," Hackney said. "I think it's not really intended to be the truth. It's the way Professor Kors wants you to see it."[104]

It was a difficult end for Hackney. He was a good man, and he cared about free speech and fundamental fairness, as his memos showed. In less contentious times, he would have ended his presidency on a more successful note. But he was loaded down with bureaucratic and political commitments that made it harder for him to be decisive in the water buffalo affair. He also had the misfortune of presiding over Penn when concerns about political correctness were starting to build outside the university. He was the victim

---

[102] Kors e-mail to Abel, April 1, 1994, "Committee/Truth"; Abel e-mail to Kors, April 4, 1994, "Inquiry"; Kors e-mail to Abel, April 4, 1994, "Inquiry."

[103] Kors e-mail to Abel, May 18, 1994, "Your Stupidity." Abel is dead now, so an interview was not possible.

[104] Edward Sherwin, "A New Book Looks Back at Penn's 'Shadow Years,'" *Daily Pennsylvanian*, December 3, 1998.

of this historical circumstance, and of political forces that he had helped to unleash and nourish. In addition, he was the victim of his priorities, which made free speech simply one value among others at the university. In the end, his attempt to balance free speech and academic freedom with racial sensitivity did not serve him well when a fundamental choice had to be made between these goods in a case that called out for a firm support of due process and free speech. In his book, Hackney accused a right-wing conspiracy in the culture wars for jumping on the water buffalo case as an example of political correctness run amok. There is truth in this allegation, especially as the issue made its way to the Senate during his confirmation hearings. He also wrote that most issues are gray, not black and white – another truthful claim.[105] But when all is said and done, the injustice of the prosecution of Eden Jacobowitz transcended the call of political opportunism and pragmatic waffling. It was simply wrong, and someone had to take a stand against it.

The "Speech Code" Dies

With or without a critical Abel Report, the water buffalo case was a bombshell that initiated major change at Penn. Hundreds of donors, alumni, and parents wrote angry letters to the trustees and the administration, sending copies to Kors. After serving as the chair of NEH, Hackney returned to Penn, where he is now a professor of history. (He refused to be interviewed after I informed him of my project.) Provost Aiken also left, and was replaced by Stanley Chodorow, an associate chancellor at the University of California, San Diego. Under the administrations of Claire Fagin and Judith Rodin (who was still, in 2004, president of Penn), several individuals involved in the administration of the judiciary and student life were replaced or given new positions. Their departures created an opportunity for Kors to build on the momentum generated by Jacobowitz's case.

The water buffalo case gave speech codes a bad name at Penn, allowing pro–free speech supporters to gain influence in the spheres of public and political opinion. Kors described the effect in words that echo the words of Timur Kuran: "They took such a hit that students were mobilized across a pretty broad spectrum. People who had lost their courage and voice suddenly found it. And administrators had more to lose supporting this [code] stuff than backing away from it." The student government opposed the administration in the case, and a group of students, some of whom Kors called "extraordinary," formed the First Amendment Task Force, which played an important role over the next few years. On May 3, the First Amendment Task Force took out a full-page advertisement in the *DP*, denouncing the embattled status of free speech on campus and declaring its commitment to free speech principles. Drawing on a strategy deployed by the Black

---

[105] Hackney, *The Politics of Presidential Appointment*, esp. introduction, and pp. 18, 77.

Student League, they also held a rally in front of Hackney's home.[106] According to most witnesses, surprisingly few minority and procode students publicly took the other side, either because of the nature of the case or because of the overwhelmingly critical publicity that the case generated almost as soon as it became a matter of public notice.[107] After Hackney left at the end of the term, interim president Fagin opened up a debate regarding the code, which featured hardy arguments on all sides of the issue. It was clear proof that at least some voices for free speech had indeed "found their courage."

Meanwhile, Kors worked closely with Fagin in the transition period to push for libertarian change. In June the university established the "Commission on Strengthening the University Community," charged with ways to restore civility and respect for differences consistent with a community "in which free exchange of ideas may flourish." On September 21, 1993, Fagin called for suggestions from the university community. She even referred to the policy as "the *speech* code" – evidence that the open debate about free speech at Penn had succeeded in changing the public name of the policy.[108] In the commission's preliminary report, issued in February 1994, it recommended that "student speech *qua* speech not be subject to formal sanction."[109]

Thereafter, Fagin had to negotiate with the forces of change and the forces of reaction. Kors described Fagin as a "good person, someone with the right instincts. Everyone liked her." But though she wanted to get the speech code matter settled before the new president arrived, she remained somewhat wary of campus opinion. Her call for discussion triggered widespread campus debate in the public forum and in such circles as student government and the university council. The latter held a quasi debate between political science professor Anne Norton (against change) and finance professor Morris Mendelson (for change).[110] Fagin received hundreds of e-mails from those on both sides of the matter during that fall term.

Kors was now in almost constant correspondence with Fagin, and in October he encouraged the wavering interim president by giving her supportive talks about the importance of courage in the face of adversity. Now was the time to stand strong in support of principles. In November, Fagin replaced the existing code with an impotent remnant that emphasized mediation – not

---

[106] Interview with Alan Kors; "New Group Is Formed to Foster Free Speech," *Daily Pennsylvanian*," September 9, 1993.

[107] Interview with Eden Jacobowitz; interview with Tina Besian; interview with Alan Kors.

[108] "For Comment: On the University's Racial Harassment Policy," *Almanac*, September 21, 1993 (emphasis added).

[109] "Preliminary Report of the Commission on Strengthening the University Community," *Almanac*, February 1, 1994.

[110] "October 13 Discussion of the Proposal to Suspend the Racial Harassment Policy," *Almanac*, October 19, 1993.

punishment – in the name of establishing community standards of civility. But Kors and Silverglate noted, "By 1994–95, almost everyone seemed to know that abolition was both inevitable and appropriate."[111] One of Judith Rodin's first acts as new president was to abolish what remained of the code. In a letter to alumni and parents dated June 30, 1995, Rodin stressed the need for "intellectual risk-taking," and concluded, "Today at Penn, the content of student speech is no longer a basis for disciplinary action."[112]

Other Successes

Although the speech code was dead, a few other issues arose or remained to be addressed. Over the next few years, Kors was also involved with several individual cases, most of which he could not discuss in order to respect the privacy of the individuals involved. Some, however, are a matter of public record. In one instance, for example, the university backed down when Kors threatened to go public about a case in which the judicial system refused to abide by a rule against all appellate cases being final. Two other cases show the strength of the pro–free speech groups that formed after the water buffalo case.

In 1995–96 Provost Stanley Chodorow followed up on the recommendations of the Abel Report by proposing a "confidentiality" rule that prohibited anyone from disclosing to outsiders information pertaining to judicial proceedings. Chodorow justified the gag order on the grounds that it was mandated by the 1974 Buckley Amendment in the national Privacy Act. Kors and members of the First Amendment Task Force fought against the measure. Andrea Ahles, a reporter for the *DP*, dealt it a fatal blow when she called the Department of Education and found out that the Buckley Amendment simply did not apply to such situations. Kors and Silverglate remarked, "In less than a month of struggle, the undergraduates had overturned the gag rule."[113]

Another issue concerned the conservative journal, the *Red and Blue*, the oldest student publication in the Ivy League. In 1995, the magazine had suffered two setbacks: someone had destroyed $100,000 worth of its archived volumes, allegedly by accident; and the Student Activities Council had stopped funding it on political grounds because it had published an article critical of Haiti's politics and culture. When the future FIRE director,

[111] Kors and Silverglate, *The Shadow University*, p. 364; "Of Record: University Statement on the Racial Harassment Policy," *Almanac*, November 16, 1993.

[112] Judith Rodin to Penn Parents and Alumni, letter, June 30, 1995, in Kors and Silverglate, *The Shadow University*, p. 365.

[113] "Student Group Calls for Judicial Charter Revisions," *Daily Pennsylvanian*, February 21, 1996; "Gag Rule to Be Lifted from Charter," *Daily Pennsylvanian*, March 4, 1996; "Provost Revises Judicial Charter Draft," *Daily Pennsylvanian*, March 5, 1996; Kors and Silverglate, *The Shadow University*, p. 358; interview with Alan Kors.

Thor Halvorssen, took over as editor in chief, he fought hard to retrieve the funding. After much debate and behind-the-scenes politicking (the details of which I may not divulge), Rodin and Chodorow both publicly criticized the decision and called for new funding guidelines that prohibited SAC from making decisions on the basis of "the content of the speech or expression of such organization."[114]

Finally, the climate after the water buffalo case promoted changes in the administrative offices that dealt with student life. On December 7, 1993, the *Almanac* announced on the front page that Penn had chosen Rodin as the new president. A no-nonsense person who valued institutional competence and success, Rodin had less patience for the moral crusades that had marked the Hackney years. The second article on the front page of the *Almanac* was equally interesting: Kim Morrison was leaving the position of vice provost for university life to become vice provost in the office of the provost. Her replacement was Valerie Swain-Cade McCoullum. Valerie Cade, as she was known, was to have oversight of all programs directed at increasing "minority permanence" at Penn.[115] An African American woman who had earlier served as interim president at Cheney University, Cade (who also declined being interviewed) cared deeply about the individualistic principles underlying the civil rights movement: social justice consistent with a commitment to the individual. She was Kors's dream come true. As soon as she assumed the new position, Kors commenced a meaningful dialogue with her. Kors and Silverglate describe her as an exceptional woman who "treated each student as an individual, not as the embodiment of an abstract group. She was a demonstrative, compassionate person, open and emotive in her expressions, and her kindness was legendary."[116]

Cade modified the residential assistance program to conform to liberal principles of individualism and published a new set of "University Life Principles" in 1996. It informed the university that the "citizens of Penn are free to individuate according to their private conscience. They are equal in their rights, dignities, and responsibilities. ... I also believe, absolutely and resolutely, in both freedom of expression and the individual's moral responsibility [to rebut] views that he or she might find abhorrent."[117] One should compare this language to that of the diversity planning administrator mentioned

---

[114] "Controversial Magazine Denied Funding," *Daily Pennsylvanian*, June 30, 1995; "Magazine Funding Approved," *Daily Pennsylvanian*, September 28, 1995. The viewpoint neutrality standard is also the First Amendment standard the Supreme Court now mandates for the allocation of student fees. See *Rosenberger v. Rector of the University of Virginia*, 515 U.S. 819 (1995).

[115] "For President: Yale Provost Judith Rodin, CW '66," and "Transition at VPUL," *Almanac*, December 7, 1993.

[116] Kors and Silverglate, *The Shadow University*, p. 365; interview with Alan Kors.

[117] Valerie Swain-Cade McCoullum, Division of University Life, "A Strategic Plan for University Life," April 1996. Quoted in Kors and Silverglate, *The Shadow University*, p. 368.

previously, who scolded a student in 1989 for expressing her belief in the "individual."

Cade proved the authenticity of her commitment in an April 1997 case in which an administrator in the Department of Administrative Support tried to fire (and investigate!) a student tutor for publishing an article critical of affirmative action in the *Philadelphia Inquirer*. Cade responded immediately and ordered everyone involved to reverse their decision, apologize to the student, and "immediately retract" the official statement made against him. Cade then told the key administrator in the case that any repetition of such behavior would result in her dismissal. Cade also contributed to broadening the outreach of the Women's Center, which previously had been harnessed to narrower identity politics interests. She also managed to pry freshman orientation programs away from groups with special agendas, returning them to the schools, which were less overtly political.[118] Overall, Cade was instrumental in turning the Penn bureaucracy in a direction that was liberal, individualistic, and intellectually diverse. Kors claims that she suffered little criticism from student groups and faculty for her efforts. The fact that she is a black woman gave her a degree of immunity, but she was also given leeway "because of the water buffalo case."[119]

She and Kors developed an ongoing relationship and exchanged numerous e-mails and correspondence. The tutor case may have been the defining victory. Kors portrayed it as a "pure win. It scared the hell out of them. It was a total win."[120] By 1998 and 1999, however, Kors began to turn his attention outside of the university with the publication of *The Shadow University* and the formation of FIRE, which was founded to carry out the vision articulated in that book.[121] Meanwhile, Penn has continued without Kors's direct support (he has not spoken to Rodin since the *Red and Blue* affair in 1995). His labors are now directed toward the national scene. He laments the lack of a lasting change in the infrastructure at Penn that could carry on the mission he brought to life during and after the water buffalo affair. His musing was sparked by my comment that Valerie Cade had decided not to be interviewed for this book:

To me, all of this hangs by a thread because the students who were motivated are gone, the Val Cades don't want to talk about this stuff now. It's not clear that at the next big incident or provocation . . . what way the university will go in a crisis is unclear. They took a massive PR hit. They were unaware of my ability to generate publicity,

[118] Kors and Silverglate, *The Shadow University*, p. 369; interview with Alan Kors.
[119] Interview with Alan Kors.
[120] Ibid.
[121] See FIRE's website: www.theFIRE.org. See also Commonwealth of Massachusetts, Articles of Organization, General Laws, Chapter 180: Foundation for Individual Rights in Education, Inc., April 8, 1999.

so over the years since 1993, when I intervened in that case of major injustices, people have tended to take care of them right away. I don't count on institutional memory, though Penn is still traumatized by the water buffalo incident. It's like gravity: the further you get away from the water buffalo case, the more my power weakens.[122]

[122] Interview with Alan Kors.

6

Renewal

The Rise of the Free Speech Movement at Wisconsin

The University of Wisconsin at Madison, one of the country's first major research universities, has long been a national leader not only in research but also in academic freedom. At the end of the nineteenth century it witnessed a major battle over academic freedom when members of the board of regents sought to oust progressive political economist Richard T. Ely because of his prolabor and prostrike views. After a trial accompanied by a great deal of publicity, the regents refused to dismiss Ely in one of the most important victories for academic freedom during an era that often pitted the academic freedom claims of the rising social sciences against the proprietary claims of capitalistic trustees.[1] In its report on the case, the regents declared that the commitment to academic freedom was the university's most important mission. The Ely case stands as a landmark in the history of academic freedom in America, something of which the University of Wisconsin is justly proud.

The regents' statement analyzed the university's role in promoting the "vast diversity of views regarding the great questions which at present agitate the mind." It also linked academic freedom to the facts of human fallibility and the inherently incomplete state of knowledge. "We cannot for a moment believe this knowledge has reached its final goal, or that the present condition of society is perfect." The report concluded with words that would eventually become the university's official motto: "Whatever may be the limitations which trammel inquiry elsewhere we believe the great state University of Wisconsin should ever encourage that continual sifting and winnowing by which alone truth can be found."[2]

---

[1] See Neil Hamilton, *Zealotry and Academic Freedom: A Legal and Historical Perspective* (Transaction Books, 1998), ch. 1.

[2] See Theodore Herfurth, "Sifting and Winnowing: A Chapter in the History of Academic Freedom at the University of Wisconsin," in W. Lee Hansen, ed., *Academic Freedom on Trial: 100 Years of Sifting and Winnowing at the University of Wisconsin–Madison* (Office of University Publications, University of Wisconsin–Madison, 1998), pp. 58–89.

Sixteen years later, another academic tribulation took place when the regents and their allies attacked sociology professor Edward A. Ross for associating on campus with Emma Goldman, the famous anarchist, and Parker Sercombe, a noted advocate of free love. Ross was saved when the faculty and students rushed to his defense, and when the president of the University of Wisconsin, Charles R. Van Hise, refused to take action against him. In response to these events, the politically active and savvy leaders of the class of 1910 had the "sifting and winnowing" statement of the regents made into a large bronze plaque and presented it to the university as a class present at graduation. Embarrassed, the regents refused to accept the plaque, which some construed as a biting criticism of their actions against Ross. The plaque was then taken to the cavernous basement of Bascom, where it "accumulated dust and cobwebs for five years."[3] In planning for their five year reunion, leaders of the class of 1910 then mounted a local and national campaign to resurrect the plaque. After much maneuvering in public and behind the scenes, the regents relented and formally accepted the plaque on behalf of the university. It was affixed just outside the main entrance to Bascom Hall in 1915, where it has remained ever since.[4]

Academic freedom has never been completely secure at any university. But some universities have fared better than others in this regard, and Wisconsin has enjoyed a prominent status among this group historically. While many prominent institutions fell prey to loyalty oaths and other affronts to academic freedom during the McCarthy era, Wisconsin was noteworthy for its refusal to do so in the face of pressure. Wisconsin also refused to deny radical student groups official standing during this period despite political pressure to do so.[5] A consensus in favor of academic freedom normally prevailed among the faculty, administration, and student body, and the university has often had many allies in the state government who have valued the university's distinctive contributions to the state and its national and international reputation. Most of the attacks against the university have come from the right, as the two leading historians of the university write in their analysis of the McCarthy era in volume 4 of their institutional history. "As previous volumes of this history recorded, the University had periodically been attacked for its alleged 'radical' orientation."[6] The attacks on Ely, Ross, and left-leaning students and professors during the McCarthy era represented attacks from *outside* the university from the right. This pattern

---

[3] Ibid., p. 77.

[4] The plaque disappeared for a short while in 1956 due to a prank, but was found. See Arthur Hove, "Now You See It, Now You Don't," in Hansen, *Academic Freedom on Trial*, pp. 90–93.

[5] See E. David Cronin and John W. Jenkins, *The University of Wisconsin, a History: Renewal to Revolution, 1945–1971* (University of Wisconsin Press, 1999), pp. 90–98. On McCarthyism and the universities in general, see Ellen W. Schrecker, *No Ivory Tower: McCarthyism and the Universities* (Oxford University Press, 1986).

[6] Cronin and Jenkins, *The University of Wisconsin*, p. 92.

fit the traditional pattern of censorship in America: the right attempting to restrict the promulgation of ideas from the radical political and sexual left. Advocates of liberation and freedom stood with liberalism, while advocates of tradition espoused censorship.[7]

But what would happen when the forces of *progressive* censorship discussed in Chapter 2 came to the University of Wisconsin? Once again, Wisconsin assumed the mantle of national leadership in declaring diversity as its new mission. In service of this new mission, it adopted speech codes and related policies as means to this end. The new restrictions on free speech and academic freedom emanated from the left and from *within* the university's own gates. What difference would this turn of circumstance make in terms of politics and points of view? Could the new restrictions on speech coexist in a principled fashion with academic freedom? Let us now turn to the story of speech codes at the University of Wisconsin.

The Rise of Codes at Madison

Like many universities, Wisconsin experienced major changes in the later 1980s. Racial and gender issues became perhaps the most prominent public issues on campus, and new leaders came to the university who were dedicated to furthering the objectives of racial and gender justice. While an overwhelming majority agreed with these goals, the real debate concerned the means the university employed to achieve these worthy ends.

Wisconsin's adventure with speech codes began when Phi Gamma Delta fraternity held a Fiji Island party on a Saturday night in May 1987. The event featured partiers in black face, an oversized figure of a Fiji Islander advertising the party on the house's front lawn, and a special "Harlem Room" where fried chicken and watermelon were served. Minority students expressed their anger and dismay, and then began reporting other incidents of racism on campus, including exposure to offensive speech. Suddenly, the university was overwhelmed by concern about racism and the harmful effects of demeaning speech. However, Patricia Hodulik (now Patricia Brady), a University of Wisconsin System attorney who was involved in formulating a speech policy, wrote, "Existing university rules and policies governing student conduct did not address harassing verbal conduct and offensive expressive behavior by students."[8]

The Phi Gamma case was the last straw for many minority students. A new generation of students such as Geneva Brown and Charles Holley had

---

[7] See, e.g., Lorenne M. G. Clark, "Liberalism and Pornography," in David Copp and Susan Wendell, eds., *Pornography and Censorship* (Prometheus Books, 1983), p. 45.

[8] Patricia Brady (Hodulik), "Prohibiting Discriminatory Harassment by Regulating Student Speech: A Balancing of First Amendment and University Interests," 16 *Journal of College and University Law* 4 (1990), p. 574.

assumed leadership of the Black Student Union (BSU), and they pounced on the case and held it up as an example of the racial insensitivity of the institution. According to Brown, "This has been a long time coming. It has happened before, but it is only because of the current racism awareness that it has come to the forefront."[9] The assistant dean of students, Roger Howard – originally a supporter of codes who reconsidered his position several years later – pointed out that the fraternity had been holding the same event for many years, but it was only in 1987 that new black leadership objected. "But in this particular year, [the fraternity] attracted the attention of a group of graduate and undergraduate students who had begun to be more active than usual on issues of race and diversity on the campus. . . . They came across the Fiji Island cartoon character in the spring of 1987, called the television cameras and staged a protest, and it really took off from there."[10]

Three days after the Phi Gamma party, five hundred students attended an antiracism rally at the student union. Activists blamed the "entire campus" for what happened, and the BSU presented a list of demands, which included the revocation of Phi Gamma's charter, the creation of a multicultural center, and the requirement that all UW undergraduates take a course on ethnicity and race.[11] On May 8 the board of regents' education committee passed a resolution that committed the university to address "subtle racism" and proclaimed that the board "condemns all acts of racism or cultural insensitivity that are occurring throughout the UW system."[12] Over the summer the university established a large, campuswide committee, eventually called the Steering Committee for Minority Affairs, to explore the BSU demands, the feasibility of special orientation sessions for minority students, and what the *Badger Herald* described as "a permanent racism grievance board." In addition, students formed a new group called Students Fighting Racism. Meanwhile, the university sanctioned Phi Gamma, revoked its official status, and mandated participation in sensitivity-oriented functions.[13]

Virtually everyone agreed that race was a major concern. The problem was that no one defined "racism" clearly, and there were calls for censorship of speech acts that lay well within the umbrella of the First Amendment's protection. (Indeed, federal courts would later rule that universities may not sanction fraternities for engaging in skits that were even more provocative and insensitive than Phi Gamma's party, for such expression is protected by

[9] "FIJI Fraternity Party Called Racist," *Badger Herald*, May 4, 1987.
[10] Roger Howard, Oral History interview with Brady Teicher, April 27, 2001, pp. 2–3, in university archive in Memorial Library, University of Wisconsin, Madison.
[11] "Minorities Blame Entire Campus," *Badger Herald*, May 6, 1987.
[12] "Regents Pledge to Address Racism," *Badger Herald*, May 8, 1987.
[13] "Campus Racism Battled," *Badger Herald*, July 2, 1987; "Committee on Racism Studies Minority Issues," *Badger Herald*, August 10, 1987; "Racism Investigated Here," *Badger Herald*, August 10, 1987.

the First Amendment.)[14] Racial tensions intensified during the fall as other incidents occurred, turning the campus into a sensitivity tinderbox. According to a *Herald* columnist, "The campus is under siege, with our conscience held hostage by a handful of anonymous (sometimes not so anonymous) racists who have real hatred in their hearts. The entire university [is] set on edge the way it is, with 45,000 sets of eyes, ears, and nostrils straining for the slightest blip, squeak or waft of racism."[15]

In early December the steering committee issued its report, named the "Holley Report" in recognition of the major role that BSU president Charles Holley had played in its drafting. It was the first time in the 140-year history of the university that a report of such magnitude had been named after a student. A level-headed man, Holley led by virtue of his character and intelligence rather than by emotional appeals. The undergraduate told me that he had paid a stiff price for his activism. Over the course of the next year, he received threatening hate calls, and someone threw a brick through his window. Unfortunately, the perpetrators of these pernicious criminal acts were never identified.

The Holley Report presented a list of recommendations, including the establishment of an ethnic studies department, a multicultural center, the creation of a more racially congenial climate, and the aggressive recruitment of minority faculty, students, and staff. Roger Howard said that the Holley Report proposed that "the University at least consider strongly adopting rules regarding discriminatory harassment, hate speech. That recommendation was picked up in the Madison Plan very carefully calling for a consideration of whether or not the University ought to adopt such rules."[16]

In January 1988 Donna Shalala, former president of Hunter College in New York City, took over as chancellor. At a meeting of the board of regents, she announced that the university planned to present its response to the Holley Report on February 9 and that her objective was to "make Wisconsin a stronger and more sensitive university." Shalala was on her way to earning a national reputation as a leader in the quest for greater diversity and sensitivity in higher education. An advocate of total quality management (a management theory that entails cooperative interaction of all units of an organization under the aegis of leadership), she brought the diversity agenda to Madison by appointing bureaucrats who shared her goals and replacing most of the college deans with people sympathetic to the movement. Some of the new administrators ranked this goal ahead of the university's

---

[14] See *Iota Chapter of Sigma Chi Fraternity v. George Mason University*, 773 F. Supp. 792 (E. D. Va. 1991).

[15] David Gammon, "Racism Overblown: Policies Attack Wrong Targets," *Badger Herald*, December 1, 1987.

[16] Roger Howard, Oral History interview; Report of the Steering Committee on Minority Affairs (Holley Report), University of Wisconsin, Madison, December 1, 1987; "Committee Issues Minority Report," *Badger Herald*, December 2, 1987.

traditional commitment to free speech, academic freedom, and due process (as the Richard Long case and other matters I discuss revealed). However, it is important to note that Shalala resisted some of the more radical proposals of the Holley Report, such as the establishment of a separate ethnic studies department that would essentially be based on the promotion of a cause; and her approach to speech codes was at times more nuanced than her critics often alleged.[17]

In early February, Students Fighting Racism announced the establishment of a "racism hotline" for reporting incidents of racial discrimination, harassment, and insensitivity. Shalala also presented the Madison Plan, the university's response to the Holley Report. Addressing a standing-room-only audience in a large hall at the Wisconsin Center, Shalala declared, "Today we do more than denounce racism, sexism, and discrimination of all kinds." The "comprehensive and bold" plan was an effort to improve the campus climate through a variety of programs, including outreach and recruitment of minority faculty, students, and staff; increased scholarships and financial aid; curricular enhancement through the development of a multidisciplinary course on "understanding other cultures"; the requirement that all undergraduates earn credit in ethnic studies through courses provided by established departments and programs; and, finally, the creation of a multicultural center, offering both academic and social functions. The plan also called for the consideration of new policies on student conduct to promote a nondiscriminatory environment.[18]

Activists greeted the Madison Plan ambivalently. Some students considered it too "assimilationist" because it linked the new programs to the broader mission of the university and provided that the ethnic studies requirement be fulfilled by courses in existing departments and programs. Mark Wenner, coordinator of the Black Graduate Council, criticized the tone and substance of the plan as "[coming] across as saying that the minorities have a problem of adjusting to the university. The minority heritages should be talked about in classrooms and celebrated," he proclaimed. "We shouldn't have this burden put on us." Wenner and his allies also derided the plan for its lack of "strong policies against harassment."[19] Another student leader declared that ethnic courses should "promote cross-cultural understanding and respect" and that they be taught from the "minority point of view." Supporting Shalala's decision against creating a separate ethnic studies department, David Gammon wrote that her critics' reasoning meant that "[s]tudents in Ethnic Studies would at best be taught in

---

[17] "Minority Issues Highlighted in UW Board of Regents Hearing," *Badger Herald*, January 27, 1988.
[18] "Madison Plan Unveiled by Shalala," *Badger Herald*, February 10, 1988.
[19] "Minority Coalition Questions Madison Plan in Its Response," *Badger Herald*, February 26, 1988.

social virtues, rather than intellectual accomplishments, and at worst be compelled to learn the basic tenets of the religion on Third Worldism, which tends only to replace old lies with new."[20] In the end, the university required all undergraduates to take one three-credit course in a subject dealing with ethnicity from a list of dozens of courses in established departments or programs.

In April 1988 another racial incident arose when several members of the Acacia fraternity at the University of Illinois disrupted several classes at the University of Wisconsin, including two in the Department of African Languages and Literature. Apparently, the fraternity conducted disruptions of classes at other schools every year as part of their initiation rituals. Campus groups interpreted the disruptions as racially motivated, and large protests and voluminous commentary shook the campus.[21]

Then one of the first incidents called into the UW-Madison racism hotline, anonymously, reported a "slave auction" held by Zeta Beta Tau in October 1988. Most of the "slaves" consisted of impersonations of famous white people, but two skits personified Oprah Winfrey and the Jackson Five, causing the caller to describe the shows as racist. Someone at the university then leaked the incident to the press, sparking an outcry against racism on campus and in town. According to Steven Hurley, ZBT's attorney in the case, the fraternity was tried and convicted in the press and campus opinion before anyone had examined the actual facts – a claim substantiated by a perusal of the local and campus press.[22] The administration did not make its own decision in the case, choosing instead to delegate the matter to the Committee on Student Organizations (CSO), the Wisconsin Students Association's panel dealing with student groups. Though under pressure to yield to the moral outrage on campus, the CSO exonerated the fraternity because a videotape of the skits showed that nothing racist had transpired. (In fact, the imitation of Michael Jackson was so funny that the members of a concerned faculty committee that viewed the tape broke into laughter while watching it.) Wisconsin Student Association copresident Margaret McCormick told the press that the CSO could not punish ZBT because "WSA is a state agency and thus has to follow state and federal laws [including the First Amendment]." In reaction, the Inter-Fraternity Council, which is a private organization overseeing fraternity life at Wisconsin, then decided to expel ZBT for five years, which meant that the fraternity lost all official privileges pertaining to fraternities at the university.[23]

---

[20] Gammon, "The Minority Coalition at Shalala's Door," op-ed, *Badger Herald*. (No date provided in my materials.)

[21] See, e.g., "UW Frat Member Tied to Disruption," *Wisconsin State Journal*, April 26, 1988.

[22] See, e.g., "Slave Auction Sale by Fraternity Called Racist," *Capital Times*, October 24, 1988. This story is but one of numerous stories and opinions that were published.

[23] "IFC Expels ZBT for 5 Year Period," *Badger Herald*, November 22, 1988.

Caught in a crossfire that it was not yet prepared to handle, the administration found itself under attack by both racial sensitivity and free speech advocates.[24] Critics claimed that the administration had handed the problem off to the student government board rather than making the politically difficult (though factually correct) decision itself. The *Herald* editorialized, "When CSO finally came out with its decision, saying that ZBT enjoys First Amendment protection, it did what Shalala should have done. And as a result, CSO members and not the UW administration were subjected to a cry of outrage from students."[25] During the controversy, one story appeared early on in the *Capital Times* in which eyewitnesses said that nothing racist had taken place.[26] But the majority of the press was accusatory until the issue died with the expulsion decision.

According to ZBT's attorney, Steven Hurley, the university leadership did not inform the community publicly why the charges had been dropped. It was a wrenching case for Hurley, for it revealed a disconcerting side to the university's pursuit of racial justice:

This was the case, strangely enough, where I went home every night with knots in my stomach because this steamrolled every day, and I saw what was happening in the media, and I saw people at the university making pronouncements about what was appropriate discipline and not really caring about the facts.... when the nine-hundred-pound gorilla of the university decides to gang up on somebody, they do it. And this university can do some wonderful things. But this university, when it decides to come to a snap judgment and be autocratic about it, gets its way. And when they are intent on doing that, it is extraordinarily difficult if not impossible to stop them.[27]

New Codes

The Madison Plan called on the faculty senate and the academic staff assembly to adopt a policy regarding harassment "on the basis of race, color, creed, sexual orientation, disability, national origin, and ancestry."[28] Following up on the Madison Plan, the regents issued the "Design for Diversity," which mandated that each of the UW system's twenty-six campuses develop antidiscriminatory harassment policies.[29] In pursuit of this mandate, the administration at Madison asked a committee of law professors, including Gordon Baldwin, Richard Delgado, and Ted Finman, to devise rules that would not

---

[24] See, e.g., "Groups Claim ZBT Auction is UW's Fault," *Badger Herald*, October 26, 1988.
[25] "Shalala Uses CSO as a Shield from ZBT Flap," *Badger Herald*, November 28, 1988.
[26] "Eyewitnesses Say Auction Not Racist," *Capital Times*, October 27, 1988.
[27] Interview with Steven Hurley, August 2001.
[28] "The Madison plan," statement by UW-Madison Chancellor Donna E. Shalala, February 9, 1988, p. 19.
[29] See Hodulik, "Prohibiting Discriminatory Harassment," p. 575.

run afoul of the First Amendment. The committee was an interesting mix: Baldwin was a noted conservative constitutional law scholar who was also active in local politics and law, whereas Delgado was gaining fame as a leader of critical race theory.[30] The committee also received suggestions from other law professors with strong antidiscrimination credentials, including Linda Greene, Patricia Williams, and Carin Clause.

The most important figure, however, was Finman, a man with a brilliant legal mind, extensive university experience, and sterling liberal credentials. Finman's belief in freedom of speech was long-standing, reaching back to the time that he wrote an amicus brief for the defendants in *Yates v. United States*, a famous Supreme Court case in which the Court reversed the convictions of several lower-level Communist Party leaders under the federal Smith Act. The case was a cornerstone in the development of the modern doctrine of speech.[31] Because Finman was disturbed by some of the arguments being advanced in support of speech codes, one of his motivations for entering the fray was to protect free speech interests from ignorance and zealotry. (In this respect, his experience was similar to that of William Van Alstyne at Duke, as reported in Chapter 1. But, unlike Finman, Van Alstyne reacted by preventing any code from emerging at all.) But the Jewish Finman also recalled the epithets of his childhood in San Francisco and believed that justice required that individuals be protected from racist expression that allegedly existed at the university. He considered it possible for reasonable individuals with the proper legal training to fashion a policy that maintained the proper balance between free speech and protection from harassment. In an interview with researcher Kiki Jamieson, Finman said,

I think initially if someone had come to me and said, "How about coming up with a code?" I would have said, "No." Later on, I became quite convinced that the code, properly limited and very narrowly drawn, could serve some important functions without violating First Amendment provisions as I saw them. . . . There are really two [important functions]. One function is to communicate to the minority community that the rest of us do care and that we understand the hurt that is caused by malicious racial epithets inflicted on them. And the other function is to communicate to the campus community the sentiment that this [sort of behavior] is unacceptable.[32]

The speech code committee drafted a faculty and a student code. Because the student code applied to the entire UW system, its formal approval required the approval of the regents and the state legislature after the measure

---

[30] See, e.g., Richard Delgado, *Critical Race Theory: An Introduction* (New York University Press, 2001); *The Coming Race War? And Other Apocalyptic Tales of America after Affirmative Action and Welfare* (New York University Press, 1996).

[31] *Yates v. United States*, 354 U.S. 298 (1957).

[32] Finman, quoted in Kiki Jamieson, "Paved with Good Intentions: The University of Wisconsin Speech Code," in Milton Heumann and Thomas W. Church, eds., *Hate Speech on Campus: Cases, Case Studies, and Commentary* (Northeastern University Press, 1997), p. 171.

passed the senate of each campus. The faculty code applied only to the Madison campus, so the faculty senate at Madison had the final vote. Code proponents were careful to claim that the measures covered discriminatory *conduct*, not speech, as the latter would raise the specter of First Amendment problems. Some of these claims were more measured and respectful of free speech than others. When the senate passed the codes in November 1988, for example, Shalala stated, "Freedom is never easy, and a great university is not a place to play with constitutional rights. It is a laboratory for open debate, a haven for diverse opinions."[33] Regent Ness Flores was less appreciative of free speech values when the board finally ratified the codes in June 1989. Claiming that the codes covered conduct, not speech, he asserted, "I think that when we hide behind the First Amendment on this issue, we are mistaken."[34] An editorial in the *Daily Cardinal,* one of the two student papers, reported a pending legal attack by the state branch of the American Civil Liberties Union in words that were unusual for a college newspaper with a great free speech tradition:

This is not a First Amendment issue at all. UWS 17 [the student code] is an important step in stopping harassment, not free speech. It strives to create a safer environment for everyone regardless of race, gender, religion, creed, disability, sexual orientation, national ancestry or age. . . . Instead of maintaining such an absolutist position, the ACLU should use this opportunity to make an intellectual jump and *redefine* free speech to account for the realities of current society.[35]

The student code empowered the university to punish a student

[f]or racist or discriminatory comments, epithets or other expressive behavior directed at an individual or on separate occasions at different individuals, or for physical conduct if such comments, epithets or other expressive behavior or physical conduct intentionally: 1. Demean the race, sex, religion, color, creed, disability, sexual orientation, national origin, ancestry or age of the individual or individuals; and 2. Create an intimidating, hostile or demeaning environment for education, university-related work, or other university-authorized activity.[36]

The faculty code used similar language but incorporated more explicit protections of academic freedom. Nonetheless, this code was much broader than the student code, as it did not even require intentional wrongdoing. It singled out the special categories of gender, race, cultural background, ethnicity, sexual orientation, and handicap. In so doing, it applied the assumption that certain forms of speech affect members of designated groups

---

[33] Shalala, in Jamieson, "Paved with Good Intentions," quoting *Wisconsin State Journal,* November 13, 1988.
[34] Minutes of Board of Regents Meeting, June 9, 1989.
[35] Editorial, *Daily Cardinal,* October 25, 1989, quoted in Jamieson, "Paved with Good Intentions," p. 572 (emphasis added).
[36] Wisconsin Administrative Code, Sec. UWS 17.06(2).

in the same way (a form of "groupthink"). This code covered "expressive behavior" that is "explicitly demeaning" in instructional and noninstructional settings and provided a complicated set of definitions and provisions of burdens of proof. The key elements of the rule dealt with the kind of expression that was prohibited, and a provision that a faculty member's claim that an expressive or teaching technique is germane to the subject matter of the course be respected unless it was "clearly unreasonable." An expression could be punishable if considered a demeaning "epithet" or if "the behavior is commonly considered by persons of a group of a particular gender, race, cultural background, ethnicity, sexual orientation, or handicap to be demeaning to members of the group." The expression could not be a single incident; it also had to be repeated and had to "seriously interfere" with someone's academic work, or create a "hostile or intimidating, or demeaning environment."[37]

No meaningful, organized opposition to the codes arose. But as the codes were being considered by the regents and the state legislature after passing the faculty senates of the system, some public concern emerged. The two major Madison newspapers opposed the student code in editorials – everyone ignored the faculty code – and four professors spoke out against it in hearings or in op-ed essays: theater professor Robert Skloot; mathematics professor Anatole Beck; English professor Peter A. Schreiber; and College of Letters and Sciences dean David Cronon. Regent Oly Fish was also an outspoken opponent, as were Madison mayor Paul Soglin – a well-known 1960s activist – and Madison's affirmative action officer, Eugene Parks.[38] In addition, during the 1988–89 academic year, political science senior Michael Aprahamian wrote a thoughtful and courageous senior honors thesis defending free speech against speech codes. Aprahamian's opposition was public in nature because he was known and respected on campus, and because he presented the arguments in his thesis in public forums, including the annual ceremony at the end of the academic year in which selected university honors students present the ideas in their theses.[39] The *Badger Herald* wrote an editorial criticizing the motives of the regents and the legislature. It also pointed out that the rule "doesn't have such a firm constitutional basis." The *Herald* wrote, "It seems either the Regents have created a setting for Gestapo tactics or they have sought to get good publicity and soothe their

[37] Faculty Legislation as Appended to Faculty Policies and Procedures, II, pp. 303–5.

[38] See, e.g., Robert Skloot, "Board of Regents Must Be Careful When Considering Students' Rights," *Capital Times*, April 18, 1989; Peter A. Schreiber, "UW's Anti-Racism Rules Unworkable," *Wisconsin State Journal*, September 13, 1989; "Soglin Praised for Opposing Rule," *Wisconsin State Journal*, July 20, 1989.

[39] Aprahamian presentation, Senior Honors Thesis Presentations, University of Wisconsin, Madison, April 1989. I was Aprahamian's thesis adviser. At this point in time, I disagreed with his position, which led to several interesting debates between us. Unfortunately, I was unable to find his excellent thesis, so I cannot cite it.

consciences by coming up with a shoddy concept that will have little real effect."[40]

Some student dissent appeared in op-eds and reports in the student papers, but it was isolated and unorganized. Student government supported the codes. Interestingly, virtually all the debate focused on the student code. From day one, commentators outside the administration called it a *speech* code, thereby guaranteeing controversy over its legitimacy. Conversely, the faculty code, to the extent that anyone even thought of it, was widely considered an appropriate *conduct* code that the university was obligated to enact under Equal Employment Opportunity Commission (EEOC) or Office of Civil Rights (OCR) guidelines. (Later, advocates maintained that the university could even lose federal funding if it abolished or unduly weakened the faculty code – a questionable claim that nonetheless carried considerable weight at a university that is second in the nation in procuring federal research money.) No one with credible legal credentials questioned these claims, so the faculty code met no meaningful public challenge.

The senate vote in May 1988 reflected the difference between student and faculty codes. The student code generated heated debate and took up most of the discussion. The debate on the faculty code, however, was perfunctory; its passage being a foregone conclusion. The student code proceeded to the regents and the legislature, where it passed without serious opposition.[41] Shortly after this meeting, Shalala linked the code movement to "a second wave of the civil rights movement," stating that resolving racial tensions was "a central issue of higher education."[42]

Legal Problems

After ratification, the faculty code quickly slipped into obscurity while the student code continued to generate controversy. The Madison speech code committee prepared a brochure that explained the new student rule and provided five examples intended to clarify what was prohibited and what was not. Unfortunately, the examples caused more confusion and revealed the potential of overbroad enforcement. Kiki Jamieson wrote, "In retrospect, the brochure seems not to have clarified the rule but instead to have illustrated its over breadth. Despite the university's arguments to the contrary, it seems clear that the rule would have covered racist and similar remarks directed at individuals in classrooms and other academic settings."[43] At least

---

[40] "Chilling New Rule Possible: Is Free Speech on Its Way Out?" *Badger Herald*, June 19, 1989.

[41] Tape of faculty senate meeting, University of Wisconsin, Madison, May 2, 1988; "Faculty Ok's Minority Relations Plan," *Wisconsin State Journal*, May 3, 1988.

[42] "UW Must Be Out Front on Civil Rights, Says Shalala," *Wisconsin State Journal*, May 9, 1988.

[43] Jamieson, "Paved with Good Intentions," p. 174.

nine students received sanctions under the code at other campuses between the time of adoption in 1989 and the lawsuit in federal court in 1990. Although some of the cases appeared to be within reach of the rule, others did not. In one case, a student at UW-Stevens Point received probation under the code for stealing his roommate's credit card and obtaining sixty dollars from the roommate's account. The defendant acknowledged that the fact his roommate was Japanese had motivated him to commit the act. His conduct was a crime but did not constitute what the code prohibited, which was demeaning speech. Another case involved sexist remarks made to a woman at a bar off campus. In another case, a student was charged with calling another student a "red neck."[44] According to Jeffrey Cassell, one of the attorneys who litigated against the code, the cases on other campuses "showed that this was not just a theoretical/academic debate. [We saw] that it was being applied in a manner that supported our argument."[45]

No one at Madison was ever "officially" charged with violating the student code, let alone sanctioned. However, I personally know of one case in which a student was pressured by a residence director to attend a sensitivity session and to speak with a counselor for engaging in an expressive act that appears to have fallen well short of the code's zone of prohibition. In the fall of 1990, freshman David Mecklenberg played an admittedly ill-advised and thoughtless practical joke by posting two fliers in his dorm that presented a doctored picture of a friend. He placed one flier on his friend's door, and the other in the hallway by the elevator. The fliers portrayed the friend, who was heterosexual, as gay, and displayed the friend offering videos of himself engaging in sex acts for thirty-nine dollars. The friend did not complain about the fliers, and there was no evidence that any gay person saw them – a finding that should have meant that the code did not apply in this case, as it prohibited only demeaning expression "directed at an individual." People in the dorm took the fliers down soon after Mecklenberg posted them. According to Mecklenberg, the resident director told him, "if I did not agree with how this incident was being resolved, that I could appeal and discuss my violation with the Dean of Students, who would probably be less understanding. It was also explained that the potential punishment for violating the student speech code in the dorms was eviction." Unsure of his rights and fearful of being evicted (eviction would have meant dropping out of school for a year because he would have still owed three thousand dollars on the room), Mecklenberg accepted the informal sanction. There is no evidence that the dean of students knew that such plea bargaining was taking place; Mecklenberg dealt only with an adviser on his floor and the resident director of the dorm. Twelve years later he related that the problem for him was not

[44] See *UWM Post v. Regents of the University of Wisconsin System*, 774 F. Supp. 1163 (E. D. Wis. 1991), p. 1168.
[45] Jamieson, "Paved with Good Intentions," p. 177.

being told that his conduct was problematic but rather the coercive way he was treated. Punitiveness outweighed any effort to persuade. "Contrary to what the university hoped would occur, my opinion of homosexuality was changed negatively because of the whole incident. As I have [now] adopted strong libertarian principles, my thoughts on homosexuality have changed again. But UW certainly had nothing to do with this change."[46]

The legal challenge to the code came on March 29, 1990, when a group of student activists involved in progressive political causes and the student newspaper (*UWM Post*) at the University of Wisconsin, Milwaukee, challenged the code on its face for running afoul of the First Amendment. On October 11, 1991, District Court Judge Robert Warren ruled that the code violated the First Amendment. Warren concluded that in addition to being vague, the code suffered from overbreadth for not being limited to fighting words, which the court defined as words likely to incite a hostile physical reaction.[47] Warren also dismissed the university's claim that Title VII's antiharassment provisions legitimated the code, pointing out that, while Title VII applies to employees and agents of the university, it simply does not cover students. Furthermore, Title VII's status as a statute means that it must always yield to the First Amendment, which is part of the Constitution. The code also clearly constituted content discrimination. Warren concluded:

The problems of bigotry and discrimination sought to be addressed here are real and truly corrosive of the educational environment. But freedom of speech is almost absolute in our land and the only restriction the fighting words doctrine can abide is that based on the fear of violent reaction. Content-based prohibitions such as that in the UW Rule, however well intended, simply cannot survive the screening which our Constitution demands.[48]

In an interview in 1994, Finman conceded that the code possessed constitutional infirmities. "When the case was challenged, my first reaction was, 'How the hell did we let this wording get through?' We should have known better. We should have seen the potential for attack there. I think the explanation is that in the process of political compromise, we had to come up with language that would satisfy the system-wide committee."[49]

Revision of the Code

Judge Warren's invalidation of the student code received national attention, and was rendered at a time when the debate over the "political correctness" mentality was rising. Although more people began questioning the

---

46 Correspondence with David Mecklenberg, March 2002. I have been given credible accounts of other cases similar to Mecklenberg's.
47 *UWM Post v. Board of Regents*, p. 1170.
48 Ibid., p. 1181.
49 Finman interview in Jamieson, "Paved with Good Intentions," p. 179.

advisability of codes, University of Wisconsin leaders remained unflagging in their commitment to them. As James Sulton, UW system president of minority affairs, stated, "The Rule was a visible sign to prospective minority students and their parents that we are willing to do something. We are anxious to show that we will protect the rights of minorities on this campus."[50] The administration quickly moved to revise the code.

In late October 1991 a small group (including Chancellor Shalala) met to consider the advisability of introducing a revised code. My own inclusion in this group represented my entry into the politics of free speech on campus. My political science colleague, Joel Grossman, who was a member of the university committee, then invited me to address the upcoming senate meeting, which was to take up the question of renewal. Grossman had quietly opposed the original codes and knew that I was no longer as firmly committed to them as before. I did not argue against a new code at this juncture but noted that any new code should not single out such categories as race, gender, ethnicity, or culture as prohibited subjects, as this would hinder debate about important and controversial issues. Several law professors defended the constitutional status of the revised code. The senate voted for the committee to craft a new code.[51]

Between the November meeting and the senate vote on the new measure on March 2, 1992, I struggled to decide what I believed. A variety of factors coalesced to compel me to declare my views publicly. I had been at Madison over six years and was known as a First Amendment scholar and supporter. I took my teaching seriously and felt that I owed it to my students to take a public stand. I was also growing alarmed at how codes were being enforced in the UW system and around the country. But I was still undecided about the validity of the underlying premises that gave rise to the codes. No network of opposition existed. Led by history professor Theodore Hamerow, the Wisconsin Association of Scholars (WAS, which is the state chapter of the National Association of Scholars) had forcefully, yet unsuccessfully, challenged several administration policies. The knowledgeable and forceful Hamerow had gained national repute for opposing the various aspects of political correctness and had established WAS as a presence on campus.[52] But WAS was perceived as too hostile to the new campus order to be a credible player. And WAS's lack of a libertarian bent at this juncture indicated that it was not inclined to make free speech a major issue. (Later, however, WAS would prove to be an invaluable ally and component

---

[50] Sulton in *Daily Cardinal*, October 23, 1991, quoted in Jamieson, "Paved with Good Intentions," p. 181.

[51] Tape of faculty senate meeting, November 4, 1991.

[52] See Patrick Houston's article on Hamerow, "He Wants to Pull the Plug on the PC," *Newsweek*, December 24, 1990, p. 52. This article appeared as part of *Newsweek*'s cover story, "Thought Police: There's 'Politically Correct' Way to Talk about Race, Sex, and Ideas. Is This the New Enlightenment – or the New McCarthyism?"

of the free speech movement.) The student code had fallen at the hands of a federal court, rather than those of a political movement, so no infrastructure or organization had arisen upon which free speech interests could build a meaningful opposition or springboard for persuasion. Salvation by the judiciary had not appeared to do much to sway public opinion.[53]

Perhaps most important, I was influenced by several remarkable students in my seminar on criminal law and jurisprudence that spring who were very active in student affairs and who opposed the codes in principle. Lee Hawkins, Bill Dixon, Simon Olson, Mark Sniderman, and Eric Jacobson composed the core of this group. Hawkins later became editorial page editor of the *Herald*, which dedicated the fall term of 1993 to discussion of the First Amendment. This group followed the revision movement with keen interest and appeared at meetings of the regents and the state legislature on the matter.

Hawkins is an African American and was, therefore, considered a beneficiary of codes. In fact, he recoiled at the racial taunting he had experienced during his years at a prep school in St. Paul, Minnesota, and had picked Wisconsin for his undergraduate education precisely because it *had* just passed a new student speech code. But as his noteworthy career as a student leader unfolded, Hawkins came to consider codes demeaning to minorities because they inherently underestimated minorities' capacity to handle the rough-and-tumble of public discourse. He also disdained others telling him how to think because of his race – or because of any other factor, for that matter. Hawkins had developed a relationship with a leading administrator, whom he considered a mentor. One day in spring 1992, Hawkins phoned me at my office, distraught. The administrator was committed to codes and had heard that Hawkins was going to declare publicly his opposition to renewal of the student code. He pleaded with Hawkins to hold his tongue, appealing to Hawkins's sense of personal loyalty and debt (the administrator had assisted Hawkins several times). Compelled to choose between his sense of loyalty and obligation to his mentor and his own intellectual and moral conscience, Hawkins was caught in a powerful dilemma. I told Hawkins that I could not tell him what to do but that I thought his mentor's actions were reprehensible. No mentor who truly respects a student should ever place that student in such a predicament. In my view, it showed how such administrators considered a cause more important than individual conscience.

After pondering his decision for a few days, Hawkins not only decided to side with his conscience, he also became perhaps the single most eloquent and forceful opponent of speech codes on campus over the next two years.

[53] On the political problems of reliance on courts, see Gerald Rosenberg, *The Hollow Hope: Can Courts Bring about Social Change?* (University of Chicago Press, 1991); Mark V. Tushnet, *Taking the Constitution Away from the Courts* (Princeton University Press, 1999).

His case was the first of many that would be repeated over the course of the next few years: individuals rose up to resist authority after being subjected to questionable treatment or investigations. Such action played a crucial moral and strategic role in the eventual abolition of the faculty code. Hawkins's posture and actions, like those of his student allies, also epitomized something else: the importance of students in the political movement supporting free speech and civil liberty. Without students like Hawkins, Dixon, Olson, Sniderman, and Jacobson (and many others whom I mention later), the free speech movement at Wisconsin would not have gotten off the ground.

The students in my seminar were very influential in pushing me closer to supporting abolition during the spring of 1992. Their combination of articulateness, commitment, courage, and sense of adventure deeply impressed me. They were disappointed at the lack of faculty resistance and opposition, and they challenged my integrity. I finally felt obligated to act. "Downs, we need you. We need someone on the faculty with First Amendment credentials. Come on over to our side. We don't understand why you keep supporting codes. Your position is inconsistent with everything you teach us."

Revising the Student Code, Revisiting the Faculty Code

The Finman committee had presented a new student code in February that painstakingly attended to Judge Warren's criticisms, making it much tighter than its predecessor by limiting it to "epithets" likely to trigger a fighting response. The revised code defined "epithet" as "a word, phrase or symbol that reasonable persons recognize to grievously insult or threaten persons because of their race, sex, religion, color, creed, disability, sexual orientation, national origin, ancestry, or age," and would create a hostile or threatening educational environment and "that without regard to the gender or other physical characteristics involved, would tend to provoke an immediate response when addressed directly to a person of average sensibility who is a member of the group that the word, phrase or symbol insults or threatens."[54]

I finally decided where I stood while preparing to be interviewed on a Wisconsin Public Radio show a few days before the senate vote. On the show, I surprised host Mark Paulsen by outlining my reasons for opposing the new code. Then when we turned to take callers' questions, something unexpected happened. We received a call from "Richard," who expressed his appreciation for my opposition to the code. But then he said something stunning: "Though I fully agree with your position, you have left something out. There is a worse code that you have not mentioned." Taken aback, I asked Richard what he could possibly mean. "There is a *faculty* code," he replied to my skepticism. "I ought to know. I was investigated under it."

---

[54] Wisconsin Administrative Code, Sec. UWS 17.06(2). Revised.

Unsure what to make of this startling revelation, I said that I would look into it. We then took other calls, most of which were also critical of codes.

That evening, Richard Long, a University of Wisconsin art professor, phoned me at home and related his story, presented in some detail in Chapter 2. He eventually told several other faculty of his plight, making the case common knowledge among free speech activists. Long eventually played an important role in the abolition movement. He was yet another example of an individual rising from persecution under the code to fight policies and actions that had violated or jeopardized his academic freedom.

Long's call to Wisconsin Public Radio was the first act in the laborious process that eventually led to abolition of the faculty code. Stage 1 was the "wilderness period": a few faculty members and students persevered to make free speech publicly recognized as an issue. They struggled futilely to forge a political movement but managed to accomplish one important objective: they put free speech recognition in the public's consciousness at the university. Stage 2 began in 1996 with the formation of a serious political movement, which was sparked by an explosive case in the history department. Stage 3 entailed the movement to become inside players as a special ad hoc speech code committee met to debate the fate of the faculty code. During this time, free speech emerged as one of the most prominent issues on campus. Stage 4 encompassed the three-month debate in the senate over the code's fate, during which a "tipping point" occurred: the public's sentiment shifted. Members of the movement felt precisely the kind of "amazement" that Kuran describes in *Private Truths, Public Lies*.[55]

Stage 1. The 1992 Senate Vote and Its Aftermath

The senate held its meeting on the second student code on March 2. Unlike the 1988 vote, this time a small, fledgling opposition was prepared to challenge the motion to adopt a new code. Political scientist Joel Grossman led the effort by writing a substitute motion that eschewed sanctions in favor of establishing informal methods of fostering a campus climate that "promotes diversity and mutual respect for all students and other members of the university community."[56] Grossman called on me to speak in favor of his motion, and I told the senate that I agreed with the objectives of the substitute motion, and that the very idea of speech codes was inconsistent with a great university. Several faculty members then spoke in favor of Grossman's motion, raising serious questions about the proposed code's moral and utilitarian

---

[55] Timur Kuran, *Private Truths, Public Lies: The Social Consequences of Preference Falsification* (Harvard University Press, 1995), pp. 49, 252.

[56] Substitute Motion by Professor Joel Grossman, in Motions Regarding Item #6, Revised Version of UWS 17.06; faculty senate meeting, March 2, 1992. *Capital Times*, March 3, 1992.

advisability in the debate that followed. No one questioned the code's constitutionality, as the law professors had all vouched for its consistency with that document. Journalism professor James Baughman (who became an invaluable ally of the free speech movement afterward) declared that he was incredulous that a major university would even consider such restrictions on free speech. Having done a calculation based on the number of incidents of offensive speech reported and the chilling effect, genetics professor Carter Denniston concluded, "The benefits are slight, the possible costs great." Medical School professor Jeffrey Patterson referred to his interactions with Soviet doctors who were pressured by the state to serve political ends. "You don't lose intellectual honesty all at once," he said. "You lose it bit by bit." Many were surprised at the level of opposition. For a fleeting moment, we entertained the illusion that we might prevail.[57]

But code supporters then played their trump cards. At least two supporters clearly implied that opponents of the code were racists for defending the free speech rights of hate speech. A member of the university committee then replied to concerns about the code's chilling effect on speech by asserting that such chilling effect was precisely what the university desired: making individuals more cautious when discussing racial and gender issues would enhance the moral environment. Applause followed these remarks. Ted Finman then clinched the victory for his side. After stressing how the code singled out only the most unacceptable epithets, he brilliantly linked this objective to his own experience of being subjected to epithets as a boy. His voice cracked with emotion as he recalled the experience. As Finman left the podium to the loudest applause of the afternoon, Mark Sniderman and I slipped each other glances and shrugged. We knew that the able and dramatic law professor had just assured our defeat.

The vote, however, was closer than anyone had anticipated: 89 to 70. It was a good battle, and a sign of what can be accomplished when even a small group is prepared to make a concerted effort. The small free speech movement enjoyed the support of several students and the editors of the *Badger Herald*.[58] When student Kathy Evans, a free speech activist, opposed the code in a Wisconsin Students Association committee debate, she was rebuffed by her peers, who considered her free speech concerns to be proracist. Evans told a writer for the *Los Angeles Times Magazine* that her friends accused her of being "full of white liberal bull shit.... People had deeply personal, preset ideas."[59] Undeterred, the intrepid Evans continued to protest restrictions on speech throughout her remaining years at Wisconsin. That summer,

[57] Tape of faculty senate meeting, March 2, 1992.
[58] See, e.g., "UWS-17 Appeal Is a Waste of Money," *Badger Herald*, October 18, 1991.
[59] Barry Siegel, "Speak No Evil: How the University of Wisconsin Tried to Outlaw Hate," *Los Angeles Times Magazine*, March 28, 1993.

Harold Scheub, professor of African languages and literature, and renowned on campus for his course on African story telling, spoke out against the new code, criticizing the way the university was creating policies that encouraged racial separatism rather than integration. In Scheub's view, speech codes discourage the intellectual honesty and openness to difference that are among the predicates of intellectual and moral growth and are essential to the cultivation of racial understanding.[60]

After surviving in the faculty senate, the revised code went on to the regents, where it was quickly approved on March 5 by a 9 to 6 vote. (Several students testified against renewal at this meeting, including Hawkins, Dixon, Sniderman, and Olson.) Then it passed on to the legislature. Although she had maintained an aloof posture, Shalala praised the regents' action, declaring, "We're talking about harassment, not impinging free speech."[61] Some students and university personnel then appeared before the State Senate Education Committee to testify against the measure, along with Eunice Edger, the state chairwoman of the ACLU. (Meanwhile, the Madison newspapers and the *Badger Herald* vigorously opposed the code in editorials.)[62] Dean of Students Mary Rouse and others testified in support of the code. But just when the legislature was poised to pass the code in late June, the Supreme Court handed down the *R.A.V. v. St. Paul* decision, which ruled that speech restrictions that single out fighting words dealing with such categories as race, gender, sexual orientation, and the like violate the First Amendment's prohibition of viewpoint discrimination (see Chapter 2).[63]

R.A.V. placed the new code in constitutional jeopardy, so the legislature remanded it back to the regents, where the vote was to repeal it on September 12. This time, university leaders reluctantly conceded to constitutional fate and dropped the pursuit of the code grail. Because no one publicly proposed adopting a code that did not single out such categories as race and gender, the student code issue was laid to rest. Even Finman appeared resigned, telling Kiki Jamieson in 1994, "Although the codes we drafted are constitutionally defensible – I don't think they offend First Amendment

---

[60] Harold Scheub, "Yes – Our University Can Deal with Hate," *Wisconsin State Journal*, June 28, 1992.

[61] "Regents Approve Controversial Hate Speech Rule, 9-6," *Capital Times*, March 6, 1992.

[62] "Senate Committee Approves New UW Hate Speech Rule," UPI report, June 10, 1992; "An Exercise in Futility," *Badger Herald*, March 16, 1992; "UWS-17, Our PC Enemy," *Badger Herald*, April 27, 1992.

[63] *R.A.V. v. City of St. Paul*, 505 U.S. 377 (1992). The next day, the Wisconsin Supreme Court handed down *Mitchell v. Wisconsin*, which invalidated Wisconsin's hate crime penalty enhancement law on the basis of *R.A.V.* A year later, the U.S. Supreme Court reversed, holding that the *R.A.V.* standard applied only to the regulation of "expression," not "conduct." *Wisconsin v. Mitchell*, 508 U.S. 476 (1993). See "Court Ruling May Doom UW Hate Rule," *Capital Times*, June 24, 1992.

principles – I've come to the conclusion that they're politically unwise be-cause the unintended consequence is to encourage people and movements to censor their ideas themselves."[64]

The University of Wisconsin has not had a student code since 1991. In lieu of a speech code, the university added a new rule to the student conduct code that prohibited "stalking and harassment," without specifying race, gender, and the like – the type of viewpoint-neutral rule that Jeffrey Rosen advocates in his book, *The Unwanted Gaze*.[65] This code poses no meaningful First Amendment problems.

The senate debate launched stage 1 of the free speech movement at Madison. Though the university had reluctantly abandoned its quest for a student code, those with free speech interests were still a small minority. Problems soon arose concerning both faculty speech and the *Badger Herald* that cast a pall over free speech at the university. The fledgling free speech movement failed to gain any traction politically, although it did manage to give free speech interests a meaningful presence in the public mind.

The most significant events took place in the spring of 1993. This was when the water buffalo case broke at Penn, which bestowed more national credibility on anticode claims. Near the end of April, the *Herald* provoked anger by publishing a cartoon by Mark Lysgard entitled "Suspended An-imation," which featured a picture of Little Black Sambo and the Chief Wahoo mascot of the Cleveland Indians. Lysgard's intent was to suggest that the image of Chief Wahoo is just as racist as the image of Sambo, but many students considered the cartoon itself to be racist.[66] Critics held an angry protest outside the *Herald*'s headquarters, burning copies of the paper and intimidating the paper's editor, Jodi Cohen. Nonetheless, Cohen refused to apologize, claiming in an editorial that the cartoon was not racist.[67] Some faculty spoke out publicly on the *Herald*'s behalf in the early going, but most commentary – including that of members of the administration – opposed the paper.[68] Once again, the university was stricken with racial guilt and recrimination, despite the fact that the cartoon's intent was *not* racist. In addition, some faculty began teaching courses on the First Amendment and free speech principles. Many student activists who later contributed to the free speech movement took such classes between 1993 and 1999.

---

[64] Finman in Jamieson, "Paved with Good Intentions," p. 185.

[65] University of Wisconsin Administrative Code, Chapter 17 (UWS 17), Sec. 17.03 (2); Jeffrey Rosen, *The Unwanted Gaze: The Destruction of Privacy in America* (Random House, 2000).

[66] Risa Berg, "Comic Strip Creates a Furor on UW Campus: Controversial Cartoon Was In-tended to Attack Racial Stereotypes," *Milwaukee Journal*, May 1, 1993.

[67] Jodi Cohen, "From the Editor," *Badger Herald*, April 29, 1993.

[68] For an interview supporting the *Herald*, see "Professor Accuses University of Failure to Protect Intellectual Freedom," *Badger Herald*, May 6, 1993.

The next term, Lee Hawkins used the *Herald* editorial page as a vehicle for promoting free speech principles and discussion.[69] In addition, several speakers came to campus that term to talk about free speech. The most noteworthy were journalist Jonathan Rauch, who had just published *Kindly Inquisitors*, and Anthony Griffin, a black attorney in Texas who was defending the state Ku Klux Klan's right to freedom of association. It was an act for which he won the national William Brennan Award that year for doing the most to promote First Amendment freedoms. It was also during this time that Lester Hunt, a philosophy professor, became known as a free speech advocate as the faculty adviser to the Jefferson Society, a student group dedicated to free speech and thought. Hunt soon emerged as a major spokesperson for free speech on campus.

Sometime in 1994 the fledgling movement's commitment shifted from one of general advocacy of free speech to a more specific focus: the faculty speech code. Richard Long's experience had been troubling, but it was not enough in itself to generate a movement. But this situation changed when Hunt *himself* became a target of the code. Hunt was investigated for racism after a Native American student accused him of racially motivated grading, of using the word "injun" in a conversation with her, and of making a joke about the Lone Ranger and Tonto in class to make a point. Hunt emphatically denied the charge of biased grading and of using the word "injun," but defended his use of the Lone Ranger–Tonto example as an appropriate pedagogical technique. Although he was completely vindicated by a fair process conducted by his department, Hunt was stunned by the accusation against him and by the fact that the lead administrator in the investigation (someone at the university level who is no longer at the university) told him that he could lose his job for his sins. Once again, the process itself was the punishment. The affair also hurt Hunt's teaching by making him so hypersensitive that he was unable to think creatively and dynamically about racial issues in class. In his case, the application of the code chilled creativity rather than fostering it. Concerned about this troubling pedagogical effect, Hunt decided to go after the code.

Selecting Hunt as a target was a major blunder for those dedicated to codes, for no one was more able and motivated to present and promote powerful arguments against codes' validity than he. To him, the battle against the code was personal as well as a matter of principle. Hunt made many public statements about free speech over the next few years, doing as much as anyone to make it a matter of public concern.[70] The case further radicalized

---

[69] Many pieces appeared in the *Herald* dealing with free speech. The paper kicked off the term with a symposium on free speech principles. "The Downs-Hawkins Symposium on Free Speech: Parts 1–5," *Badger Herald*, August 30–September 8, 1993.

[70] See, e.g., Lester Hunt, "New Code Must Halt Informal Punishment," *Daily Cardinal*, October 28, 1997; "Repealing the Codes of Silence," *Liberty*, May 1999, pp. 35–38. These are but two of several pieces Hunt wrote.

Hunt and made the cause even more urgent. Still, the free speech movement did not gain political ground. For example, WAS responded with indifference during the 1994–95 academic year when two members of the movment attended a WAS meeting to ask the group if they would be interested in joining the fight against the faculty code.

Nevertheless, two events in late 1994 and in 1995 continued to keep awareness of free speech issues alive in the public eye. First, economics professor W. Lee Hansen organized a two-day conference in September on academic freedom, drawing on speakers from the university and across the nation. The conference commemorated the one hundredth anniversary of the regents' "sifting and winnowing" plaque on Bascom Hall. The meeting linked the commitment to academic freedom to the university's history and tradition – a connection that the free speech movement would take advantage of in subsequent years. There were several panels, including one on the student speech code.[71] Interestingly, no one mentioned the faculty code on the panel or in the conference; invisibility remained its fate.

The event in 1995 was the first public expression made against the faculty code, which appeared in the last edition of the *Herald* for the fall term. The *Herald* published a long anonymous interview with Richard Long in which Long related the story of his case in great detail.[72] The interview also contained a copy of the code, which the paper labeled "UW-Madison's Faculty Speech Code." *Herald* reporter Tim Graham conducted the interview under the aegis of a faculty member in the movement and with the consent and encouragement of the paper's editor in chief, Richard Schwartz, another free speech ally. An inside source told Graham that the interview roiled some members of the administration. The cat was now out of the bag. What the movement needed now was a catalytic event or two.

Stage 2. The Forging of a Movement

The turning point came in late 1995 and 1996 with the advent of two important developments. The first was the University Athletic Board's contract with Reebok, in which the company gave the university several million dollars and free shoes and athletic gear, in exchange for which the university's teams would wear Reebok insignia. The contract contained a "No Disparagement by University Clause" (6.2) that included the following wording: "[the] University will promptly take all reasonable steps necessary to address any remark by any University employee, agent or representative . . . that disparages Reebok." Some members of the board added a clause after concerns

---

[71] The book compiled from this conference is Hansen, *Academic Freedom on Trial.*

[72] Tim Graham interview with Richard Long, "The Dangers of 'Window Dressing': A Tenured UW Professor Relates His Experience with the University's Faculty Speech Code," *Badger Herald*, December 12, 1995.

were raised about free speech. "Nothing herein is intended to abridge anyone's First Amendment rights."[73] The additional clause did little to assuage
the concerns of free speech advocates, however, for the original antidisparagement clause remained in effect. Student Shira Diner presented the
strongest dissent to the antidisparagement clause during the board's vote.
Diner was a leader in student government and a fearless advocate of free
speech. At the undergraduate graduation ceremony in May 1997 – attended
by several thousand people – she attacked the university's lethargy in defending free speech and academic freedom during an address she gave as the
student government president. (See Chapter 8.)

Even before the Reebok contract was official, Richard Schwartz raised
questions about its legal and normative advisability in a *Herald* article.[74] As
soon as it was enacted, members of the still fledgling free speech movement
made it a public issue. Then something unusual happened. Over the summer,
several faculty members who had remained silent about free speech problems
organized a mass e-mail campaign that led hundreds of faculty members to
e-mail Chancellor David Ward, urging him to rescind the offending clause. In
the face of such opposition, Ward complied. (Unlike the other speech codes,
the final say in this matter was his.) The Reebok case was an important
victory for free speech supporters. It helped raise consciousness about free
speech problems on the left and may have caused members of the left to be
more amenable to claims concerning other infringements of free speech. It
also helped put those who supported codes and other speech restrictions on
the defensive. The campaign also revealed the potential usefulness of e-mail
in political campaigns.

Meanwhile, the case that would change everything was brewing in the
history department. In early 1996 a group of activists undertook a secret
investigation of professor Robert Frykenberg for alleged gender bias. The
case is delicate and complex, and I have no desire to open old wounds. And
some of those on the other side of this case have come over to our side in
subsequent years. So I focus only on the highlights and minimize the naming
of names. Frykenberg was never formally charged under the speech code,
although he maintains to this day that the investigation proceeded under its
spirit. Like the less well known Long case, the affair tore the department
apart. The investigation was conducted in a troubling way, and Frykenberg
was unfairly accused.

The affair originated when a faction of faculty members in the graduate council (a committee with authority over the graduate program) became
angry over the way the university had handled a sexual harassment claim
the previous year involving a male faculty member of the department and

---

[73] Reebok Contract, Sec. 6.2. Provided in Hansen, *Academic Freedom on Trial*, p. 11.
[74] "Final Reebok Deal Still in Negotiations," Schwartz on Sports column, *Badger Herald*, February 15, 1996.

a female graduate student. They decided to target Frykenberg for an investigation because of unsubstantiated rumors about his "traditional" way of dealing with women students – he was considered aloof, perhaps condescending, and unresponsive to feminist ideology – and because he had not supervised a woman graduate student for some time. At important points in the investigation, the faction refused to allow certain male council members to attend meetings addressing the investigation, in apparent violation of the state public meetings laws. The council possessed no authority to embark on such an enterprise; eventually, the university administration pressured the department to pursue the investigation. Frykenberg remained in the dark about what was transpiring until late in the process.

The case began to break open when David McDonald, the associate chair of the department who is widely respected for his judgment and sense of fairness, learned of what was transpiring and believed that it was wrong. McDonald felt hemmed in by his official position, so he sought out someone he knew had the ability and motivation to pursue the matter. He informed history professor John Sharpless that he "might be interested" in attending the meeting of the graduate council, which was taking place at that time. Sharpless understood that something was afoot and showed up at the meeting, only to be informed that he was not allowed in the room because it was a meeting that concerned only women. Sharpless complained that such exclusion was contrary to state public meetings law, yet to no avail. Rebuffed, he eventually informed Frykenberg of what was going on. Deeply shaken by learning that a secret investigation of him was being conducted, Frykenberg turned to his friends at the Wisconsin Association of Scholars, especially his fellow historian, Stanley Payne, perhaps the world's leading scholar of Spain and European fascism.[75] A group opposed to the investigation then organized around Payne and his allies, which was opposed by the advocates of investigation, who also began constructing a survey of gender relations in the department. Reaching for outside allies, WAS informed the National Association of Scholars of the case. James Billington, the librarian of Congress, personally wrote a letter to the chancellor, beseeching him to order a halt to the investigation, but without success.[76]

Some longtime friends ceased talking to one another as factional conflict and fractious departmental meetings tore the department apart. Things got so tense that graduate students – caught in the crossfire – began making anonymous calls to the student newspapers. With no place else to go, Frykenberg retained the services of attorney Steven Underwood of the Madison law firm Neider and Boucher, who became committed to Frykenberg's cause.

---

[75] See, e.g., Stanley G. Payne, *A History of Fascism, 1914–1945* (University of Wisconsin Press, 1995).

[76] This exchange, as well as an array of other material pertaining to the case, is in a file that I have in my temporary possession.

They filed a lawsuit against several administrators through the state attorney general's office and the investigation immediately came to a halt.[77] The university then settled the case by agreeing to vindicate Frykenberg and pay his legal fees, which had amounted to twelve thousand dollars.

Like Richard Long, Frykenberg was devastated by the investigation. He described the political aspects of the case in an interview and stressed a theme that is perhaps the single most important point in this book: a problem arises when philosophical and political differences are dealt with not by discussion and debate but by the recourse or reference to coercive, punitive measures and powers that in effect "criminalize" disagreement:

This matter could have been handled so easily just by talk, discussion of what's going on. But... you get into February and March, and finally there's departmental meetings. And on one end of the department there are some very strong and courageous people who have been denied access to meetings that were held in secret, in violation of the open meetings law. And, of course, it was at one of those meetings that [professor John] Sharpless [took a stand]. . . . Sharpless's turn ideologically, his Damascus road experience, was essentially turfed out of one of those meetings. . . . And a number of others – Stan Kutler, Maureen Mystrom, Johann Summerville, Larry Dickey. There were people who stood up on my side in the department meetings. And then it was amazing to see how many guys with whom I've had good relationships over the years just quiver like rabbits. Just laid down and prepared to roll over.[78]

Frykenberg said the case "could have destroyed the department." This was averted when a few of the most respected moderates in the department came to Frykenberg and asked, "Bob, what would it take to end this matter?" Frykenberg told them that the investigation and inquiry had to stop and that the university had to agree to reimburse his legal bills. The university's acceptance of these conditions led to the settlement of the case. Frykenberg's recollection of the case closely resembles Richard Long's reconstruction of his own case. Frykenberg recalled,

Seriously enough, this is where we come to the Leviathan. I don't think they cared a whit about whether I lived or died. It was nothing personal. In fact, they probably even liked me. I was just a bystander who happened to be in the way of the great wheels of the juggernaut as it began to roll, and if I had to be sacrificed for the cause, then who cares? And who would notice? The sheer callousness of that I found outrageous.[79]

---

[77] See, e.g., Robert E. Frykenberg, Notice of Claim, Pursuant to Sec. 893.82, Wis. Stats., filed against several individuals at University of Wisconsin, Madison, April 23, 1996. Settlement Agreement, September 12, 1996. These materials are in a packet provided by University Counsel.

[78] Interview with history professor Robert Frykenberg, University of Wisconsin, Madison, March 2002.

[79] Ibid.

According to Sharpless, one of the most disconcerting aspects of the case was that individuals in the department who could have made a difference refused to speak up and demand that the principles of fundamental fairness be observed until it was too late. Even then, some members of the department took action to resolve the crisis not because of a commitment to fairness but for another reason: concern for the department's reputation and prestige.[80]

The Frykenberg case alienated many members of the department across the political spectrum. It also provided the spark that activists needed to ignite a free speech movement, bringing together Frykenberg, Payne, and others with political connections on campus. In the early summer of 1996, Payne and Frykenberg convened a meeting at the University Club attended by about thirty faculty members of various political inclinations. A sense of betrayal and urgency hung over the gathering. At this meeting, activists formed the Faculty Committee for Academic Freedom and Rights (later renamed the Committee for Academic Freedom and Rights, CAFR – the term I use hereafter). CAFR is dedicated to championing and defending academic freedom and constitutional rights on the UW-Madison campus and in Wisconsin. CAFR quickly retained the services of attorney Steven Underwood, who proved to be a dedicated and able friend and ally. CAFR has taken on several legal cases, including three cases on other Wisconsin campuses. There is no group like CAFR on any other campus in the United States. The group received $100,000 in outside funding from the Bradley Foundation of Milwaukee; most has been spent on individual cases.

Payne was named president of CAFR (a position that I assumed in 2000, when Payne became secretary). The gathering voted art history professor Jane Hutchison treasurer, and me as secretary. I interpreted my position as political and media mobilizer. Payne and Hutchison are distinguished in their fields and fearless in defending principles of academic freedom. (Hutchison is the former president of the Wisconsin chapter of the American Association of University Professors, a group that has retreated from prominence during the battles discussed in this book.) In addition, CAFR named Gordon Baldwin – one of the initial framers of the codes – as its legal adviser. (Recall that he also assisted Richard Long.) CAFR also has an "executive committee," which meets whenever a crisis or matter of importance emerges and decides what action to take. Its membership consists of Lester Hunt, Mary Anderson, Jane Hutchison, Stanley Payne, Bob Frykenberg, Gordon Baldwin, Lee Hansen, Marshall Osborne, and me. Other members of CAFR include Michael Fox, Booth Fowler, Eric Triplett, Larry Kahan, Richard Long, Ted Hamerow, Anatole Beck, Steve Bauman, and many more sporadic supporters.

[80] Discussion with history professor John Sharpless, University of Wisconsin, Madison, February 2002.

CAFR was the vehicle with which to forge a political movement. Its first move was to publish a statement of purpose, the heart of which declared:

We hereby announce the formation of a new faculty group called the Faculty Committee for Academic Freedom and Rights. In recent years, faculty at the University of Wisconsin have been subjected to sometimes alarming threats to their academic freedom and their constitutional rights. These threats, which continue, have come from a variety of sources at departmental, administrative, and campus-wide levels. Such infringements too often wrongfully harm the reputations, rights, and professional goals of individuals, and they do equal damage to the intellectual community as a whole. Strong institutional protection of such rights as freedom of speech and inquiry, due process, and equal protection of the law is essential to fostering the principles and goals of a community of scholars.[81]

CAFR members possess what is perhaps the single most important attribute in these matters: one can rely on them under pressure and in the face of hostility. CAFR waited until its funding arrived in the middle of the fall semester to make its existence known to the public, at which time it announced its founding in the student papers simply by publishing the statement of purpose that appeared in a quarter-page advertisement. The news struck the campus like a lightning bolt. The *Wisconsin State Journal*'s new higher-education reporter, Jennifer Galloway, immediately wrote a front-page article about the committee, quoting CAFR's officers. Hutchison's quotation was the most poignant: "We've decided not to involve ourselves with the university because that would make us part of the problem," she told Galloway. Galloway's article concluded by alluding to the Frykenberg case.[82] The chancellor contacted Payne and discussed the problems of the university over lunch, and I appeared on the *Tom Clark Show* on Wisconsin Public Radio to talk about the situation and the Long, Frykenberg, and Hunt cases. It was a heady time, to be sure. My emotions were magnified by a touch of trepidation as well because we had so openly challenged our own university in highly charged times.

Just before Thanksgiving, a dean accused CAFR at a major meeting of the College of Letters and Sciences of betraying the university, suggesting that it had also violated the agreement in the Frykenberg case, which prohibited the parties from publicly discussing the case. CAFR wrote a response, which the dean graciously copied and disseminated to the chairs along with his own comments about academic freedom and the contemporary university.[83]

---

[81] CAFR Statement of Purpose, composed in July 1996.
[82] Jennifer A. Galloway, "UW Faculty Defend Free Expression," *Wisconsin State Journal*, November 16, 1996.
[83] Dean Philip Certain, "Who Speaks for Academic Freedom?" speech to chairs of the College of Letters and Sciences, November 26, 1996; Donald Downs, "The Response of the Faculty Committee for Academic Freedom and Rights to Dean Certain's Speech, 'Who Speaks for Academic Freedom?'" presented at meeting of the department chairs of the College of Letters and Science, December 6, 1996.

Several days after the public announcement of CAFR's formation, the Wisconsin Association of Scholars brought the noted Harvard professor and civil liberties lawyer Alan Dershowitz to campus. He gave a passionate speech on speech codes and free speech in the Great Hall in the Union, and denounced the faculty speech code, calling it the "worst speech code in the country." The widely reported speech was a headline story on the front page of the *Herald*.[84] Suddenly, the faculty speech code was, amazingly, on the defensive in a very public way. The free speech issue had crossed a critical threshold in terms of public awareness.

In reaction to all the publicity, university committee chair Evelyn Howell, encouraged by university committee member Mary Anderson, invited several members of CAFR to address the committee. An invaluable CAFR member, Anderson had herself previously survived an attempt by the committee to expel her on questionable grounds. She received a letter from the committee informing her that a conflict had developed concerning her that made her presence on the committee no longer advisable. The committee did not tell her what this "conflict" was. It was virtually unheard of for a member to refuse a request to resign in this context, but Anderson attained Gordon Baldwin's services, pro bono, as legal counsel and successfully challenged the expulsion effort. At one point, the committee even convened a special, closed session of the faculty senate to vote on a motion to expel Anderson. Even then Anderson was not told the nature of the charges and so could not prepare a defense at the meeting. Despite this, the senate meeting foundered in its expulsion effort when Baldwin warned senators that they would be subject to a defamation suit if they defamed Anderson. The senate decided, therefore, to discuss the matter without using names, including Anderson's. As a result, no one was able to fathom what was going on. (After the meeting, the discusson without names led someone else to falsely believe that the meeting was about him, not Anderson!) In the end, the university committee was compelled to drop the matter, and Anderson served out her term, an outcome that was very helpful to the free speech cause in more respects than one. Anderson related her experience in words that echo both Long and Frykenberg:

It was like being put in prison for no reason. I had no idea what it was I was supposed to have done. Gordon Baldwin kept telling me to keep asking them what it was I did, and they never told me. They had closed sessions of the UC about this. Nobody would tell me what it was all about! Gordon asked them to take the matter to Chapter 9 [the university's rules for dealing with faculty discipline]. But they would not do it. With due process, there's some protection. You know the charges, you get to tell them your side of the story.[85]

[84] "Dershowitz: Abolish Speech Codes," *Badger Herald*, November 22, 1996.
[85] Interview with University of Wisconsin geology professor Mary Anderson, November 2002.

Anderson was yet another example of a faculty member fighting back after suffering mistreatment in a prominent way. She described the entire affair as "Kafkaesque," but learned a Nietzschean lesson: "This affair helped me later. I survived this, so I can survive anything."[86] The experience also made her a member of CAFR.

CAFR members' next meeting with the university committee over the faculty speech code in early 1997 went well, as members of the committee were moved by Hunt's and Long's stories. The university committee also met with a dean, the vice chancellor for legal affairs, the head of the equity and diversity resources committee, and with Payne and me. By May the university committee decided to appoint a special ad hoc committee to explore what to do about the faculty code.[87]

The question of who would make up the ad hoc committee was crucial, and the appointment decisions were politically influenced from the start. The university and university committee did not favor radical change, so the selections leaned in favor of moderate reform. (Interestingly, virtually everyone except some student activists realized that some reform was needed, given the flawed investigations.) Anderson called some CAFR members and asked them whom she should recommend as committee members, and she decided to suggest Hunt, journalism professor Robert Drechsel, and me. Drechsel was not an outspoken free speech activist, but he believed strongly in free speech, and he was committed to fairness and good judgment. The university committee decided to pick Drechsel and me. It considered Hunt but decided against selecting him because he had been a target of an investigation under the code. Nonetheless, both Hunt and W. Lee Hansen attended virtually every one of the twenty-seven committee meetings and interacted with the free speech faction on a constant basis.

In the spring of 1997, seventeen individuals were named to the ad hoc committee, along with two nonvoting ex officio members: Ted Finman and the dean of the School of Letters and Sciences, Phil Certain. Finman would become the de facto leader of the moderates on the committee. The university committee itself appointed the nine voting faculty members and the two ex officio members, and left it up to the student government and a committee representing academic staff to appoint three students and five staff members. The ad hoc committee met over the entire 1997–98 academic year, biweekly the first semester and more often the second.

Four key events preceded the first ad hoc committee meeting in September 1997. First, a seventy-four-year-old professor whose name I may not divulge brought CAFR its first legal case. The professor had had an emotional relationship with a female graduate student and had asked her to marry him.

---

[86] Nietzsche famously remarked, "What doesn't kill me, makes me stronger."

[87] Letter of Evelyn Howell, University Committee Chair, to faculty chosen for the Ad Hoc Committee to Review Prohibited Harassment Legislation, May 30, 1997.

When she encountered academic problems, she filed a complaint against him. Although the professor's behavior may not have been appropriate, the university reacted as if he had committed a crime. One afternoon in late 1996, the chair of his department appeared at the classroom door while the professor was teaching and summoned him to an office. There the professor was questioned in the presence of an armed guard. He was informed that the student had accused him of making inappropriate comments, such as telling her to "straighten up," "start working harder," and "to stop messing around with her boyfriend."[88] As with Long, no formal complaint was filed, but the university proceeded under the aegis of the faculty code. The professor contacted CAFR, and its executive committee met with Underwood. CAFR decided to pursue the case. After studying the case, Underwood wrote a letter to the university, accusing it of an improper application of the code. After all, he said, a survey of various cultures had failed to find a single one in which a proposal of marriage was considered "demeaning," the key type of expression forbidden by the code. Underwood's intervention compelled the university to retreat, and the professor agreed to be found guilty of "bad judgment" and to have a letter placed in his file. The case was alarming for the extreme lack of judgment the university displayed, especially given the fact that this happened shortly after the Frykenberg settlement.

The second important event was a students' campaign against the code. Amy Kasper was an undergraduate student, born in Korea, but raised in the Upper Peninsula near the Wisconsin-Michigan border. Like Lee Hawkins, she disdained being stereotyped by anyone for progressive or conservative reasons. Kasper had become passionate about freedom of speech and the inviolability of her intellectual and moral conscience. In the spring of 1997, she masterminded a major media event that did as much as anything to raise the community's consciousness about the code. She began by placing a poster in scores of lecture rooms that said, "Why Should YOU Care about the Speech Code?" The posters provided background information, and announced a website at which students could learn more about the code's negative effects. It also listed several problems with the code, including that it "*corrupts* the primary purpose of the university," "is *condescending* to minority students," and "denies YOU the opportunity to fully develop the communication skills necessary to battle hateful and outrageous speech."[89] In all this, Kasper was assisted by her boyfriend, Jason Batton, who became another solid ally the next year in the drive toward abolition.[90]

---

[88] See the unpublished paper by Anat Hakim, "Code Red" (for further discussion, see Chapter 7 and note 38). The professor also spent considerable time consulting with Payne and me. Letter from dean to professor [x], March 20, 1997.

[89] "Why Should YOU Care about the Speech Code?" Poster displayed campuswide (emphasis in original).

[90] See Jason Batton, "Speech Code Review a Travesty," *Badger Herald*, October 24, 1997.

Kasper then arranged a teach-in on free speech, with Hunt and me as the presenters. Hunt and I wrote an op-ed piece in the *Herald* in anticipation of the event, and Kasper succeeded in getting local media – including a local network television news show – to cover the event.[91] The gathering succeeded in increasing public awareness. Equally important, the event generated extensive media coverage, which portrayed the rule as a punitive "speech code" that unfairly victimized unpopular individuals and the state of intellectual honesty at the university. Over the next few days, several colleagues who had never talked about free speech asked members of CAFR how the teach-in had gone.

The other two events concerned the composition and political bent of the ad hoc committee. The first involved the choice of the student committee members. Everyone knew that the view of the students would have a lot to do with the fate of the committee. Early in the summer, a representative of CAFR met with the feisty new president of the student government, Christine Fredenberg, and another student whose name I cannot recall. CAFR feared – unrealistically, as it turned out – that the student leaders might be inclined to choose code advocates to sit on the ad hoc committee, and so the CAFR representative simply requested that they keep an open mind and give applicants who were suspicious of speech codes a fair hearing. (It would have been inappropriate to pressure them to take a side.) In the end, Fredenberg selected three anticode students for two reasons: she was a free speech supporter and libertarian who believed strongly in self-reliance; and the three libertarian applicants showed themselves to be much more knowledgeable about the issues than the pro-code applicants. The students were Amy Kasper, law student Rebecca Bretz, and undergraduate Jason Shepard. (The next year, Fredenberg led an effort by the Associated Students of Madison's Shared Governance Committee to advocate abolition of the code and presented that group's views at an ad hoc committee meeting.)[92]

These three students were ideal committee members from CAFR's perspective. A law student and member of the conservative Federalist Society, Rebecca Bretz had no patience for victim ideology and paternalistic, protective attitudes toward students. Shepard was also a former editor of the *Herald* and a homosexual who had recently come out of the closet in the paper. A gifted public speaker, the liberal Shepard possessed a contagious passion for free speech, self-reliance, and individualism. Over the next two years, he would have to endure the vilification of gays and lesbian activists

[91] "Exposing the UW Faculty Speech Code," Wednesday, April 16, 1997, 7:00 P.M., Room 2080 Grainger Hall. Lester Hunt and Donald Downs, "Speech Code Promulgates Weakness," op-ed, *Badger Herald*, April 15, 1997; "UW Profs, Students: Speech Code Hurtful," *Capital Times*, April 17, 1997; "Code Restricts Free Expression," *Daily Cardinal*, April 17, 1997.

[92] Letter of Christine Fredenberg to Ad Hoc Committee on Prohibited Harassment Legislation, March 20, 1998.

who accused him of being a traitor to his identity group. But like many gay and lesbian political actors, Shepard considered free speech an indispensable right for the oppressed.[93] To Shepard, speech codes were a paternalistic insult.

One could not stress strongly enough how important these students were to the movement. The fact that the three students on the ad hoc committee strongly opposed codes helped the cause immeasurably. (The students' "group identities" also enhanced the credence of their position.) More than one senator told CAFR members that he or she had changed his or her mind about the code when Shepard stood up at the first senate meeting and eloquently proclaimed that codes demeaned members of minorities like himself. These students also worked as hard as anyone else when it came to the time-consuming committee work and political work outside the committee.

The final key event involved the selection of a chairperson for the ad hoc committee at the first meeting in September. A few days before the first meeting, Mary Anderson e-mailed me with an "urgent" message. She said that the university committee and the administration did not want major change and that there was a movement afoot to make Evelyn Howell the chair of the ad hoc committee to help achieve this objective. "You must not let this happen," Anderson warned. We decided that I would not be the right person to make a counternomination, so Mary suggested that I contact Charles Bentley, a distinguished colleague of hers in geology and geophysics, and ask him to nominate someone else. Bentley, Shepard, Kasper, and I decided that Robert Drechsel should be our man. When philosophy professor Claudia Card nominated Howell early in the meeting, we were ready. We politely contended that Howell's selection could compromise the perception of the committee's neutrality, as she had just served as the chairperson of the university committee. Under the circumstances, Howell had no choice but to agree, and Bentley then nominated Drechsel. No other serious candidates emerged, so Drechsel became chair. His selection would prove to be crucial to the abolition movement.

Stage 3. The Ad Hoc Committee

The ad hoc committee's task was to propose reforms that the faculty senate would consider the next year. The committee's meetings were open to the public, and several visitors attended its meetings over the course of the year. (As mentioned, Hunt and Hansen came to most meetings.) Drechsel assigned members to various subcommittees, including subcommittees to propose a preface, to draft a new substantive code, to draft a new set of procedures,

[93] See Paul Siegel, "Why Lesbians and Gay Men Need Traditional First Amendment Theory," in David S. Allen and Robert Jensen, eds., *Freeing the First Amendment: Critical Perspectives on Freedom of Expression* (New York University Press, 1995), pp. 224–52.

and to conduct research on such matters as faculty codes at other schools and complaints to deans about faculty expression. I was a member of the committee to draft the substantive part of the code, along with history professor Charles Cohen and law professor Carin Claus. Our sessions were lengthy and full of vibrant ideas. Both Cohen and Claus accepted the need to strike a better balance between academic freedom and sensitivity, but they were more moderate than I.

Serving on the ad hoc committee was an extraordinary and memorable experience for many of us. Meetings were often intense and intellectually passionate. They were also extremely time-consuming, with the full committee meeting twenty-seven times and subcommittees meeting often as well. The radical faction was in the minority from the beginning, so one of its goals was to draw as many members as possible to its side in order to weaken the force and appeal of the majority's eventual report to the senate. But the radical faction also entertained the possibility of forging a consensus on the committee if the other side accepted sufficient change. Some of this faction were torn by a conflicted sense of loyalty: on one hand, they felt an obligation to their colleagues on the other side, and to be open to a good compromise that might represent the views of the larger university community. On the other hand, the radicals felt an obligation to procure the strongest protection that they could for freedom of speech in the classroom and to satisfy their growing list of libertarian constituents.

Apparently sensing the danger of sending two reports to the senate, Finman and his allies dedicated themselves to building a consensus and made many concessions to attain it. In response, the radical faction adopted a dual strategy: it worked to get the other side to grant further concessions while holding out for even more radical change. This strategy may not have been fair to the colleagues on the other side, but it worked to the faction's advantage. It put them in a surprisingly advantageous position, for in the end the so-called Majority Report embodied significant change, even if the changes fell short of the radicals' aspirations.

The three students and I were committed to radical change from the start, either abolition or radical reform. Drechsel and mathematics professor Steve Bauman leaned in our direction but were more undecided, as were Charles Bentley and Bill Steffenhagen, an academic staff member. This meant that the radical faction might be able to garner up to 8 votes out of 17 if it could not reach an agreement with the other side, led by Finman, Claus, and Cohen. (Howell and Card also played important roles for the majority, as did Afro-American studies professor Stanley James and art historian Gail Geiger.)

After the chairperson was selected, the committee engaged in discussion, conducted research, brought in informational speakers, and carried on deliberation in the full committee and subcommittees. The next major debate of the full committee occurred in early November when it addressed the first report of the drafting subcommittee, which presented a provisional new code to focus the deliberation. The report's major revisions included tightening the language of prohibited expression by replacing the key term "demeaning" with "degrading"; making the judgment of the average member of the general university community the standard for determining what is degrading rather than the average member of the ascriptive group to which the complainant belongs; requiring that the standard of proof be "clear and convincing" evidence; and adding a requirement that the vilification and harm to the educational environment be *intentional*. When Cohen presented the draft to the full committee, several members gasped, "We cannot support this draft. This proposal would gut the code." The fundamental difference between the two sides became starkly clear at this point. The committee devoted the rest of the fall term to research, presentations by faculty and staff with special knowledge about relevant issues (including Richard Long, Lester Hunt, Assistant Dean of Students Roger Howard, and the head of the Office of Diversity and Equity Resources), and further deliberation. By the end of the first semester, abolitionists decided that they had to raise the ultimate controversial issue, even if it meant getting shot down: outright abolition of the code as applied to the classroom. This move would change the nature of the debate.

The question of abolition was the first important matter of the next term. Jason Shepard introduced the motion formally at the March 20 meeting, and Kasper, Drechsel, Bauman, Steffenhagen, and I spoke on its behalf. It was at this meeting that Christine Fredenberg presented the student government's governance committee's call for abolition. While the previous discussions about word changes had amounted to quibbling, the call for abolition unleashed discussion about fundamentals, compelling the committee to wrestle with principles of freedom within the university. The motion failed, but the debate raised the stakes and escalated the tension and consequences of the committee's agenda. At this time the local press started noticing the committee. For example, *Isthmus* (Madison's popular *Village Voice*-style weekly) had published three articles in the fall about the speech code and the Frykenberg, Hunt, and Long cases. (One story featured a picture of Hunt covering his mouth.) An anonymous source on our side whose identity I may not divulge alerted *Isthmus*'s editor Marc Eisen to the issue.[94]

After the debate on abolition something strange and regrettable happened. Perhaps sensing that the abolitionist faculty might be more willing to accept a deal after losing the vote against abolition, Finman redoubled his efforts to get Drechsel and me to agree to a deal. He offered reforms that further limited the code's reach. One addressed language, another tightened the burden of proof. Without giving the matter sufficient thought, Drechsel and I

[94] See Marc Eisen, "In No Other Country...," *Isthmus*, October 10, 1997; "A Fight over Faculty Speech," *Isthmus*, January 2, 1998.

agreed to the deal without even discussing the decision with the students. Confident in his new majority, Finman took charge of the next committee meeting, introducing each new measure and quickly registering the votes for each one. He wanted to secure his side's victory by wrapping things up as quickly as possible. When Shepard and Kasper expressed their chagrin at what was transpiring, Finman told them that a deal had been arranged and that Drechsel and I were with him. And that was all there was to it. Drechsel and I began to feel sheepish as we realized that we had betrayed the students, to say nothing of our beliefs. So when it came time to vote for the entire package of changes at the end of the meeting (the previous votes were for each change separately, so we needed a final vote for the changes taken as a whole), Drechsel and I voted "abstain" rather than "yes" for the package, leaving Finman and his allies dangling. This meant that a final vote had to be postponed to the next week. When we left the meeting, Lee Hansen came over and said, "Well, you guys have done as well as could be expected, given that the other side has people who are more seasoned in university politics." It was a backhanded compliment from someone who was disappointed in what we had wrought. As the reality of our betrayal sank in over the weekend, Drechsel and I decided that we would have to back out of the deal.

When I arrived at my office on Monday morning, an e-mail from Shepard awaited me: "Downs, I can't believe that I have to say this, but I have no choice. Amy, Rebecca, and I are very upset about what happened last Friday. We feel that you have betrayed our cause."[95] I e-mailed Shepard and Kasper back and told them that we had made an inexcusable decision in a moment of weakness and that we were going to back out of the deal at the next meeting. It was not too late. We felt bad about letting Finman down and knew that we had now treated him unfairly as well. It was an important lesson concerning the hazards of losing one's moral compass in the confusion and pressure of events.

Although the deal was broken, the committee still struggled to find common ground but ineluctably split into two clearly distinguishable sides, one favoring more moderate change, the other radical change. As the ad hoc committee prepared its final report for the university committee and the senate, seven members began meeting on their own: Shepard, Kasper, Bretz, Drechsel, Bauman, Steffenhagen, and I. They soon dubbed themselves the minority faction, and began to draft a Minority Report that they could present to challenge the majority on the committee. In the end, then, there were two separate reports. (Though all members of the faction provided input into the report, Drechsel performed the lion's share of the actual

---

[95] I quote this e-mail from memory, as it – along with other e-mails that I did not save to a separate disk – disappeared when my entire e-mail program crashed a year later. Later, I cite e-mails that survived because I printed them out before the crash.

drafting.) Both reports had an ample preamble affirming the importance of academic freedom. The multipaged Majority Report protected all expression "germane" to the class, however controversial, except

the use in addressing a specific student, of an epithet or a comment concerning a specific student that clearly derogates and debases the student on the basis of the student's gender, race, religion, ethnicity, sexual orientation, or disability, thereby impugning the student's status as an equal participant in the class, shall not be considered "germane." Therefore, such expression is not protected unless the instructor has a reasonable pedagogical justification.[96]

The Minority Report, considerably simpler and shorter, was protective of all but the most extreme forms of verbal abuse. The presumption of germaneness could be overcome only by showing with "convincing clarity" that the instructor *intended* to harm a student by "derogating and debasing" him or her and that *no conceivable* pedagogical justification existed for the expression. This approach did not assume harm on the basis of a stereotypical group-based response but rather required that the complainant demonstrate harm in his or her individual case.[97] The Minority Report was about as close to outright abolition as a policy could get. It differed from the Majority Report primarily through the inclusion of the intent requirement and a requirement that harm to the educational environment be proved. The minority faction considered resurrecting abolition as a policy but, at this point, did not think that such a stand was politically feasible. A stance in favor of abolition also might have splintered the minority faction itself, as some members still entertained the possibility of joining the Majority Report. Hence, the minority faction's interpretation of the political situation inside and outside of the faction foreclosed the possibility of abolition at this stage.

Although Drechsel, Bauman, and Steffenhagen had contributed to the Minority Report, they still considered joining the majority before the penultimate committee vote on May 18. The ad hoc committee met with great frequency as it moved toward the final vote, while the minority stayed in constant contact. Although every vote mattered, Drechsel's vote was the prize that both sides coveted. He was the chair of the committee and respected for his solid, conscientious judgment and his knowledge of freedom of speech. But he continued to ponder, even agonize over, the right decision. Then, at 10:30 P.M. of the night before the vote, Drechsel called me at home to inform me that he was going to side with the Minority Report. I was overjoyed, knowing that Drechsel's decision meant that our faction now could mount a more plausible challenge to the Majority Report. When Drechsel

[96] Report of the Ad Hoc Committee on Prohibited Harassment Legislation, May 11, 1998.
[97] Minority Report, Ad Hoc Committee on Prohibited Harassment Legislation, September 24, 1998.

voted against the motion in favor of the Majority Report at the May 18 meeting, one could almost feel the air leave the majority's sails. Bauman and Steffenhagen also voted with the Minority position, meaning that the Majority Report garnered 10 votes to the Minority Report's 7. Though "losers," the radical faction left the meeting feeling very upbeat, whereas the majority walked out with their heads bowed, defeated in their attempt to find a consensus that preserved a code with some teeth.

Over the summer, both sides tidied up their reports and wrote responses and counterresponses to each other's reports. Everything was then sent on to the university committee for presentation to the senate. By September, Bentley had changed his mind and joined the minority, making the final split 9-8 – a virtual wash. In November 1998 a few members of each side met with the university committee, which decided to endorse the Majority Report. Committee member Bernice Durand, who had played a significant role in the Majority Report and in the enactment of the speech codes, was the minority's strongest opponent.

Sometime during the late spring or early summer, the radical faction made a move that would change the nature of the politics and debate: it sought out national publicity. Knowing that the outside world and the press were much more skeptical of speech codes than universities, the faction informed the *Chronicle of Higher Education* of what was going on in Madison; and in September 1998, *Chronicle* reporter Robin Wilson came to the campus to cover the story, which led to a cover article in October.[98] This article spawned a flurry of other national media coverage. By the end of 1999, national media addressing the issue included the *New York Times*, *Boston Globe*, *Associated Press*, *Wall Street Journal*, *Village Voice*, *Reason*, *Liberty* (an article by Hunt), National Public Radio, and the *National Journal*, as well as the *Chronicle of Higher Education*. The radical faction also fed information to local media, which were usually on its side. Outside and local media were instrumental to the success that the free speech movement enjoyed because the mere exposure of the issue exerted pressure on the university.

It was now time to enter a new arena: the faculty senate, which would ultimately have to decide.

[98] "Rethinking Limits on Faculty Speech: U. of Wisconsin Debate Reflects Changing Views of Political Correctness and Academic Freedom," *Chronicle of Higher Education*, October 2, 1998, p. A1.

7

Abolition in the Wisconsin Faculty Senate and Its Aftermath

The movement to the senate represented the widening of the debate, as the entire campus confronted the question of what to do about the speech code. It was the most publicly anticipated series of senate meetings at Wisconsin in many years. Entering the fourth stage of the movement also meant engaging in a new kind of politics.

Stage 4. On to the Senate

During the fall, both sides finished their reports for the university committee and the senate. Before the first senate debate, scheduled for December 7, Ted Finman and Charles Cohen went to the *Wisconsin State Journal* in the hope of persuading associate editor Thomas Still to endorse the Majority Report. They did a good job and persuaded Still to at least momentarily question his standard opposition to codes. But Still then called members of the Minority Report and asked them to make an argument for their position. They explained that certain unpopular ideas could still be punished under the Majority Report and that the climate was such that no one should trust the enforcers. (Of course, this argument applied to *any* code, including that proposed by the minority.) Still and his fellow editor, Sonny Schubert, soon became strong supporters of radical change and eventually wrote several key editorials in support of abolition.[1]

Ironically, three free speech crises that erupted on campus in the fall of 1998 also were turned to the radical faction's advantage as the senate debates loomed. On September 10, students disrupted a speech by Governor Tommy Thompson commemorating the 150th birthday of the university. Thompson contacted Chancellor Ward and urged the university to provide

[1] See, e.g., "Word Flap Is Reason against Speech Code," editorial, *Wisconsin State Journal*, February 3, 1999; "UW Must Aspire toward Ideals," editorial, *Wisconsin State Journal*, February 7, 1999.

an environment conducive to rational debate.[2] Three weeks later, dozens of organized students shouted down University of California regent Ward Connerly in the Union Theater during his talk criticizing affirmative action. Afterward, Connerly declared, "This place is unlike anything I've ever seen. People here have no respect for different views."[3] The incident made national news and compelled the chancellor to criticize publicly the suppression of speech. CAFR members who were senators made statements at the next senate meeting, decrying these actions.

The next day, the *Herald* published a cartoon by Brad Menken of an African American student tearfully denouncing Connerly's right to speak. The cartoon figure included exaggerated features, thereby provoking the anger of students already enraged by the mere presence of the leader of California's statewide initiative against affirmative action. (Menken's defenders pointed out that all of his cartoon figures, like those of many cartoonists, had exaggerated features, so no racial insult was intended. Ben Thompson writes in his history of *Herald* disputes, "big noses and big mouths are a staple of Menken's work.")[4]

The evening of the day the cartoon appeared, a coalition of twelve students took over the *Herald*'s headquarters, demanding that the editors agree to publish an apology virtually dictated by the coalition. Shaken and guilt-ridden, the newspaper hostages agreed. One editor described an intimidating scene. "There were 6'3" men that were right in my face and grabbing newspapers and shouting, 'Look at this!' and then they would chuck it at you and sort of push desks around. There was definite physical intimidation."[5] Feeling pressure and morally chastised, the staff did not see fit to call the police, and the board agreed to write an apology that it negotiated with the protesters. After the intruders left, opinion editor Katie Fetting quickly regretted the capitulation and unsuccessfully tried to convince the board to change its mind. ("I started to get angry. They walked into our house and told us what to do.") Despite her efforts, an apology appeared on October 5.[6] In response, Fetting composed a "dissenting view" for the *Herald* to publish on the opinion page next to the apology. But the board would not let her publish it as a member of the board alongside the apology, so Fetting decided to resign and publish the statement as a regular student opinion piece. Her resignation and dissent appeared on October 7. In her interview with Ben Thompson almost four years later, her recollection evoked memories of

[2] "UW Celebration Ends in Arrest," *Badger Herald*, September 11, 1998.
[3] Gwen Carleton, "Storm Erupts over Affirmative Action," *Capital Times*, October 1, 1998. See also Karen Kersting, "Protesters Boo Speaker Off Stage," *Wisconsin State Journal*, October 1, 1998.
[4] Benjamin Thompson, "Paper of Protest: A Short History of Free Speech Disputes at the *Badger Herald*" (Senior thesis, University of Wisconsin, Madison, May 2002), p. 10.
[5] Katie Fetting, in Thompson, "Paper of Protest," p. 11.
[6] Ibid., p. 15; editorial, *Badger Herald* October 5, 1998.

the *Daily Californian's* actions during the Horowitz affair in February 2001: "All these people who'd given such lip service in the past to the 'glory of journalism' and 'our duty' and the 'greater good' were the first people to cave. [They were] always talking about what great things we did – 'we are providing a forum!' and all this crap – and then when this came up, they were like, 'oh gee,' and totally bent over. They totally fell over."[7]

Several *Herald* workers were traumatized by the incident and had trouble sleeping for several weeks. The paper's staff became fearful of offending anyone for the rest of the academic year. Ironically, the paper's leadership that year had prided itself on being the most progressive in the paper's history and often commented about the benighted views of previous generations. (The *Herald's* tradition normally has oscillated between right of center and right. That a right-of-center student paper has become the student paper of record on a campus noted for its liberal-progressive orientation is a story in itself, and one reason so many controversies have surrounded the paper over the years.) But none of this mattered in the face of unexpected pressure. By the time CAFR members learned what had transpired, the *Herald* had already capitulated, so that organization decided to lie low on this issue. But the local papers leapt to criticize the *Herald*. The *State Journal* editorial stated, "something is terribly wrong on the UW-Madison campus when a free and rambunctious press can be muzzled by students who feel empowered to camp out at the newspaper office until they bully their way to a retraction." John Nichols of the *Capital Times* and the *Nation*, a frequent supporter of free speech on campus, wrote, "UW officials seem to be signaling that they want a debate that is tepid, disengaged and intellectually irresponsible. As the lamentable resignation of Katie Fetting indicates, the editors of the *Herald* have gotten the message."[8]

Meanwhile, the minority faction and its allies continued preparing their arguments for the upcoming senate meeting, as did the supporters of the majority position. It was an exhilarating time. At the beginning of the meeting, Shepard, Kasper, and Bretz presented the senate with a memorandum stating the reasons that the student members of the ad hoc committee opposed the Majority Report. One reason was that "The Majority proposal stereotypes minority students by assuming that we will inherently have the same reaction to certain types of speech."[9] In presenting the memorandum to the senate, Shepard made a remarkably eloquent speech in favor

---

[7] Katie Fetting, "Former Editor Clarifies Point," letter to the editor, *Badger Herald*, October 7, 1998; Katie Fetting, in Thompson, "Paper of Protest," p. 23.

[8] "Regret the Image, Not the Idea," editorial, *Wisconsin State Journal*, October 7, 1998; John Nichols, "UW Tarnishing Tradition of Passionate Discourse," *Capital Times*, October 8, 1998. On the faculty denouncing the Connerly incident at the senate, see Gwen Carleton, "UW Faculty Decry Students' Heckling," *Capital Times*, October 6, 1998.

[9] Jason Shepard, Amy Kasper, and Rebecca Bretz, Memorandum to Faculty Senate, December 7, 1999.

of free speech that influenced voting decisions. Shepard chastised the university for inculcating the ethic of sensitivity over free speech and thought. (In this regard, his speech matched the graduation speech two years earlier of his friend, Shira Diner.) Shepard began by talking about the failure of education and leadership concerning academic freedom and wide-open discourse:

The three of us students are all members of minority groups... so we have a unique perspective on this issue.... If I have learned anything during my four years at the University of Wisconsin, it is that we here are so very afraid of the people who think differently from us. When somebody expresses an idea that we disagree with, we are not taught by the status quo of this university to respond back with reasoned debate.

Shepard then addressed the relationship between the citizenship of minority students and the free speech ethic of republican virtue:

One of the things that we were initially surprised by is the stereotyping that members of the Majority did on us as three minority students [on the ad hoc committee]. Initially, they blindly assumed that we would support a speech code that was intended to protect us. In the most general sense, I, as a gay student, see this policy as paternalistic. And I think it reinforces the stereotype that all minority students think the same, and don't have the capacity or the desire to stand up to bigotry on our own. That's the thing the speech code does: it assumes that all of us will have the same reaction to offensive speech.

Finally, Shepard spoke about the relationship between the speech code debate and academic freedom:

The Majority earlier today stated that this debate is not about the extent of academic freedom. But that is *exactly* what this debate is about.... This is about the freedom of us as students and faculty, together, to search for the truth without Big Brother stepping in and telling us which ideas are too hurtful for us.[10]

After Shepard's oration at the December 7 meeting, the university committee introduced the issue to the senate. Then Drechsel and Cohen spoke eloquently on behalf of their respective sides.[11] Drechsel outlined the minority's case with meticulous skill. Cohen then defended the Majority Report as a pathbreaking attempt to articulate the contours of academic freedom in a formal fashion. It was an important, even profound statement of professional responsibilities in teaching and would serve as a good model of how to teach. But the senate would prove itself uninterested in such profundity when it came to the matter at hand, which most senators construed as the

---

[10] Tape of Jason Shepard speech at faculty senate meeting, December 7, 1999 (emphasis in Shepard's tone on tape).
[11] "Prohibited Harassment Legislation," University Committee Recommendation, December 7, 1999.

problem of punitive enforcement of even thoughtful codes and the revival of the fundamental principle of free thought and inquiry at the university. Finman and I spoke when Cohen and Drechsel had finished, after which the floor opened up to any senator who wanted to speak. Suddenly something stunning happened: to everyone's surprise, all but one of the senators who took the microphone attacked the Majority Report, with most calling for abolition or something close to it. (And even the one pro-majority speaker mainly raised a question rather than strongly endorsing the majority position.) A previously silent group of faculty now felt empowered to speak out.[12] Unable to report the commentary in its entirety, I quote here only the most salient of the watershed comments.

Mathematics professor Anatole Beck criticized the Majority Report's response to a hypothetical situation: a professor who condemns homosexuality after being asked by students to state his honest opinion on the subject. (The majority position left this situation open to interpretation.) Beck ignited a round of laughter when he answered his own question with sarcasm: the only rational response by a faculty member in this situation was to tell the student, "under the laws of the University of Wisconsin, I do not dare answer your question, and I will not." Larry Kahan of biomolecular chemistry said that the majority position would make him afraid to say intellectually honest things about alcoholism in his class discussions about drunk driving, for alcoholics could be considered "disabled," a protected category under the code. Kahan (who later joined CAFR) said he favored outright repeal over even the Minority Report.

Professor Ken Thomas, of rehabilitative psychology (who also later became a member of CAFR), declared that speech codes contradicted the historical mission of the university, which was the "sifting and winnowing of ideas." Elaborating, he stated, "to discover the truth, it is necessary to get all ideas on the table, not just those that are socially acceptable. Moreover, how does one attempt to change another's attitude or perspective if the other is so afraid to express his or her opinion or biases? An idea cannot be challenged unless it is expressed." He also quipped that "guests on the Jay Leno Show probably fear censorship less that UW professors." Thomas later said that his two proudest moments in his thirty years at Wisconsin were this speech and his later vote to abolish the faculty speech code. Other critiques were raised by English professor Richard Knowles and professor of educational administration Dean Bowles. Knowles made his usual eloquent, sarcastic comments about a policy he considered dubious. Bowles said that he would favor abolition but was worried that the university could lose federal funding if it abolished the code. Accordingly, he supported the Minority Report, pending what the senate later concluded about the status of federal funding at the university.

---

[12] See Timur Kuran, *Private Truths, Public Lies: The Social Consequences of Preference Falsification* (Harvard University Press, 1995).

CAFR leader Lester Hunt weighed in by saying he was still debating between the minority position and outright abolition. He then cut to what would later prove to be the decisive argument against preserving a code in the classroom: *its coercive power.* The code debate raises "one of the fundamental issues of political philosophy: what are the limits of society's rights to coerce people to do things?" Hunt recalled Western movies in which saloons required drinkers to "leave your guns at the door." Similarly, at a university there should be "no weapons in the forum. You may not use force. Bad views must be answered with good views." A code puts "a weapon in the hands of students who don't like the views that you are expressing." Hunt's speech came from the heart of experience, as he had personally felt the brunt of coercive enforcement (see Chapter 6). Speech codes were as much about moral bullying as protecting sensibilities.

Classicist Silvia Montiglio stated that she intentionally provoked her students all the time with controversial, unpopular ideas and personal teasing designed to loosen the class. Students truly enjoyed it and never evinced an incapacity to handle her pedagogical provocations. Montiglio questioned whether any problem with offensive teaching existed on campus and speculated that the whole code movement was propelled for ideological reasons, asking "whether [the problem] is being made up by an ideologist, which I suspect very much." One of the more poignant statements came from political scientist Ken Mayer, another CAFR ally. University committee member Bernice Durand had just spoken in favor of the Majority Report by referring to Supreme Court Justice Louis Brandeis, who had defended incremental reform enforced by government as constitutionally acceptable. But Brandeis had made this comment in the context of government regulation of the economy, not free speech, an area in which Brandeis was as close to an absolutist as any justice in history. (In my view, Durand had been poorly advised by her legal allies to invoke Brandeis in this fashion in the midst of a debate over free speech.) Mayer said that Durand's comment reminded him of an even more apt statement by Brandeis in a famous Fourth Amendment civil liberty case: "Men born to freedom are naturally alert to repel invasion of their liberty by evil-minded rulers. The greatest dangers to liberty lurk in the insidious encroachment by men of zeal, well-meaning but without understanding."[13]

Music professor Javier Calderon got the last word. Recalling his harrowing experiences living under dictatorships in South America and the fascist Franco regime in Spain, Calderon decried the lack of appreciation of free speech and civil liberty on campus. Referring to the Majority Report, he declared:

There is no notion of the damage done by restricting speech. From having lived in South America for many years, and in Spain during the Franco regime under military governments, I could imagine that, yes, I would any minute take racial or religious

---

[13] *Olmstead v. U.S.*, 277 U.S. 438 (1928), Brandeis, dissenting.

or nationality insults thrown at me than to be living again under the terror of having
my life taken away or being incarcerated for having the courage to speak. I think the
Majority Report goes way too far, and it does not pay enough respect to the precious
Bill of Rights of the Constitution. [The First Amendment] is the oxygen that feeds all
the Bill of Rights and human rights.[14]

Overall, it was a dramatic and memorable meeting. A bit later in the
Cardinal, I wrote that the senate "spoke with the language of free men and
women" and that Wisconsin "could become the very first university in the
country to take back a code by a faculty vote rather than a court order."[15]
After the meeting, members of the minority faction gathered together in
the hallway outside the senate chamber to ruminate about the radical shift
of sentiment. They had to pinch themselves to prove that what they had
just witnessed was real. They vowed to heighten their commitment. That
evening, Hunt, Harvey Silverglate, and I conducted a three-way telephone
conversation. Silverglate was excited about what was happening at Madison,
as he and Alan Kors considered the Wisconsin free speech movement the first
meaningful application of the principles propounded in their recently published book, *The Shadow University*. Silverglate pledged to help the minority
faction in any way that he could and to write a legal report that it could take
to the university committee and the senate. The report focused on whether
the university risked losing federal funding if it abolished the code or replaced
it with an insufficiently restrictive code.[16]

New Ideas and the Question of Federal Funding

Over the Christmas break, the leaders of the minority faction redoubled their
efforts. Taken aback by the outpouring of sentiment at the December meeting, the university committee asked the two sides to focus more narrowly on
the legal issues posed by a code, and to present their positions at the next senate meeting on February, so the minority faction spent the entire Christmas
break preparing its legal report. Its leaders also called several experts, including Eugene Volokh of UCLA Law School, the Center of Individual Rights
in Washington, D.C., and Silverglate. The report treated constitutional issues, harassment law, the chilling effect of codes, and the question of the
withdrawal of federal funding. (Kors and Silverglate report in *The Shadow
University* that *New York Times* columnist Anthony Lewis found out from
the Department of Education that the government had no requirement that

[14] All these statements are quoted from the tape of the faculty senate meeting, University of
Wisconsin, Madison, December 7, 1999.

[15] Donald Downs, "UW Professors Help Reassert 'Free Thought,'" *Daily Cardinal*, January 19,
1999.

[16] See "Harvey Silverglate's Memorandum to Free Speech Advocates, University of Wisconsin,
Madison, January 26, 1999," on FIRE's website: www.theFIRE.org.

universities adopt such speech codes.)[17] The report concluded that the Majority Report posed potential constitutional problems, especially because it raised the specter of the kind of viewpoint discrimination prohibited by *R.A.V. v. St. Paul*. More important, the report challenged the majority's claim that the university could lose federal funding if it radically reformed or abolished the code. Minority leaders succeeded in their goal of presenting a legal analysis that challenged the monopoly that the law professors had long enjoyed in this domain. They presented their report to the university committee, accompanied by Silverglate's forty-page legal analysis.[18]

The question of federal funding was unsettled in the law, so both sides had to extrapolate into an area painted gray. What was known was that the Office of Civil Rights (in the Department of Education) had become more aggressive in regulating and monitoring sexual and racial harassment during the 1990s, led by its commissioner, Clinton appointee Norma Cantu. Cantu empowered "stakeholders" to bring cases and declined to provide specific content to harassment law in order to encourage enforcement on a case-by-case basis. In response, universities often developed policies that were broader than necessary to uphold the purposes of the original law.[19] In addition, OCR had long required institutions receiving federal funding to establish internal mechanisms for dealing with cases of harassment and had used the threat to withhold funding as a weapon to compel compliance. The settlement that took place in the Santa Rosa Junior College case described in Chapter 2 is a prominent example.[20] So there was some authority for the view that Wisconsin could lose funding if it abolished or severely restricted its policies on harassment, at least at that point in time.

The problem was that Wisconsin has a separate university policy dealing with sexual harassment based on national OCR guidelines, and no one advocated changing these rules; furthermore, in the minority faction's view, we were dealing with a *speech* code, *not* a *harassment* code (see Chapter 2). Accordingly, either the OCR guidelines for harassment were irrelevant to the faculty speech code – in which case there was no threat of funding cutoff whatsoever – or the status of the faculty code was ambiguous in this regard. If the latter were true, it was a question of which side the university should

[17] Alan Charles Kors and Harvey Silverglate, *The Shadow University: The Betrayal of Liberty on America's Campuses* (Free Press, 1998), p. 93.

[18] Donald Downs and Robert Drechsel, "Minority Position on the Law," presented to university committee and faculty senate, University of Wisconsin, Madison, February 1, 1999. For the majority's position, see Carin Claus, "What Does the Law Say?" presented to university committee and faculty senate, University of Wisconsin, Madison, February 1, 1999.

[19] Terence J. Pell, "A More Subtle Activism at the Office of Civil Rights," 10(3) *Academic Questions* 83 (Summer 1997).

[20] "Harvey Silverglate's Memorandum to Free Speech Advocates, University of Wisconsin, Madison," pp. 18–19. In general, see also Eugene Volokh at http://www1.law.ucla.edu/˜volokh/hartass/cyberspa.htm.

err on, in which direction to take a risk. Silverglate addressed all of these issues in his memo: "[T]he real question is not whether campuses may outlaw *actions* that could cause a 'hostile educational environment,' but rather whether *words* may be banned under this rubric. I am *not* suggesting that the University repeal its harassment code, but, rather, that it repeal only that portion of the harassment code which seeks to ban pure speech."[21]

Silverglate then posed the fundamental choice the senate had to make. At worst, it was unclear what would happen if the code were abolished, and "to the extent the question is genuinely in doubt, colleges and universities have a moral obligation to defend academic freedom and freedom of speech, rather than jump at the slightest invitation to join the ranks of censors." But he also argued that the matter probably was not gray once all the dust settled. "[I]t is inconceivable that a college would be punished with the loss of federal funds merely for seeking to litigate its right, if not its obligation, to protect rather than ban such speech." Furthermore, he argued that if the government did require a code that restricted free speech, such action would constitute a violation of the First Amendment. As the federal court concluded in invalidating Wisconsin's student speech code in 1991, Title VII's provisions governing discrimination in employment (which parallel the requirements of Title IX in education) are statutory provisions that are trumped by the First Amendment.[22]

In the end, the senate concluded that academic freedom was worth the risk. Universities, after all, are different from regular businesses and corporations: their sine qua non is to protect free inquiry in order to pursue the truth. Only an unthinkably coercive federal agency would punish a university for abolishing one part of its overall harassment policies on the basis of a well-thought-out process dedicated to protecting intellectual freedom.

In July 2003 the Office of Civil Rights helped to clarify this question, although it did not specifically address the issue of federal funding per se. But the office did make a strong statement about the difference between illegal harassment and free speech. Gerald A. Reynolds, OCR assistant secretary, wrote an "open letter" to colleges and universities across the land reaffirming the "central importance" of free speech and stating that such institutions must not limit speech protected by the First Amendment in their drives to prevent or punish harassment. The letter stated in a relevant part:

OCR has consistently maintained that the statutes that it enforces are intended to protect students from invidious discrimination, not to regulate the content of speech.... OCR has recognized that the offensiveness of a particular expression, standing alone, is not a legally sufficient basis to establish a hostile environment

---

[21] "Harvey Silverglate's Memorandum to Free Speech Advocates, University of Wisconsin, Madison," p. 8.

[22] Ibid., pp. 16, 19–24. See *UWM Post Inc., et al. v. Board of Regents of the University of Wisconsin*, 774 F. Supp. 1163 (1991), p. 1177.

under the statutes enforced by OCR.... OCR regulations and policies do not require or prescribe speech, conduct or harassment codes that impair the exercise of rights protected under the First Amendment.[23]

The February Meeting

Earlier in the fall, Silverglate had contacted *New York Times* education reporter Ethan Bronner. Bronner decided to come to the senate meeting in February to gather information for an article he planned to write in the *Times Education Supplement*.[24] More importantly, two senators from the sciences, agronomist Eric Triplett and Larry Kahan of biomolecular chemistry and the Medical School (the latter had spoken at the December 7 senate debate), contacted leaders of the minority faction over the break, volunteering to join them in an effort to construct an abolition motion to take to the senate in March. Triplett and Kahan were articulate allies who were unafraid of challenging university authority. An organized movement toward abolition had begun.

At this time, Kasper and Shepard began lobbying student groups. Unlike the previous year when Christine Fredenberg had convinced a major organization in student government to endorse abolition of the code before the ad hoc committee, the student government in 1998–99 was led by identity politics groups who opposed radical change. Furthermore, the *Herald* was still shell-shocked from the fallout of its decision to apologize for the cartoon the previous fall. The *Cardinal* was another story, however. Its editor, Andrew Browman, had been writing stirring, provocative articles and editorials on behalf of the free speech movement for over a year, including one that was accompanied by a riveting cartoon of a professor's mouth being closed shut by a hideous-looking zipper. That year the *Cardinal* continued to provide the most thorough and engaged coverage of both the ad hoc committee and the senate debates and deliberations.[25] Other writers for the *Cardinal* demonstrated support for the free speech movement, including Sarah Maguire, Kristen Stippich, Christopher Drosner, and Adam McCalvry.

The February senate meeting was another turning point. Local and national media were on hand, including Bronner of the *New York Times* and a representative of the Associated Press. Robin Wilson of the *Chronicle for Higher Education* was also keeping a close eye on the meeting and

---

[23] Open Letter from Gerald A. Reynolds, Assistant Secretary of Office for Civil Rights, United States Department of Education, July 28, 2003, available on the main website of the Foundation for Individual Rights in Education, www.theFIRE.org.

[24] Ethan Bronner, "Big Brother Is Listening," *New York Times Educational Supplement*, April 4, 1999.

[25] See, e.g., Andrew Browman, "The End of UW Faculty Speech Codes?" *Daily Cardinal*, March 12, 1997; "UW Professors Scared into Silence," *Daily Cardinal*, April 30, 1997.

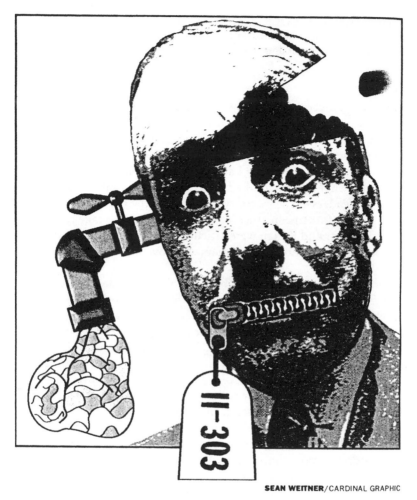

SEAN WEITNER/CARDINAL GRAPHIC

Cartoon accompanying op-ed by Andrew Browman in the *Daily Cardinal*, "UW Professors Scared into Silence," March 12, 1997. Illustrator: Sean Weitner. Reproduced with permission.

called members of the minority faction later that evening to learn what had happened. CAFR brought in Silverglate to witness the meeting and to give a speech at the Union. He blasted the code, calling the legal case the majority made at the senate meeting "legal malpractice." Student free speech advocate Jamie Fletcher had contacted media about the visit, and the *Wisconsin State Journal* covered the speech on the top of its front page.[26] The next morning,

---

[26] "Lawyer Urges Censorship of Speech Code: Calls UW Faculty Senate Rules to Limit Speech Unconstitutional," *Wisconsin State Journal*, February 2, 1999. See also "Silverglate Criticizes Campus Speech Codes," *Daily Cardinal*, February 2, 1999.

Silverglate continued his campaign on the minority's behalf by appearing on the *Tom Clark Show* on Wisconsin Public Radio. (A busy and noted civil liberties lawyer, Silverglate was exceptionally generous in the time and effort he expended on the Wisconsin free speech movement's behalf. It could not have asked for a more reliable and able ally.) The debate concerning the legal aspects went well in the senate, with the minority faction holding its own. In the period of time allotted for short comments by nonsenators, most speakers supported abolition or radical reform. John Sharpless of the history department (who was, at that time, a viable candidate for Congress) declared himself an abolitionist along with others.

Finally, student opponents of meaningful reform made a stunning blunder that might have helped the abolitionist cause as much as any other single event. Before the legal panels met to present their positions, an alarmed Shepard e-mailed the leaders of the minority faction, informing them that the head of the Black Student Union was going to present a "horror case" of a professor violating her dignity in class. Radical reformers knew that one strategic story could doom their cause. (During its investigations, incidentally, the ad hoc committee had not found any meaningful examples of such abuse in class over the course of several years. The relevant subcommittee contacted forty-six department chairs, and only two reported having received any student complaints about demeaning instruction. And neither of these cases appeared outrageous. As Drechsel often said, the speech code appeared "to be a solution looking for a problem.")[27]

Drechsel, Shepard, and I sat together near the front of the room when the head of the minority coalition introduced Amelia Rideau, the vice chairperson of the Black Student Union, who attempted to demonstrate why even the Majority Report was too protective of faculty expression in the classroom. Shaking with outrage, Rideau informed the audience that a professor, English professor Standish Henning, had recently offended her deeply by using the word "niggardly" while teaching Chaucer. Because Chaucer used this very word, the professor tried to explain its meaning and continued to use it after Rideau informed him that the word offended her. "I was in tears," she told the senate. "It's not up to the rest of the class to decide whether my feelings are valid." (Recall that under the faculty code then existing, what is "demeaning" was to be determined by the offended group, not by an independent consideration of what is reasonable.) Only a week before, a similar fracas driven by misunderstanding had erupted in Washington, D.C., over a city administrator uttering the

---

[27] On the lack of reported harm, see Report of the Ad Hoc Committee on Prohibited Harassment Legislation, October 7, 1998, p. 2. "Of the 46 department chairs responding, 44 reported no complaints during the past five years from students regarding faculty members' expression." Faculty Senate Agenda Materials, December 7, 1998, UW-Madison Fac. Doc. 1402.

same word in public, making that city government the curiosity of the country.[28]

As soon as the offending word slipped from her lips, free speech advocates knew that Rideau's attempt had backfired. The accusation triggered a local and national media storm, and critical messages from alumni poured into the chancellor's office from across the country. Sharpless posed a question about where such misguided sensitivity would end: "What other words are to be purged from our language? *Thespian*?" The next day, the *State Journal* editorialized, "Thank you, Amelia Rideau, for clarifying precisely why the UW-Madison does not need an academic speech code. . . . Speech codes have a chilling effect on academic freedom and they reinforce defensiveness among students who ought to be more open to learning."[29] The code had become an embarrassment to the university. Later, several senators said that it was this event that pushed them off the fence of indecision. According to reliable reports, two members of the majority had pleaded with Rideau not to make her speech, recognizing the potential consequences.

The Revival of Abolition

The next month, many people who had either favored the code or remained undecided turned against it. The code was the talk of the campus. A few days before the actual vote, CAFR brought in Jonathan Rauch of the *National Journal* to speak about free speech and harassment. Rauch used the occasion to write a column on the code vote in that journal.[30] Leaders of the minority faction then began to lobby senators and others. Shepard worked to convince the somewhat gun-shy *Herald* editorial board to come out of its shell and endorse abolition;[31] and Kasper interacted with several senators whom she knew, in particular an untenured faculty member who strongly opposed the code but was reluctant to make her stand publicly visible. (The next year the *Herald* reasserted its tradition of championing free speech under the able leadership of Alex Tenent.)

The senate proceedings in December and February opened the door to something that had retreated into the background the previous spring: *the reemergence of an abolitionist movement.* In response to what had transpired, Hunt, Triplett, Kahan, and I formed a "Group of Four" senators to sponsor a motion that would effectively abolish the code in instructional settings.

---

[28] Tape of faculty senate meeting, February 1, 1999.

[29] "Word Flap Is Reason against Speech Code," *Wisconsin State Journal*, February 2, 1999. See also, John Sharpless, "Presuming the Worst Is No Way to Serve Anyone's Best Intentions," op-ed, *Wisconsin State Journal*, February 3, 1999; Denise K. Magner, "Wisconsin Student Complains about Professor's Use of Word 'Niggardly,'" *Chronicle of Higher Education*, February 12, 1999, p. A12.

[30] Rauch, "An Earthquake in PC Land," *National Journal*, March 6, 1999.

[31] "No Code Only Choice for Free Speech," editorial, *Badger Herald*, February 25, 1999.

(Drechsel, Kasper, and Shepard were equally involved but did not serve as senators.) Kahan and Triplett were seasoned in the senate and added strong doses of experience and ability to the cause. Hunt did the lion's share of the work of draftsmanship. This group met with Drechsel, Kasper, Shepard, and a growing list of members of CAFR in a few chaotic meetings, drafting a motion that retained all the positive changes of the ad hoc committee's reports, especially the preamble. It concluded with a call for abolition in the classroom: "Accordingly, all expression germane to the course . . . is protected from disciplinary action provided the instructor has a pedagogical purpose for its use."[32] The Group of Four sent the motion to the university committee, which surprisingly endorsed the motion in principle. (By now, chair Steve Robinson had gravitated to the abolitionists' position, and was setting the stage for them to prevail if they made the right arguments in the senate.) Things looked promising for the abolitionists indeed.

But when the university committee formally considered the motion at a special meeting called on the Friday afternoon before the Monday, March 1 vote, the redoubtable Ted Finman showed up to counter the abolitionists' move. He convinced the committee to add a clause that abolitionists believed could undermine everything: a statement that all expression would be protected unless it constituted unlawful discrimination under state law, federal law, or court opinions, or was otherwise unprotected by the First Amendment. Although this amendment appeared innocuous, even redundant, on paper, it would have given virtual carte blanche to the Office of Equity and Diversity Resources to interpret expression as it saw fit, for the uncertainties of the law in this domain at that time left a wide range for interpretation. The central issue of the free speech movement all along embodied a single proposition: the university had shown that it could not be trusted to enforce such codes in a principled fashion.[33] The abolitionists decided that they would have to present an alternative motion to challenge this new motion. Over the weekend, Hunt, Drechsel, Kahan, Triplett, Kasper, Shepard, and I worked hours to draft a motion to counter Finman's motion. In one e-mail, Drechsel wrote that "the UC's proposal [Finman's motion] may – may – be even worse than the Majority recommendations."[34] Abolitionists felt under the gun, and the package they managed to fashion was not as elegant and clear as it could have been. Regardless of this concern, abolitionists

---

[32] Faculty Senate Agenda Materials for March 1, 1999, UW-Madison Faculty Document 1402b, p. 2.

[33] In his book on the theory of free speech, Frederick Schauer concludes that distrust of the government making censorial decisions except when absolutely necessary is the single most plausible argument supporting the free speech principle. See Frederick Schauer, *Free Speech: A Philosophical Inquiry* (Oxford University Press, 1982).

[34] Drechsel e-mail to Kasper, Shepard, and Downs, February 2, 1999.

went into the meeting buoyed by the feeling that they could perhaps rewrite institutional history.[35]

Stage 5. The Senate Vote

The senate vote was a climactic moment. During the intense two-week period leading up to the senate vote, one could palpably feel a shift in campus sentiment as numerous groups outside the free speech movement gathered to discuss the faculty speech code. Leaders of the movement felt the very sense of surprise and amazement that Timur Kuran describes in *Private Truths, Public Lies*.[36] But even though campus opinion now appeared to lean toward abolition, the two-hundred-member senate consisted of many campus activists who were committed to codes. Abolitionists knew the vote could go either way.

Despite years of work, it all came down to the next hour or two of debate. Parliamentary debate can be unpredictable. Carefully crafted positions can be sideswiped at the last second by a skillful argument or maneuver. Accordingly, abolitionists dedicated the final week before the decisive vote to mapping their strategy, reading *Robert's Rules of Order*, and leading comparatively virtuous lives. Although they had laid the necessary groundwork, they knew that luck would also have to be on their side if they were to succeed the next day. A few days before the vote, Mary Anderson, herself a senator, sent an e-mail to several abolitionists that succinctly stated the task at hand. "Remember that you folks are in the driver's seat. You have your motion on the agenda, and in the hands of the senators. The University Committee wants to back a winner. . . . Don't give up anything you believe in! Good luck! . . . The real 'battle' will be on Monday, not with the UC on Friday. Be ready for surprises and parliamentary tricks."[37]

A perceptive former student, Sheerly Avni, told me that abolitionists should not assess success in the narrow terms of the outcome of a vote: what mattered was that they had already managed to change the terms of the debate and the public conversation. Indeed, abolitionists had persuaded the original supporters of the code to support what seemed to be major reforms in the name of intellectual and academic freedom and had managed to place the debate over speech codes and free speech at the center of the university's

---

[35] In his article on the anticode movement, Kors writes that abolitionists compromised with Finman in the end. This is not true. The abolition motion we took to the senate was intended to *counter* Finman, not accommodate him. This motion was unclear simply because the abolitionists themselves could not agree on simpler language. Abolitionists had long considered Finman an adversary by this point. Alan Charles Kors, "Cracking the Speech Code," *Reason*, June 1999.

[36] Kuran, *Private Truths, Public Lies*, pp. 49, 252.

[37] Mary Anderson e-mail to Downs, Hunt, Kahan, Drechsel, and Triplett, February 25, 1999.

public agenda. Abolitionists agreed with Avni's point, of course, but still wanted to win. They had come too far to settle for a moral victory. After much reconsideration and many false steps, they had come to the conclusion that compromise, though often desirable, was not acceptable in this case.

If anything, abolitionists had come to the meeting overprepared. The Group of Four – Hunt, Triplett, Kahan, and I – seated themselves strategically in the front of the room. Kasper and Shepard stood in the back of the room along with a former student, Anat Hakim, a graduate of Harvard Law School who had returned to Madison to practice law. Hakim had aided the abolition movement in several ways, and she had married graduate student Martin Sweet, who also had given meaningful support to the cause.[38] (Back when the ad hoc committee was first meeting in the fall of 1997, Sweet and Hakim had encouraged the leaders of the free speech movement to push hard for abolition, but at that time the latter had had insufficient faith in that possibility. Time had proved Sweet and Hakim prescient.) Next to Hakim stood Mitch Pickerill, a political science graduate student and constitutional law expert, another reliable abolitionist activist. More than a year earlier, the independently minded and gutsy Pickerill had helped keep the abolition cause alive by writing an op-ed in the *Daily Cardinal* that exposed the thought control aspects of the sensitivity training for teaching assistants. Stressing the "intellectual dishonesty" of the sessions, Pickerill reported his own experiences and presented bitingly critical statements by other political science graduate students, including free speech advocates Paul Martin and Evan Gerstmann.[39] Kasper and Shepard stood next to Pickerill and Hakim, poised to shuffle messages among abolitionist senators and supporters, back and forth. Other students and former students had been offering abolitionists valuable advice and encouragement throughout this period and over the years, especially Shira Diner, Adam Loewy, Kevin St. John, Kate Ross, Tim Graham, Neil Toppell, Adam Rich, Tim Hudson, Bob Schwoch, Mike Gauger, Evan Gerstmann, Julie Berger-White, Ian Rosenberg, and Avni. These and other students (many of whom are mentioned in this discussion) made important contributions to the abolition movement in terms of politics and encouragement over the course of several years, helping to keep the message of free speech alive. In many respects, they were the kindling out of which the fire ignited.

The meeting opened with the university committee offering a motion based on the Finman-inspired compromise. The Group of Four then offered

---

[38] See the unpublished paper about the code movement by Anat Hakim, "Code Red" (1999), which describes the origins of the free speech movement at Madison and the cases with which CAFR has dealt. (Red is one of the university's colors; the Badgers are also called "Red.")

[39] Mitch Pickerill, "Sensitivity Charade: TAs Fed UW-Madison's PC Agenda," *Daily Cardinal*, weekend, October 24–26, 1997.

an amendment that embodied abolition in the classroom, albeit in somewhat cumbersome language. After extensive and intense debate, that motion failed by several votes. Despite their laborious efforts, the abolitionists had come up short! Deflated, they had no choice but to push for the best compromise they could attain. The debate and momentum swung back and forth for over an hour. Confusion competed with clarity of vision. At times the senators resembled the serious and dedicated people they imagined themselves to be, while at other times they seemed more like characters in a *Saturday Night Live* skit making fun of academics trying to conduct an important debate.

Before anyone knew it, the time to adjourn approached. It appeared that a "compromise" would prevail, virtually by default. Abolitionists feared that compromise would be essentially cosmetic, that it would leave the door open for the unprincipled application that had prevailed in recent years.

But just as an unsatisfactory compromise appeared imminent, the winds sharply shifted. Michael Onellion, a physics professor who had never before spoken out on the issue, rose to his feet. He spoke pointedly of the witch hunts that can arise in the shadows cast by codes, and how he himself had been the target of a fraudulent, racially motivated complaint in his department. Onellion said that he simply could not trust administrators to apply any type of code in a principled and fair manner. It was a matter of simple self-interest and self-defense. Onellion then offered a motion that cut to the heart of the matter and resurrected the choice of abolition in plain language. His motion simply stated: "*Accordingly, all expression germane to the instructional setting – including but not limited to information, the presentation or advocacy of ideas, assignment of course materials, and teaching techniques – is protected from disciplinary action.*"[40]

In the back of the room, Anat Hakim instantly grasped that Onellion's surprise motion revived abolition. She turned to Jason Shepard and Amy Kasper. "You've got to go down there and tell our senators that they have to jump all over this motion."[41] Shepard nodded his assent, and bounced down the aisle to my side. "Downs, I just talked to Anat. This is it! This is abolition!" he whispered excitedly in my ear. "You've got to speak for the motion. This is our last chance!" I nodded agreement. This was indeed the decisive moment, presenting itself on the heels of luck. But the new motion had taken abolitionists by surprise. How could a seemingly more radical motion prevail when their less clearly radical one had failed? Once again, leaders of the free speech movement had underestimated the senate and a too-often ignored rule of political action: sometimes people will vote against less radical change but endorse more radical change because the latter

---

[40] Amendments to UW-Madison Faculty Policies and Procedures, II-303–306 ("Prohibited Harassment: Definitions and Rules Governing the Conduct of UW-Madison Faculty and Academic Staff"), May 3, 1999.
[41] Hakim, "Code Red."

seems more worth the risk. (Kasper later said that the anonymous senator with whom she had been working to line up votes had been unenthusiastic about the original abolition motion because it was not clear enough. But this professor was willing to go to the mat for the Onellion motion.)

Onellion turned the tide, unleashing new debate. His point was similar to the defining point Lester Hunt had made at the December 7 senate meeting: such codes introduce the specters of coercion and bullying into teaching and the exchange of ideas. When one senator asked what body would apply any version of a code that fell short of abolition, university committee member Bernice Durand declared that the faculty could rely on the Office of Equity and Diversity Resources to do the job. According to Alan Kors, this comment "probably secured the abolitionists' victory."[42] Hunt and I spoke again, along with a few others.

As debate ensued, an opponent from the Law School sensed the turn of sentiment and rose to thwart it. He moved for an adjournment of the meeting, but his motion failed. Then he called for the end of debate and an immediate vote. This motion prevailed.

The vote would be close. And suddenly a new difficulty appeared. Abolitionists had to contend with another problem of all faculty meetings that go on too long into the late afternoon: senators leave to attend to their families and other obligations. It was after 5:30, and there was a very real chance that the senate would lack a quorum. Abolitionists dreaded having to wait another month for the next meeting. For one thing, Ted Finman was on vacation, and could be counted on to sway at least a few votes at another meeting. And the senate has a way of turning against supporters of causes and motions that drag on too long. There is an unwritten rule: "Make sure you have your act together and do not waste the senate's time." Abolitionists were in danger of transgressing this rule in the event of yet another senate meeting on the code. So would a majority for abolition prevail? And was there a quorum so the vote would actually count?

The vote was taken by a showing of hands. I turned around to canvass the room and was amazed. More hands were raised in favor of this motion than for the previous less radical motion. It even appeared that Onellion's motion might pass! Then in the far corner of the room, just above the outstretched hands of voters, I spotted the usually circumspect, taciturn Amy Kasper jumping up and down next to Jason Shepard. I quickly concluded that Onellion's motion must have won. It did, 71-62. "Is there a quorum?" someone asked immediately. The senate's parliamentarian replied that a quorum required 130 votes. There were 133 total votes. The abolition vote had made a quorum by a mere three votes! Our Law School colleague had blundered,

[42] Alan Charles Kors, "Cracking the Speech Code: When the University of Wisconsin Sat Down to Evaluate Its Repressive Speech Code, Nobody Expected Free Speech to Win. Here's How It Happened," *Reason*, July 1999.

his greater parliamentary skill notwithstanding. Had he not called for a vote and allowed the debate to continue a bit longer, the quorum could have easily evaporated.

Applause broke out in the senate chamber, a reaction reserved for only the most important votes. Senators realized that something important, even historic, had taken place. One essayist had written in a journal before the vote that the university stood a chance of reversing a major part of the legacy of Donna Shalala, not a small thing.[43] In 1988 Shalala had said, "This campus has a reputation of being a model – it redefined the role of universities."[44] It had just done so again. A dozen members of the abolitionist coalition came together in front of the room to offer congratulations, including CAFR heavyweights Mary Anderson, Stanley Payne, and Robert Frykenberg. Richard Long came down and ceremoniously bowed before the abolitionist senators, saying that he never thought he would live to see such a day. The abolitionist opponent from the Law School came over and scolded me for not accepting a compromise motion that "would have represented a broad consensus of the campus community." As we walked out, a student opponent hissed in my face, and Onellion found himself surrounded by a group of angry students shouting that he had failed to understand the prerogatives of white power. Later that evening, abolitionist leaders spent time talking to Rauch, Silverglate, and Robin Wilson of the *Chronicle*. In his column in the *National Journal*, Rauch called the event "An Earthquake in PC Land."[45] The next morning, the front-page headline in the *Wisconsin State Journal* confirmed what had happened: "Speech Code Is History."[46] That summer, an editorial appeared in the *Wall Street Journal*, written by Dorothy Rabinowitz, who had helped to break open the water buffalo case at Penn and the sexual misconduct case at Columbia:

[T]he story of this successful battle [was] one in which one faculty member after another found his voice. A story in which, by an alchemy known only in a free society, accommodation and silence dropped away, and formerly quiet citizens spoke their minds. They used to make movies with scenes like these, speeches like some of those heard here, way back when filmmakers were given to celebrating American values and character.

It may be, of course, that at the University of Wisconsin, adherents of the speech code will look for ways to bring it back in some other form. That can't matter now that Wisconsin's faculty has shown what can happen under the leadership of a few intrepid rebels against the forces of dimness.[47]

---

[43] John Sanders, "Wisconsin's Choice," *Freeman*, February 1999, pp. 42–44.

[44] "Shalala, Rouse Hear Input and Gripes," *Badger Herald*, March 29, 1988.

[45] Rauch, "An Earthquake in PC Land." See also Robin Wilson, "Wisconsin Scales Back Its Faculty Speech Code: Professors Now Have Blanket Protection for All Comments That Are Germane to a Course," *Chronicle of Higher Education*, March 12, 1999.

[46] "Speech Code Is History," *Wisconsin State Journal*, March 2, 1999.

[47] "A Speech Code Dies," editorial, *Wall Street Journal*, July 16, 1999, p. A14.

The Aftermath

Despite the abolitionists' hopes, the success of the Wisconsin free speech movement did not lead to similar movements at other universities. But the movement did have at least two significant impacts on the University of Wisconsin: in *education* and in *politics*. The movement was responsible for educating the university about the reasons for free speech. It also set an example of standing up for free speech principle in the cauldron of campus politics. Because the Wisconsin chapter of the American Civil Liberties Union declined to assist the movement in court (and even politically!), the movement had no choice but to mount a political attack against the code and censorship, thereby reversing what initially appeared to be an impregnable campus orthodoxy in favor of such restrictions. Although some critics dismissed the abolition vote as merely "symbolic," its advocates had reason to believe that the vote was considerably more substantial. First, the free speech movement had had to persuade a majority of the faculty senate to support abolition, a result that indicated that attitudes have changed in this body, which had once overwhelmingly supported the student and faculty codes. And the senate reflected the beliefs of the faculty as a whole. It was in this respect that Sheerly Avni's observation mentioned earlier made sense: the movement's success in altering the nature of the debate was an important part of its labors. Although it is still embattled, the free speech position now has a meaningful presence in the public mind of the university. When a free speech controversy arises, people expect members of the movement to make their views known. Free speech principles have public recognition in campus politics.

Second, the effort necessitated the creation of a political movement that remained in place after the abolition vote. Centered on the Committee for Academic Freedom and Rights, this infrastructure has provided a vehicle that has helped the movement win some other important battles. Several CAFR members now serve routinely in the faculty senate, and have cooperated with other senators in important cases involving civil liberty. In addition, CAFR heavyweights Lester Hunt and Jane Hutchison subsequently served on the university's equity and diversity resources committee, with Hunt as the chair. This committee is the primary committee dealing with diversity-related issues and student life. Hunt and Hutchison have gained respect in the university administrative establishment for the way they have handled themselves in this office, showing that a strong free speech and civil liberty position is not inconsistent with the acceptance of diversity and equality. In addition, other CAFR members have worked with the university committee on other academic freedom issues that I discuss shortly.

Let me now look briefly at the most important conflicts that arose after the abolition vote.

Further Efforts and Successes

CAFR has been involved in several other individual cases at the University of Wisconsin and other schools in the state. Its most recent case is *Marder v. The Board of Regents of the University of Wisconsin System*, which involves the termination of a tenured professor at the University of Wisconsin, Superior. The case raises serious questions about fundamental fairness and due process. CAFR worked with mathematics professor Anatole Beck, a new member of CAFR and a longtime faculty activist for academic freedom and due process, in persuading the faculty senate at Madison to pass a resolution criticizing Marder's treatment by the regents and the UW-Superior administration. The senates of several other UW campuses followed suit. CAFR and its attorney Steve Underwood have also worked with state employee unions to challenge the board of regents in the *Marder* case. CAFR tried – unsuccessfully – to enter the case as intervenors on Marder's side. (Intervention would have made CAFR, in effect, a coplaintiff in the case.)[48] During the 2003–4 academic year, CAFR and Beck were involved in further efforts to promote academic freedom in the wake of the *Marder* case.[49] University committee and CAFR leaders worked together on unusual motions designed to give the faculty a stronger role in determining the meaning and extent of academic freedom at the university. CAFR attorney Steve Underwood was the major intellectual force in discerning how state law provides the faculty at the University of Wisconsin with a unique opportunity to define and shape the content of academic freedom in a manner that could influence the future disposition of cases.[50] On the basis of this effort, in April 2004 the faculty senate approved amendments to the university's faculty policies and procedures that more strongly affirmed academic freedom as a right, emphasizing the centrality of due process and individualism as backbones of this freedom.[51]

CAFR has also had some other notable political successes. Just a month after the speech code abolition vote on March 1, 1999, the administration and the university committee presented a proposal to change some of the procedures governing the investigation and adjudication of faculty members

[48] See, e.g., Notice of Motion and Motion to Intervene in Case of John Marder v. Board of Regents of the University of Wisconsin System, Case No. 01 CV 222, Douglas County, WI. January 4, 2002. Steven C. Underwood, Neider & Boucher, S.C., on behalf of Committee for Academic Freedom and Rights.

[49] On September 29, 2003, the faculty senate voted to adopt three resolutions criticizing the regents for the way that they handled the Marder decision. Beck was the author of the original resolutions that the university committee then modified on its own with the eventual support of the senate and members of CAFR.

[50] See Donald Downs, Lester Hunt, and W. Lee Hansen, "Motions concerning Academic Due Process and Faculty Governance," presented to university committee of the University of Wisconsin, September 22, 2003.

[51] University Committee Recommendation to Amend Faculty Policies and Procedures 8.01, 8.02, and 9.01. Faculty Document 1771a. Approved by Faculty Senate, April 5, 2004.

accused of violating university rules (Chapter 9 of Faculty Policy and Procedures). The changes included weakening the right of legal representation and limiting the right of the accused to know the identity of the accuser. CAFR's executive committee and Underwood met for several hours and drafted a counterproposal that CAFR president Stanley Payne presented to the university committee. Faced with a CAFR challenge of the proposal at the next faculty senate meeting, the university committee decided to postpone consideration of the matter until the next academic year. It then established a new ad hoc committee to deliberate further on the changes and placed Payne on it. The reforms that emerged a year later were not ideal from CAFR's standpoint but were notably better than the original reform package.[52]

CAFR achieved an even more important victory in the fall of 2000. Over the summer, students who had opposed the abolition of the faculty speech code convinced the dean of students office and the chancellor to adopt a new program called MARC, for "Make a Respectful Campus." The program entailed setting up thirty-five boxes at strategic locations around the campus, accompanied by brochures that encouraged informers to make anonymous complaints about people for transgressions ranging from crimes to harassment to offensive speech. The Orwellian implications of the MARC program were immediately evident to many faculty and students, and CAFR set to work to forge opposition.

CAFR's first act was to communicate with senior Hasdai Westbrook, the editorial page editor of the *Herald* that fall. Westbrook attacked the program in a biting editorial, charging that the program "smells like an agenda . . . MARC exists to monitor attitudes, not crimes – attitudes that the dean of students office thinks are unacceptable. . . . MARC reports will simply be an emotional cudgel with which to bludgeon anyone who objects to the program's methods."[53]

CAFR leaders then notified the *Isthmus* editor, Marc Eisen, who assigned reporter Jay Rath to do a story on MARC. (Eisen has been a longtime press contact for the free speech movement.) Rath tried to write a neutral story but did not succeed in disguising his disdain for the program. The article that appeared was a lead story entitled "Sifting, Winnowing, and Informing."[54] It caused an immediate stir on the campus. The local ABC news affiliate presented a story on the boxes, and CAFR also engaged in an e-mail campaign that brought numerous faculty members on board to resist the program. (One ally in engineering vowed to read something haunting on the floor of

---

[52] See Memoranda from Steven C. Underwood, Neider & Boucher, S.C., to Stanley Payne and Donald Downs, Committee for Academic Freedom and Rights, May 27, 1998; April 2, 1999; April 12, 1999; April 13, 1999.

[53] Editorial, *Badger Herald*, September 21, 2000.

[54] Jay Rath, "Sifting, Winnowing, and Informing: Controversial Program Lets Students File Anonymous Reports," *Isthmus*, November 13, 2000.

any faculty senate discussion of the program: letters written by his ancestors who had been persecuted during the seventeenth-century Salem Witchcraft Trials.) A faculty revolt against the policy was a very real possibility. With these events in the background, four members of CAFR (Lester Hunt, James Baughman, Jane Hutchison, and I) met with the new chancellor, John Wiley, who had opposed the program the previous academic year when he served as provost. Wiley listened to our concerns and promised to conduct an inquiry into the viability of the program. Within one month, Wiley ordered the dismantling of the MARC program. As mentioned in Chapter 1, Wiley has proved to be receptive to civil liberty concerns.

In 2003 and 2004 CAFR has been involved in something that could represent the next wave of "back door" speech codes. In November 2001 the University of Wisconsin Medical School enacted a code governing "Professional Behavior." Violations ranged from committing violent acts and thefts to not acting in "a collegial, professional manner and respecting individual rights to hold opinions that differ from their own." One example of a violation in an early draft was "making derogatory references or using obscene or sarcastic language when filling out an anonymous evaluation form."[55] The policy authorized the school to sanction or discipline students officially for such transgressions, which it proceeded to do in a case that CAFR entered in 2002.[56] The code allowed punishment for conduct even outside of academic performances on exams or in the classroom. Discipline for such conduct is normally subject to the procedural protections afforded by university-wide rules, but the school tried to get around these requirements by labeling the conduct "academic."[57] Because it represents an attempt to circumvent the normal rules of procedure, this type of code is potentially more problematic than the old speech codes, for those could be enforced only by following the procedural requirements governing the disciplining of faculty or students.

Members of CAFR worked with the university committee on the issue, arguing that the Medical School needed to adhere to the procedural protections of university rules. After the university committee sent a letter to the school, it agreed that it would abide by these rules and modified the code to make it more consistent with due process norms. CAFR and the school are still engaged in discussion as of June 2004. Similar issues concerning "professional conduct" codes have arisen in recent times in other departments as well. In another case, members of CAFR managed to get a department to abandon its original plan to inflict formal sanctions – again,

---

[55] University of Wisconsin Medical School, Professional Behavior Requirements (Faculty Action, November 2001).

[56] In *Board of Curators v. Horowitz*, 435 U.S. 78 (1978), the Supreme Court ruled that "academic evaluations" are generally within the judgment of educational authorities, but that "disciplinary determinations" call for some due process protections.

[57] University of Wisconsin System, Sections 14 (Academic Misconduct) and 17 (Misconduct).

without going through the normal procedural channels – on students whose offensive speech violated the department's new "professional conduct" code. In dealing with these cases, CAFR activists were ably assisted by three graduate student allies and confidantes: Martin Sweet, Janet Donavan, and John Evans. "Professional conduct" codes could be the next wave of codes. Like some kinds of "harassment" codes, they attempt to disguise restrictions of speech protected by the First Amendment by calling it something else.

The *Badger Herald* and the Horowitz Affair

CAFR was also involved in the conflict over the *Badger Herald*'s publication in February 2001 of David Horowitz's paid advertisement against monetary reparations for slavery (see the Appendix). Like the *Daily Californian*, the *Herald* published the ad without paying much attention to its content or its possible effects. But there the similarity ends.[58] After witnessing the devastating consequences that attended the paper's public apology for publishing a cartoon falsely considered racist in the fall of 1998 (see Chapter 6), the *Herald*'s new leaders had slowly recovered their journalistic mettle. The road back began with the renewal of their commitment to free speech under the leadership of editor in chief Alex Tenent during the 1999–2000 academic year. The paper was back to its traditional standards by the fall of 2000.

Aware of what was happening at Berkeley, leaders of the Multi-Cultural Student Coalition demanded that the *Herald* publicly apologize for publishing Horowitz's ad. Later, they held a rally of about 150 students in front of the *Herald* headquarters, during which a dozen police officers were needed to preserve order and to prevent outsiders from getting inside the building. But the *Herald*'s leadership and staff resisted this pressure. At one point, a top member of the staff who had spoken with student critics of the paper called an emergency meeting of leading staff while the editor in chief was out of town. His objective was to replace the *Herald*'s leadership with students who would reverse course and apologize. This effort was thwarted only after the editor in chief managed to make it back to the meeting by driving a hundred miles through a snowstorm while her allies held their ground before she could arrive. The influential leader of the Multi-Cultural Student Coalition, Tshaka Barrows, then prepared an advertisement that excoriated the *Herald* as a "Racist Propaganda Machine":

On the last day of Black History Month, the *Badger Herald* printed and profited from a racist advertisement that attacked students of color, specifically Black students. Historically, the *Badger Herald* has been involved in promoting racist ideology and destroying the morale of students of color who have attended this University....

[58] "Ten Reasons Why Reparations for Blacks Is a Bad Idea – and Racist, Too," *Badger Herald*, February 28, 2001.

Due to the history of abuse and disrespect, students and staff are calling for the UW administration to put the *Badger Herald* on probation.[59]

Barrows first presented the piece to the *Herald* for publication, but the *Herald*'s leaders refused to publish it for two reasons. First, they considered the statement to be false and malicious, and publishing such pieces was contrary to the paper's general policy. Second, publication of the attack would deeply wound the staff's morale during this time of crisis. The *Herald* staff believed that Barrows, a master strategist, had intentionally written the ad in a way that would place the *Herald* in an inescapable dilemma: if it published the ad, the staff would be demoralized; if it did not publish the ad, then the *Herald*'s defense of its own free speech would appear hypocritical.[60] Barrows succeeded in wounding his adversaries, for the *Herald*'s refusal to publish the statement exposed it to the criticism of several national and local commentators who criticized the *Herald* for not being consistently true to free speech. In but one of several national critiques, journalist Tom Regan wrote in the *Christian Science Monitor*, "[t]he *Badger Herald*'s explanation just doesn't cut it. Instead of looking like a champion of free speech, the paper looks closed minded and one-sided."[61] The paper suffered a moral black eye that it could have avoided.

Barrows's explosive statement on behalf of the Multi-Cultural Student Coalition then appeared in the *Daily Cardinal*. After this, *Herald* editor in chief Julie Bosman and managing director Alex Conant called another meeting to explain to the entire staff why the paper should hold its ground. About seventy-five members of the *Herald* staff attended this eventful meeting. Several students, including Conant, Jay Senter, and Katie Harbath, assisted Bosman. Conant had had extensive experience running political campaigns and provided strategic advice to Bosman throughout the confrontation. Conant and Bosman had been in contact with the leadership of the *Daily Californian* and knew that the *Daily Cal*'s staff had insisted on an apology. "The first thing I thought about was what happened in Berkeley," Conant said. "They lost their staff support. . . . the staff demanded that they apologize."[62] Bosman also spent considerable time reading news clips about previous incidents at the *Herald*. She was struck by the effects of the *Herald*'s apology in 1998 and was determined to avoid the mistakes the paper's leaders made then. "In my down time I would go through and

---

[59] "The *Badger Herald*: UW Madison's Independent Racist Propaganda Machine," *Daily Cardinal*, March 6, 2001.

[60] Interview with *Herald* leaders Julie Bosman, February 2002; Alex Conant and Ben Thompson, April 2002.

[61] Tom Regan, "An Opportunity Missed at the University of Wisconsin Badger Herald," *Christian Science Monitor*, April 27, 2001. See also Joan Walsh, "Who's Afraid of the Big Bad Horowitz?" *Salon.com*, March 9, 2001.

[62] Interview with *Herald* editor Alexander Conant, in Thompson, "Paper of Protest," p. 38.

read those articles to get a sense of the history of the paper. That helped guide me as to what to do in various situations. I knew what *not* to do."[63] Conant said that "the one thing that a paper should never do is to apologize in the face of pressure. You just can't ever do that. Nothing good comes from it."[64]

After the meeting with the staff, the editors knew that they had to write an editorial defending their refusal to apologize. Bosman contacted CAFR and met with an officer of CAFR for over an hour in the evening to discuss the content of the editorial that would appear the next morning. During this episode, the *Herald* also received calm and able advice from its longtime faculty adviser, Larry Meiller, a professor of agricultural journalism and the host of a well-known show on Wisconsin Public Radio that is carried around the country. (The show focuses on gardening but also deals with important political and legal issues as they arise.) CAFR promised Bosman and the *Herald* its unqualified support, in whatever capacity they deemed necessary, and encouraged Bosman and the *Herald* to "take the First Amendment High Road." This meant opening the *Herald*'s pages to all commentary about their decision, including that which was most critical of the paper, something Bosman and Conant had already planned to do. Despite the disagreement over the handling of Barrows's statement, I was impressed with Bosman's and Conant's resolve and grasp of the issues that were at stake. Most important, they exemplified in the flesh a major proposition of this book: that free speech and due process can prevail only if individuals entrusted with their care are willing to stand up and protect these principles – and the individuals at stake – *in the face of pressure.*

Bosman, Conant, and the other leaders at the *Herald* felt a sense of fiduciary duty to defend the First Amendment. Bosman said that there was never any doubt in her mind that the *Herald* had done the right thing in publishing the ad and in not apologizing under pressure. Those faculty and students who assisted in the politics and in writing the editorial were filled with nervous excitement as they anticipated the impact the editorial would have the next day, knowing that all hell would break loose on campus over the *Herald*'s stand. Later that night, Bosman, Conant, and copy chief Michael Harrison worked six hours chiseling the editorial into perfect shape. "The First Amendment First" appeared the next morning, March 6. I quote it in part:

At the *Badger Herald*, we only regret that the editors of the *Daily Californian* allowed themselves to give into pressure in a manner that unfortunately violated their professional integrity and journalistic duty to protect speech with which they may disagree.

[63] Interview with *Herald* editor in chief Julie Bosman, February 2002 (emphasis by Bosman).
[64] Interview with Alex Conant, April 2002.

The knee-jerk response by the *Californian* is frighteningly indicative of the growing tendency of college newspapers to allow the opinions they publish to be stomped out for fear of being called names. . . .

We understand and lament the fact that because of our commitment to free speech, we run the risk of occasionally offending readers. It is not our goal. But while we do not want to offend for the sake of offense, we refuse to censor unpopular ideas simply because someone may be offended.[65]

This editorial won many awards, including second place for editorial of the year from the Associated Collegiate Press, and first place for editorial of the year from the Wisconsin Newspaper Association.

The *Herald*'s show of strength impressed many members of the paper's staff and the public. Katie Harbath said, "I was never so proud to work for a newspaper. I called Alex and Julie and told them how proud I was. I was so excited. This is what we are supposed to be doing, inciting debate. Just to have this happen and to do the right thing was incredible to me. . . . They don't teach this in journalism school: the responsibility that we have to free speech."[66]

A week after the editorial appeared, the *Wall Street Journal* published an op-ed piece by Bosman that defended the *Herald*'s stance, compared the *Herald*'s actions with those of the *Daily Cal*, and addressed the problem confronting universities: "We were also under pressure to abase ourselves. But the *Herald* editorial board refused to run an apology. . . . The issues raised here go to the heart of a critical question: Are American university campuses free and open to a spirit of inquiry, or closed places where activist cohorts can determine what is, or isn't, acceptable?"[67]

Although no one performed a public opinion poll, it is evident that the *Herald*'s strong stand earned it respect in the community. The paper received hundreds of e-mails from the Madison area and from around the nation, of which well over 90 percent were favorable. The *Wisconsin State Journal* published an editorial entitled "*Badger Herald* Does a Free Press Proud."[68] The next school year, Alex Conant became editor in chief, while Katie Harbath became managing editor and Ben Thompson assumed responsibilities as editor of the editorial page. They dedicated themselves to two tasks: continuing to provide controversial opinion; and reaching out to the minority community by providing more coverage of issues of interest to that constituency, and giving the minority voice enhanced access to the opinion page. That fall, Conant and Thompson attended my seminar on criminal law and jurisprudence along with Tshaka Barrows, their arch critic the previous year. Though still at odds, these students developed some mutual respect for one

[65] "The First Amendment First," editorial, *Badger Herald*, March 6, 2001.
[66] Interview with *Herald* managing editor Katie Harbath, May 2002.
[67] Julie Bosman, "The (No) Free Speech Movement," *Wall Street Journal*, March 14, 2001.
[68] "*Badger Herald* Does a Free Press Proud," editorial, *Wisconsin State Journal*, March 13, 2001.

another, and by the end of the semester, the three were holding meetings and discussions about campus issues. Barrows even agreed to write an op-ed for the paper criticizing the administration's response to campus climate issues.

The university had settled down by April 2001. Then, on May 1, a group of seventy-two administrators (including the dean of students, the director of undergraduate admissions, and the director of the Wisconsin Union) published an advertisement in the student newspapers that criticized the publication of Horowitz's advertisement and other *Herald* transgressions as affronts to civility and decency. The signers included their official university titles next to their names. Although the administrators acknowledged that the First Amendment protected the publication of Horowitz's advertisement, they implied that it was a form of hate speech that lay beyond moral acceptability. "Freedom asserted without care and thought for others can become destructive to the community and our joint humanity."[69]

The advertisement made it clear where the signers stood in the trade-off between free speech and sensitivity. *Village Voice* columnist Nat Hentoff has been America's keenest student of campus free speech and civil liberty controversies for decades and has been a confidant of the free speech movement at Wisconsin. After reading a copy of this advertisement, he wrote in his column that the ad constituted "the likes of which I have never seen before in a campus newspaper."[70] In addition, three political science professors (Howard Schweber, Ken Mayer, and me) wrote a letter to the *Herald* defending the paper. The *Herald* defended itself and attacked the administration in an editorial: "While it is a little unnerving to have powerful administrators . . . attempt to intimidate us with their titles and vague statements, it is even more unsettling to discover such a blatant disregard for freedom of speech among many members of the administration."[71]

In May 2001 Hasdai Westbrook got the last word that semester on the Horowitz affair by writing the most hard-hitting op-ed to appear on the issue and the administrators' actions. In language echoing the theory of republican citizenship, Westbrook accused the *Herald*'s critics of treating students like "children" and maintained that such treatment undermined the proper mission of the university, which is to prepare students for dealing with the rigors of the pursuit of knowledge. "Censorship and cowardice are not the values the University of Wisconsin should be promoting. A university is supposed to confirm us as adults by helping us to pursue knowledge. Instead the UW

---

[69] "Improved Campus Climate: A Statement," in *Badger Herald* and *Daily Cardinal*, May 1, 2001.

[70] Hentoff, "Chilling Free Speech on Campuses: Sensitivity above All?" *Village Voice*, May 31, 2001.

[71] "UW Should Foster, Not Hinder, Speech," editorial, *Badger Herald*, May 7, 2001. And letter by three political science professors, "Professors Defend First Amendment," letter to the editor, *Badger Herald*, May 8, 2001.

administrators wish to act as speech inquisitors, protecting us as children from the menace of ideas."[72]

CAFR members then met over the summer and decided to publish their own advertisement in response to the administrators. They sought signatures quietly, only by word of mouth, as they did not want the administration to get wind of their plans. But they still managed to get forty-three signatures in an advertisement that appeared in the first editions of the student newspapers in September. They naturally agreed that the university should "promote a welcoming and respectful climate on campus" but declared that "we strongly disagree with the principle behind the administrators' ad: namely, that some ideas must be suppressed or self-censored because they offend or anger others."[73] This advertisement stunned the administrators involved and caused some to announce that the Horowitz affair was now a dead letter. The local and national reaction to their posture against free speech had proved to be somewhat of an embarrassment.

The final act in the Horowitz drama at the university came about when the University Distinguished Lecturers Series committee members invited David Horowitz to give a lecture in December 2001. Though tensions were high, both student newspapers and some faculty members worked behind the scenes to foster tolerance for Horowitz's right to speak. The event went remarkably well and packed the Union Theatre, which seats more than a thousand people. During the lengthy question-and-answer period, about twenty questioners strongly challenged Horowitz's position and general politics. But each person critically engaged Horowitz's ideas, not his character. And a majority of these critics prefaced their questions by actually thanking Horowitz for coming to the university to challenge their views in the public forum of ideas. They paid explicit tribute to the principle of free speech before engaging the arch provocateur in intellectual combat. In response, the *Herald* wrote an editorial entitled "A Victory for Free Speech":

Last night's event could prove to be the pivotal battle for intellectual freedom on our campus. Only by challenging our beliefs can we gain knowledge. And now that pursuit can continue with the assurance that this campus had shown a commitment to true intellectual diversity.

UW administrators should take note. Clearly, UW students can handle controversial ideas and contentious debates. It is past time the administration stop insisting UW students see no evil, hear no evil and, most importantly, say no evil.[74]

---

[72] Hasdai Westbrook, "UW Administrators Fail to Protect Speech," *Badger Herald*, May 10, 2001.

[73] *Badger Herald*, August 31, 2001; *Daily Cardinal*, September 4, 2001. The advertisement had no title. "Faculty Group Rekindles Horowitz Ad Controversy," *Capital Times*, August 17, 2001. I wrote an op-ed on this matter and the Horowitz affair, "'Free Speech and Racial Sensitivity Aren't Mutually Exclusive," *Capital Times*, May 10, 2001.

[74] "A Victory for Free Speech," editorial, *Badger Herald*, December 11, 2001.

Although the students at the *Herald* deserve the primary credit for the lesson in free speech that they taught the university, CAFR provided an assist. In his column in the *National Journal* on the politics surrounding the Horowitz affair, Jonathan Rauch pointed to the political climate that this organization had helped to create at the university:

The [*Badger*] *Herald*'s community is not the same as the *Daily Cal*'s community. At Wisconsin, an energetic free-speech faction has emerged in the past few years. In 1999, the Wisconsin faculty rose up to abolish its speech code, an apparently unprecedented event in American academe. When the *Badger Herald* came under fire this month, an aggressive free speech group, called the Faculty Committee for Academic Freedom and Rights, immediately offered the paper its full support.[75]

---

[75] Rauch, "A College Newspaper Messes Up, and So Might You," *National Journal*, March 24, 2001.

PART III

CONCLUSIONS

8

Civil Liberty and Political Strategy on Campus

The preceding chapters raise several general and specific points that can contribute to our understanding of the relationship between political mobilization and the status of civil liberty in the university. Let us begin with the nature of adjudication. Although debate rages about how much due process students and faculty are entitled to under the Constitution or through accepted ethical norms, many of the cases discussed highlight the critical need to ensure separation of the prosecution and adjudication functions. This point emerges most poignantly from the chapters dealing with the sexual misconduct policy at Columbia and the water buffalo case at Penn. Such separation is an underlying principle of the right to a fair trial and should apply to all universities.[1] The Penn case also reveals how even the narrowest of codes (in that case an "intent" code) can be abused if the requirement of fundamental fairness is ignored.

Pragmatism and Absolutism

In addition, the case studies here allow us to examine another point that is seldom addressed: the distinction between cases worth fighting for and those that merit a less adversarial approach. William Gormley writes in his book on administrative reform that most social and political problems call for "prayers" rather than "muscles" because problems are often complex, and reform can inadvertently make things worse. In a complex world, the spirit of compromise is often a virtue.[2] This is also a constant refrain in former

[1] On the primacy of the independence of the adjudicator, see Charles H. Whitebread and Christopher Slobogon, *Criminal Procedure: An Analysis of Cases and Concepts* (Foundation Press, 2000), ch. 27. On due process and higher education, see Curtis J. Berger and Vivian Berger, "Academic Discipline: A Guide to Fair Process for the University Student," 99 *Columbia Law Review* 289 (1999).

[2] William T. Gormley, *Taming the Bureaucracy: Muscles, Prayers, and Other Strategies* (Princeton University Press, 1989).

University of Pennsylvania president Sheldon Hackney's book on the water buffalo case and the politics of his nomination to the NEH. According to Hackney, Alan Kors and his allies are too quick to see civil liberty disputes as black and white, a battle between good and evil:

> On the contrary, this [the book] is a story about the gray area, about how hard it is to be a centrist when the forces of politicization are so strong. . . .
> I am undone by my training as a historian, which impels me to try to understand all sides of an issue. I am also defeated by my belief, matured in long years of struggle, that truth is more likely to be found in the contingencies and double-folds of reality than in the assertion of simple principles.[3]

Although Hackney's approach is usually the best way to proceed, choices sometimes have to be made that draw lines. There are times when a more hardheaded, adversarial posture is called for ("muscles"), especially when constitutional or individual rights are clearly at stake.[4] Sometimes civil liberty questions *are* black-and-white. Recall that Hackney wrote his assistant Steven Steinberg, "If this guy [Eden Jacobowitz] gets convicted it will be a horrible miscarriage of justice." What would Hackney have done if the judicial hearing panel had proceeded to convict Jacobowitz? Would a conviction have been acceptable because such issues are usually "gray"? On the contrary, such cases as the Jacobowitz case call for clarity of vision and commitment. Most of the cases presented in this book have involved clear violations of legal or moral rights under established rules. In addition, the administrative response to such cases was often simply unsatisfactory. In the end, deciding which of the two approaches to take – compromise based on the complexity of the situation or taking a strong position based on the clear justice of the case – requires practical wisdom and judgment that are often difficult.

In this book I have not discussed the several cases in which the Committee for Academic Freedom and Rights has chosen not to get involved, either because CAFR disagreed with the claims brought to its table or because the situation was indeed too ambiguous or two-sided to justify taking a stand. And in a few instances, CAFR limited its involvement in individual cases to a relatively modest posture, once again in deference to the complexities of the case. Only when CAFR leaders discern a clear problem do they shift into an adversarial political or legal mode.

Many people reject legal formalism and clarity across the board in favor of more pragmatic or nuanced approaches to resolving legal and normative disputes. And most cases probably call for this type of balancing of the equities at stake. The danger arises when the nuance and subtlety of pragmatism

---

[3] Sheldon Hackney, *The Politics of Presidential Appointment: A Memoir of the Culture War* (New South Books, 2002), pp. 18, 77.

[4] Gormley, *Taming the Bureaucracy*.

or other ostensibly more sophisticated antiformalist theories blind those who ascribe to them to severe deprivations of liberty that can occur. It is noteworthy in this regard that critical race theorist Richard Delgado has praised what he perceives as a theoretical shift in much First Amendment theory (outside the courts at this point) away from formalism and toward pragmatic balancing and "legal realism," which eschews a strong presumption in favor of free speech. "The prevailing First Amendment paradigm is undergoing a slow, inexorable transformation. We are witnessing the arrival, nearly seventy years after its appearance in other areas of law, of First Amendment legal realism."[5] Delgado praises this alleged movement because such a jurisprudence would eliminate any special constitutional status for free speech, dissolving it into the elixir of numerous other political claims. On the evidence of this book, such a policy would expose unpopular speech to bullies posing as moralists.

In *Free Speech in Its Forgotten Years*, David Rabban shows how John Dewey and other pragmatists undervalued the importance of free speech before World War I on the grounds that free speech libertarianism was too individualistic and antisocial. But the repression of dissent during World War I and its aftermath caused Dewey and his followers to reassess the importance of free speech to democracy and to conclude that free speech and related liberties should have special weight in any pragmatic balance. Dewey's intellectual odyssey in this regard demonstrates how one's views on free speech can change when one witnesses unjustified repression of dissent and persecution of dissenters;[6] indeed, actual experience is also a major component of pragmatism. Bearing witness to such injustices certainly motivated CAFR to become active at Madison. In cases that call for firmness, a strong commitment to civil liberty helps to guide one's moral compass when one must deal with contentious situations.

The Importance of Politics

The Penn and Wisconsin stories demonstrate that individuals matter. Kors was important because of his understanding of the issues at stake, and his willingness to devote his time and energy to liberty and due process. "You have to remain vigilant to protect liberty," he related.[7] Kors was not alone, and was well advised by his mentor Michael Cohen, his friend Harvey Silverglate, and others. Freedom is not manna from heaven: someone or some group must be willing to stand up and protect it when it comes under

---

[5] Richard Delgado, "First Amendment Formalism Is Giving Way to First Amendment Legal Realism," 29 *Harvard Civil Rights–Civil Liberties Law Review* 169 (1994), p. 170.

[6] See David M. Rabban, *Free Speech in Its Forgotten Years* (Cambridge University Press, 1997), chs. 5–7.

[7] Interview with Alan Kors, July 2001.

fire. Power in some form must be exercised. At Wisconsin, opposition has been more of a collective undertaking, but the principle is the same. And now FIRE embodies this principle on a national level. (FIRE was established to replicate on the national level what CAFR has done in Wisconsin.) FIRE has an organizational core in Philadelphia, a national base of contributors, and select allies in local areas that assist in cases that arise on campuses around the country. The organization has also developed extensive ties with media across the country, and an extensive website that has gained national attention.[8] When it comes to campus liberty issues, FIRE has surpassed even the American Civil Liberties Union as a leader, although the two organizations have been allied in many cases, such as the Columbia sexual misconduct policy.

The cases in this book also suggest what individuals or groups need to do to prevail in the struggle for liberty on campus. A key individual or core group is necessary to lay the foundation upon which to build a cogent force that might succeed. A central core keeps the vision alive when it is marginalized and can provide the basis upon which a movement can eventually grow when propitious events or circumstances arise that can transform or tip the confluence of forces.[9]

The evidence in the case studies suggests at least five attributes such individuals or groups should possess. First, they need an *understanding* of the issues at stake. Second, they require the ability to *recognize* a problem when it arises. This is not always easy, for there will often be compelling reasons for taking the other side, and the most important issues may be hidden in a cloud of confusing or uncertain evidence. Furthermore, the rationalizations and avoidances of the administration may make it difficult to understand what is actually happening. The legalistic interpretation of the Abel Report at Penn, which either refused or was unable to acknowledge the lack of fairness at the heart of the case, is a good example of this problem. Kors was able to see through the smokescreen of rationalizations to the heart of the matter. In many of the cases described in Chapters 6 and 7, members of CAFR grasped the deeper issues at stake while many faculty colleagues remained silent due to the ostensible complexity of the issues, or because they were reluctant to step up. Yet CAFR is careful not to act unless its members believe that important rights have clearly been violated. (In fairness, some of CAFR's critics have accused its members of exaggerating the deprivation of liberty in a couple of cases. Perhaps this is an occupational hazard.)

Third, someone or some group must be willing to take what may be an unpopular stand. This can be especially difficult when criticism comes from one's local community. When Kors was nominated to be on the national

---

[8] See www.theFIRE.org.
[9] Timur Kuran, *Private Truths, Public Lies: The Social Consequences of Preference Falsification* (Harvard University Press, 1995).

board of the NEH in the late 1980s, a critic publicly opposed his nomination, calling him an enemy of women and minorities. No doubt many people agreed with this assessment. If Kors had let such criticism mute his activism, Eden Jacobowitz might have been found guilty of racial harassment. At Wisconsin, CAFR leaders have had to endure similar criticism. In at least one instance, one CAFR member had to contact the police after receiving dozens of harassing telephone calls. Such problems come with the territory. Members of FIRE have also had to endure often severe criticism, as the portrayal of the Columbia case in Chapter 3 revealed. And, of course, many students in this study stood up to defend their own rights or the rights of others in the face of pressure. Most noteworthy were the editors of the *Patriot,* the leaders of the *Daily Californian* (the second time around), and several students at Berkeley; the handful of civil libertarians at Columbia; the Students for the First Amendment at Penn; and numerous students in the free speech movement at Madison, including (more often than not) the leadership of the *Badger Herald* and the *Daily Cardinal.* Student mobilization is essential and inspires other students, especially when linked to faculty mobilization.

Fourth, individuals must be willing to make such issues a meaningful part of their agenda. Edward J. Cleary, the attorney who won the famous *R.A.V.* case, has written that there is a difference between Supreme Court justices who take the First Amendment into consideration and those who believe it is something to fight for. The latter type of justice "displays the *requisite passion.*"[10] Cleary also had to endure sometimes severe criticism from the public and even from peers for pressing the appeal all the way to the Supreme Court. The same point applies to the defense of civil liberty in the university. someone or some group has to "have the requisite passion" to spend the time and energy that such defense requires. Kors said, "I would just wake up and figure how to outsmart them – everyday. That was my life for a couple of months."[11] The speech code abolition movement at Wisconsin devoured hundreds of hours of participants' time. At Columbia, the supporters of the sexual misconduct policy prevailed because the other side did not match their commitment. It was only after a few students joined hands with FIRE that opposition was able to build on the criticisms initiated by a few faculty members. Meanwhile, no one at Berkeley has undertaken the burden of advocating free speech in an organized fashion that might give public presence to its underlying principles.

Finally, advocates must have the *strategic understanding and skills* to make a meaningful defense of civil liberty. It is interesting to note that while Kors

---

[10] Edward J. Cleary, *Beyond the Burning Cross: A Landmark Case of Race, Censorship, and the First Amendment* (Vintage, 1994), p. 44 (emphasis added). Cleary's case was *R.A.V. v. City of St. Paul,* 505 U.S. 377 (1992).

[11] Interview with Alan Kors.

had substantial experience in campus politics and in civil liberty disputes, even he was unprepared to anticipate fully the strategic opportunities that in some ways fell into his lap as the water buffalo case unfolded. But he quickly took full advantage of what came his way, and he learned quickly in the face of experience. Kors, Silverglate, and Thor Halvorssen then applied what they had learned to the building of FIRE. At Wisconsin, civil liberty advocates had to learn as they went along the trail of the abolition drive, and often benefited from simple luck. A corollary of this point is that the core activists must be able to learn quickly while maintaining a reliable moral compass that aids in the navigation of uncertain and sometimes confusing situations.

Beyond these activist attributes, the case studies also provide other examples of key strategic tactics in the politics of academic civil liberty. Contrary to the recommendations of the Abel Report at Penn, civil liberty advocates should make every attempt to stop improper action by the administration as soon as possible, using all valid resources, including persuasion, political pressure, attorneys, and exposure. Institutions and the individuals who run them have enormous incentives to promote their agendas and to protect their reputations and hides, so one cannot always count on them to do the right thing in the face of pressure from angry constituents. As James Madison famously wrote, the first "difficulty" in framing a government is to "enable the government to control the governed." The second difficulty is "to oblige it to control itself."[12]

Second, those whose rights have been violated or jeopardized, or who have been persecuted for their beliefs, need the support of others. Both Pavlik and Jacobowitz were left alone at Penn until Kors came to their aid. Jacobowitz related, "As soon as I convinced Kors to represent me, I felt like everything was going to be okay. I felt ten times better and will be forever in debt to him for that. My attitude at that point was that the school had no idea who it was messing with."[13] As seen in Chapter 3, Columbia student Karl Ward felt that he "was no longer alone" when he read about FIRE's attack on the Columbia sexual misconduct policy. FIRE has provided such cover and assistance to others at many of the schools it has targeted. At Wisconsin, CAFR has received many such comments from individuals it has supported in recent years.[14] For example, recall the case of the seventy-four-year-old

---

[12] James Madison, Federalist 51, in Clinton Rossiter, ed., *The Federalist Papers* (New American Library, 1961). Government incentive to protect its own institutional interests is also a major factor behind the incarceration of innocent people in criminal cases. See, e.g., Barry Scheck, Peter Neufield, and Jim Dwyer, *Actual Innocence: Five Days to Execution, and Other Dispatches from the Wrongly Convicted* (Doubleday, 2000).

[13] Interview with Eden Jacobowitz, November 2001.

[14] This is a major theme in Neil Hamilton's book on threats to academic freedom. See Hamilton, *Zealotry and Academic Freedom: A Legal and Historical Perspective* (Transaction, 1998), chs. 1, 2.

University of Wisconsin professor improperly accused of harassment, discussed in Chapter 6. When he attended the retirement party of Robert Frykenberg two years later, he sought out CAFR leaders and made a point of thanking them for the support they had given him in his case. "You have no idea how important your support was to me," he said. "I was all alone and had no idea what to do."

A third strategic point for civil liberty groups to consider is that it is essential to take full advantage of networking and other opportunities that arise to present the case, including turning questionable actions by the administration or relevant committees against them. Outside action can be enormously effective. Kors and Silverglate stress that "sunlight is the best disinfectant."[15] The media provide an invaluable source to publicize problems and to assist in building pressure against individuals and groups intent on violating fundamental liberties. Timur Kuran and Joseph Gusfield have demonstrated that movements or cases need to reach a critical point where they resonate in the public consciousness.[16] Kors became adept at making connections with a handful of faculty and students; it was the First Amendment Task Force that successfully battled the confidentiality rules the provost enacted at Penn in 1995 and 1996. At Wisconsin, CAFR has developed extensive ties with students, faculty, the student newspapers, and local media (and some national media). Garnering such support is FIRE's forte, of course.

As the Abel Report at Penn shows, members of the university community, faculty as well as administrators, often consider "going outside" a kind of betrayal. But there is nothing wrong with going public if the institution is betraying its own principles (as written in official publications, founding documents or monuments, and pronouncements), and attempts to address the problem internally prove futile or unproductive. Recall how Kors labored to get Penn to correct its ways, to no avail, and how Columbia activists castigated FIRE and considered such individuals as Jaime Schneider and Karl Ward to be traitors for "taking the case outside."

During the controversy over the MARC anonymous complaint box program at Wisconsin, CAFR leaders received a telephone call from Alan Kors at FIRE, who had just held a meeting with Harvey Silverglate, Nat Hentoff, and Thor Halvorssen to discuss what was happening at Madison. Kors offered FIRE's assistance in the battle against MARC. CAFR leaders replied that they would welcome such assistance if it was needed but that they wanted to try working with the administration before resorting to outsiders. CAFR thought that it owed this to the administration – especially because the new chancellor, John Wiley, had opposed the program as provost the previous

---

[15] Alan Charles Kors and Harvey A. Silverglate, *The Shadow University: The Betrayal of Liberty on America's Campuses* (Free Press, 1998), ch. 15.
[16] Kuran, *Private Truths, Public Lies*; Joseph Gusfield, *The Culture of Social Problems: Drinking – Driving and the Symbolic Order* (University of Chicago Press, 1981), p. 3.

semester – and believed that it would develop further its organizational muscles and confidence if it succeeded on its own. But CAFR would have had
no reservation about bringing FIRE on board had the necessity arisen.

Typically, the outside world and the press value free speech and liberty
more than universities these days; recall journalist Jonathan Yardley's comment about universities' reaction to the Horowitz ad quoted in Chapter 4:
"[T]he American college campus is a foreign country; they do things differently there."[17] Consequently, extending the struggle to the outside world
builds on James Madison's famous insight in Federalist 10: expanding the
scope of the conflict and the constituency is a classic way to check local
power and to promote broader, more universal principles of justice over
local domination.[18]

It is important to note that CAFR has consistently eschewed one source
of outside support: the government. There are several reasons that CAFR
has turned down more than one offer to enlist the government in its free
speech and civil liberty battles at Wisconsin. First, the government often
lacks the ability to fathom adequately what is at stake. It often addresses
problems with an ax when a scalpel is called for. Second, the government
possesses coercive power, and setting the precedent of overt government
involvement poses potential danger to institutional freedom, for one component of academic freedom involves the university's relative autonomy
vis-à-vis the government.[19] Of course, this book has concerned itself with
the problems that arise when individual academic freedom or other rights
are jeopardized not by outside government intervention – the paradigm of
McCarthyism – but rather from *within the institution itself*. In CAFR's view,
however, calling on outside government intervention in this context is too
risky. The coercive power of speech codes and related policies is a problem, but so is the coercive power of the state. Accordingly, the Collegiate
Speech Protection Act of 1994, which would have provided legal recourse
for students in nonsectarian colleges to fight speech codes, was a bad idea.
Fortunately, this so-called Hyde Amendment did not pass.[20] In 2003 an inter-
mediary on the University of Wisconsin board of regents contacted CAFR on
behalf of David Horowitz, who wanted the university to be among the first
to adopt his organization's new national "Academic Bill of Rights" (sponsored by "Students for Academic Freedom"), which includes protection of
free speech and the promotion of intellectual and ideological diversity on
campus. CAFR declined to be a vehicle for this effort for two reasons: the

---

[17] Jonathan Yardley, "Politically Corrected," *Washington Post*, March 5, 2001.
[18] James Madison, Federalist 10, in Rossiter, *The Federalist Papers*. The classic book that develops
this point in the context of a range of political and policy issues is Grant McConnell, *Private
Power and American Democracy* (Knopf, 1966).
[19] See, e.g., David M. Rabban, "A Functional Analysis of 'Individual' and 'Institutional' Academic Freedom under the First Amendment," in William W. Van Alstyne, ed., *Freedom and
Tenure in the Academy* (Duke University Press, 1993), pp. 227–301.
[20] See Kors and Silverglate, *The Shadow University*, pp. 351–52.

Academic Bill of Rights entailed outside overview of policies and courses; and Horowitz's effort appeared to be too politically partisan.[21]

Fourth, winning the battle of "naming" is important. Advocates of broad speech codes have often called them "harassment" codes, which ostensibly cover only conduct, not speech. But many such measures are, in truth, speech codes in disguise. In the aftermath of the water buffalo case at Penn, even the interim president at Penn called it a "speech code" in the *Almanac*. Precisely the same transformation of language took place at Wisconsin. The student speech code at Madison was controversial from its inception partly because it was commonly called a "*speech* code." The faculty code had a different status for a long time because it was widely known as a "*harassment* code." One reason that the free speech movement at Wisconsin succeeded in abolishing the code in the classroom was because it was able to persuade many people to call the measure a *speech* code – which, of course, it was.

Finally, in many cases, honest appeals to the principles of freedom and fundamental fairness will resonate and be considered by those who listen, even in institutions that are bent on applying agendas that undercut these values. Many universities and colleges have historical traditions of honoring such values, and traditions have a way of lingering in the collective memory of institutions.[22] Numerous individuals will also honor such values, whatever the public philosophy of the institution, even if they remain silent out of fear or a reluctance to make waves. Kors claimed at Penn that many such individuals "found their courage."

At Wisconsin, the abolition movement reached its peak during the university's sesquicentennial. Leaders of the movement and the local press repeatedly referred to this fact in their public and political statements. In an article written for the *Wisconsin Interest* right after the abolition vote at Madison, Thomas W. Still, a *Wisconsin State Journal* associate editor, made precisely this type of appeal. Still, one of the free speech movement's most loyal local media supporters, wrote:

A great university such as the UW-Madison must constantly recommit itself to the ideals that define our society, from the rule of law to political democracy. . . . For the UW-Madison to remain a true university, that commitment to what binds us as a state, nation, and civilization must not waver in the years ahead.

Almost 150 years to the day after its first class of 17 men began classes, the University of Wisconsin disposed of its speech code. There could have been no better sesquicentennial gift to the faculty and students who will follow.[23]

---

[21] See, e.g., "Students for Academic Freedom Year-End Report," at www.studentsforacademic-freedom.org/reports/SAFyearendreport2003to2004.htm.

[22] On the incentives of institutions, see the burgeoning literature on the "new institutionalism." See, e.g., James G. March and Johan P. Olsen, *Rediscovering Institutions: The Organizational Basis of Politics* (Free Press, 1989).

[23] Thomas W. Still, "Turning Back the Tide of Political Correctness," *Wisconsin Interest* 8 (1999), pp. 25–26.

Speech and Civility at the University

Some will point out that I have provided many criticisms of present policies designed to promote mutual respect and diversity on campus but that I have not presented any alternative suggestions for achieving this objective. So let me conclude by reflecting on what types of expression or expressive acts might properly be subject to restriction.

Before I deal with this question, however, I need to address why speech codes and compromises of due process are the wrong way to proceed. If the experience with speech codes and related policies teaches us anything, it is the lesson – central to liberal jurisprudence – that Lester Hunt decreed at the pivotal meeting in December 1998 at which the senate debated the faculty speech code for the first time: liberal freedom is simply not compatible with the expansion of punitive rules beyond prohibiting the infliction of serious direct harm.[24] And a long line of First Amendment theory and case law holds that offensive or demeaning speech does not cause the types of harms that should be subject to the legal sanction.[25] Hunt hit the nail on the head: the regime of speech codes thrusts coercion, bullying, and politicization into the academic marketplace of ideas. This concern recurs in considering the water buffalo case at Penn. Even assuming for the sake of argument that Eden Jacobowitz's comments were indeed highly inappropriate, new questions arise when authorities dealt with the problem by enlisting the punitive judicial system, replete with all the trappings of coercive power that the university can muster.

Speech codes allow partisans, in effect, to "criminalize" moral and political disagreement and feeling offended in a manner similar to the way in which the now discredited federal independent counsel law criminalized political and policy differences; rather than besting an opponent in the marketplace of ideas or the political process, partisans who enjoy the support of authorities can take the coercive way out by turning the law against their foes. Congress let the independent counsel law die in the late 1990s after each side of the political aisle had suffered under its misplaced moralism.[26]

If someone causes true offense, it is best to resort to informal remedial responses. Such informal means might include confronting the offender, seeking a broader discussion, marshaling social support, or seeking campus authorities as informal intermediaries to bring the sides together and work out their differences. Given their strong commitments to racial and ethnic diversity, contemporary universities will always have individuals who are willing to play constructive roles in such cases. What universities do not need is speech codes, for such policies corrupt the painstaking process of building

---

[24] See, e.g., Herbert Packer, *The Limits of the Criminal Sanction* (Stanford University Press, 1968).

[25] See, e.g., *Cohen v. California*, 403 U.S. 15 (1971).

[26] See, e.g., Stephen L. Carter, "The Independent Counsel Mess," 102 *Harvard Law Review* 105 (1988).

mutual respect by tempting authorities to indulge in moral bullying. Recall that Eden Jacobowitz offered several times to meet with the complainants in his case at Penn and to apologize for any misunderstanding. Instead, the case was submitted to the throes of a punitive process. Recall also the case of David Mecklenberg (see Chapter 6), whose later respect for homosexual rights arose *in spite of* the university's quasi-coercive tactics under the aegis of Wisconsin's first student speech code. (In this case, no informal process was possible because no gay student had seen the offensive posters.) As Mecklenberg remarked in Chapter 6, "Contrary to what the university hoped would occur, my opinion of homosexuality was changed negatively because of the whole incident. As I have [now] adopted strong libertarian principles, my thoughts on homosexuality have changed again. But UW certainly had nothing to do with this change."[27]

A university is a humanitarian institution that has several obligations that are sometimes in conflict: pursuing truth, preparing students for competent participation in constitutional citizenship, and promoting civility and mutual respect.[28] The evidence in this book shows how speech codes and related policies compromise all of these obligations. Such policies have promoted limited political agendas over the pursuit of truth, and do not envision or treat students as young adults who possess the inherent strength to handle the responsibilities of constitutional citizenship. The evidence in this book also makes another point abundantly clear: universities are failing to instill in students adequate understanding of the principles of liberal freedom. The problem is not how a student will stand in any particular controversy but rather whether he or she will assess controversies with sufficient appreciation of the constitutional claims at stake. As Shira Diner proclaimed in her speech to the graduating class of 1997 at Wisconsin (see Chapter 6), universities have been busy requiring sensitivity sessions for incoming students while neglecting to teach them the fundamental principles of free speech and academic freedom. After praising various programs in academics, student life, and athletics at Wisconsin, Diner zeroed in on her central parting concern before an audience of several thousand students, family, and friends. After the address, some members of the administration who sat on the stage would not look at her, though others congratulated her. Diner's remarks are worth quoting at length, for they stood as one more milestone in the drive toward the abolition vote that took place two years later. They also exemplify the significance of student awareness and courage:

While it is important to celebrate these accomplishments by the different subsections of our student body, there is a danger which comes from glorifying separation and

---

[27] Correspondence with David Mecklenberg, March 2002. I have been told of other cases similar to Mecklenberg's, but these are hearsay.

[28] On universities' obligation to foster respect, see Nathan Glazer, *Remembering First Things* (Basic Books, 1970).

division. I propose today that we celebrate the one idea that we all should take pride in being a part of. That idea is our shared learning and growing process which had been shaped by Academic Freedom.... Through its long history, the cornerstone of this institution of higher learning has been the idea that the truth can be found through critical thinking and learning....

It is the responsibility of the institution to foster the academic freedom that it claims to have. Before we began school, many of us went through the SOAR program [freshman orientation]. As we were being taught how to treat people with sensitivity, why were we not reminded that we needed to open our minds to all ideas, even those that hurt?... In [my] four years the ideas of free speech and thought have been sliding down the slippery slope which will inevitably lead to [the university's] downfall.... For the past four years we have been cheated out of the education which this University should be providing because of a speech code imposed on the faculty which restricts what they can and cannot say in our classes. We have a right to be challenged with ideas that are not easy and that may hurt us. We deserve nothing less if we expect to find the truth.[29]

Supporters claim that codes at least attempt to promote civility. Civility is pitted against the pursuit of truth. But this book has shown how the enforcement of codes has often encouraged incivility in its own right. The treatments of Eden Jacobowitz, Murray Dolfman, Richard Long, Robert Frykenberg, and others hardly furthered civility at Penn and Wisconsin. The politics and discourse accompanying social censorship at Berkeley and the passage of the sexual misconduct policy at Columbia also unleashed incivility, as dissenters were treated as unworthy of moral or intellectual respect. When universities develop policies that are designed to protect select groups of students who are deemed especially in need of the protection of authority, they ignore their other obligation to treat all students equally as young adults. In the end, these policies harm their would-be beneficiaries because they assume that such students are incapable of handling the rigors of open debate and due process. Recall Columbia professor James Applegate's observation that Columbia's sexual misconduct policy treated women accusers as "juveniles" – a claim echoed by such feminist scholars as Vivian Berger and such national activists as Feminists for Free Expression.

Punitive codes must not be "speech codes" at all: they should be limited to forms of expression closely linked to illegal action, and which have traditionally been the subject of prohibition.[30] Threats of violence, badgering, harassment as traditionally understood (i.e., "to tire with repeated exhausting efforts; to weary by importunity; to cause to endure excessive burdens or anxieties"),[31] and invasions of privacy are examples. It is especially

---

[29] Shira Diner, Senior Class President's Address to Senior Class, University of Wisconsin Graduation Ceremony, May 1997.

[30] See, generally, Kent Greenawalt, *Speech, Crime, and the Uses of Language* (Oxford University Press, 1989).

[31] *Webster's New International Dictionary of the English Language*, 2d ed. unabridged (G.&C. Merriam, 1961).

important to distinguish threats or intimidation from offensiveness. Offensiveness is often linked to ideas that one finds objectionable, and it is notoriously difficult to define.[32] Intimidations and threats are different in both respects. Furthermore, it is the duty of government and institutions to protect their constituencies' basic sense of security. Speech or symbols targeted at individuals that would cause a reasonable person in the target's situation to feel physically endangered on that occasion fall outside the realm of tolerable discourse. Placing a Ku Klux Klan sign or burning a cross in front of a dorm are examples of threats that do not merit First Amendment protection.[33]

After federal courts thwarted its quest of a student speech code, the University of Wisconsin system enacted a measure prohibiting threats, harassment, and stalking, without specifying the special categories of race, gender, and the like.[34] This type of code protects individual integrity but in no way restricts upsetting or offensive ideas. It is similar to Jeffrey Rosen's proposal for harassment that I discussed in Chapter 2: it is narrowly crafted to cover only serious harm to individual safety, privacy, and autonomy; and it is not politically biased by being applied only to the select categories of race, gender, sexual orientation, and the like. It is time to move beyond a focus on these particular categories in this area of policy and public concern and to extend the same protections of law upon all individuals regardless of their ascriptive characteristics.[35] And this approach protects everyone's safety, privacy, and autonomy regardless of the reasons or ideas behind the violations of these values.[36]

It is also very important for university administrators, faculty, and students to affirm their belief in the rights of all individuals and to make clear their moral intolerance of speech acts that make individuals feel excluded on improper grounds. Universities have an obligation to make all members of the community feel welcome and respected. But such obligations should be promoted not by coercive codes that affect a wide range of speech but rather through exhortation, setting positive examples, and demonstrating moral support for individuals who are in need of such support. If speech acts cross the line that separates offensiveness and rudeness from threats and intimidation, then actual legal intolerance is called for.

There is nothing wrong with the university promoting a broader, more substantive concept of civility. Indeed, civility is important to an institution dedicated to liberal education. But universities must pursue such a worthy agenda informally, through the example of their own conduct, through the nourishment of informal networks of mutual respect and support, and by

---

[32] See, e.g., *Cohen v. California*, 403 U.S. 15 (1971).
[33] See, e.g., *Virginia v. Black*, 538 U.S. 343 (2003).
[34] University of Wisconsin Administrative Code, Chapter 17 (UWS 17), Sec. 17.03 (2).
[35] This approach is central to the vision of *R.A.V. v. City of St. Paul*, 505 U.S. 377 (1992).
[36] See Jeffrey Rosen, *The Unwanted Gaze: The Destruction of Privacy in America* (Random House, 2000).

their public advocacy of tolerance and civility. Universities must also promote tolerance of diverse opinion, including opinion that dissents from the university's preferred agenda or the agendas of preferred groups. Thus far, universities have not done a good job performing what is admittedly a delicate balancing act. They will not do so until they begin to take the principles of liberal individualism and freedom seriously once again.

Appendix

The following is the text from the full-page advertisement opposing monetary reparations for slavery that David Horowitz sent to numerous student newspapers in February 2001, discussed in Chapters 1, 2, 4, and 7. Publication of the advertisement by such papers as the *Daily Californian* (University of California, Berkeley), the *Brown Daily Herald* (Brown University), and the *Badger Herald* (University of Wisconsin, Madison) sparked an emotional reaction that typified the crisis of free speech at institutions of higher learning in the United States.

Ten Reasons Why Reparations for Blacks Is a Bad Idea for Blacks – and Racist Too

One

There Is No Single Group Clearly Responsible for the Crime of Slavery
Black Africans and Arabs were responsible for enslaving the ancestors of African-Americans. There were 3,000 black slave-owners in the ante-bellum United States. Are reparations to be paid by their descendants too?

Two

There Is No One Group That Benefited Exclusively from Its Fruits
The claim for reparations is premised on the false assumption that only whites have benefited from slavery. If slave labor created wealth for Americans, then obviously it has created wealth for black Americans as well, including the descendants of slaves. The GNP of black America is so large that it makes the African-American community the 10th most prosperous "nation" in the world. American blacks on average enjoy per capita incomes

in the range of twenty to fifty times that of blacks living in any of the African nations from which they were kidnapped.

Three

Only a Tiny Minority of White Americans Ever Owned Slaves, and Others Gave Their Lives to Free Them

Only a tiny minority of Americans ever owned slaves. This is true even for those who lived in the ante-bellum South where only one white in five was a slaveholder. Why should their descendants owe a debt? What about the descendants of the 350,000 Union soldiers who died to free the slaves? They gave their lives. What possible moral principle would ask them to pay (through their descendants) again?

Four

America Today Is a Multi-Ethnic Nation and Most Americans Have No Connection (Direct or Indirect) to Slavery

The two great waves of American immigration occurred after 1880 and then after 1960. What rationale would require Vietnamese boat people, Russian refuseniks, Iranian refugees, and Armenian victims of the Turkish persecution, Jews, Mexicans, Greeks, or Polish, Hungarian, Cambodian and Korean victims of Communism, to pay reparations to American blacks?

Five

The Historical Precedents Used to Justify the Reparations Claim Do Not Apply, and the Claim Itself Is Based on Race Not Injury

The historical precedents generally invoked to justify the reparations claim are payments to Jewish survivors of the Holocaust, Japanese-Americans and African-American victims of racial experiments in Tuskegee, or racial outrages in Rosewood and Oklahoma City. But in each case, the recipients of reparations were the direct victims of the injustice or their immediate families. This would be the only case of reparations to people who were not immediately affected and whose sole qualification to receive reparations would be racial. As has already been pointed out, during the slavery era, many blacks were free men or slave-owners themselves, yet the reparations claimants make no distinction between the roles blacks actually played in the injustice itself. Randall Robinson's book on reparations, *The Debt*, which is the manifesto of the reparations movement is pointedly sub-titled "What America Owes to Blacks." If this is not racism, what is?

Six

The Reparations Argument Is Based on the Unfounded Claim That All African-American Descendants of Slaves Suffer from the Economic Consequences of Slavery and Discrimination

No evidence-based attempt has been made to prove that living individuals have been adversely affected by a slave system that was ended over 150 years ago. But there is plenty of evidence the hardships that occurred were hardships that individuals could and did overcome. The black middle-class in America is a prosperous community that is now larger in absolute terms than the black underclass. Does its existence not suggest that economic adversity is the result of failures of individual character rather than the lingering after-effects of racial discrimination and a slave system that ceased to exist well over a century ago? West Indian blacks in America are also descended from slaves but their average incomes are equivalent to the average incomes of whites (and nearly 25% higher than the average incomes of American born blacks). How is it that slavery adversely affected one large group of descendants but not the other? How can government be expected to decide an issue that is so subjective – and yet so critical – to the case?

Seven

The Reparations Claim Is One More Attempt to Turn African-Americans into Victims. It Sends a Damaging Message to the African-American Community

The renewed sense of grievance – which is what the claim for reparations will inevitably create – is neither a constructive nor a helpful message for black leaders to be sending to their communities and to others. To focus the social passions of African-Americans on what some Americans may have done to their ancestors fifty or a hundred and fifty years ago is to burden them with a crippling sense of victim-hood. How are the millions of refugees from tyranny and genocide who are now living in America going to receive these claims, moreover, except as demands for special treatment, an extravagant new handout that is only necessary because some blacks can't seem to locate the ladder of opportunity within reach of others – many less privileged than themselves?

Eight

Reparations to African-Americans Have Already Been Paid

Since the passage of the Civil Rights Acts and the advent of the Great Society in 1965, trillions of dollars in transfer payments have been made to African-Americans in the form of welfare benefits and racial preferences (in contracts, job placements and educational admissions) – all under the rationale of redressing historic racial grievances. It is said that reparations are necessary to achieve a healing between African-Americans and other Americans. If trillion dollar restitutions and a wholesale rewriting of American law (in order to accommodate racial preferences) for African-Americans is not enough to achieve a "healing," what will?

Nine

What About the Debt Blacks Owe to America?
Slavery existed for thousands of years before the Atlantic slave trade was born, and in all societies. But in the thousand years of its existence, there never was an anti-slavery movement until white Christians – Englishmen and Americans – created one. If not for the anti-slavery attitudes and military power of white Englishmen and Americans, the slave trade would not have been brought to an end. If not for the sacrifices of white soldiers and a white American president who gave his life to sign the Emancipation Proclamation, blacks in America would still be slaves. If not for the dedication of Americans of all ethnicities and colors to a society based on the principle that all men are created equal, blacks in America would not enjoy the highest standard of living of blacks anywhere in the world, and indeed one of the highest standards of living of any people in the world. They would not enjoy the greatest freedoms and the most thoroughly protected individual rights anywhere. Where is the gratitude of black America and its leaders for those gifts?

Ten

The Reparations Claim Is a Separatist Idea That Sets African-Americans against the Nation That Gave Them Freedom
Blacks were here before the Mayflower. Who is more American than the descendants of African slaves? For the African-American community to isolate itself even further from America is to embark on a course whose implications are troubling. Yet the African-American community has had a long-running flirtation with separatists, nationalists and the political left, who want African-Americans to be no part of America's social contract. African Americans should reject this temptation.

For all America's faults, African-Americans have an enormous stake in their country and its heritage. It is this heritage that is really under attack by the reparations movement. The reparations claim is one more assault on America, conducted by racial separatists and the political left. It is an attack not only on white Americans, but on all Americans – especially African-Americans.

America's African-American citizens are the richest and most privileged black people alive – a bounty that is a direct result of the heritage that is under assault. The American idea needs the support of its African-American citizens. But African-Americans also need the support of the American idea. For it is this idea that led to the principles and institutions that have set African-Americans – and all of us – free.

Index

INDEPENDENT STUDIES IN POLITICAL ECONOMY

For further information and a catalog of publications, please contact:
THE INDEPENDENT INSTITUTE
100 Swan Way, Oakland, California 94621-1428, U.S.A.
510-632-1366 • Fax 510-568-6040 • info@independent.org • www.independent.org